Dynamic Scheduling
with Project 2000
The Book by and for Professionals

Dynamic Scheduling with Project 2000

Copyrights

Author

Eric Uyttewaal, PMP
Director, Microsoft Project Certification
International Institute for Learning, Inc.
Ottawa, ON, Canada
Tel. 613-692-7778
Email: EricU@iil.com

Disclaimer

The author has made a sincere effort to ensure the accuracy of the material provided
herein. However, the author assumes no responsibility whatsoever for the use of this
material or for decisions based on its use. There are no warranties, either expressed or
implied, regarding the contents of this product, its marketability or its fitness for any
particular purpose. The author or anyone involved in the creation, production, distribution
or delivery of this material shall not be liable for any reason.

Short Table of Contents

Dynamic Scheduling with Project 2000	1
Chapter 0 About This Book	31
Chapter 1 Concepts of Project Management	45
Chapter 2 Setting up a Project	55
Chapter 3 Entering Tasks	105
Chapter 4 Entering Estimates	137
Chapter 5 Entering Dependencies	169
Chapter 6 Entering Deadlines and Constraints	207
Chapter 7 Entering Resources	233
Chapter 8 Entering Assignments	267
Chapter 9 Optimizing the Schedule	299
Chapter 10 Reporting	393
Chapter 11 Updating the Schedule	441
Chapter 12 Evaluating the Project	509
Chapter 13 Summary	513
Appendix 1: Shortcuts of Project 2000	519
Appendix 2: Certification Curriculum Sample Exam Questions	529
Glossary	539
Index	547
Contents of the CD-ROM	554

Long Table of Contents

Dynamic Scheduling with Project 2000   1

    Dedication   19

    Foreword   20

    Acknowledgements   21

    Microsoft Project 2000   23

    Is this Book for You?   23

    What you will find in the Book   24

    Who is the Author?   25

    The Author's Perspective on Scheduling   26

    The Project 2000 Certification Curriculum   27

        Three Levels of Certification   27

        How Many are Currently Certified?   27

        What are the Certification Requirements?   29

        Qualifying Instructors   29

        Consulting   30

    Give us Your Feedback   30

Chapter 0 About This Book   31

    Learning Objectives   31

    Outline of this Book   32

        Initiating   33

        Planning   34

        Executing and Controlling   35

        Closing   37

    Exercises   39

    Conventions in this Book   40

        Symbols and Text   40

Step Formulation   41

Screen Snapshots and Illustrations   42

Meet the Cartoon Characters…   43

Chapter 1 Concepts of Project Management   45

Projects   46

Examples of Projects   46

Program Management Versus Project Management   48

Guide to the Project Management Body of Knowledge   48

The Pulling Forces of a Project   49

Dwight was Right, but is he Still?   50

Scheduling is Modeling   51

Why do we Schedule?   52

How Strong are the Forces in my Project?   53

Project Management Software   54

Chapter 2 Setting up a Project   55

Objectives   55

File Management   57

MS Project as a Relational Database   57

File Structure   58

Project Files   59

Opening a Project File   59

Saving and Replacing a Project File   59

Saving in a new Directory or under a new Name   61

Closing a File   61

Project Templates   62

Creating a Project Template   62

Using a Project Template   63

The Project 2000 Interface   65

The Main Screen 65
Project 2000 Views 70
Navigating the Views 83
Using Help 87
Setting up a Project 89
Creating a new Project File 89
Choosing the Options 91
Options for a new Project 92
Setting the Date Order 93
Leveling Option: Automatic or Manual 94
Workload Leveling 94
Leveling Option 94
Creating the Project Calendar 95
Exercises 100
Review 100
Relocation Project – Scope Statement 100
Relocation Project – Tools, Options 102
Relocation Project – the Project Calendar 103
Chapter 3 Entering Tasks 105
Work Breakdown Structure (WBS) 107
Breaking Down into Phases or Deliverables? 109
Breaking Down the Work 110
From WBS-Chart to WBS-List 111
Types of Tasks 111
Types of Task Bars 113
Types of Milestones 114
Formulation of the Task Names 115
The Right Level of Detail 116
Why is the Right Level of Detail Important? 118

Entering Tasks 119

    Entering Summary Tasks 119

    Entering Detail Tasks 119

    Entering Milestones 120

    Entering Recurring Tasks 122

    Entering Split Task Bars 123

Creating an Outline 125

    Outline Structure 125

    Indenting a Series of Detail Tasks 126

    Indenting and Outdenting by Dragging 126

    Outdenting Tasks 126

    To Hide or Reveal Detail Tasks 126

    To Hide all Detail Tasks 127

    To Reveal the Next Level 127

    To Reveal a Certain Level 127

    To Reveal all Levels 127

    What you do with a Parent, you do with the Entire Family 127

Changing the WBS 128

    Editing a Task Name 128

    Inserting Multiple Tasks 128

    Deleting Tasks 129

    Copying or Moving Tasks 129

Using Task Calendars 131

    Creating a new Task Calendar 131

    Using a Task Calendar 132

Exercises 133

    Review 133

    Relocation Project – Entering the WBS 133

    Case Study "My First Time …" 135

    Troubleshooting 135

Chapter 4 Entering Estimates   137

What are Estimates?   139

Choosing the Options   139

Difficult Situations   141

The Human Tendencies in Estimating   142

    "I can't predict the future!"   142

    "I am always off!"   143

    "Can't you do it?"   144

The Difference Between Duration and Work   145

The Formula Behind the Screens   145

An Example of an Estimation   146

A Process for Estimating   147

    Estimating: Types of Tasks   147

    Preparing the Gantt Spreadsheet   149

    Fixed Work Tasks   151

    Fixed Duration Tasks   152

Estimating: Difficulties and Techniques   152

    In Which Time Unit to Estimate?   154

    What to Include? Pure Work Time or Gross Work Time?   156

    Unknown Events: The Rolling Wave Approach   157

    Unknown Resources   158

    Unknown Experience and Skill Levels   158

    Unknown Learning Curves   159

Copying and Moving Data   160

    Editing Fields of Multiple Tasks at Once   160

    Copying With Fill Down   161

    Fill Up or Fill Down Using the Fill Handle   161

    Copying or Moving Cells   161

    Copying or Moving the Data of a Column   162

Copying Between Projects — 163

Exercises — 165

    Relocation Project – Entering Estimates — 165

    Case Study – Escalated Estimates — 167

Chapter 5 Entering Dependencies — 169

Dependencies — 171

    What are Dependencies? — 171

    Why Should I Use Dependencies? — 172

    Choosing the Options — 173

Types of Dependencies — 174

    Absolute Lead or Lag Time — 175

    Relative Lead or Lag Time — 175

    Choosing the Right Type of Dependency — 176

    Steps for Choosing the Right Type of Dependency — 177

    Categories of Dependencies — 177

Entering Logic — 180

Entering Dependencies in the Gantt Chart — 181

    Using the Link Tool — 181

    Using the Mouse — 182

    Using the Task Information Form — 183

    Using the Task Form — 184

Entering Dependencies in the Network Diagram — 185

    The Network Diagram — 185

    Viewing the Network Diagram Toolbar — 185

    Displaying More Tasks on the Screen — 185

    To Set Dependencies in the Network Diagram — 186

    To Delete Dependencies in the Network Diagram — 187

    Checking the Logic — 188

Checks on Dependencies — 189

Limitations of Dependencies   190

Logic on Summary Tasks   191

Printing the Network Diagram   193

    The Layout of the Boxes   193

    The Layout of the Diagram   198

Exercises   203

    Review   203

    Relocation Project – Dependencies   203

    Case Study CoalPower   204

Chapter 6 Entering Deadlines and Constraints   207

What are Deadlines and Schedule Constraints?   209

Choosing the Options   210

Scheduling Regimes   210

Types of Constraints   211

    Tendencies   211

    One-Sided Constraints   211

    Rigid Constraints   212

No-Earlier-Than Constraints   212

No-Later-Than Constraints   213

Must Constraints   213

In Which Situations do you Need Constraints?   214

    Milestones and Constraints   215

Deadlines   216

    Entering Deadlines   216

    Managing Deadlines   217

Constraints   218

    Entering Constraints   218

    Setting Constraints by Dragging Task Bars Horizontally   218

Setting Constraints by Entering Dates 219

Setting Constraints Using the Task Fields 219

Setting Constraints Using the Task Information Box 220

To Check all the Scheduling Constraints 220

To Delete Constraints 221

Limitations of Constraints 221

Printing the Gantt View 222

To Adjust the Text Styles 222

To Wrap Task Names Around 222

To Adjust the Column Width 223

To Position the Divider on a Column Split 223

To View the Whole Project Timescale 224

To Format the Timescale 224

To Format the Task Bars 225

To Show Milestone Diamonds on Summary Task Bars 226

To Adjust the Page Setup 227

Exercises 230

Relocation Project – Constraints and Deadlines 230

Relocation Project – Printing the Gantt Chart 231

Chapter 7 Entering Resources 233

What is a Resource? 235

When to add a Resource? 235

Choosing the Options 236

Types of Resources 238

What if you Don't Know who you will get? 239

Change the View to Enter Resources 239

Resource Fields 239

Entering Resources 242

Downloading the Resources From the Mailing List 242

Keying in the Resources Manually	243
Resource Calendars	245
Resource Availability	247
Temporary and Varying Availability	248
Part-time Availability	248
Full-time Availability	249
Overtime Availability	249
Consolidated Resources	252
Cost Management	252
Cost Situations	252
Printing the Resource Sheet	257
Customizing the Table	257
Sorting Resources Alphabetically	258
Formatting the Text	259
Formatting the Gridlines	259
Choosing the Page Setup	260
Preview the Resource Spreadsheet	261
Exercises	262
Review A	262
Review B	263
Relocation Project – Entering Resources	263
Relocation Project – Printing the Resource Sheet	265
Troubleshooting	266
Chapter 8 Entering Assignments	267
What is an Assignment?	269
Full-time or Part-time Assignment	270
Choosing the Options	271
Types of Detail Tasks	272
Estimating and the Types of Tasks	274

Designing the View for Assigning Resources   275

Entering a Fixed Duration Task   276

Entering a Fixed Work Task   277

Entering a Fixed Units Task   277

Overview Assigning   278

Assign Using the Assign Resources Dialog   279

Assigning Resources by Dragging   279

Assigning Multiple Resources to Multiple Tasks   279

To Enter the Units on an Assignment   280

To Delete an Assignment   281

Assign Using the Task Form   282

Fields on the Task Form   282

To Assign   283

To Delete an Assignment   284

Entering Multiple Uneven Assignments   284

Assigning to Recurring Tasks   285

Changing an Assignment   286

Printing the Assignments   289

Exercises   293

Review A   293

Review B   293

Relocation Project – Entering Assignments   294

Relocation Project – Changing Assignments   296

Troubleshooting   297

Chapter 9 Optimizing the Schedule   299

The Pulling Forces   301

Overview Optimizing Schedules   303

Choosing the Options   304

Optimizing for Time   305

Techniques   305
The Critical Path Method (CPM)   306
Forward Pass   307
Backward Pass   308
Calculating Slack   309
The Critical Path   310
Constraints and Negative Slack   310
Steps to Optimize for Time   311
Shortening the Duration of the Project   322
Monte Carlo Simulation   333
Assumptions of the Critical Path Method   337
Optimizing for Time and Cost   338
Steps to Optimize for Time and Cost   338
Sorting on Cost   339
Lowering the Cost of a Project   340
Optimizing for Time, Cost and Resources   343
Steps to Optimize for Time, Cost and Resources   344
Workload Leveling   344
The Work Field   345
Checking the Workloads: Resource Graph   345
Manual Leveling   347
Automatic Leveling Scenarios   352
How Leveling affects the Critical Path   358
The Resource-Critical Path (RCP)   360
Finding the Resource-Critical Path   361
Highlighting the Resource-Critical Path   363
Methods to Optimize on Time, Cost and Resources   370
Consider the Impacts   378
Exercises   380
Review   380

Relocation Project – Understanding the Gantt Chart   380

Relocation Project – Shorten the Duration   381

Relocation Project – Ideas for Shortening the Duration   382

Relocation Project – Lowering the Cost   384

Relocation Project – Ideas for Lowering the Cost   385

Relocation Project – Leveling Manually   387

Relocation Project – Leveling Automatically   387

Intranet Project – Shorten the Duration   388

Intranet Project – Ideas for Shortening the Duration   389

Case Study Multinational – IT   390

Troubleshooting   391

Chapter 10 Reporting   393

Project Communications Management   395

Creating One-page Printouts … Always!   395

Hiding your Time Buffer?   396

Methods to Hide the Time Buffer   397

How to Defend Visible Buffers   400

Communication Vehicles in Project 2000   400

Printing a Report   402

Previewing Reports   402

To Customize a Report   404

Report Customization Options   405

Printing a View   407

Tables   408

Filters   410

Groups   412

Views   414

Sort the Records   416

Apply any Formats   417

Choose the Page Setup Settings   419

Copying Views Between Projects 421

Examples of Useful or Hard-to-Get-At Printouts 422

Printing 432

Specify Columns to Spell-Check 432

To Check the Spelling in the Schedule 432

Inserting Page Breaks Manually 432

Inserting the Project Logo Into the Header 433

The Timescale is Too Short or Too Long 433

Print Preview 434

Printing the Current View 435

Print Options 436

Sending a Project File to Colleagues 436

Review Exercises 438

Relocation Project – Reporting an Executive Overview 439

Relocation Project – Reporting Cost by Function 440

Chapter 11 Updating the Schedule 441

Overview of Updating 443

The Baseline 444

Viewing the Baseline 444

Setting the Baseline 445

Maintaining the Baseline 446

Choosing the Reporting Period 447

Showing Progress 448

Graphically 448

Mathematically 448

Updating Strategies 449

Tasks Update 449

Preparing to Update Tasks 449

Choosing the Options for Updating Tasks 450

Collecting the Data   451

Change the View to Tracking Gantt   451

Setting the Status Date for Updating   452

Set the Task Type for all Tasks   453

The Formulas Behind the Screen   454

Task Updating Situations in Practice   455

Tasks that Ran as Scheduled   455

Tasks that Run as Scheduled   456

Tasks that Run Behind   456

Tasks that will Run Longer or Shorter   458

Tasks that Started Late or Early   460

Tasks that Finished Late or Early   461

"My Reality is More Complex… "   462

Checks on a Tasks Update   463

Assignments Update   464

Preparing for an Assignments Update   464

Choosing the Options for an Assignments Update   465

Creating the View   465

Set the Task Type for all Tasks   468

The Formulas Behind the Screens   469

Collecting the Data   470

Paper Timesheets   471

Assignments Update Situations   471

Assignments that Ran as Scheduled   471

Assignments that Run as Scheduled   472

Assignments that Run Behind   472

Assignments that Will Run Longer   472

Assignments that Started Late   473

Assignments that Finished Late   473

Electronic Timesheets: the Workgroup Features   474

Workgroup Features   474

The Workgroup Toolbar   474

Configurations   475

Types of Workgroup Messages   478

Communicating Assignments and Getting Commitments   479

Communicating Changes in Assignments   492

Collecting Actual Progress Data   495

Reporting Status and Latest Forecast   504

Updating the Costs   505

Cost Updating Strategies   505

Setting the Options for Assignments Cost Updates   505

Preparing the View for Updating Costs   506

Exercises   507

Review   507

Relocation Project – Updating Tasks   507

Relocation Project – Optimizing for Time Again   508

Chapter 12 Evaluating the Project   509

Project Evaluation   510

Evaluation Points   510

Chapter 13 Summary   513

Checklist for Dynamic Project Models   513

Work Breakdown Structure (WBS)   514

Estimates   515

Dependencies   515

Deadlines and Scheduling Constraints   515

Resources   516

Assignments   516

Optimizing   516

Reporting   517

Updating   517

In Closing   518

Appendix 1: Shortcuts of Project 2000   519

    To Move Around in a Project   520

    Standard Toolbar   521

    Formatting Toolbar   523

    Network Diagram Toolbar   524

    Resource Management Toolbar   525

    Tracking Toolbar   526

    Workgroup Toolbar   527

    File Page Setup Tools   528

Appendix 2: Certification Curriculum Sample Exam Questions   529

    The Testing Process for Certification   529

    Orange Belt Sample Exam Questions   531

Glossary   539

Index   547

Contents of the CD-ROM   554

    The Certified Schedules   555

Dedication

In Dutch:

Ik draag dit boek op aan mijn ouders die me de mogelijkheid hebben gegeven te studeren wat ik wilde.

Ik draag dit boek ook op aan Shelley. Shelley, terwijl jij onze baby verwende in je buik, heb ik nog een baby gemaakt … zij het van een andere soort.

In English:

To my mother and late father who made sure I could study what I wanted.

To Shelley, while you were nurturing our baby in your belly, I created another one … of a different kind.

Foreword

Finally, we have a book on MS Project written by a Project Management Professional! Over the years, I have been disappointed with books written on the scheduling software. Past books seem to have been written by non-practitioners using examples that were somewhat removed from real-world applications or with examples that were so simplistic that the reader was left with a false impression of the true applications and capability of the software. In this book, however, there exist a lot of practical examples from real-life projects. You will quickly discover that the author exhibits the necessary experience to give you the insights you need to manage your projects more effectively.

This book will convince you that project management can be done more efficiently using software. Historically, PERT-charts were hanging in the war rooms of large project teams. These charts were excellent tools that provided insight into the downstream impacts of any changes made. Schedulers had to become skilled at identifying the impacts and the associated risks. This book is proof that project management can be made simpler by using Project 2000.

This book creates a common language (Level 1) that will help you to establish common processes for the scheduling of projects (Level 2). The summary of the book contains 'guidelines for dynamic schedules' that should be considered for the scheduling of your projects. This book will help you move into the 3rd Level of the project management maturity model. This is where the book adds value over the many books that have been published on scheduling in general, and on MS Project in particular. It combines scheduling best practices with the how-to in Project 2000.

The scheduling guidelines are an integral part of the MS Project certification curriculum that the International Institute for Learning (IIL) has put together. Since many organizations are sending their project managers and schedulers to IIL's courses, the guidelines have been embraced by several organizations. What seems to be evolving is a body of knowledge on scheduling with Project 2000.

Harold Kerzner
December, 2000
Cleveland, OH

Acknowledgements

I would like to thank all the people I had the pleasure of meeting during my MS Project courses and consulting. The discussions we had provided valuable input for this book. Many people have opened my eyes to some remarkable insights. Where I remembered individuals, I have recognized them in this book. Unfortunately, I have forgotten where many thoughts and insights originated. To all of those who should have been mentioned, I apologize.

Some people were actively involved in creating this book and need special recognition:
- I thank the technical editors for their contributions to the accuracy of the text in this book. Because of their help, I have used the word "We" throughout the book when making recommendations. What I recommend is really a culmination of experiences and insights of the team of instructors at IIL. Some instructors have helped me ensure that this textbook on Project 2000 will be as successful as the Project 98 course manuals.
  Let me thank the technical editors personally here:
  - ◇ Ron Gardiner, thanks for your razor-sharp observations.
  - ◇ Jeff Turner, thanks for your concern about making it teachable. Jeff created the helpful illustrations on the Critical Path and slack calculation.
  - ◇ Gardy Joseph, thanks for your feedback on the big picture. Thanks to you, I found a better structure for the chapter on optimizing.
  - ◇ Terrell Smith, thanks for trying out all the steps and picking up on the loose ends!
  - ◇ Tim Stahl, thanks for your comments on the first part of the book.
- Laurene Burnside my English language editor (and dear mother-in-law). She managed to pick up all the tiny little oversights that I had become blind to. She has read more books than I will ever read in my life. Since English is my second language, I really needed her and Julia.
- Julia Perce for the final editing and format checks. She has an eye sharper than anyone I ever met.
- Paul Mason for the creative cartoons that illustrate many of the points made. Often when I received a new batch of sketches, I had some good laughs.
- Rina van Adrichem for creating and inserting many of the snapshots of the buttons and for checking the consistency in the steps and formats.
- LaVerne Johnson, thanks for your confidence that it would be a worthwhile book. Thanks also for the assistance in getting it published.

◆ And thanks to you as the reader for buying this book. You should not find any technical errors in this textbook, but in case you do, please let me know by email via EricU@iil.com. Thank you!

Microsoft Project 2000

Microsoft Project is a tool that helps you perform planning and control of your project. This software can help create budgets, Gantt Charts, network diagrams and resource histograms. It will provide reports tailored to your needs and allow you to depict the progress of your project. The strengths of the software are:

◆ The ease-of-use and flexibility in scheduling and re-scheduling.

◆ The user-friendly reporting features.
 With Project 2000 you can extract almost any information from the project database and present it in a concise report.

◆ The Web features, as embodied in Project Central, that allow dispersed teams to collaborate through the Internet.

Project 2000 is a powerful tool, and like other tools, requires knowledge and skill to use it correctly. The software is not a magic bean that will grow a successful project. Experience has taught me that a successful project results from the combination of sound project management knowledge, and a skilled and committed project team that is equipped with the right tools.

Is this Book for You?

This book is different from other books written on Project 2000. It not only shows you how to use MS Project, but also adds insights and experiences from real-life project management. This book teaches you how to manage projects using Project 2000.

This book is intended for project managers who use Project 2000. It is aimed at the novice to intermediate user of MS Project, but I like to think that an advanced user may find it worthwhile. The advanced user may discover better words or ways to explain the basic features of Project 2000 to colleagues.

The book is written for people who schedule and manage a single project. We intend to publish additional books to cover more advanced features like how to roll up multiple projects and how to customize MS Project using macros.

Another target group is students at colleges and universities and computer-training classes. For professors and instructors, I have added case studies at the end of the chapters. At the end of the book you will find sample exam questions on Project 2000 as we are using in the certification curriculum at the International Institute for Learning.

In short, this book is for:
◆ project managers who manage a single project
◆ novice to advanced users who practice project management
◆ college and university students and professors

What you will find in the Book

This book does not explain all features of Project 2000. I have made a careful selection of features that will benefit users most when managing a single project. It is not a complete reference on Project 2000. The book is aimed at the busy practitioner who is looking to get up to speed quickly with practical guidance. I present the most important features to create project documents efficiently. These are the features that will benefit you in practice.

Many people have asked me for a good process to follow for creating schedules. The structure of the book matches the order of steps we recommend you take. The recommended process is as simple as following the Short Table of Contents of this book.

I have kept the text as succinct as possible. Less text is more, in my opinion, and the last thing I want, is to waste your precious time. I have inserted graphics throughout the text wherever I felt I could save words with an illustration.

This book has an attitude. It is not just a description of the features of Project 2000. I will recommend certain features and I will argue against using some other features. An important criterion I use for my recommendations is that the schedule you build with Project 2000 should be a good model of your project. A good model is a schedule that is easy to maintain during the execution of the project, hence the title of the book 'Dynamic Scheduling with Project 2000'. Static schedules do not maintain themselves, but dynamic schedules do.

Some features are nice to have but create schedules that are hungry for maintenance. During project execution, you don't have much time left to maintain your schedule. Therefore, I don't recommend features that create schedules that continue to need attention. I have found the judicious application of features critical in using MS Project. I have tried to be objective in my assessment. As a matter of courtesy, I always send my recommendations to Microsoft as well.

Now that you know that you are reading a book with an attitude, you may be interested in how the attitude came about.

Who is the Author?

The author is a project management practitioner. Over the past 10 years I have managed many projects using MS Project and I have taught thousands of people in its use. The insights you will find in this book are a combination of my own findings as well as the collective wisdom of my colleagues at the International Institute for Learning, and the participants in the courses I taught.
Even though this is the first edition to be published, you could look upon it as the 10th edition of the course material that I have written and used since MS Project 3.0. In a sense, this book has been in the making for eight years.

In September 1993, I became the first Canadian to be certified in MS Project by Microsoft. At that time, the current version was 3.0. When 4.0 came out, I re-certified. More eager than ever, I awaited the exam for Project 98 … and waited … and waited, but it was never released. I realized that I was probably not the only person who was looking for it. I also found that practitioners and organizations need a meaningful certification curriculum. Particularly, those organizations that are setting up a *Project Management Office* (*PMO*) need a thorough professional development curriculum. In the last few years, I have seen many PMO's sprouting. I have helped several in formulating scheduling guidelines. I decided to address the need for a curriculum in the marketplace …

In 1998 I developed a certification curriculum in MS Project. I approached the International Institute for Learning (IIL) to market it. They hired me as the Director of MS Project Certification. Since then we have held many certification classes in North America and in Europe. In these workshops, I have had the pleasure to work with some of the finest schedulers from these continents.

The consulting and training I have done included people from a wide variety of sectors: information technology, telecommunications, banking, automotive, construction, manufacturing, pharmaceutical and government. As a result, you will find a wide variety of examples in this book. It does not cater to one sector in particular.

The Project Management Institute (PMI) certified me as a Project Management Professional (PMP) in March of 1994.

The Author's Perspective on Scheduling

In my years of consulting and training, I made some observations:

◆ Some large schedules I have seen did not have a Work Breakdown Structure (WBS). All tasks were on the first (and only) indentation level. A well-known automotive company used schedules like these. Sorry, no names! Organizations were not using the basic concept of Work Breakdown Structures. Such a schedule is difficult to explain to anyone not interested in the detail activities.

◆ Many schedules created by 'experienced' project managers turned out to have only a few dependencies (links between tasks). As a consequence those schedules had many schedule constraints that kept the task bars on their dates. Constraints, however, made the schedule very rigid. Every time a change occurred, the entire schedule needed to be updated before it depicted the project well, once again. Isn't this reminiscent of the time in which we made schedules on paper? Such schedules are nice charts of the project, but definitely are not a useful model of the project. These people spend too much time on scheduling. And they have to spend this time when they don't have a moment to spare — during project execution.

◆ Many organizations invest in making schedules, but put them aside when the project execution starts. Project managers tend to get very busy with fighting fires. If you don't update your schedule, you don't have forecasts of your project. You need constant forecasting to control your project. A dynamic schedule is easy to maintain and provides continuous forecasts.

These observations, among others, on the current state of the art in scheduling, led me to believe a certification curriculum was much needed. Such a curriculum can elevate the user's skills to new heights.

The Project 2000 Certification Curriculum

Three Levels of Certification

The curriculum consists of three levels. Each level is designed with a specific target group in mind:

◆ Managing a Single Project with MS Project (Orange Belt)
◆ Managing Multiple Projects with MS Project (Blue Belt)
◆ Masters Certificate in MS Project (Black Belt)

In the Orange Belt workshop we bring people who make nice charts of their projects to the level of making dynamic models of their projects. If a person is certified on the Orange Belt level, we guarantee that the person has a demonstrated capability to create good models of their own projects. The Orange Belt is tailored to project managers and schedulers.

The Blue Belt is designed for people who manage multiple projects. These people have successfully managed single projects, and have ended up, as a reward, managing multiple projects at a time. They can be program managers as well as staff working in a PMO. In the Blue Belt we equip people with the know-how to integrate schedules as well as with the tools and techniques to handle these large schedules.

The Black Belt level is suitable for corporate power-users and MS Project trouble-shooters. It is also for people in the PMO who want to make program management more efficient by developing tools and custom solutions on the foundation of MS Project. In other words, the Black Belt is for people who need to know everything about Project 2000.

This book will cover all of the content presented in the Orange Belt level workshop as offered publicly by IIL.

How Many are Currently Certified?

As of January 2001 there have been 273 people certified on the Orange Belt level, 137 on the Blue Belt and 53 on the Black Belt level. The curriculum has been very well received. The following are some quotes from participants.

Orange Belt

I now feel like I am in control of the MS Project program rather than it controlling me. Richard Jones, Project Manager, Logicon, USA

This program taught me more about MS Project in the first four hours than I had picked up in three years of using the product. Preferred Anonymous, USA

The Orange Belt course was full of tips, which immediately made me more productive. Jill Mitchell, Business Analyst-Project Coordinator, GE Capital IT Solutions, USA

This course should be a requirement for professional companies that understand the expense associated with missing schedules. Steve Magee, Program Manager, Dura Automotive, USA

Blue Belt

I really did enjoy the course and have already applied some of the value with my current team and client base. Can't wait until October! Kim Buchalski, Manager Project Office, Alpha Technologies, USA

Superb instruction and excellent course content. A must for even experienced MS Project users. Bill Reinhart, Project Manager, SBC/Ameritech, USA

I have managed projects for a number of years, but the course was of such high quality that I now feel the quality and accuracy of my project plans will be enhanced. Dave Kempster, Consultancy & Research Manager, Centrefile Limited, UK

The IIL MS Project Certification series should be required by every project manager who uses the product! Stephanie Iverson, Director Program Management, Marriott Vacation Club International, USA

Black Belt

Truly challenging from the beginning to the end. Paul Groothuis, Manager Project Control, Allied Signal, USA

Although there are millions of copies of MS Project sold, only a few thousand people really know how to use it. If you want to become a real 'master' user of MS Project, this is the class for you. Jacob Myers, Program Manager, Limited Technology Services, USA

What are the Certification Requirements?

The certification levels have a combination of knowledge and skill tests:

◆ The Orange Belt candidates must submit a schedule of their own project that meets the guidelines for good scheduling practices (a skill test). Many organizations use Orange Belt certification to ascertain that people can create schedules that meet the standards set by their own PMO.

◆ The Blue Belt participants must pass a multiple-choice exam that covers the Orange and the Blue Belt materials. The multiple-choice exam is described as *'challenging'*. The exam discriminates very well between people who studied in preparation and those who didn't. Sample exam questions can be found on page 529 in the Appendix 2: Certification Curriculum Sample Exam Questions . The questions only cover the Orange Belt content that is in this book.

◆ The Black Belt experts must create a custom solution for their own projects in the macro language of MS Project — Visual Basic for Applications (VBA). With VBA you can make Project 2000 sing and dance. For example, you can add and customize fields, create new dialog boxes and have Project 2000 calculate project health indicators. This is another skill test.

The blend of one knowledge test and two skill tests has proven to be very well liked and beneficial for the individual <u>and</u> their organizations.

Qualifying Instructors

In order to maintain quality in the delivery of our training programs, we select instructors based on several criteria. A first criterion is that candidates must have hands-on experience in managing projects. Secondly, candidates must be using MS Project on an almost daily basis. Thirdly, they have to have earned credentials in training groups in MS Project. Fourthly, every trainer has to be certified in MS Project on a higher level than the level he or she will be teaching in this certification curriculum. A final criterion is that the candidate must go through a train-the-trainer session. If you are interested in becoming a certified instructor, please send me your resume at EricU@iil.com.

Consulting

Not every organization is the same or has the same requirements for project schedules. We help people understand how tools like MS Project can best be implemented in their organization. The output of the consulting can take the shape of:

◆ Recommendations for implementation

◆ Project Management Handbook
   A handbook is a document containing best practices, scheduling guidelines, methodology or project management framework specifically for your organization.

◆ Templates and customizations of the MS Project interface
   Templates can contain custom views, tables, filters and groups. Macros can be added if the basic functionality in MS Project does not support what is needed in your organization.

◆ Training
   After the tools are developed, people often need training in how to use them. We create or adapt the course material and train the project managers and schedulers.

◆ Coaching, Mentoring and Helpdesk
   A final step is often to coach and mentor on the job, or provide technical support. People tend to get stuck sometimes, when they strike out on their own to model their projects. If so, we are here to help.

Give us Your Feedback

You are the person who can make the next edition of this book better. Please give us your feedback.

If you have any further questions, don't hesitate to contact me. If you would like to discuss any recommendations we made, let's email.

Thanks for choosing this product from the International Institute for Learning. And thank you for the time you will spend reading it, I hope you will find it well worth the effort!

Eric Uyttewaal, PMP
Director, Microsoft Project Certification
International Institute for Learning
EricU@iil.com
www.iil.com

Chapter 0 About This Book

Learning Objectives

The following are the learning objectives we aim to accomplish with this book. After reading this book you will:

◆ understand project management terminology

◆ be able to create a model of your own project:
   ◇ choosing the options and creating the project calendar
   ◇ entering tasks, estimates, dependencies, constraints, resources and assignments

◆ know how to optimize the schedule to meet deadlines and budget restrictions while keeping the workloads of the resources within their availability

◆ be able to create reports and custom views on the project

◆ know how to use and update the schedule when the project is running

In general you should feel comfortable with Project 2000 after you are finished with this book. We will now outline the topics that will address these objectives.

Outline of this Book

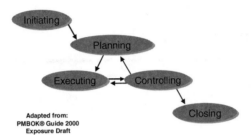

First you initiate the project, then you plan it and while you execute it you control it. At the end, you close it out. The illustration shows the five processes as distinguished by the Project Management Institute (PMI) in the Guide to the Project Management Body of Knowledge (PMBOK®), 2000 Edition. We have used these five processes to structure the book. We treated creating the project plan as a mini-project in itself and we mapped all the steps that you need to take to create a schedule to these processes. The result can be seen in the following illustration.

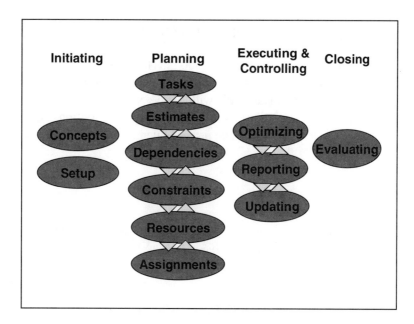

This illustration provides an overview of the contents of this book. Each balloon is a chapter. The overview illustration will be shown at the start of every chapter to indicate where we are. It will pull us back into overview mode before we delve into the next topics.

In this book, we will follow the sequential approach that we recommend you use when you model your project with Project 2000. We will now elaborate on the steps in the approach.

Initiating

Concepts (Chapter 1)

In this chapter we will explain some basic concepts of project management. Even though this book is not meant to be a project management theory book, we will provide as much as you need to utilize Project 2000 well.

In this chapter we will also explain the different purposes you can have using Project 2000. We will aim at the most ambitious one — forecasting a project by building a dynamic model in Project 2000.

Setup (Chapter 2)

In this chapter we will introduce the Project 2000 interface. We will discuss file management and templates. Setting up a new project includes naming the project and entering the project start or finish date. We will invite you to think about the default settings that are active in Project 2000, because some important options need to be set at this stage before any tasks are entered. The project calendar for the project will be created.

Planning

In this part we will enter all the schedule data into Project 2000. This step involves most of the work. There are six types of data Project 2000 needs to create the schedule. We will discuss each of these in six different chapters.

Tasks (Chapter 3)

Task names answer the question: What needs to be done? The task list is developed from the Work Breakdown Structure (WBS). The structure can have several hierarchical levels as in an organizational chart. In Project 2000 the levels are called outline levels. This chapter will show how to create a structured task list and how to enter it into Project 2000. We will also discuss how to move and copy tasks in your project.

Estimates (Chapter 4)

Estimates answer the question: How long will the task take? They can be made in business days (duration) or in person days (work). There are many factors to consider when estimating. We will provide a process in this chapter that will make estimating easier. We will also discuss the human side of estimating and the biases that occur in practice. We will suggest how to handle these biases.

Dependencies (Chapter 5)

Dependencies deal with the question: In what sequence do the tasks have to be done and how will the tasks affect each other? We will explore this important feature in this chapter. Dependencies are the logical cause-and-effect relationships between tasks. Scheduling with project management software does not require dates to be entered for each task. By entering dependencies, as opposed to dates, you build a very powerful model of the project. If you change the duration of one task, Project 2000 will reschedule all affected dependent tasks. The secret of dynamic schedules will be revealed in this chapter.

Constraints (Chapter 6)

Constraints can be dates imposed on the project or promises made for certain dates. Constraints can also be used for restricting Project 2000's freedom to move task bars around in the timescale. We will discuss the new feature of deadlines. The Gantt Chart is finalized in this chapter and we will show you how to create a printout of it.

Resources (Chapter 7)

Resources are the answer to: Who will do the work? Resources can be human resources, facilities, machines or materials. In this chapter we will discuss all these types of resources and how to enter them into Project 2000. We will conclude with how to print the list of resources.

Assignments (Chapter 8)

This last type of project data answers the question: Who does what? Multiple resources can be assigned to work on a task and vice versa, many tasks can be assigned to one resource.

Project 2000 does its own thing when you work with assignments. Behind the screens it uses a formula with which it recalculates data you may have entered. We will explain the when and how, and provide you with the insight to help you predict what Project 2000 will do. The goal of this chapter is to make it help you as a tool … like it should.

Resources do the work and have to be assigned to the appropriate tasks. We will discuss the mechanics of assigning resources.

Executing and Controlling

Optimizing the Schedule (Chapter 9)

After entering all the data, Project 2000 shows a schedule that ends before or after the project deadline. The schedule may be under or over the budget. Changes may have to be made to stay within the restrictions of deadline and budget. Making changes to accomplish this is called optimizing the schedule.

We will present three different approaches for optimizing schedules. You should choose the approach that best fits your own project.
◆ Optimizing for Time
◆ Optimizing for Time and Cost
◆ Optimizing for Time, Cost and Resources
Each approach also includes consideration of the scope and the quality.

In *Optimizing for Time* we will explain the Critical Path method briefly and show how to highlight the Critical Path in your schedule. Sometimes the Critical Path is fragmented and we will show you how to make it go from the start of the project to the end. We will then present many different ways in which you can bring down the duration of your project.

In *Optimizing for Time and Cost* we will make the optimization a bit more complex (or more interesting) by incorporating the cost dimension of projects. We will explore the methods available to bring down the cost without compromising too much on scope, quality, or time.

Optimizing is more complex when you also want to ensure that the required resources are available and not overloaded with work. Over-allocating resources can compromise the scope of the project or the quality of the deliverables, and will often lead to missing deadlines. In the section on *Optimizing for Time, Cost and Resources* we will address the issue of over-allocations by leveling the workloads. And we will introduce the new concept of a Resource-Critical Path that appears like a regular Critical Path but also takes resource constraints into account.

After this chapter the schedule will be ready to print.

Reporting (Chapter 10)

In this chapter we will not change the data of the schedule; we will only adjust the appearance of the schedule. Views and reports can, for example, be used to communicate to resources what to do, what to deliver and when and with whom to cooperate. Filters hide certain tasks and display other tasks and can be used to provide the overview to executives — or the detail of a problem to the team members. Tables can be used to communicate certain data by inserting or deleting fields. The tasks or resources can be grouped on any commonalities found in the data. Formats can be applied to lead the eye of the reader to the important parts of the schedule.

The first prints of the project will be used to get the project approved. The following printed reports are the periodic status reports.

Updating (Chapter 11)

As soon as the project is approved, a baseline schedule is created from the schedule. The baseline schedule serves as the standard of comparison to track progress. Progress information has to be entered into MS Project, which is known as *updating* the plan. Just like bookkeeping, this should be done on a regular basis. An updated schedule shows the actual performance compared to the baseline.

After updating, you need to establish whether another round of optimizing is needed in case there are slippages. During the execution phase of the project, reports will support the decision-making in and about the project, such as modifying the activities or approving the next phase.

During the Execution and Controlling phase of the project, many cycles will be made among the last three project management activities of Optimizing, Reporting and Updating. Delivering a project involves many iterations of making progress (updating), monitoring the progress (reporting) and taking corrective actions (optimizing).

Closing

Evaluating (Chapter 12)

Evaluating your projects is the only way to become a better project manager. It can prevent you from running into the same traps with your next project. Looking back can also improve your skills in setting dependencies and estimating. These are the hardest skills to acquire as a project manager. It has been predicted that the most competitive organizations will be the *'learning organizations'*.

It is important to take some time to look back and see what went well, what went wrong and why. Attention should be paid to the completeness of the task list, the correctness of the network of dependencies and the accuracy of the estimates.

Evaluating is also looking forward to see how problems can be predicted and prevented in the future through lessons learned.

Summary (Chapter 13)

In this chapter you will find a summary of the good scheduling guidelines, as discussed throughout the book. Our instructors use this checklist to certify course participants on the Orange Belt level in the certification curriculum.

Appendix 1: Shortcuts of Project 2000

A summary of keyboard shortcuts and toolbar buttons.

Appendix 2: Certification Curriculum Sample Exam Questions

This appendix contains sample exam questions on Project 2000. These questions are representative of the exams we conduct in the certification curriculum at the International Institute for Learning. The questions pertain to the contents of this book, which corresponds to the Orange Belt level of certification. The real exam is taken at the end of the Blue Belt level and also includes the Blue Belt course materials on managing multiple projects.

Glossary

Index

Contents of the CD-ROM

Exercises

You will find exercises at the end of each chapter. Several projects will be worked out step-by-step throughout the exercises to familiarize the students with MS Project. There are four types of exercises:

◆ **Review**

These exercises are meant to consolidate the knowledge you gained in each chapter. Some are hands-on exercises to challenge you to use the steps in MS Project. Some review the theoretical concepts.

◆ **Hands-on exercise project: the Relocation Project**

You can test yourself and see if you can create a schedule with Project 2000 on the Relocation Project. The Relocation Project is an office move that you will lead as the project manager. You will be moving about 100 people who work in your office to a new location that you have yet to find. You can find the solutions to these exercises on the CD-ROM in the back of the book.

◆ **Troubleshooting**

These exercises will help you understand some of the pitfalls in MS Project. These exercises help you prepare for providing technical support to other MS Project users. All the troubleshooting exercises are situations I have run into over the years of staring at people's schedules. The typical troubleshooting situation is one in which the schedule stubbornly refuses to do what you expect.

◆ **Case Study**

The case studies are meant to give an idea of what is going on in the practice of project management and, in particular, the implementation of MS Project. The case studies are real-life cases from my consulting experience. In all cases, I have disguised the organizations involved.

In the back of the book, in Appendix 2, you can find sample exam questions as used in the certification curriculum at the International Institute for Learning. If you want to check to see if you answered the multiple-choice questions correctly, please visit our website www.iil.com. Trainers, instructors and professors can acquire a separate Instructor's Manual from the International Institute for Learning with all the answers to the review questions, the multiple-choice questions, troubleshooting exercises and the discussions on the case studies. The case discussions in the Instructor's Manual contain information on what really happened in each case. If you want to receive a copy of the manual, please contact the International Institute for Learning at www.iil.com or call 1-800-385-4350 in New York.

Conventions in this Book

Symbols and Text

The following graphics can be expected:

 The light bulb shows a tip, a recommendation to the user. It may be a time-saver, or achieving better project information.

 An exclamation mark shows a warning to the user of Project 2000. Heeding the warnings may keep you out of trouble like unexpected results, loss of data or quirks in Project 2000.

 Indicates that the feature is new in the Project 2000 release. For people who are upgrading to Project 2000 and who want to focus on just the new features, this graphic is the thing to look for.

File   Bolded words are words that can literally be found on your screen in Project 2000 — either as a menu item or as a label in a dialog box.

Quotes   Italicized words are literal references. These can be literal quotes from people, data you literally need to enter into Project 2000 or literal words from the index at the back of the book. The indexed keywords are italicized so you can find them easily in the text.

Step Formulation

We have not used our creativity in the stepwise instructions; in fact we have followed very rigid guidelines to be as clear and consistent as possible. These guidelines are:

◆ For menu items we used the verb "Choose". Example: Choose **File, Save As**; the **Save As** dialog appears, and a snapshot of the dialog is shown.

◆ For the toolbars we used the verb "Click" as in: Click 🗁

◆ For buttons in dialog boxes, we used the verb "Click" as in: Click 💾 S̲ave

◆ For tab pages in dialog boxes, we used the verb "Click" as in: Click **Advanced**

◆ For shortcut key combinations we used the verb "Press":

  ◇ For a single keystroke: Press F2

  ◇ For two keystrokes: Hold down Alt and press F

  ◇ For three: Hold down Alt + Shift and press →

◆ For entering text into the fields that have a name, we used "Key in" as in:
Key in Relocation in the field **File Name**.

◆ For check boxes that are checked or not and where the user can choose one or more, we used the verb "Check" or "Uncheck" as in:
Check ☑ **Display Help on Startup**
Uncheck ☐ **Display Help on Startup**

◆ For radio buttons where the user has to choose one of many options, we used the verb "Select" as in: Select ◉ **Automatic**

◆ For lists in dialog boxes that do have a label, we used:
Select from the list **Insert Field** ID ▼ a column to be inserted.

◆ For lists on toolbars that do not have a label, we used:
Select from the list All Tasks ▼ the filter **Resource Usage...**

Screen Snapshots and Illustrations

We used many illustrations in this book. All the illustrations show only a few tasks extracted from a larger schedule. This allows us to keep the illustrations concise and to the point.

All the dialog boxes are shown with screen snapshots to ensure that you are in the right dialog when you follow the steps.

Where snapshots of screens are shown, we have tried to show only the relevant portion of the screen.

We have annotated the snapshots so you can easily find the option or field referred to in the text.

Meet the Cartoon Characters...

Throughout this book you will find little stories with cartoons. The main characters in these stories are Bob, a very dynamic and successful project manager. This is Bob (any resemblance with existing people is purely coincidental):

As you can see, the man is busy communicating in several different ways at the same time. The smile on his face radiates success. Notice the certificate on the wall.

The second project manager looks rather confused and overwhelmed. His name is Nob (any resemblance with existing people is, again, purely coincidental):

As you can see, Nob has not mastered the latest communication technology, which is epitomized in the way he uses the computer monitor. For him it just is a pin board for yellow stickies.

Bob and Nob will share with us in their project adventures. You will find several cartoons spread throughout the book. I hope you will enjoy them during this serious project management stuff as much as I did when I first saw them. Paul Mason created these wonderful cartoons.

I wanted a successful project manager and a loser. We discussed what their gender should be. There was no way we could come out unscathed by using both genders. Was the successful project manager going to be a man and the loser a woman? Or was the loser going to be a man and the winner a woman? We realized it was a lose-lose situation, and eventually we decided to make both of them men. I apologize to those women who would have liked to see the successful project manager to be female. However, the stories that come with the cartoons could apply to both genders.

Throughout the book I will randomly use *he* or *she* in my examples.

Chapter 1 Concepts of Project Management

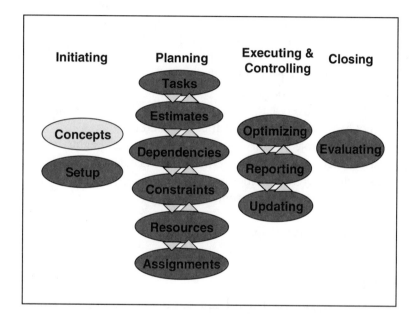

The first *Initiating* phase starts with the *concepts* of project management. The first step is making sure every stakeholder is clear on these concepts.

After this chapter you will know:

◆ the difference between projects and ongoing operations

◆ about the Project Management Body of Knowledge (PMBOK)

◆ recognize the driving forces in projects

◆ the purposes of scheduling

◆ what project management software can do

Projects

A project is the vehicle to create change. Project team members create unique deliverables. When the deliverables are ready, the project is over. A project team is a temporary organization within an existing organization. Some organizations have projects as their core of operations, like construction and consulting companies. In other companies, projects are often used to implement changes, like relocations and reorganizations, or for creating new systems, such as information and financial systems. The manager of today has, apart from his operational management, often one or more projects in progress as well. A project has these characteristics:

◆ It has a concrete objective or goal.
◆ The objective is a relatively new or unique challenge for the organization in the sense that is has not been done to those specifications before.
◆ The end date of the project is forecasted before the project begins.
◆ The project product is divisible into *deliverables*. The deliverables can be further broken down into concrete activities and tasks.
◆ A temporary team performs the activities in a project.

To manage any endeavors like these, Project 2000 can be a helpful tool to create a solid project plan.

Examples of Projects

Below we will give many examples of projects from different industries.

◆ **Organizational change projects:**
  ◇ Implementing a new financial system
  ◇ Implementing ISO 2000
  ◇ Implementing a Total Quality system or continuous improvement
  ◇ Implementing supply-chain management
  ◇ Designing and implementing a project management methodology
  ◇ Creating a Project Management Office (PMO)
  ◇ Office relocation project
  ◇ Business process re-engineering
  ◇ Designing and implementing a new job classification system

◆ **Regulations implementation projects:**

  ◇ Projects to make changes to the manufacturing process in order to meet environmental standards

  ◇ Realizing equal-opportunity in the workplace

◆ **Event projects:**

  ◇ Conferences

  ◇ Writing the yearly financial report

  ◇ Creating a broadcast or news conference

  ◇ Formal presentation to investors

◆ **New product development:**

  ◇ Developing a new pharmaceutical drug

  ◇ Developing new computer hardware

  New product development typically involves Research and Development (R&D). There are typically go/no-go gates and if-then-else branches in R&D-projects.

◆ **Information systems projects:**

  ◇ Programming a desktop application

  ◇ Implementing a LAN or WAN

  ◇ Developing the company's e-Commerce website

◆ **Construction projects:**

  ◇ Designing and constructing buildings

  ◇ Designing and constructing new infrastructure objects like bridges and roads

  ◇ Construction of a new plant

  ◇ Construction of a new manufacturing line

◆ **Education projects:**

  ◇ Develop and pilot new courseware

  ◇ Organizing training workshops for different target groups across several sites

◆ **Maintenance-type projects:**
  Project managers who schedule maintenance projects often deal with many small projects or 'jobs'. Sometimes the maintenance project can stop an entire plant, as is the case when a condenser needs to be replaced in a coal-fuelled power plant. Such a project can take up to five weeks during which the operations are suspended. Thus the project needs to be planned carefully. Every day, early or late delivery has huge financial consequences.

Program Management Versus Project Management

A program is a group of similar or related projects managed in a coordinated way. Projects can be integrated to programs for a variety of reasons:

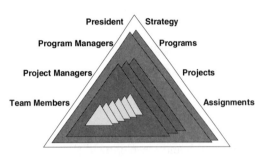

- ◆ a need for overall reporting on all projects
- ◆ a need to model the impacts a project has on other projects
- ◆ a need to monitor resource utilization when several projects share the same resources

This book will deal with project management only i.e., managing a single project.

Guide to the Project Management Body of Knowledge

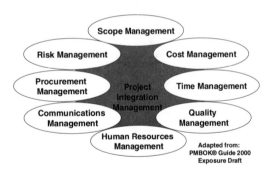

Adapted from:
PMBOK® Guide 2000
Exposure Draft

The Project Management Institute (PMI) has issued the Guide to the Project Management Body of Knowledge, or PMBOK. The PMBOK has become a global standard on project management. Each project has to deal with all nine knowledge areas as specified in the PMBOK. This book is entirely based on and aligned with the 2000 Edition of the PMBOK published by the PMI.

The PMBOK® Guide describes project management as "*The application of knowledge, skills, tools and techniques to project activities in order to meet the project requirements.*"

The Pulling Forces of a Project

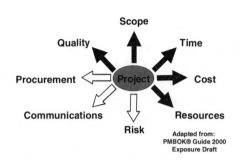

Scope
Quality
Time
Procurement
Project
Cost
Communications
Resources
Risk

Adapted from:
PMBOK® Guide 2000
Exposure Draft

All the areas in which project managers need to have knowledge and skills can also be seen as the areas that require attention from the project manager. The areas even pull the project in opposite directions and can be traded off against each other. The illustration shows this.

MS Project isn't a tool to help you manage all of the areas. For example, Project 2000 does not have many features to manage the quality, risk, procurement and communications side of projects. It does not capture data on risk events, quality standards, contracts or document versions.

The four areas that can be managed well, however, with Project 2000 are:
◆ *Scope*: what to accomplish
◆ *Time*: the deadline
◆ *Cost*: budget restrictions
◆ *Resources*: availability (or capacity) and workloads of the resources

The area of *Quality* can be managed only somewhat with Project 2000. Quality control activities can be scheduled but the tool, as it comes, does not capture quality standards of deliverables, for example. The application is not a quality management system.

The three areas of Risk, Procurement and Communications are the weakest parts of Project 2000. An important activity in risk management is to analyze adverse events and to rank and then manage them. Project 2000 alone is not suitable for this purpose. It can do some PERT-analysis and, yes, there are add-ons that do Monte Carlo risk analysis. We will explain both of these in Chapter 9 Optimizing the Schedule.

In project procurement you want to create and track your contracts. There is no feature in Project 2000 that handles contracts. You can just create hyperlinks to MS Word files that contain the contracts. Project 2000 by itself is not a procurement management system.

Project 2000 is not a document handling system either. Even though Project 2000 has new and strong communication features with Project Central, it still misses the handling of revisions needed for comprehensive document management.

Dwight was Right, but is he Still?

"In preparing for battle, I have always found that plans are useless, but planning is indispensable."

President Dwight D. Eisenhower (1890-1969)

In the time in which Dwight Eisenhower lived (1890-1969), project plans only existed on paper. Paper plans are static and therefore dead. They are a snapshot of the project and the project's vision of the future when the plan was written. A written plan printed on paper is a project-plan-of-the-past. At best, written plans are *"history-books-written-ahead-of-time"*. In his time, Dwight was right.

With the advent of computers, we can now create plans that are alive and dynamic. Let's start thinking of a project plan as an online database that contains current status data and prediction algorithms. This project-plan-of-the-future has a model of your project that is up-to-date and that allows you to make forecasts for the future performance of the project at any time during the life of the project.

The project-plan-of-the-future is a powerful tool for project managers. I like to think that, if Dwight was still alive, he would likely admit: "In preparing for the global market place, I have found that planning is indispensable and that dynamic plans are the critical success factor."

Scheduling is Modeling

As a project manager you should attempt to create a model of your project situation, not just draw a chart that is nice to look at. Nice charts are very useful for selling purposes, but not for managing purposes. The differences between a 'Static Chart' and a 'Dynamic Model' of your project are:

◆ **A model is a simplified reality**
Architectural models are small three-dimensional versions of the final building. Similarly, project models should be simple versions of a complex reality.

◆ **A dynamic model has to be kept up-to-date**
A schedule that is not maintained is static and will be useless soon after it is made. **A dynamic model needs to be responsive**
A responsive model updates itself as much as it can. Schedules can do this if they are created with as many dependencies as needed and as few fixed dates as possible.

◆ **A dynamic model has predictive power**
Schedules need to show the latest forecasts of the finish date and expenses of the project. Only then can a schedule truly be a powerful decision-support system for the project manager. It is nice to have a prediction that holds true in, let's say, 9 out of 10 cases. This requires the model to use empirical data that are translated into parameters and algorithms that provide the predictive power. An example of such an algorithm is the 15%-rule on Earned Value from Fleming and Koppelman [1]. The 15%-rule states that if you are 15% into your project, you should be able to predict the final cost of your project within a margin of plus or minus 10%.

◆ **Executives need online access to a dynamic model**
There is whole new class of business intelligence tools arriving in the marketplace that allow you to slice and dice the data any way you want. They also allow you to drill down into the project database to see detail, if needed. These powerful features are accessible through a user-friendly interface with which executives could familiarize themselves in order to keep their fingers on the pulse of the project. Executives can then do their own analysis and what-if scenario development.

---

[1] See their book "Earned Value – Project Management", PMI, 1996

What we attempt to do in this book is to show you how to create a dynamic model of your projects. A model that meets all the criteria of a dynamic model as explained above. That is what we will set out to do in the chapters that follow. Models are always built for a purpose. We first have to ask ourselves why we are scheduling.

Why do we Schedule?

There are four reasons why people prepare schedules of their projects. The reasons can be ranked by level of challenge (lowest first):

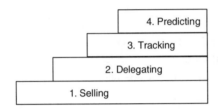

1. **Selling**
   Aspiring project managers want to sell upper management an idea in order to start a new project. A consulting firm may try to sell a new project to a client. The selling is supported by making the timing visible in a Gantt Chart and the cost visible in a budget. Selling requires the least amount of detail in your schedule and does not require the schedule to be dynamic.

2. **Delegating**
   When you have the Work Breakdown Structure (WBS) in MS Project, you can easily create assignments for team members. When you have all the assignments, you can easily create to-do lists for each resource. This by itself is a great benefit.

3. **Tracking**
   In order to track your project you can enter the current status in MS Project and report on it. The output of tracking would be status reports. A status report shows how far the project has progressed.

4. **Predicting**
   You can use MS Project to model your project in such a way that you forecast the

project end date and total cost. You have to set the schedule up in such a way that it immediately shows what impact actual events have on the project end date and cost.

The levels are listed in increasing challenge or difficulty. The lower down the list and the higher up the staircase, the more ambitious you are with the software. Predictive power is the highest level of purpose for using scheduling software. If you want to predict the outcome of your project, you have to set up your schedule in a particular way. For example, you have to use dependencies wherever applicable. We will provide you with all the guidelines to help you set up schedules that will give you predictive power. Will prepare you for the most ambitious scheduling purpose.

The next thing we should do, is explore the field of forces that surrounds our project. This will help us model the important aspects of our project.

How Strong are the Forces in my Project?

As we described in the previous paragraphs, scheduling as modeling is supposed to simplify the reality. One of the first things a project manager needs to do is find out how strong each of the forces is. Recognizing the dominant force and modeling the project accordingly will determine the success of the schedule in a significant way. For example: If a nuclear power station has to be renovated, it is clear that the scope and the quality cannot be tampered with, because of the immense consequences an error could or would have. Meeting the quality standards of the International Agency for Atomic Energy will be a dominant force, even if this leads to higher-than-anticipated cost and/or a delay in the project.

Remodeling a Nuclear Power Station

For most projects, however, the dominant force is less obvious. Depending on whether scope, time, money, quality or resources is the dominant force, different schedules may be the result. Sometimes two forces are equally important. It is therefore a good question to ask before starting: Which force is dominant? Or, if that question is difficult to answer, ask yourself: Which force is least dominant?

Project Management Software

In any project, these six questions are important:
1. What needs to be done? Deliverables and Tasks
2. In which order? Dependencies
3. How long will it take? Duration/Work
4. Who is going to do it? Resources/Assignments
5. When will it happen? Start and Finish dates
6. How much will it cost? Rate x Assignment Effort

The user will have to enter the answers to the first four questions, and Project 2000 will automatically answer the last two questions and create the schedule and the budget.

Notice that when you schedule electronically you hardly ever enter start and end dates for tasks. You enter durations and dependencies instead. The software then calculates the start and finish dates by itself based upon those durations and dependencies. A schedule with dependencies is flexible and "knows" how to update the other tasks automatically when preceding tasks are changed.

Based upon resource cost rates and assignments you entered, the software calculates the total cost, per deliverable and for the whole project. Project 2000 calculates a lot of data automatically.

Scheduling software is efficient in reporting. The software behaves like a database in this respect; you can pull data from the database focusing on any kind of activity, any period or any resource you want. The type of information in a report can be changed as well, like scheduled dates or cost figures. Reports allow you to compare actual against planned progress.

Chapter 2 Setting up a Project

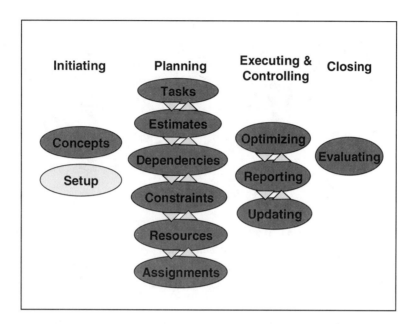

Objectives

After this chapter you will:

◆   be able to open and save a project file

◆   be familiar with the main screen, menu, toolbar and views

◆   know how to move around in a project file

◆   be able to set up a new project and choose the right options

◆   be able to create the project calendar and task calendars

◆   know how to use and create a project template

◆   know how to access help in MS Project

Chaos in the Date Order

An international team is working on a software development project. The team is led by Nob who is from North America. One of the overseas team members, Carl, lives and works in Germany. Carl is two weeks late with a deliverable, although he never reported any issues or expected delays. Nob braces himself for a difficult phone call while he dials the German telephone number.

"Hi Carl, how are you doing?"

"I am fine; how are you?"

"I am fine too. Where is the data model you were supposed to have finished two weeks ago, on 7/8/2000?"

Carl, taken by surprise, stutters: "Which d-d-data model are you referring to?"

"The data model for the Intranet Purchasing website!" Nob exclaims in disbelief.

"I am still working on it. The deadline is August 7th – two weeks from now! I will be ready with it then."

Nob protests. "No, no ... you were supposed to be done two weeks ago – on July the 8th!"

Carl is upset and counters: "The schedule shows '7/8/2000' – the seventh of August, right?"

"No, ... 7/8/2000 is the 8th of July!"

File Management

MS Project as a Relational Database

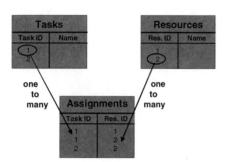

At first glance, Project 2000 bears a striking resemblance to a spreadsheet. However, instead of seeing it as a spreadsheet, we suggest you think of Project 2000 as a relational database. A relational database has several different tables that are related to each other through certain fields. In MS Project these are the ID-fields [2].

There are three reasons for seeing the tool as a relational database:

1. The data is relational by nature.
    There are three types of data in MS Project: tasks, resources and assignments. There are one-to-many relationships between these entities: one task can have many resources assigned and one resource can be assigned to more than one task.

2. Each type of data has its own tables.
    Tasks can be found in task views, resources in resource views. Assignments do not have their own views. The assignments can be shown in between the tasks in the Task Usage View or in between the resources in the Resource usage View.

3. Project 2000 acts as a relational database.
    Deleting a field from a table does not delete the data; it just hides the data from view. Conversely, if you delete a column in a spreadsheet application you delete the data, but if you delete a field from a query in a database, you are just not showing the data. Tables in Project 2000 are like queries in a database.

---

[2] In fact the **Unique ID** fields, because the **ID** values change constantly.

File Structure

Project 2000 has project files and project template files:

Project Files (.MPP)
◆ data: tasks, dependencies, resources, assignments
◆ objects: Views, Tables, Filters, Fields, Calendars, Groups, Reports, Custom forms, Maps, Visual Basic modules
◆ project-specific options

Project Template Files (.MPT):
◆ data
◆ objects: all objects plus Toolbars and Menu
◆ project-specific options

Default Template File: GLOBAL.MPT
◆ (default) objects
◆ generic (default) options

The file extensions are well thought out: a project file has an **.MPP** extension, which stands for **M**icrosoft **P**roject **P**roject. A template file has an **.MPT** extension, which stands for **M**icrosoft **P**roject **T**emplate. Project and template files can contain project data, as well as objects and options. The objects can be viewed in the Organizer by choosing **Tools, Organizer**.

Project templates are standardized schedules that are protected against accidental changes. Project templates are used in organizations that run similar projects over and over, like construction companies. The project templates can contain schedule data, objects and project-specific options.

The *global.mpt* is the default template and is always open when Project 2000 is running. The objects of the *global.mpt* are exposed and ready to be used in new project files. The *global.mpt* also contains the menu bar and the toolbars that are active in your projects. It can have a custom menu bar, and custom toolbar objects, if desired.

The difference between a project template and the *global.mpt* template is that the latter cannot contain schedule data like tasks and dependencies.

Objects can be transferred from one file to another with the **Organizer** (on the **Tools** menu).

Project Files

Opening a Project File

1. Choose **File, Open**; the **Open** dialog appears:

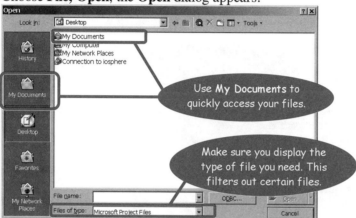

Use **My Documents** to quickly access your files.

Make sure you display the type of file you need. This filters out certain files.

2. If the project is on a drive or directory other than the current one, select it from the list **Look in:** (C:)

3. Double-click on the name of the file to open
    OR

    single-click on the name and click Open

Saving and Replacing a Project File

1. Click on the **Save** tool OR choose the menu items: **File, Save**

2. If your file existed already, the file on the hard disk will be updated with the changes.

If you save a schedule for the first time, you are prompted for a filename in the **Save As** dialog:

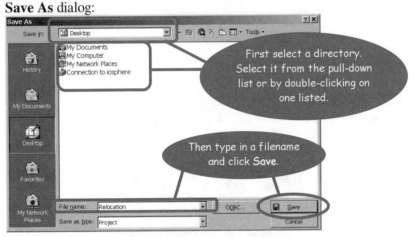

3. A prompt appears that asks you to save with or without a Baseline:

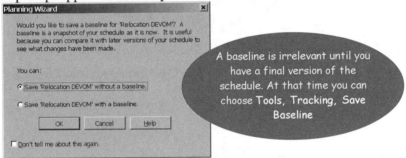

4. Save it with a baseline if you have an approved version of your schedule, if not, check ☑ **Don't tell me about this again** and save the baseline when you have the schedule approved. You can set the baseline yourself by choosing **Tools, Tracking, Save Baseline**. For more on baselines, see Chapter 11 Updating the Schedule.

 Each project file will be saved with the extension **.MPP** unless specified otherwise.

Saving in a new Directory or under a new Name

1. Choose **File**, **Save As**; the **Save As** dialog appears (see above).

2. Select the drive and directory from the list
    Save In ▭ (C:) ▼ at the top of the dialog.

3. Type a name in the field
    File Name: ▼
    at the bottom of the dialog.

4. Click 🖫 Save

Closing a File

1. Choose **File, Close**. If you have made changes to the open project, MS Project will
    prompt you to save the changes. The **Microsoft Project** dialog appears:

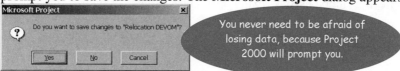

You never need to be afraid of
losing data, because Project
2000 will prompt you.

2. To save changes, choose Yes . If the project hasn't been saved as a file before,
    the **Save As** dialog appears. Type a name for the project and choose a subdirectory.
    To discard changes, choose No .
    To interrupt the closing, choose Cancel .

Project Templates

Project templates are useful as a quick-start on your project plan. If you run similar projects over and over again templates are useful as well. Templates are meant to be protected from accidental tampering so you can use them again and again and they will be the same every time.

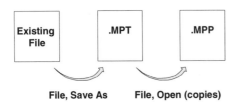

File, Save As   File, Open (copies)

The way the templates are protected is simple. When you open a project template file, Project 2000 copies it; you never open the template itself. You can see this because when saving the file you will always be asked for a (new) filename. In this way the templates are safe and can be used by many different people.

Creating a Project Template

1. Choose **File, Save As;** the **Save As** dialog appears

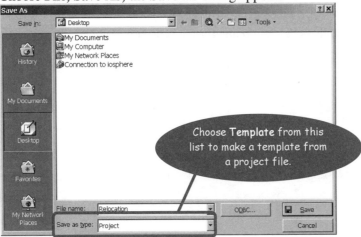

Choose **Template** from this list to make a template from a project file.

2. In the list **Save as type:** `Microsoft Project Files (*.mp*)` ▼ select **Template (*.MPT)**.

Notice that in Project 2000 the directory is immediately changed to the default directory for your templates, as specified in **Tools, Options**, tab **Save**.

3. Type a name for the template in the field
   File name: [_____] ▼

4. Click [💾 _Save_] ; the **Save as Template** dialog appears that prompts you as to
   what data to save in the template:

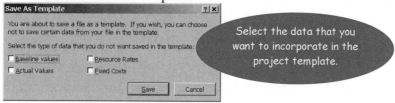

5. Check the data to include and click the **Save** button again.

 Templates can be created centrally to promote consistent work breakdown structures,
common options, standard resource names, and the use of standard reports and project
calendars.

Using a Project Template

1. Choose **File, New ...** as if you are opening a project file. The **New** dialog appears:

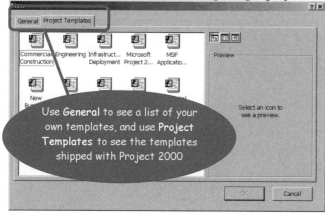

2. The templates you created yourself should be listed in the list on the tab **General**.
   Click the tab **Project Templates** to see a list of templates shipped with Project 2000.
   It has ready-to-go templates for construction, new product and software development
   among others. Templates have the extension **.MPT**.

3. Select one template and click [OK]; the file opens, and the schedule appears
    with the options and project calendar set. There may be tasks, dependencies, estimates
    and generic resources that are assigned in the project template as well.

The Project 2000 Interface

The Main Screen

We suggest that you open one of the project templates at this point to follow the instructions for navigating the Project 2000 interface.

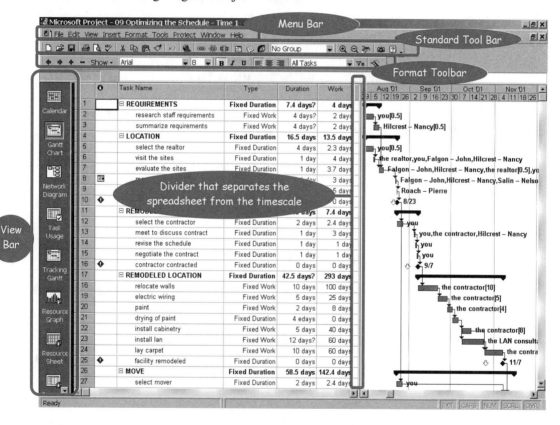

Working With the Menus

To choose a menu item, just click on it with the mouse or hold down the [Alt] key and press the underscored character of the menu item.

Working With the Toolbar

To invoke the action of the tool, click with the left mouse button on the tool you need. If you are not sure which button to click, hover the mouse pointer on top of the button without clicking; a tool tip will remind you what the button does. An example of a tool tip for the 🐾-tool is: Go To Selected Task.

Each toolbar now has on the right-hand side the **Add or remove buttons** tool ☑. This button allows you to customize your toolbar very quickly. You can also reset your toolbar to its original with this button.

Working with the View Bar

The view bar on the left is meant to quickly change views. To display or hide the view bar choose **View, View Bar** or make a right-click on the view bar and choose **View Bar.**

In my opinion, this View Bar wastes valuable screen space. It carries only buttons for some views, so it does not save many clicks. I normally turn it off. Microsoft added it to be consistent across their office applications. From here on, I will show the view bar turned off in the screen snapshots.

Working with Scroll Bars

The scroll bar consists of three parts

scroll arrow buttons: click and scroll one row

scroll box: drag

scroll bar shaft areas: click and scroll a screen

While you are dragging the scroll boxes of the time scale, you will see a yellow feedback box pop up that will tell you where you are. The vertical scroll box shows the ID-number of the task to browse to:

```
ID:    4
Name: LOCATION
```

The horizontal scroll box tells you the date to travel to:

```
Aug 1 '01
```

Using Right-Mouse Clicks

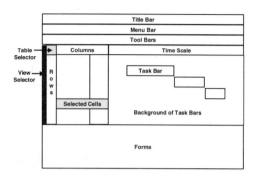

For those who are right-handed the right-mouse button (as opposed to the left-mouse button) under your middle finger can pop up shortcut menus. You can make a right-click in all the places that are labeled in the illustration on the left. It is a stylized version of the Gantt Chart; you can make many more right-clicks in other views. Try it out instead of clicking yourself silly through the menus. Save your mouse muscles!

Moving Around in a Project

The following convention is used in the table:

[Alt] + [→] means hold down [Alt] and press [→].

Move to	By keyboard	By mouse
Next row	[Enter]	Click
Next column	[Tab]	Click
Next time unit in time scale	[Alt] + [→] or [Alt] + [←]	Click on an arrow button of the scroll bar [▶]
Next screen in time scale	[Alt] + [Page Up] or [Alt] + [Page Down]	Click at the left or right of the scroll box [■] on the scroll bar
The start date of the project	[Alt] + [Home]	Left align the scroll box [■] on horizontal scroll bar
The end date of the project	[Alt] + [End]	Right align the scroll box [■] in the scroll bar
The first task of the project	[Ctrl] + [Home]	Drag the vertical scroll box [■] to the top
The last task of the project	[Ctrl] + [End]	Drag vertical scroll box [■] to the bottom
A specific task, resource or date	[F5] OR [Ctrl] + [F]	**Edit, Go To** OR **Edit, Find**
The other split window	[F6]	Click in the other split window to make it active
The task bar of a selected task		Click [icon] **Go To Selected Task**

Moving Around in a Dialog Box

The following convention is used in the table:

`Alt` + `Tab` means hold down `Alt` and press `Tab`.

Action	By keyboard	By mouse
Move to next field in dialog box	`Tab`	Click in the field
Previous field	`Shift` + `Tab`	
Move to any field in a form	`Alt` + press underlined letter of the field name	Click in the field
Increase or decrease value in a field	`Alt` + `↑` `Alt` + `↓`	Use the spin button ⬍
Move to next tab in a dialog box with page tabs	`Ctrl` + `Tab`	Click on the tab

Selecting Data

The following convention is used in the table:

`Alt` + `Tab` means hold down `Alt` and press `Tab`.

Select	By keyboard	By mouse
A task		Click on the ID number of the task or click on the task bar.
An entire row or record	`Shift` + space bar	Click on the row heading
An entire column	`Ctrl` + space bar	Click on a column heading

When you select an entire row as explained above, all the cells of a task (about 243) are selected, even the ones that are not visible. It is important to select a task in the proper way before moving or copying it.

Project 2000 Views

The view of a project is a predefined layout that presents the project from a certain angle. The fields in views allow you to enter, review or report your project.

View	Shows
Calendar	the tasks shown as bars on a calendar
Gantt Chart	the tasks over time, plus spreadsheet columns
Network Diagram	the network of dependencies between tasks (dependencies are shown as arrows)
Task Usage	the assignments on each task
Tracking Gantt	the original (baseline) schedule and current schedule
Resource Graph	the workloads for resources in a bar chart format
Resource Sheet	the spreadsheet with resource information
Resource Usage	the workloads for resources in numbers over time

We will discuss each of these views on the pages that follow.

Calendar View

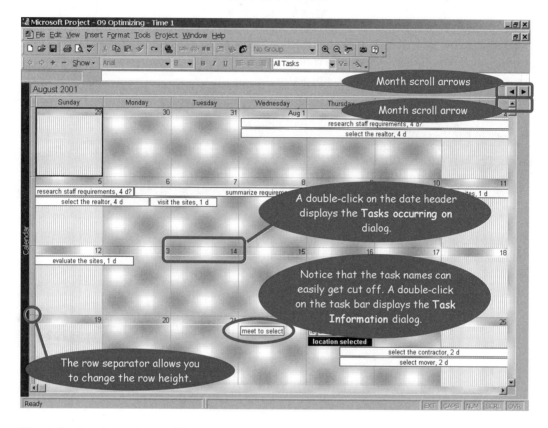

To apply the view, choose **View, Calendar**.

Notice that the *Calendar* view is different from the **Standard Project Calendar** that contains the holidays and working times. The calendar view shows task bars as in the Gantt Chart, though in a format that is similar to conventional calendars.

To See All Tasks on a Day

The calendar view is not suitable for showing the entire schedule. As you can see in the snapshot below, not all task bars always show. This occurs if too many tasks take place on the same day. If there is too little room vertically, Project 2000 displays a ▓ in the date heading, as in the following snapshot:

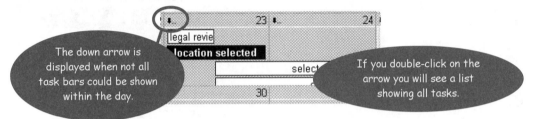

Point to the area where the date is displayed and double-click; a list showing all the tasks on that day appears:

Notice the check mark in front of the tasks that were already visible; focus on the tasks without check marks!

Because of the lack of space, we recommend you use this view to create to-do lists for resources. To-do lists typically have only one or two tasks per day. We will explain and create one in the Reporting chapter on page 425: To-Do Lists in the Calendar View.

To Create Tasks

Creating new tasks in this view is not recommended because the tasks end up at the end of the list and you will still have to move it to the right place in the work breakdown structure (WBS).

To Edit the Data of a Task

1. Double-click on a task in the spreadsheet; the **Task Information** dialog appears:

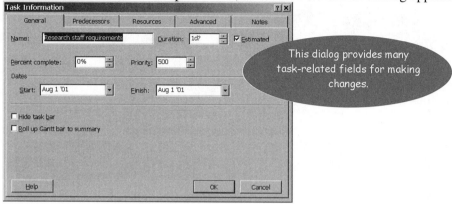

2. Make the changes, and click ▭ OK ▭.

To Move Task Bars

If you move task bars by dragging them by their border, you are setting
start-no-earlier-than constraints on the task. This happens just like in the Gantt Chart.
You can drag one when you point to the border of a bar and see the mouse pointer ✛.
You can drag a bar within the same day(s) or across days.

The Gantt Chart

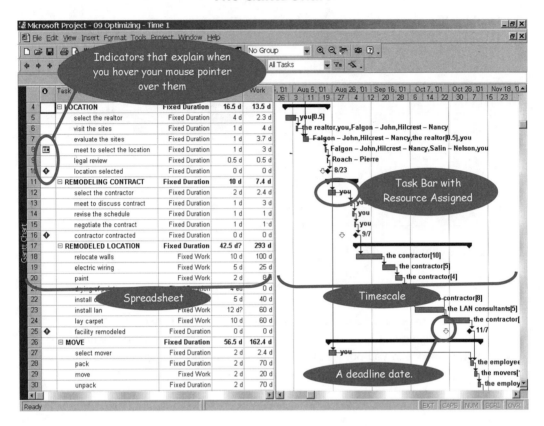

To apply the view, choose **View, Gantt Chart**. The *Gantt Chart* shows tasks over time. The duration of each task is reflected in the width of its task bar. The Gantt Chart also shows the list of tasks that is also referred to as the Work Breakdown Structure (WBS). The WBS typically has multiple levels of summary tasks and indented detail tasks.

To See more Spreadsheet of Timescale

You can change the amount of the spreadsheet you see on the left of the screen. If you reveal more of the spreadsheet it will be at the expense of the timescale on the right. You can do this by pointing to the divider line between the spreadsheet and the timescale; you should see the mouse pointer change to a ◀▶. Click and hold down to drag it to the desired position.

Collapsing and Expanding Levels

Click on the minus button ⊟ next to the summary task name to hide its detail tasks. Click the plus button ⊞ of a summary task to reveal its detail tasks.

Seeing More Spreadsheet or Timescale

To see more spreadsheet, drag the border that separates the spreadsheet from the timescale to the right. It works like a sliding door. To see more timescale, drag the border to the left.

 To position the border exactly in between two columns in the spreadsheet, double click on the border.

Zooming the Timescale

To zoom the timescale in to smaller time units to see the details, click ⊕.
To zoom the timescale out to larger time units to get an overview, click ⊖.

 To fit the entire project timescale within the screen so you always see task bars when paging up or down, choose **View, Zoom,** and select ⦿ **Entire Project**.

Finding the Task Bars

If you don't see any task bars in the Gantt timescale, the timescale shows a time period when no tasks are scheduled. If you put the horizontal scroll box at the extreme left on the scroll bar, you will always see the start date of the project.

If you hold the left mouse button down on the scroll box in the horizontal scroll bar, it will tell you the exact date, including the year you currently have on your screen.

 If you quickly want to see the task bar of a task, select the task and click the tool **Go To Selected Tasks** .

Network Diagram

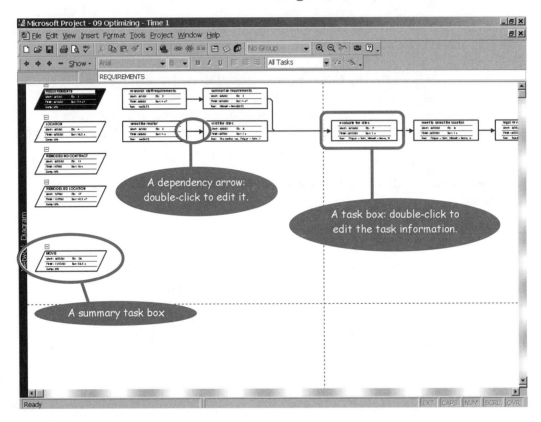

To apply the view, choose **View**, **Network Diagram**. This view used to be called PERT Chart in previous releases. Network Diagram is a better name, because PERT refers to a particular technique that we will discuss on page 305.

The *Network Diagram* shows the network of dependencies between tasks. The dependencies are depicted as arrows. However, when you enter this view for the first time, you often don't see many.

Zoom out using the **Zoom Out** 🔍 tool; the text becomes illegible when zoomed out too far, but if you point the mouse pointer on a task a box pops up that allows you to read the task data. An example of such a pop-up box is:

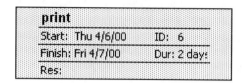

To zoom back in, use the **Zoom In** tool 🔍.

By default, the Network Diagram displays the different types of tasks in differently shaped boxes:

◆ summary tasks in a parallelogram

◆ detail tasks in a rectangle

◆ milestones in a hexagon

The critical tasks have a red border instead of the (default) blue.

This view is typically used to check the logic in the network. You can easily add and delete dependencies. We will discuss this view in more detail on page 185: Entering Dependencies in the Network Diagram.

Task Usage

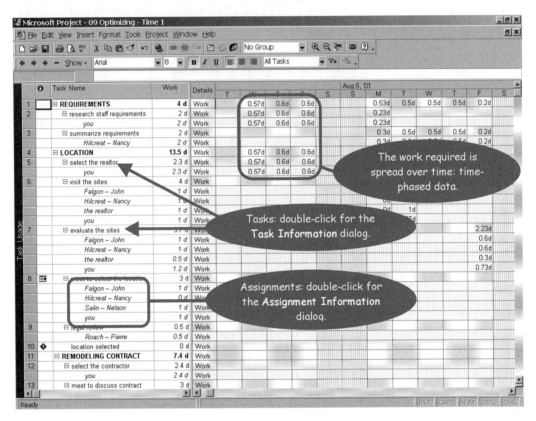

To apply the view, choose **View**, **Task Usage**.

Notice how the *Task Usage* view shows the assignments in italicized text in between the tasks. The Task Usage and the Resource Usage are the only views that show the assignments as separate line items.

The timescale on the right shows how Project 2000 schedules the tasks and assignments. It shows the detailed numbers behind the task bars of the Gantt Chart. This view helps in understanding the Gantt Chart and troubleshooting it.

If you click the **Zoom Out** tool, Project 2000 immediately calculates the totals for the new time unit. To zoom back in, use the **Zoom In** tool.

You can report the spread of the effort across the life of the project. The view is often used for reporting a time-phased budget by activity. We will detail the steps on page 431: Workload Histogram.

Tracking Gantt

To apply the view, choose **View, Tracking Gantt**.

The *Tracking Gantt* view is used during the execution of the project to track the progress against the original schedule (the baseline). Notice that the task bars are split in two halves, a top half that represents the current schedule and a bottom half for the baseline. If you don't have a baseline in your schedule it only shows thin task bars for the current schedule. We will discuss the use of this view extensively in Chapter 11 Updating the Schedule.

Resource Graph

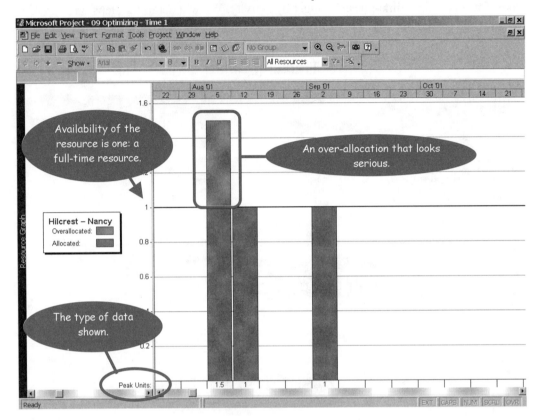

To apply the view, choose **View, Resource Graph**. The *Resource Graph* shows
bar charts of the workload over time for all resources.

If you don't see any bars, hold down Alt and press Home to jump to the project start
date. If you still don't see any bars use the tool **Zoom Out** until you do.

By pressing Page Down or by using the bottom left horizontal scroll bar you can browse from
resource to resource.

Notice that the Resource Graph shows the **Peak Units** by default. Peak Units means that
if you zoom out the timescale and go from days to weeks the highest daily bar will be
shown as the workload for the week. The more you zoom out, the more pessimistic the

depiction of the workload becomes. You can change the Peak Units by choosing **Format, Details**. If you select **Work** you will see the 'real' totals charted.

Resource Sheet

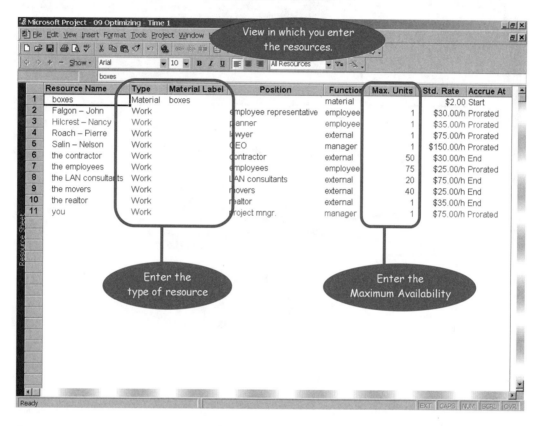

To apply the view, choose **View, Resource Sheet**.

The *Resource Sheet* is used to enter the resources needed in a project. Resources can be human resources, facilities, machines and material resources.

Important fields in the Resource Sheet are:

◆ **Type**; you can indicate if a resource is a material resource or a resource that works on tasks.

◆ **Max.Units**; the maximum units represents the availability of the resource.

Resource Usage

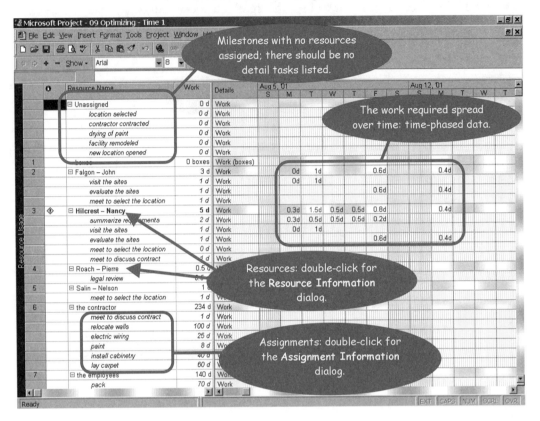

To apply the view, choose **View, Resource Usage**.

The *Resource Usage* view shows the amounts of work or cost over time. As in the Task Usage view, this view shows the assignments as separate line items in italics.

This view allows you to analyze the workloads and solve any over-allocations. We will discuss the how-to on page 344 and following.

Navigating the Views

To Switch Views

Choose **View**; notice the check mark in front of one of the views that is the current view on your screen. Click on the view you want to switch to.
OR
Right-click on the blue bar in the left of your screen and select the view in the pop-up menu.

Single View Versus Combination View

A *single view* is a one-view screen.

A *combination view* is a screen with two views. A combination view consists of a top and a bottom view. The bottom view only shows information pertaining to the tasks (or resources) selected in the top pane. This interaction between top and bottom view can be very useful for:

◆ Data entry with a sheet view in the top and a fill-in form view in the bottom. The Task Entry view (**View, More Views, Task Entry**) is a combination view with the Gantt Chart in the top and the Task Form in the bottom.

◆ Analysis with a task view in the top and resource view in the bottom to check assignments. Or with a resource view in the top and a task view in the bottom to check over-allocations (**View, More Views, Resource Allocation**).

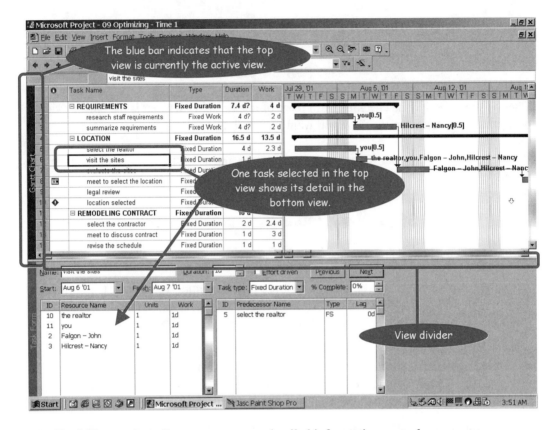

The **Task Entry** view allows you to enter detailed information on tasks: resource assignments and dependencies. The task you select in the top view, the **Gantt Chart**, is shown in the bottom view, the **Task Form**. The top and bottom pane interact, whatever you select in the top is shown in more detail in the bottom. This makes combination views well suited for analysis of schedules.

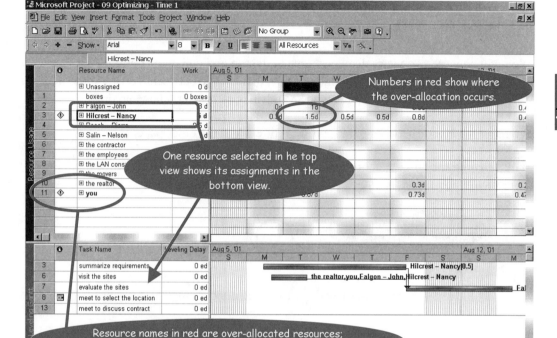

The **Resource Allocation** view has the **Resource Usage** in the top view and the **Leveling Gantt** view in the bottom. This combination view allows you to analyze and resolve over-allocations. The interaction between the top and bottom pane is such that the assignments on the task selected in the top are shown in detail in the bottom.

To Switch to a Combination View

You can create a custom combination view by splitting the window.
Choose **Window, Split**.

Or you can point with the tip of the mouse pointer to the sliding window handle at the bottom right of your screen (the little horizontal bar under the scroll down button).

The mouse pointer will become a double-headed arrow ↨. Drag it up or double-click on it.

You will now see two views displayed, one in the top and one in the bottom. You can change the size of each view by pointing to the divider line between the views; the mouse pointer should change to ↨. When you see this mouse pointer, click and drag.

To move the cursor between panes, press F6 or click in the other pane.

 You can drag the horizontal border and the vertical dividers both at the same time. Put your mouse pointer on the intersection between the two divider lines:

Intersection between divider lines

You should see a mouse pointer like ⁺↟⁺↖. Drag the dividers to the sizes you need.

To Exchange one of the Views in a Combination View

1. Click on the view you want to exchange. This will make it the active view. You should see the blue vertical bar on the far left of the screen jump to the view you clicked in.

2. Choose **View** and click on the view you want to apply.
   OR
   Right-click on the blue bar and click in the pop-up menu on the view to be displayed.

To Switch Back to a Single View

Drag the view divider line to the top or to the bottom using the mouse pointer ↨, depending on which of the two views you want full-screen
OR
Double-click on the view divider when you see the mouse pointer ↨
OR
Choose **Window, Remove Split.**
OR
Hold down Shift and click on menu item **View** and select another view.

Using Help

Help Index

1. Choose **Help**, **Contents and Index** to get a list of topics; the **Microsoft Project Help** dialog appears in its own window:

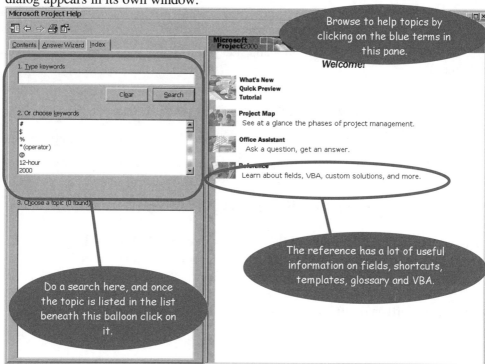

2. Click, for example, in the **Welcome!** screen on the item **Reference** to receive details on fields, shortcuts, templates, glossary and the macro programming language (Visual Basic for Applications or VBA)

3. The terms with a blue solid underline (like Templates) are topics you can jump to by clicking on them. The blue terms without underline (like Critical Path Method) are explained in a pop-up, when you click on them.

To Search for Help Information

1. Choose **Help, Contents and Index**.

2. Click on the tab **Index**.

3. Type a word or phrase you want to search for in the field:
   1. Type Keywords

   [_____] The words that most closely match the text you type are immediately displayed in the list below as you are typing.

4. Select and double-click on a topic from the list
   2. Or choose keywords

5. Select an item at the bottom in the list
   3. Choose a Topic; on the right-hand side you will now see the help text you asked for.

Help Texts About Screen Items

1. Hold down `Shift` and press `F1`; the mouse pointer has a question mark attached now.

2. Click on the screen item you want to know more about.

Help With Scheduling: PlanningWizard

The PlanningWizard can help you find your way around MS Project. It can also help you create your first schedule. The Wizard gives you choices of things to do if there is any ambiguity. It presents choices to solve the problem.

Turn the Wizard on or off by choosing **Tools, Options, General,** and (un)checking **Advice from PlanningWizard**.

Help With Project Management

Project 2000 comes with a complete road map for project management. You can find the steps to put a comprehensive project plan together by choosing **Help, Getting Started, Project Map**.

Help With your Computer System

1. Choose **Help, About Microsoft Project.**

2. Click `System Info...`.

Setting up a Project

The process for setting up a new project is:

1. Creating a new project file and setting the:
   ◇ **Project, Project Information**
   ◇ **File, Properties**

2. Setting the options: **Tools, Options**

3. Setting Leveling options: **Tools, Resource Leveling...**

4. Setting the Project Calendar: **Tools, Change Working Time**
   ◇ Business Days
   ◇ Working Hours
   ◇ Holidays

We will now discuss these steps in more detail.

Creating a new Project File

1. Click ☐
   OR
   Choose **File, New**: the **New** dialog appears:

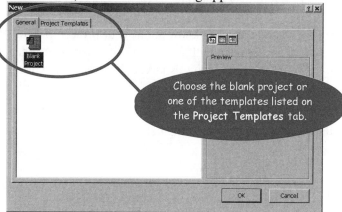

Choose to create the schedule from a blank project or from one of the project templates
shipped with MS Project. Select the **Blank Project** or one of the templates using the
Project Templates tab.
Click OK .

2. The **Project Information** dialog (on the **Project** menu) appears:

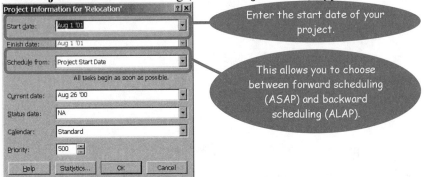

Enter the start date of your project.

This allows you to choose between forward scheduling (ASAP) and backward scheduling (ALAP).

3. Enter basic project information in this dialog. There are two choices in the list **Schedule From**:

◊ **Start Date**: (*scheduling forward*)
MS Project will schedule all tasks as soon as possible (ASAP) after the project start date. After you have entered all the tasks, MS Project will show what the earliest finish date will be for the project.

◊ **Finish Date**: (*scheduling backward*)
MS Project will schedule all tasks as late as possible (ALAP) working backwards from the project finish date. After you have entered all the tasks, MS Project will show what the start date of the project should be.

The choice you make depends on what you know about your project: the start date or the finish date. Neither approach will prevent the common occurrence that the initial schedule is too long, requiring you to squeeze the project into the time frame that is available for the project. This makes the choice between entering the start or the finish date less important.

4. Choose **File, Properties** the name of the project in the field **Title** and your name as the **Manager**.

5. Click [OK].

In an existing project file, choose **Project, Project Information…** to change project-level data, for example, if the start date of the project changes.

Choosing the Options

The way Project 2000 operates is affected a lot by the settings in **Tools**, **Options**. The steps to change the options are:

1. Choose **Tools, Options…**; the **Options** dialog appears:

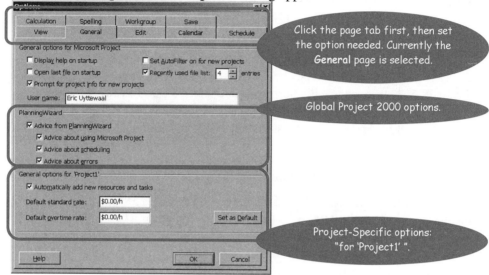

Click the page tab first, then set the option needed. Currently the *General* page is selected.

Global Project 2000 options.

Project-Specific options: "for 'Project1' ".

2. Select the category of options by clicking one of the tabs.

3. Set the options.

4. Click [OK].

There are two types of options:

◆ *Global options* that take effect in all projects. These options are stored in the GLOBAL.MPT.

◆ *Project options* that affect the active project only. You can recognize these because they start with a section divider that has the name of the project file. These options are stored in the project file (.MPP).

By clicking [Set as Default] you can make project-specific options the default for new projects. This button saves the project-specific options also in the global template file GLOBAL.MPT. The GLOBAL.MPT file is used as the template for a blank new project. For existing project files, the project-specific options will not be overridden by clicking this button.

Options for a new Project

Tab	Set to
Schedule	☑ **Show Scheduling Messages** will give helpful messages when it notices a problem in the schedule.
View	**Date Format:** `Mon 1/31/00` ▾ To avoid confusion about dates in international projects, a date format should be chosen with the month spelled out i.e., 31 Jan '00. Americans will interpret a date like 7-8-2000 as July 8, 2000. Europeans, South Americans and people from Québec, however, will interpret it as August 7th and will think they have an extra month.
General	**User Name** `                    ` Enter your name. ☑ **Advice from PlanningWizard** For novice users a great help, otherwise uncheck.
Calculation	⦿ **Automatic** will ensure that you see the effect of the last changes made. With the current speed of computers the need for manual calculation is evaporating.
Calendar	**Hours per Day** `8.00` ⬍ MS Project uses this number to convert days entered in the **Duration** and **Work** fields into hours. If this number does not represent the hours of a Full-Time Equivalent (FTE) employee, your schedule will not be accurate. **Hours per Week** `40.00` ⬍ MS Project uses this number to convert weeks into hours. If this number does not reflect your situation, the schedule will not be accurate. It should correspond to the **Hours per Day** setting. **Days per Month** `20` ⬍ MS Project uses this number to convert months into days. This number should reflect your situation. `Set as Default` Sets the calendar options above as the default settings for any new schedules you create. The existing schedules are not affected because this option is stored in the project files as you can see in the label of the section divider, **Calendar Options for 'Project 1'**.

This table indicates the most important options you must set (or accept) when initiating a new project.

 The **Calendar** option, **Hours per Day** has to be decided upon first and cannot be changed without re-entering all durations. You have to specify how many work hours there are in a workday. If you start with the wrong number, MS Project will interpret the durations you enter incorrectly. It uses this setting to convert between time units. For example, if the **Hours per Day** is set to 7.5 hours and you enter a duration of 4 days, MS Project knows this equals 30 hours. You must consider this option before entering data.

Most options we discuss in this chapter are global, which means that they apply to all your projects, existing and new. You can see this in the **Options** dialog box by reading the labels in the section dividers; on the **Schedule** tab it reads:
Schedule Options for Microsoft Project.

Setting the Date Order

The date order (ddmmyy or mmddyy) cannot be set inside Project 2000. You have to set it in the Windows Control Panel. This means that it will affect the date order in all of your Windows applications.

1. Click ▇**Start**.

2. Choose **Settings, Control Panel**; the **Control Panel** folder appears.

3. Double-click on:
   ● Regional Settings in Windows 98, or
   ● Regional Options in Windows 2000.

4. Click the page tab **Date** and select the date order from the list
   Short Date Style M/d/yy ▼ in Windows 98 or
   Short Date Format M/d/yy ▼ in Windows 2000.

5. Click ▇ OK ▇; all lists in Project 2000 that provide choices for date formats will now only show items in the date order you choose.

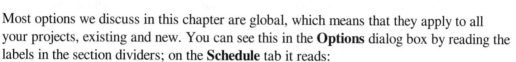

Leveling Option: Automatic or Manual

Workload Leveling

Workload leveling is making changes to the schedule in such a way that the workloads of

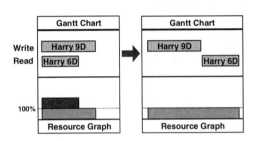

the resources are within their availability. In the illustration, you can see that on the left Harry has to work fulltime on two tasks that are scheduled in parallel. It causes a workload that exceeds his availability, which is called an *over-allocation*. The over-allocation was solved on the right by delaying the task *Read* until after *Write*.

Leveling Option

1. Choose **Tools, Resource Leveling…**; the **Resource Leveling** dialog appears:

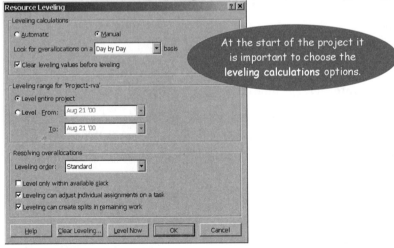

2. At the top in **Leveling calculations**, select ◉ **Manual**.

We recommend you use manual leveling at this time; when we come to Chapter 9 Optimizing the Schedule, we will generate some scenarios using automatic leveling and discuss the various options in more detail.

Creating the Project Calendar

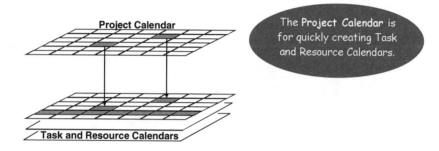

Project Calendar

Task and Resource Calendars

> The Project Calendar is for quickly creating Task and Resource Calendars.

The **Tools, Change Working Time** dialog allows you to set the *Project Calendar*. On the Project Calendar you indicate:

◆ the *business days* —
   Which days are working days in a regular workweek?

◆ the standard *working hours* —
   What are the typical working hours for project team members?

◆ the national *holidays* —
   What days are non-working days throughout the year?

Apart from the Project Calendar there are:

◆ *Task Calendars*
   These can be used to schedule individual tasks. For example, outdoor construction tasks can only take place when the weather permits. A task calendar could be created for all tasks affected by winter weather. We will discuss these on page 131.

◆ *Resource Calendars*
   These are calendars for each individual person. A resource calendar typically contains individual working days, hours, and vacations. We will explain these on page 245.

The business days, working hours and national holidays of the project calendar will be transferred to all the task and resource calendars. The changes you make on the Project Calendar apply to every task and every resource in the project. At this point we will only edit the Project Calendar, later we will create Task and Resource Calendars.

On the resource calendars you can override the Project Calendar and individualize the workdays, working times, and vacations for each resource.

MS Project uses the Project Calendar to schedule tasks that do not have a task calendar or resources assigned. MS Project uses the Resource Calendars when a task has resources assigned.

In summary, the Project Calendar has two functions:

◆ It is a time-saving device to change all resource calendars.

◆ It is used to schedule tasks without a task calendar and without assignments.

Hours/Day Option Versus Working Time

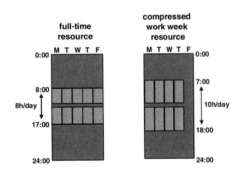

What is confusing to many people is this. If you change the number of hours per day, Project 2000 does not update the working times on the Project Calendar by itself. Project 2000 uses the hours per day option for conversion purposes only. When you enter a duration of *1w*, it will convert it to hours. If the setting in Tools, Options is 40h/w then it knows that 1w = 40h. Project 2000 then goes to the Project Calendar to schedule the 40h of the task within the working hours.

Entering the Working Hours

1. Choose **Tools, Change Working Time...**; the **Change Working Time** dialog appears:

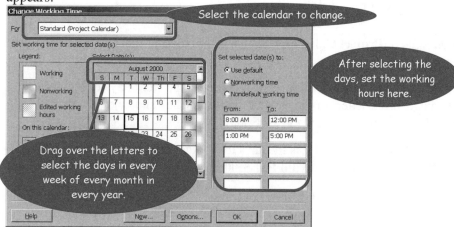

2. Select from the list: **For:** 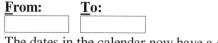 **Standard (Project Calendar)**; this is the calendar that acts as the Project Calendar.

3. Select the work days Monday through Friday by dragging with the mouse from the **M** to the **F:** | M | T | W | Th | F |

4. MS Project has a default calendar with 8 hours per day and working hours from 8AM-12PM and 1PM-5PM. For any diversion from these defaults, select
   ⊙ **Nondefault working time**.

5. Type the normal work times into the boxes:
   From: **To:**

   The dates in the calendar now have a gray hatching pattern in the background and are **Edited working hours**.

6. Click OK or select another calendar from the list.

7. Answer Yes to the prompt to save the changes.

Entering the Business Days

1. Choose **Tools, Change Working Time...**; the **Change Working Time** dialog appears.

2. Select at the top of the dialog under:
   For: Standard (Project Calendar)
   the **Standard (Project Calendar)**; as this is the calendar that acts as the Project Calendar.

3. If you have a Monday to Friday workweek, select the work days of the week by dragging over the letters of the days of the week. Click and hold down on the **M** for Monday and stop at the **F** for Friday: M T W Th F

4. Select ⦿ **Use default**; this sets the days to working days with default working hours of **8:00 AM-12:00 PM** and **1:00 PM-5:00 PM.**

5. Click on the S of Saturday, then hold down Ctrl and click on the S of Sunday and select ⦿ **Nonworking time.**

When you select the days by their letter at the top, you have selected 'eternity'! The changes you make apply to those days in every week in every month and in every year!

Entering the Holidays

1. Choose **Tools, Change Working Time...**; the **Change Working Time** dialog appears.

2. Select at the top of the dialog under **For:** Standard (Project Calendar) the **Standard (Project Calendar);** as this is the calendar that acts as the Project Calendar.

3. Take out your calendar to find the national holidays. Find the first month in which there are national holidays by clicking on the scroll arrows ▲ or ▼ OR by pressing Page Up or Page Down. To go faster, drag the scroll box ▬.

4. Select the holidays by dragging over them or by holding down Ctrl and clicking on them.

5. Select ⦿ **Nonworking time**; the days are now gray as nonworking time. Repeat steps 3 and 4 for the rest of the holidays.

The holidays set on the Project Calendar are carried over onto the individual Resource Calendars.

Even if the Project Calendar is changed after Resource Calendars are created, the changes will show up automatically in the Resource Calendars.

The national holidays and the company holidays should be marked on the Project Calendar. Days should be marked as nonworking days if they apply to (almost) everybody involved in the project: either national holidays or company holidays. On *Resource Calendars* the Project Calendar can still be overridden. Therefore the Project Calendar should merely be looked upon as a time saver for creating Resource Calendars.

The calendar information is saved in the project file. If you want to distribute a calendar among colleagues you have to transfer it via the Organizer: see page 163.

Exercises

Review

How can you change the default calendar; i.e., how can you edit the *Standard Project Calendar* in the *global.mpt*?

Relocation Project – Scope Statement

You are put in charge of relocating your office. You have to find a new location and organize the move. The following is the scope statement created for the project. Your CEO has already signed the scope statement.

Scope Statement for the Relocation Project of DEVOM Inc.
Project accounting code: MOVE001

The Business Need for the Relocation
DEVOM Inc. is growing and needs more facilities to accommodate the expanding workforce.

The Project Objectives

◆ to be moved to and operational in the new location by Nov 1st, 2001
◆ to stay within the available budget of $100.000 for labor cost
◆ to have an 80% satisfaction rate from the personnel for the new work environment

The Project Deliverables
◆ a project plan (including WBS, network diagram, Gantt Chart, budget, resource list and assignments)
◆ a new rented or leased location that has a maximum capacity of 150 work spaces
    - the location should be accessible to disabled people
    - the location should have parking facilities for at least 50 cars
    - the location should have modern work cubicles and an open workspace
◆ contracts with the landlord, the general contractor and the moving company
◆ the physical move of people and equipment

The Project Constraints
◆ the work on the project is to be started not earlier than August 1, 2001
◆ the personnel have to be asked for input as to the location and facilities needed

---

◆ the disruption to the normal operations of DEVOM should be minimized and may not exceed a loss of 200 person days caused by the project
◆ clients will have to be able to contact DEVOM at any time by phone, fax and e-mail
◆ the purchase of new materials and equipment shall be budgeted and approved separately
◆ the new location will be within the boundaries of the city and suburbs
◆ the need for expansion is so urgent that the project has priority over normal operations
◆ any changes to the project objectives will require the approval of the CEO

The Project Assumptions
◆ the market will continue to grow at the same rate
◆ the current furniture can be reused
◆ the current work stations can be reused
◆ the current LAN and servers will be replaced

Date: ....

Your signature   signature N.R. Salin:

...   *NRSalin*

Project Manager, Relocation Project   CEO, DEVOM Inc.

You decide to make a project plan and to put the tasks into Project 2000 to keep track of them.
1. Sign the scope statement and take charge of this project.
2. Create a new MS Project file.
3. Set the start date for the project to *August 1, 2001*
4. The title of the project: *Relocation Devom Inc.*
5. You are the responsible project manager; fill in your own name under **Manager**.
6. Enter *Devom Inc.* under **Company**.
7. Save the file as *Relocation.MPP*

Relocation Project – Tools, Options

Continue to work in the file *Relocation.MPP* and enter the options:

Page tab	Set to
Schedule	☑ *Show scheduling messages*
	Show assignments units as a: Decimal [3]
	Duration is entered in: Days
	Work is entered in: Days
	Default task type: Fixed Duration
	☐ *New Tasks are effort driven*
	☑ *Tasks will always honor their constraint dates*
View	*Date Format: Jan 31 '00* [4]
General	*User name: you* [5]
	☑ *Automatically add new resources and tasks*
Calculation	⦿ *Automatic*
Calendar	*Hours per day: 7.5* [6]
	Hours per week: 37.5 [7]
	Days per Month: 20

---

[3] In this project we will use mostly individual and group resources and we will therefore use decimals rather than percentages.

[4] If you don't have the mmddyy items here, you could go to the Control Panel, Regional Settings (Windows 98) or Regional Options (Windows 2000) to change the date order.

[5] Enter your own name here instead of 'You'. You can refer to it in the headers and footers of all reports you create.

[6] Enter this by typing instead of using the spin buttons.

[7] Same

Relocation Project – the Project Calendar

Continue to work with your file *Relocation.MPP* and enter the following data:

1. Set the working hours on the Standard (Project Calendar) to:
   8:00 to *12:00* and
   13:00 to *16:30*

2. Take out your calendar and enter the national holidays for the months August, September and October on the **Standard Project Calendar**. If you want to achieve an exact match with the solution file, enter the national holidays of the USA, they are:

   ◇ *Labour Day, September 3rd 2001*

   ◇ *Columbus Day, October 8th 2001*

   ◇ *Veterans Day, November 11th 2001*

3. Compare your file with the solution file *03 Entering Tasks.MPP* in the subdirectory *Relocation Project* on the CD-ROM.

Chapter 3 Entering Tasks

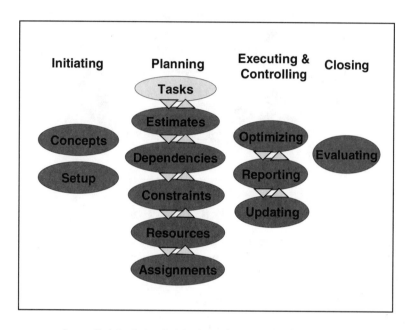

As you can see, we have finished the *Initiating* phase and will now begin the *Planning* phase. It starts with entering the tasks. We recommend you enter the data in the order as shown in this overview: first tasks, then estimates, dependencies, constraints, resources and assignments.

After this chapter you will:

◆ be able to create a Work Breakdown Structure (WBS)

◆ know about summary tasks and detail tasks

◆ know about milestones and deadlines

◆ be able to create an indented outline structure for the WBS

◆ know how to edit, copy and move tasks

Many Trees, but ... no Forest

Bob and Nob work together on a team that is organizing a conference. Bob is the project manager and Nob has taken on the scheduling. Nob has worked hard on his draft schedule. Bob has asked him to break down the work.

"Here is my list of 900 tasks for our project, Bob."

"Wow, 900 activities! I see you have been busy!"

Nob says with pride in his voice: "Yeah, it was a lot of work, but we did it..."

Bob lowers his voice and asks, "Where are the checkpoints and the deliverables? I can't find them in this long list of tasks."

"Oh, there are some meetings ... there ... there ... and there", he says as he points at the meeting tasks in the list.

Bob follows his finger and summarizes, "That one is for the program of the conference, that one ... for the marketing and this one ... for the logistics, isn't it? Why don't you make those deliverables and indent all activities as a group under their deliverables?"

"OK, I can do that!"

"Would you create more groups and summary tasks for each deliverable? It makes the WBS easier to read and allows us to keep the overview. It also gives total duration and cost on each deliverable."

Work Breakdown Structure (WBS)

The situation with Bob and Nob illustrates that it is important to find the right level of detail in the list and to create a logical grouping to keep the overview of the entire project. This grouping is known as the Work Breakdown Structure (WBS).

Before entering tasks into Project 2000 you should create the WBS. The WBS is a breakdown of the project product into deliverables that defines the work scope of the project.[8] Once you have the deliverables, you can then come up with the activities and tasks you need to create those deliverables. The WBS is the most important document in a project. It is the contract between the project manager and the customer. In the case of an internal project, the WBS is the agreement between the project manager and upper management. The illustration below shows a WBS for aircraft manufacturers.

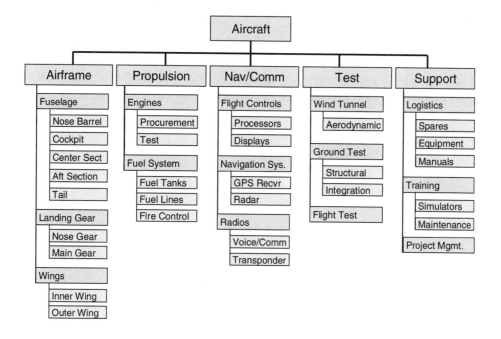

---

[8] See the PMBOK® Guide, 2000 Edition

The WBS specifies what should be done and, implicitly, what should NOT be done. If the client requests output during project execution, the WBS should be clear about whether the output was meant to be delivered or not. If it is not in the WBS, it is out of scope; if it is not explicitly in, it is implicitly out. This is generally accepted project management practice.

You may have been forced by your client to deliver something that was never promised; this is known as *scope creep*. In that case you probably have learned to specify explicitly in the project plan which elements are out-of-scope. Otherwise you will continue to be burned by scope creep.

 In Project 2000 you can capture the scope of the project in the **Task Name** column. Out-of-scope elements can be captured using the **Notes** tool.

Deliverables are tangible components of the project product that are handed over to the client during or at the end of the project. The deliverables are broken down further into components and eventually into tasks.

In the example, the WBS is shown as a chart, the WBS-chart. MS Project does not have such a view, but there are two add-on tools *WBS-Chart* [9] and *Project+* [10] you can buy that will allow you to lay out the WBS in a graphic format. The graphic format is easy to read and understand for most people because it resembles an organizational chart.

---

[9] WBS-Chart is marketed by Critical Tools Inc, please refer to www.CriticalTools.com.

[10] Project+ is marketed by International Institute for Learning, Inc., please refer to www.iil.com

Breaking Down into Phases or Deliverables?

The PMBOK® Guide defines 'deliverable' as *any measurable, tangible, verifiable outcome, result or item that must be produced to complete a project or part of a project.* Sometimes it is difficult to identify the deliverables in a project. But if you don't try to find the deliverables, you won't. So ask yourself the question, *what are the deliverables in this project?* If you cannot identify deliverables, you can always divide a project into phases. Phases are distinct periods in a project; a more vague concept than deliverables.

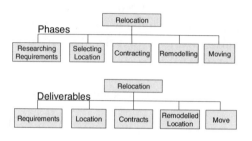

We recommend creating a deliverable-oriented WBS rather than a phase-oriented WBS. A deliverable-oriented WBS is often clearer and has activities that are focused on producing components of the project product. Phases are merely time-oriented groupings of tasks, whereas deliverables are tangible and easier to assign to teams. An office relocation project could be broken down into phases or into deliverables as is shown in the illustration. In most cases, you can do either, and we then recommend using the deliverable-oriented breakdown.

The elements of the WBS focus the team members. What if you were made responsible for "researching requirements" or for delivering the "requirements" in the office relocation project? The latter is a deliverable and is a firmer commitment. Or, imagine you are subcontracting out work. Wouldn't you prefer to commit a subcontractor to delivering something rather than to doing something without a specific end result? Deliverables specify the end result better than phases.

Another reason to use a deliverable-oriented WBS is that it makes it easier to formulate milestones. Wherever a deliverable is ready, handed over, or accepted, you could insert a milestone for the event. Examples of milestones are *requirements summarized, report ready, preliminary design accepted,* and *document delivered.*

In large projects you can often see that the first break down level is phases, which are broken down on the next level into deliverables. The WBS then contains both phases and deliverables, with the deliverables on the lower level. This is a deliverable-oriented breakdown because the lower level has the deliverables.

Breaking Down the Work

In the top-down approach, you enter the deliverables first and you determine all the tasks needed to accomplish the deliverables. In the bottom-up approach, you brainstorm about all the tasks and then you group them under their deliverables. Each deliverable becomes a summary task.

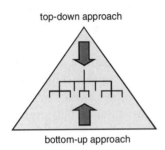

top-down approach

bottom-up approach

The two opposite approaches can lead to the same result. A person who is a novice to the type of project often prefers the bottom-up method. An experienced project manager usually takes the top-down approach. It requires experience to divide the work from the top-down.

Either approach can be successful; there is no one best way.

From WBS-Chart to WBS-List

The WBS-chart has to be converted to an indented list of tasks. The illustration shows

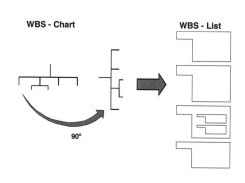

how the chart is converted to an indented list. The visual breakdown structure is rotated 90 degrees and the lower levels then become indentation levels. The add-on tool *WBS-Chart,* mentioned before, does this automatically for you.

The Gantt Chart view or the Network Diagram view can be used for entering the tasks. You may find the Gantt Chart view the most comfortable window for creating the WBS, because you can create and see

the levels of the breakdown structure. The hierarchical structure is shown through indentation of the tasks in the list. The further indented to the right, the lower the level of the task. To switch to the Gantt Chart choose **View, Gantt Chart**.

Types of Tasks

If you analyze an indented list of tasks, you will find that a standard building block

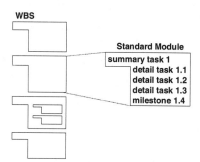

returns. The standard module consists of a summary task, the deliverable or phase, with, as subtasks, the detail tasks and a milestone. The summary task summarizes the cost and duration of all its detail tasks. That is where the name *Summary Task* originates.

Build your plan in a modular way and use the following standard module of tasks. Your WBS will consist of several of these standard modules:

Standard Module		Example
Summary Task	1	REPORT
detail task	1.1	gather data
detail task	1.2	categorize data
detail task	1.3	write report
milestone	1.4	report ready

We will now discuss the types in more detail:

◆ *Summary Tasks*

Summary tasks are often not tasks but things. To make a plan better understood by stakeholders, it is recommended that you group tasks and give each group a task name that summarizes it. They can be deliverables or phases and they give the plan a logical structure. MS Project sums the costs and work from the detail tasks within the summary tasks. This explains the term "summary task"; the cost and work are summarized. MS Project summarizes the duration of the detail tasks as well, but not through addition. If tasks are scheduled in parallel, the summary task duration is not the sum of the durations of the detail tasks, but the time span of the detail tasks included in the summary. MS Project calculates the summary duration. You cannot fill it in for a summary task. MS Project grays out the buttons in the field, which tells you it is a calculated field that you cannot change.

◆ *Detail Tasks*

A detail task is any task that is not a summary task, in other words, any task that does not have lower-level tasks. People perform the detail tasks and it should be possible to estimate the duration and the cost for each detail task.

Detail tasks come in the following types:

◇ Fixed Duration tasks
◇ Fixed Units tasks
◇ Fixed Work tasks

We will discuss these types of detail tasks on page 147 and on page 272.

◆ *Milestones*

A milestone is any important date in your schedule. Milestones are often evaluation points, critical points that executives and clients monitor. They can be the dates on which the deliverables have to be ready. A milestone has a zero-duration; it is a point in time, an event and not an activity.

Types of Task Bars

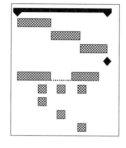

1 Summary Task
   1.1 Detail Task
   1.2 Detail Task
   1.3 Detail Task
   1.4 Milestone
2 Split Task Bars
3 Recurring Task
   3.1 Recurrence 1
   3.2 Recurrence 2
   3.3 Recurrence 3

The shape and color of the task bars can be changed through the menu items **Format, Bar Styles**. The default appearance of the bars is shown in the illustration. We will discuss spit task bars and recurring tasks as well.

◆ *Summary task bar*
Notice that the summary task bar summarizes all its detail tasks. It starts when the first detail task starts and ends when the last detail task or milestone ends.

◆ *Detail task bar*
A detail task is the lowest level of task in the WBS. The length of a detail task bar represents its estimated duration.

◆ *Milestone diamond*
Milestones appear as diamonds. Milestones have a zero-duration and feature prominently in the Gantt Chart.

◆ *Split task bars*
A split task bar has multiple parts. The work on a split task bar is scheduled to be interrupted and will resume at a later date. For example, electricians cable a building, but after the inspection they have to come back to install the cover plates.
The Project 2000 tool **Split Task** ▦ should be called *split task bars*, because the tool really splits the task bars rather than the tasks.

◆ *Recurring task bars*
Recurring task bars have multiple parts that occur at a regular interval, such as status meetings.

Types of Milestones

Milestones are used in a schedule for indicating events like decisions, approvals, target dates and ceremonies. The different types of milestones used in schedules are:

◆ **Decision points**
These are important events on which decisions are made about the remainder of the project. The decision can be:

   ◇ Go/No-Go: that can end a project, or

   ◇ Go-Left/Go-Right: in which the how-to or direction is determined for the rest of the project

◆ **Target dates**
These are soft deadlines that are inserted to break up a long series of tasks. They focus the efforts on finishing a component of a deliverable. The project manager decides with the team where to insert these target dates. Teams need several target dates in order to meet the deadline of the deliverable; they are interim evaluation points. Target dates function as reminders and should keep everyone focused and on track.
As a general rule of thumb, we recommend you enter at least one target date milestone for each deliverable; insert one milestone among the detail tasks of each summary task.

◆ **Do-or-Die Dates**
These are hard deadlines, and are often contractual dates, by which you are committed to hand over a deliverable. These dates should be clear in the schedule at all times.

◆ **Deliveries**
We recommend you enter the delivery dates of external supplies as separate milestones in the WBS. You would normally set a Start-No-Earlier-Than (SNET) constraint on them.

◆ **Ceremonies**
Ceremonies are short official events. If the duration of the ceremony is negligible, it can be entered as a milestone (with a zero duration). An example is the official opening of a new plant.

◆ **Project end date**
This is the delivery date for the project product. Meeting the project end date is

always a challenge in project management. All the chains of dependencies come together in the project end milestone.

Formulation of the Task Names

Attention needs to be paid to the wording of the task names, especially which tense is used for the verbs:

◆ **Summary Tasks**
Use nouns for deliverables, for example *location* or *detailed design*.
If you use phases instead of deliverables, use the imperfect tense (*-ing*). This tense best indicates that it is something ongoing; typical for phases. Examples are, *Researching* or *Remodeling*.

◆ **Detail Tasks**
The recommended tense for the verb in a detail task name is the present tense (or imperative tense). The present tense indicates action and that is exactly what you want in a detail task, for example *contact the publisher*, *evaluate the alternatives*, or *purchase equipment*. It is like an order or a command. A resource assigned to the task interprets it as an instruction and a request.

◆ **Milestones**
Typically the milestone is formulated following the syntax:
< deliverable> <past tense verb>.
Where *< deliverable>* is a noun that describes the deliverable, and the *<past tense verb>* describes what happened to the deliverable at that point in time. The tense for the verb used in milestones is the past tense (or perfect tense). Typical verbs for milestones are: *delivered, accepted, completed, done, sent, shipped,* and *finished*. Alternatively you could use the word *ready* to indicate completion, as in *report ready*. Examples of milestones are *module completed, printer delivered* or *report accepted*.

The Right Level of Detail

Too little detail ?

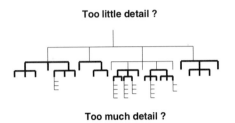

Too much detail ?

One of the biggest challenges in preparing the project schedule is finding the appropriate level of detail in the WBS. The WBS should not have too much or too little detail! In the illustration, the right level is represented with the fatter lines on the middle levels. Finding the balance is an art for the project manager. Below are some guidelines to follow.

Too Little Detail?

If you think you have a schedule that does not have enough detail, ask yourself the following questions while you go through the list of tasks:

◆ Can I estimate the duration, effort and cost of the detail tasks?
   If you know estimating is too hard without breaking it down into smaller tasks, you should do so.
◆ Can I find the dependencies between the tasks?
   Each detail task will end up being a node in a network of dependencies. Dependencies are links that indicate how tasks affect scheduling.
◆ Can I assign the task to somebody?
   Eventually, we will assign each detail task to a resource and if you can't assign it to an individual (or an organizational entity in large projects) you may have too little detail in the WBS.

We will discuss estimating, dependencies and assignments in later chapters.

Too Much Detail?

If you think you may have a WBS that is too detailed, ask yourself the following questions while you go through the list of tasks:

◆ Is this task necessary in the WBS?
◆ Is this task merely a reminder or a to-do list item, or is it a real task that will take significant effort?
   If the items do not take much time or effort, you have not created a WORK Breakdown Structure. You have created a checklist with too many detail tasks!

   Checklist items can be entered in the **Notes** field using the ▨ tool.

◆ Do I want to update all these detail tasks during project execution?
If you are not willing to update the tasks during the busy project execution, this is the
time to remove them from the WBS.

The 1%-10% Rule

There is another guideline. I call it the *1%-10% rule*. The duration of any detail task
should be between a minimum and a maximum duration. The minimum is 1% of the
project duration. The maximum is 10% of the project duration. For example, if you have
a project that you think will take 3 months, you can calculate the range. Three months is
about 65 business days with 20-22 per month. The minimum duration is 1% of 65 or 0.65
day, let's say half a day. Detail tasks should not be less than half a day. If they are
smaller, you should lump them together into a larger task. The maximum is 10% of 65 or
6.5 days, let us round it to five days or one week. Detail tasks have to be one week or less
in duration. The beauty of this rule is that it can be applied to projects of any size.

You can find the project duration easily by choosing **Project, Project Information** and
clicking Statistics... .

Not Longer Than a Reporting Period

Detail task durations should never be longer than one reporting period[11]. If you report the
status of your project every week, your reporting period is one week. If a detail task is
longer than a reporting period, you may notice an out-of-control task only two reporting
periods later.

---

[11] I learned this guideline from Frank Walker, President, GTW Corporation

Why is the Right Level of Detail Important?

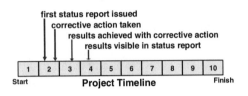

first status report issued
corrective action taken
results achieved with corrective action
results visible in status report

| 1 | 2 | 3 | 4 | 5 | 6 | 7 | 8 | 9 | 10 |

Start   **Project Timeline**   Finish

The rationale behind finding the right level of detail is to create enough checkpoints for monitoring and controlling the progress of the project. Systems theory tells us that we need feedback loops to control a process. In project management we need several feedback loops to control the project and ten is a good number. This may seem like a lot but it really isn't.

In our ten-period project, the first status report normally becomes available halfway through the second period. If the report shows a slow start, action must be taken in the rest of the second period and you will likely see the results of this corrective action in the third period. The report on the third period becomes available in the fourth period. So problems in the first period will be corrected visibly in the fourth period. There is always a delay in determining the problem, taking action and seeing the result of the action. If you have ten checkpoints you really only have six or so manage-points. You need, therefore, a safe number of reporting periods. Ten periods seems to work in most projects.

And what if you did not take the right corrective action? In that case, you end up with only a few chances to make things right for the client. Of course, successful project managers know what the status of their project is. They know it at all times, if they are in touch with their team. This communication increases the number of feedback loops dramatically. Building in ten formal feedback loops seems like a good way to facilitate communication with the client.

Entering Tasks

Entering Summary Tasks

For summary tasks you only need to enter the task name, most other fields are calculated.

1. Choose **View, Gantt Chart**.

2. Click on the cell in the **Task Name** column where you want to enter the summary task.

3. Type the name of the summary task.

4. Press ⌷Enter⌷ to go to the next task; the name is the only field you need to enter for summary tasks.

Entering Detail Tasks

For detail tasks you typically enter the task name and the duration or work estimate. For the work estimate we first need to insert the field **Work**.

1. Click anywhere in the column **Start** and choose **Insert, Column**
   OR
   Right-click on the **Start** column heading and choose **Insert, Column...**, the **Column Definition** dialog appears:

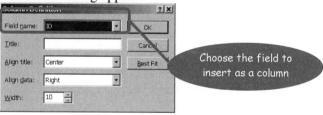

2. Select from the list **Field Name** ⌷ID⌷ the item **Type** and click ⌷ OK ⌷.

3. To insert a line for a detail task, position the cursor where you need a new row and click.

4. Choose **Insert, New Task**, or press ⌷Insert⌷.

5. Enter the **Task Name** and press ⌨Tab to go to its **Duration** or **Work** field.

6. Enter a **Duration** or **Work** estimate and press ⌨Enter. We will discuss estimating in the next chapter and will focus, in this chapter, on breaking down the work properly.

7. If necessary, adjust the indentation level clicking on the button:
    ➡ to indent the task
    OR the button
    ⬅ to outdent the task.

We recommend you enter tasks in their chronological order as much as you can. You will have difficulties with tasks that are going to be done in parallel. In those cases, let the logic of the breakdown structure prevail over the chronology of the tasks. Most projects have tasks that run in parallel. The more tasks you can do in parallel, the faster you will finish the project!

 Don't enter **Start** or **Finish** dates for detail tasks; this will set schedule constraints that make the schedule rigid. Let the tasks move freely, based upon their dependencies, this will be covered in Chapter 5 Entering Dependencies.

Entering Milestones

For milestones, you typically enter the name of the milestone, a zero in the duration field and a deadline or constraint date.

1. In the **Gantt Chart** select the task in the list prior to where a milestone has to be inserted.

2. Press ⌨Insert and enter the name of the milestone.

3. If necessary, adjust the indentation level to the same level as the detail tasks above it, use ➡ and ⬅.

4. Enter a duration of 0 (zero); this will toggle the *No* in the field **Milestone** to *Yes*. The task is now marked as a milestone.

5. Click or hold down `Shift` and press `F2`; the **Task Information** dialog appears:

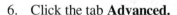

6. Click the tab **Advanced.**

7. Set an appropriate deadline on the milestone. Under **Deadline**, enter the target date and press `Enter`. The deadline shows up in the Gantt Chart timescale as a green ⇩. As soon as the deadline is violated a red ◆ will appear in the **Indicators** column.
    OR
    Set a constraint under **Constraint Type** by selecting a type of constraint from the list. Enter a date under **Constraint Date**. A constraint will prevent the network of dependencies from changing the date on the milestone. Constraints can cause scheduling conflicts.

 There is also a **Mark as Milestone** feature on the **Task Information dialog** , **Advanced** tab that will change a regular detail task bar into a diamond. We recommend you don't use this, because it will shrink a 10-day task bar into a 0-day diamond while keeping a 10-day duration. This makes the Gantt Chart look confusing. When dependencies stem from the task; it looks like there is a gap between the two tasks. The **Mark as Milestone** stores a *Yes* or *No* in the **Milestone** field. Instead of using **Mark as Milestone**, we recommend you use the field **Marked** or one of the **Flag** fields to handpick tasks that are important for reports.

See Chapter 6 Entering Deadlines and Constraints on page 207 for more discussion on constraints and deadlines.

Entering Recurring Tasks

Recurring tasks are tasks that take place regularly and repeatedly, for example every other week (biweekly) or monthly. Typical examples of recurring tasks are the *status meetings* or *progress meetings*.

1. Choose **Insert, Recurring Task**; the **Recurring Task Information** dialog appears:

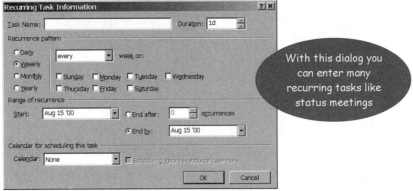

2. Type the name in the **Task** Name field.

3. Type the duration in the **Duration** field or use the ⬆⬇.

4. Under **Recurrence Pattern** select the interval at which the task recurs; the dialog changes and presents appropriate choices.

5. Under **Range of Occurrence** choose the length of the period for the recurrences or the number of recurrences.

6. Click ⬜ OK ⬜.

Some remarks about recurring tasks:

◆ Notice that recurring tasks are, in fact, a special kind of summary task. It only has a different task bar that shows all the task bars of its detail tasks. Project 2000 sets constraints on each recurring task that will keep them in their place on the timescale.

◆ Notice that the duration of the recurring (summary) task has no meaning; it encompasses the entire period of the tasks.

◆ The recurring detail tasks will not be included in the leveling process, because MS Project sets the field **Level Assignments** to *No* as a default. If you assign resources to the recurring detail tasks and level the workloads fully, you will still see slight over-allocations on the dates of the recurring tasks. To resolve this, use **Edit,**

Fill, Down to enter *yes* in the field **Level Assignments** for all recurring detail tasks and level the workloads again. We will discuss leveling in more detail on page 344: Workload Leveling.

Three questions are important in regard to recurring tasks:

◆ When do you need recurring tasks?
Normally, recurring tasks are used for meetings, like status meetings. You don't need them for overhead tasks, because there are easier ways to deal with those, for example, by assigning resources part-time to summary tasks.

◆ Will you set dependencies on them?
Dependencies are only necessary when deliverables are due for a meeting; you can indicate this by making the deliverables predecessors of the meeting task.

◆ Will you assign resources to them and level the workload?
Assigning resources is OK, but realize that MS Project will not level recurring tasks by default!

Entering Split Task Bars

You can split any existing task bar into two or more parts. You cannot set dependencies on the start or the finish of the split.

1. Click the **Split Tasks** tool ▦; a yellow pop-up appears and the mouse pointer now looks like: I▸

2. Point to a task bar and click and drag where you want the split to occur; the second part of the task bar splits off and, in the yellow pop-up, you are shown what the new start and finish dates of the part will be when you release the mouse:

Task: ▨▨▨▨▨▨▨▨▨	
Start:	Wed 4/5/00
Finish:	Sat 4/8/00

3. Drag it to where you want to schedule it and release the mouse button; the task bar is now split in two parts. Notice that the two parts are connected by dots:
▨▨▨▨......▨▨▨▨

If you change the start date of the task, the parts will move as a group and keep their relative distance. To remove a split, just drag the split part to the left reconnecting it to the other part.

You cannot set dependencies on the start or finish of the split. Therefore, we recommend you split the task into multiple tasks, rather than splitting the task bar into multiple bars. For example, electricians cable a building, but after the inspection they have to come back to install the cover plates. You could do this with one task through splitting its task bar, but it would be better if you split the task into two tasks: *pull cables* and *install cover plates*. Now you can set dependencies between the tasks and create a fully dynamic model.

During the planning of the project you will not need split task bars often. We recommend you split the task in multiple tasks rather than splitting the bar into multiple bars during the planning. You will use splitting the task bars mostly during project execution, when you update the schedule with actual progress. For example, when resources are temporarily taken off a task to take care of a problem elsewhere, you can show this by splitting the task bar.

Creating an Outline

Outline Structure

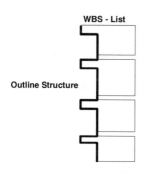

Outline Structure

The hierarchical chart of the WBS is entered into MS Project as a list of tasks. The hierarchy of the chart is preserved through indentation in the list of tasks. The tasks on a lower level are indented to the right. The more to the left, and less indented, the more important the item is.

The tasks on the lowest level are called *detail tasks*. Detail tasks do not have sub-tasks. Tasks that have lower-level tasks are called *summary tasks*. Tasks can be promoted to a higher level by outdenting them, or can be demoted to a lower level by indenting them. Thus, an outline structure is created.

Purposes of the outline:

◆ Outlining makes the plan easier to read; it provides an overview rather than details. The CEO likes an overview of the phases or deliverables, and would like to leave the detail tasks for the project manager.

◆ Outlining generates extra aggregate information on the summary tasks. You can see immediately what a deliverable costs or how long a phase takes. These numbers are often useful. MS Project automatically calculates the fields of the summary tasks.

◆ Summary tasks can be collapsed and expanded on an as-needed basis.

Indenting a Series of Detail Tasks

1. Select the detail tasks by dragging anywhere over them in the spreadsheet.

2. On the **Formatting** toolbar you click ➡

   OR
   Hold down ⎡Alt⎤ + ⎡Shift⎤ and press ⎡→⎤.

After indenting, the summary task shows a duration that summarizes all its detail tasks.

Indenting a task cannot be done by inserting spaces in front of the task name. MS Project will not recognize this as a lower-level sub-task.

Indenting and Outdenting by Dragging

1. Select the tasks by dragging over them in the spreadsheet.

2. In the **Task Name** column, point to the first half of the task name, the mouse pointer changes to a two-headed arrow: ↔. Make sure you see this mouse pointer before proceeding and not the ✛.

3. Click, hold down and drag the task to the right for indenting or to the left for outdenting. A vertical gray line gives you feedback as to how much the task will be indented or outdented when you release the mouse.

4. Release the mouse button when the gray line shows the right level of indentation.

Outdenting Tasks

1. Select the tasks by dragging in the spreadsheet.

2. On the **Formatting** toolbar click ⬅
   OR
   Hold down ⎡Alt⎤ + ⎡Shift⎤ and press ⎡←⎤.

To Hide or Reveal Detail Tasks

Click the minus button ⊟ in front of the summary task name to hide its detail tasks
OR
Select the summary task and hold down ⎡Alt⎤ + ⎡Shift⎤ and press ⎡-⎤.

The detail tasks can be displayed again by clicking the ⊞
OR

Select the summary task and hold down ⎡Alt⎤ + ⎡Shift⎤ and press ⎡+⎤.

 If you use the numeric keypad on the keyboard, make sure the numbers lock (**Num Lock**) is off.

To Hide all Detail Tasks

1. Click on the heading of any column; the entire column should be highlighted now.

2. On the toolbar click ⎡−⎤.

To Reveal the Next Level

Click on the title of any column and click ⎡+⎤.
OR
On the toolbar, click ⎡**Show ▾**⎤ and select the next level down.

To Reveal a Certain Level

1. Click ⎡**Show ▾**⎤.

2. Choose the level you want to see.

To Reveal all Levels

1. Click ⎡**Show ▾**⎤.

2. Select ⎡⁺⁺⎤ **All Subtasks**.

What you do with a Parent, you do with the Entire Family

When you manipulate summary tasks, you have to realize that what you do to a summary task affects its detail tasks as well. If you delete a summary task, you are deleting its detail tasks as well. The same applies to cutting and copying, see page 130. If you indent a summary task, you indent the detail tasks as well.

Changing the WBS

Editing a Task Name

1. You can replace a task name by typing over it. If you need to make small editorial changes to a task name, press ⒡.

    The cursor blinks as a line in the cell | write report|

    OR

    Click once on the field and, after one second, another time and an insertion point will appear in the cell | write report|

    OR

    Click in the entry bar at the top of the screen; the cursor blinks as a vertical line:

    | ✖ | | write report|

2. Move the cursor by clicking with the mouse or using the arrow keys on the keyboard. Make the changes and press ⒠.

Inserting Multiple Tasks

We already discussed how to insert one task; you press ⒤.

1. Point to the row before which you wish to insert multiple tasks, click and drag down to highlight as many rows as needed.

2. Press ⒤ and as many rows as you had selected are inserted.

 If you insert tasks between linked tasks, MS Project may set dependencies automatically if the **Autolink** option is turned on. Choose **Tools, Options, Schedule,** to verify if **Autolink inserted or moved tasks** has a checkmark or not. Always check the dependencies after adding, copying or moving tasks (or turn **Autolink** off, if you don't want MS Project to link).

Deleting Tasks

1. Select the tasks by dragging over any of its data.

2. Choose the menu items **Edit**, **Delete** or press .

Copying or Moving Tasks

For copying or moving tasks it is important to select the entire task (including its fields that are hidden from view). If you want to copy or move the whole task you have to select it by clicking on its first column with the ID numbers and the gray color. This will highlight all the visible data of the task and select all the fields of the task, even the ones that are not displayed.

If the first column is not gray, you will have to lock the column first. The gray color tells you:

◆ that the column is locked,
◆ that it will not scroll off the screen,
◆ that its data cannot be edited, and
◆ that you can select the entire task by clicking on it.

Locking the first Column of a Table

1. In the Gantt Chart, click on the menu items **View, Table: <name of the table>, More Tables**.

2. Click Edit....

3. Set it to ☑ **Lock first column**.

4. Click OK and then Apply; if you click now on the locked title the whole row is selected.

Copying Tasks

1. Select the tasks by dragging over the ID numbers in the first locked column (with the gray color) using the ✛ mouse pointer.

2. Release the mouse button; the tasks are now highlighted.

3. Hold down the ⌈Ctrl⌉ key and click anywhere on the selected ID numbers; you should now see the following mouse pointer 🔲. Drag the copied tasks to their new place.

OR

Choose the menu items **Edit**, **Copy** or click 🔲. The task is now stored in the clipboard. Select the task before you wish to insert and choose **Edit**, **Paste** or click 🔲.

Moving Tasks

1. Select the tasks by dragging over the ID numbers in the locked, first column (with the gray color) using the ⊕ mouse pointer.

2. Release the mouse button; the tasks are now highlighted.

3. Click and hold anywhere on the ID numbers of the selected tasks; you should now see the following mouse pointer: 🔲.

4. Drag the tasks to their new place.
   OR
   Click on the menu items **Edit**, **Cut** or click 🔲. The tasks are now temporarily stored in the clipboard. Select the task before you wish to insert and choose **Edit**, **Paste** or click 🔲.

 To keep the dependencies as they are when moving tasks, choose **Tools, Options**. Click on the tab **Schedule** and deselect ☐ **Autolink inserted or moved tasks**. Always check the dependencies after adding, copying or moving tasks.

To Copy or Move a Summary Task Family

Select the summary task by clicking on its ID-number in the locked, first column. Hold the ⌈Ctrl⌉ key down to copy. Click again and drag the summary task. Project 2000 will immediately highlight all the detail tasks and move or copy them as well. If you use the clipboard instead, the detail tasks will also be copied or moved.

Using Task Calendars

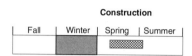

Construction

Fall	Winter	Spring	Summer

MS Project 2000 allows you to schedule tasks using *Task Calendars*. It is not recommended to create a task calendar for each individual task. Often you will use a task calendar for many similar tasks. For example, in a construction project you could create a winter weather task calendar for all outdoor construction activities affected by winter weather.

Creating a new Task Calendar

1. Choose **Tools, Change Working Time**; the **Change Working Time** dialog appears:

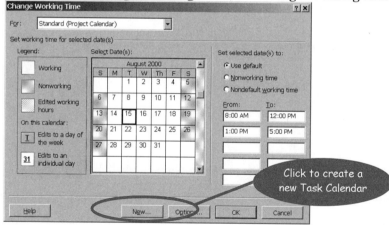

2. Select a base calendar that is closest to what you need for the new task calendar in:

For | Standard (Project Calendar) | ▾ |.

3. Click 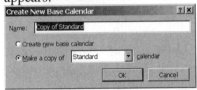 at the bottom of the dialog; the **Create New Base Calendar** dialog appears:

4. Enter a descriptive name for the task calendar and select
   ⦿ **Create new base calendar** or ⦿ **Make a copy of** the calendar you selected under step 2.

5. Click [OK]; you have now created a new calendar.

6. Enter the change on the new task calendar and click [OK] when done.

Using a Task Calendar

1. In the Gantt Chart view, click on the column before you wish to insert the **Task Calendar** column

2. Choose **Insert, Column;** the **Column Definition** dialog appears:

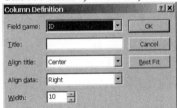

3. Select the item **Task Calendar** from the list **Field Name** and click [OK].

4. Click in the **Task Calendar** field [None ▼] of a task and select a task calendar from the list provided.

Exercises

Review

1. What are the differences between a to-do list and a WBS?

2. You ask a person to manage a project. The objective of the project is to write a document. There are an author, an editor and a graphic artist in the team. After a while, the person presents four different first-level breakdowns to you and asks you to choose one. Which one will you choose?
   ◆ first draft, final draft, final document
   ◆ writing, editing, formatting, printing
   ◆ draft text, edited text, final text, charts
   ◆ table of contents, body of text, summary

Relocation Project – Entering the WBS

1. Continue to work with your file, *Relocation.MPP* or open the file, *03 Entering Tasks.MPP* in the subdirectory *Relocation Project* on the CD-ROM.

2. Enter the WBS into Project 2000 as shown in the table below [12].

3. Indent the detail tasks under their summary tasks. The summary tasks are the tasks with names in capital letters.

4. Compare your file with the solution file, *04 Entering Estimates.MPP* in the sub-directory *Relocation Project* on the CD-ROM.

Below, you will find the WBS for the Relocation Project.

ID	Task Name
1.	*REQUIREMENTS*
2.	*research staff requirements*
3.	*summarize requirements*
4.	*LOCATION*

---

[12] Notice the capitals are used to indicate which tasks will eventually become summary tasks. The capitals are used for exercise purposes only; Project 2000, by default, bolds the summary tasks to make them stand out. This will happen upon indenting tasks.

ID	Task Name
5.	*select the Realtor*
6.	*visit the sites*
7.	*evaluate the sites*
8.	*meet to select the location*
9.	*legal review*
10.	*location selected*
11.	*REMODELING CONTRACT*
12.	*select the contractor*
13.	*meet to discuss contract*
14.	*revise the schedule*
15.	*negotiate the contract*
16.	*contractor contracted*
17.	*REMODELED LOCATION*
18.	*relocate walls*
19.	*electric wiring*
20.	*paint*
21.	*drying of paint* [13]
22.	*install cabinetry*
23.	*install LAN*
24.	*lay carpet*
25.	*facility remodeled*
26.	*MOVE*
27.	*select mover*
28.	*pack*
29.	*move*
30.	*unpack*
31.	*new location opened*

---

[13] You might wonder if *drying of paint* should be entered as a task because it happens by itself. I merely use it here to illustrate the use of an elapsed duration. Alternatively, you could enter it as lag on a dependency.

Case Study "My First Time ..."

Norm was tense when he drove home from work. He was assigned to be the project manager on a project for the first time. He felt the assignment was recognition of his outstanding technical expertise. In the evening he would start breaking down the work. This project, though, was different than other projects he had worked on. He had an idea of what deliverables and activities would be needed, but was worried whether he knew or would find them all. He decided he wanted to stay ahead of his team and create a WBS so his team would be impressed. That night he worked very hard and lost some sleep over his WBS. The next day, he presented it and introduced it as "Here is what we are going to do ...." His team is quick to point out that he forgot to incorporate the logistics, documentation and training components in his WBS.

Questions:

1. What do you think about Norm's decision to create a WBS by himself? What led him to do it by himself?

2. Would you have done it by yourself if you were in his shoes?

Troubleshooting

1. Open the file *MySchedule.MPP* in the sub-directory *Troubleshooting* on the CD-ROM. Change the start date of a task. Why does the taskbar not move in the timescale?

2. Open the file *MyOutline.MPP* in the sub-directory *Troubleshooting* on the CD-ROM. Explain why the outline does not function as an outline with summary tasks that can be collapsed and expanded?

Chapter 4 Entering Estimates

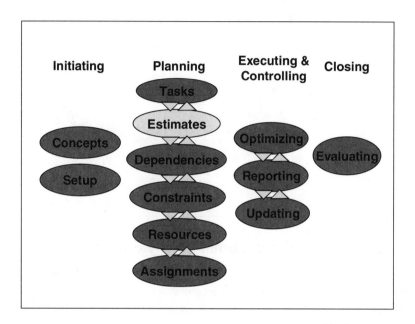

We have the Work Breakdown Structure (*Tasks*) entered into our project file and the next step is to enter the estimates.

After this chapter you will:

◆ know a process for estimating duration and cost

◆ be aware of the human tendencies when estimating

◆ be aware of difficulties in estimating

◆ know the techniques by which those difficulties can be addressed

◆ know how to move and copy cell data

Your Guesstimate is my Estimate

Ricky is a junior programmer who is hired right out of college where he studied computer science. He has limited work experience in programming. He is working on an e-commerce application. His project manager, Bob, asks him for an effort estimate and a target date on one of the screens of the application.

Ricky thinks for a second and says, "I think it will take me ten hours of effort to make it. It is noon, so ... I'll be done tomorrow at noon."

Bob asks, "Ten hours of full-focus effort or ten hours in which you will still be doing troubleshooting as well, like you have been doing all along?"

Ricky's face looks horrified, "Do I have to keep doing that as well?"

"Your telephone will continue to ring, or are you going to unplug it? And what about meeting with the tester? Did you include that?"

Ricky is getting nervous about his estimate. "I think it will take me 14 hours then, and I will be done at the end of tomorrow."

"Hold on, did you think of tomorrow's goodbye lunch for Harry and the doctor's appointment you have first thing in the morning?"

"Ok, ok ... it will be ready before lunch on the day after tomorrow." Ricky utters as his final commitment.

What are Estimates?

Estimates are predictions of how much time a task will take. The predictions can be made in terms of the duration of a task or in terms of the effort required to perform a task. The difference between duration and effort can easily be demonstrated with an example. If you have 3 carpenters working for 2 business days (duration), the effort is 3 x 2 = 6 person days of effort.

A duration estimate would be expressed in *business days* (working days), which will often be the weekdays. A business day has 8 hours in Project 2000 by default. A duration estimate can be filled into the field **Duration**; the default time unit is **Days**. To enter a duration of five days (1 week), you could enter:

◆ *5 days*
◆ *5d*
◆ *5*
◆ *1w*

Notice that MS Project displays it as *days* and not as *business days.* It will help you understand Project 2000 if you think of the duration as the number of business days.

An effort estimate would be expressed in *person days* or *person hours*. A person hour is one person working one full hour. The effort estimate is filled into the task-related field **Work** in Project 2000. The default time unit of the **Work** field is **Hours**. To enter work on a task of 16 hours, you could enter:

◆ *16 hours*
◆ *16h*
◆ *16*
◆ *2d*

Notice that MS Project displays it as *hours* and not as *person hours.* It will help you understand Project 2000 if you think of the work as the number of person hours (person days) needed for a task.

Choosing the Options

Before entering the estimates, it is important to be aware of how Project 2000 will function. Choose **Tools, Options**. We recommend you set or accept the following options.

Tab	Option
Schedule	**Duration is entered in:** Project 2000 will use this as the default time unit for duration. With the default duration time unit set to *days*, you can type in *5* instead of *5d* to get 5 days. You don't need to type a *d* in the duration fields. Choose the unit to fit the majority of your inputs.
	Work is entered in: Same, but for the Work field.
	Default task type: Most people enter the duration immediately and Project 2000 should not change it, unless required. We recommend setting it to **Fixed Duration** if you normally enter duration estimates[14].
	☐ **New Tasks are effort driven** This option changes resource units on assignments; we recommend you turn it off. This option works the same as **Fixed Work** tasks and it is preferable to use that feature.
	Set as Default Sets the options above as the default setting for any new schedules you create. The existing schedules are not affected because these options are stored in the project files, as you can see in the section divider label **Scheduling Options for 'Project 1'**.
Edit	**Allow cell drag and drop** This allows you to move or copy the selected cells by dragging the selected area by its border. This option is global, as you can read in the label of the section divider **Scheduling Options for Microsoft Project**.
	View options for Time Units for **Minutes, Hours, Days, Weeks, Months, Years** This allows you to change the way time units are shown in your project. The shorter you make the time unit, the more space you save. I set them habitually to the shortest label.

---

[14] The PMBOK® Guide 2000 of the PMI has *Activity Duration Estimating* as one of the core planning processes.

Difficult Situations

Estimating is one of the most difficult skills in project management. It is difficult in projects because, by definition, projects are about doing new things or doing things in a new way. *"How do I estimate?"* is the question I am asked most often in my project management courses. Estimating is particularly difficult in the following situations:

◆ Entirely new tasks not done very often by the organization, like moving or implementing new hardware and software. For this type of task you need to buy some outside expertise and have these consultants help you plan the project.

◆ Tasks that have uncertain outcomes, like R&D-type tasks.

◆ When a team member is assigned who has little or no experience with estimating the tasks in his responsibility. Below we will discuss how to deal with inexperienced team members.

The first time you ask a new team member how long a task will take, the team member may be very reluctant to provide an answer. It is, however, more important that people start giving you their estimates, than that those estimates are very reliable. Estimating is a skill and the only way to acquire skills is by doing. That is how we learned to drive cars. After the person starts making estimates, he should check how good they were. As a project manager with experience in estimating, you can help in this process of continuous improvement. You should be a mentor for novice estimators.

In this release of MS Project you can capture that you are not sure of the estimate. You can have the program treat an estimate like a 'guesstimate'. You indicate that by adding a "?" to the entry, for example you enter *"3d?"* in the duration field, if you are not entirely sure of the 3-day estimate. In its default settings, Project 2000 will add question marks to those cells in which it calculated the value itself.

Let's explore the human side of the estimating activity.

The Human Tendencies in Estimating

"I can't predict the future!"

Often new team members have difficulties coming up with estimates. This is particularly true for team members who are new to the type of tasks to which they are assigned. This is very common because a fundamental characteristic of a project is that it is unique, it has never been done exactly like that. So there is always improvisation and learning on the job in projects.

If a team member has difficulties producing estimates, one technique that often works is to ask for two or three estimates instead of one. The second estimate should be a pessimistic estimate: *What if many things went wrong, how long would it take then?* The person will soon consider disasters like *What if all resources go on strike?* or *What if I get run over by a bus?* or *What if the whole world crashes down?* You can tell the team member that: *If those things happen, you will not be there, the project is not needed any longer and you don't need to estimate anymore!* Have a good laugh about those extreme situations and move on with estimating. It is fine to think of those circumstances but don't consider them for a pessimistic estimate.

You probably noticed that I suggest you ask the question, *What if MANY things went wrong, how long would it take then?* 'Many things go wrong' is not the same as 'everything goes wrong'. Therefore, I tend to call it a 'pessimistic' estimate rather than a 'worst-case' estimate. Asking for the worst case will get people thinking of natural disasters and that sort of thing. The estimating becomes a hilarious event and may make the process loose its credibility. An alternative question for the pessimistic estimate would be to ask: *What is a safe estimate?*

You could even ask for a third estimate, an optimistic estimate: *What if many things go smoothly, how long would it take you then?* or *What would be an aggressive estimate?*

Asking for more than one estimate gives you a better idea what to expect. It also helps you determine the size of the padding or buffer you need to apply to the duration estimate. With a three-point estimate you can even do a PERT-analysis. Or you can apply Monte Carlo simulation on the schedule. We will discuss both on page 305. In summary, when a team member feels insecure about an estimate:

◆ You ask for more than one estimate on the task: a pessimistic one. Perhaps even an optimistic estimate.

◆ You pad the realistic estimate using the pessimistic estimate, such that you have a reasonable probability to realize the padded estimate.

◆ When the target date is not exactly met, you forgive the estimator. You use the padding you applied as the project manager to swiftly forgive. If you are not forgiving, the person may stop providing estimates. If you cannot get estimates from one of your resources at all, you are less likely to be successful as a project manager than when you get estimates that are less reliable. When you know the estimate is less reliable, you can pad it to create a reliable schedule.

◆ You sit down at the end of the project with the resources who were insecure about estimating, and have a look at their estimates. You help determine how they can improve their estimates the next time around. Evaluation serves as a learning opportunity.

"I am always off!"

People are optimistic or pessimistic by nature. Their personality greatly affects their estimating. When you have a new team, it will be difficult to determine the optimism-factor of the personalities that provide you with estimates. Asking for more than one estimate (optimistic, realistic, pessimistic) gives you a better understanding of the time-risk of a task.

In my observation, people are quite constant in their tendency to err toward either pessimism or optimism. Once you have found out the tendencies of your team members, as a project manager, you should be able to correct each estimate with a "personality-factor". If you get an estimate from a young team member who you know is very optimistic, you can ask questions to make him realize that the estimate may be optimistic. Ask similar questions as Bob did in the story at the start of this chapter. Together you may come to the conclusion that time needs to be added before entering it into MS Project. If the person is pessimistic you could ask questions that may lead to subtracting time. In any case, you should leave the final decision with the estimator; otherwise you take the ownership and responsibility away from the team member. Next time, the person may refuse to cooperate.

You can also determine someone's tendency by studying their track record of estimates and the actual durations realized.

"Can't you do it?"

I have seen organizations getting stuck in scheduling a project when they use estimates produced by people OTHER than the people who do the work. People who tend to produce unsolicited "estimates" are:

◆ **Executives**: *"Can't you do it in two weeks?"*
Project managers all know the stress that occurs when executives impose their "estimates" on your project. Some executives will try to play on your guilt with this sentence in order to get you to commit to a crazy deadline.

◆ **Sales representatives**: *"The client gets what she wants."*
Project managers all know the disastrous effects that occur when sales people have presented their own "estimates" to the client without consultation. As a project manager you cannot win in such a situation. These "estimates" are no estimates; they are commitments to please the client and win a sale at the project manager's expense.

Estimates from sales people and executives often suffer from wishful thinking in an attempt to please the client and close the deal. Their estimates should be treated as targets, not as estimates. Enter these as deadlines in Project 2000. See page 216: Deadlines.

As a project manager, you have to come to rely on the estimates of the resources in your team. If you feel the estimate is high you can always explore with the team members to see if there are other/better/smarter ways of working. In an open discussion, it is often possible to decrease estimates with new ideas.

Now that we have discussed some of the human tendencies in estimating, let us explore how MS Project handles the estimates you enter.

The Difference Between Duration and Work

The *duration* is the number of time units of working time. Duration is expressed in business days or in business hours.

The *work* is the number of person hours or person days planned or spent on a task. Work is synonymous to *effort* in Project 2000.

For example, one person who works for two *business days* (duration) delivers two *person days* of effort (work). One more example, two painters who work for three business days (duration) to paint your house, spend six person days of effort (work).

The business days are entered in the **Duration** field and the effort is entered in the **Work** field.

The Formula Behind the Screens

Project 2000 uses the formula: *Duration x Units = Work.*
◆   *Duration* is how many business days you have to finish the job,
◆   *Units* is how many resource units you have,
◆   *Work* is how much effort it will take.

The formula is meant to make your life easier, because you only have to provide two out of the three variables in the formula and Project 2000 will calculate the third one for you. However, if you are not aware of this formula, your life will be more complicated.

The first variable in the formula is a given in most project situations. It is the estimate you come up with. In any given situation, you know the *duration*, *units* or *work*.

The second variable is the one to decide on: for example when you know you have a six person day job, and you decide to assign two people to it. Project 2000 can do the math for you and will calculate a duration of three days.

The third variable is calculated by Project 2000 to balance the equation and is automatically entered. Project 2000 tries to spare you some data entry.

In summary, the formula behind the screen assumes you work like this:

◆ you estimate and enter the first value,
◆ you decide the second value, and
◆ you let Project 2000 calculate the third value

If you override the third value that is calculated by Project 2000 and enter a different value, Project 2000 will recalculate the first or the second to maintain the balanced equation. The field it will recalculate depends on the task type: fixed duration, fixed units or fixed work.

An Example of an Estimation

Let us assume you want to repaint one room in your house during your vacation. You wonder when you could be done repainting the room. You need to know the number of calendar days.

Estimating the number of calendar days, however, is very difficult and you have to step back and try to estimate the number of workdays (business days). Once you know the number of business days and on which day of the week you start, you can convert the business days into calendar days.

Estimating in business days, however, may be difficult as well because you don't know how much effort (work) the job entails. You try to figure it out and realize that you must start looking at parameters, like area to be painted, the color difference between the old and new color, the number of coats needed and what you will do with the wallpaper. After you have decided all of those factors, you figure it will take, let's say, 10 person days.

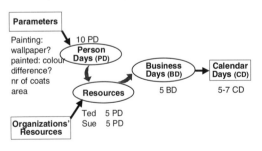

You still cannot say how many business days this requires because you have not asked how many family members or friends (resources) will help you. You ask around and you find that your significant other is willing to help and that you will share the workload. This means that both of you will take five person days of effort; ten person days of effort can be delivered by two people in five business days.

If you start on Monday and you decide not to work on the weekend, you can have your house painted by Friday (5 Calendar Days). However, if you start on Tuesday you will be done on Monday of the next week (7 Calendar Days). You now know what you wanted to know: the project end date.

The last conversion from business days to calendar days is taken care of by Project 2000. Once you have filled in the project calendar, you can count on the eager and rapid cooperation of Project 2000. The challenge in estimating with Project 2000 lies in solving the puzzle of person days, resources units and business days. We will present a process for solving this puzzle. The whole process is summarized in the illustration below.

A Process for Estimating

Estimating: Types of Tasks

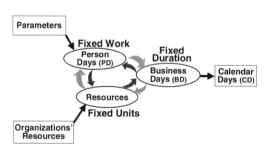

Eventually, you need to know the start date and the finish date of a task in order to fit it into the time line. To get to those dates, you need to find out the number of calendar days a job will take. It is too difficult to estimate the number of calendar days. You will immediately get bogged down into questions like, *When will we start this task? If we start it on a Monday it will take 2 calendar days, but if we start it on a Friday, it will take 4 calendar days!* You don't want to deal with those issues at this point. So you should instead try to estimate the number of business days, and have Project 2000 do the conversion from business days to calendar days. The software does an excellent job at this once you have filled in the project calendar. We filled it in when we setup the project (see page 95: Creating the Project Calendar).

In some situations it is possible to estimate the number of business days (or business hours) directly, for example, for tasks like *meeting*, *training*, and *presentation*. For a meeting you set the duration to, let's say, 2 business hours.

For many other tasks, it is impossible to estimate the number of business days immediately. Those are the tasks for which it is important to know how much effort it will take and how many resources are available to do the work. You have to step back and estimate the amount of work first.

In order to estimate the work (effort) in person days, you may find that you have to look at the parameters of the job. For a programming job you can look at how many input screens the application will have. For a construction project you can look at how many cubic feet of concrete you will need to pour. For each job there are relevant parameters to consider. You may have to ask the client more questions.

Looking at the parameters of the job is important. Each industry has its own metrics to refine the estimates of a job. The construction industry has its quantity surveyors; they can tell exactly how much a brick wall will cost given the square footage. The software industry works with function-point metrics. Once they know the number of function points of a software application to be built, they have their rough estimates. Dividing the function point total by 150 approximates the number of analysts, programmers and technicians they will need. And raising the function point total to the power of 0.4 gives a rough estimate of the time in months that the team will need.[15]

Once you determined the amount of work, you have to decide how many resources will be assigned to the job. After that, you can usually determine how many business days the task will take (duration).

I have given you an example in which you estimate the amount of work first, then you decide about the number of resources, and the number of business days is calculated as a result. This situation is called a *Fixed Work* task, because you estimate the work first.

What you estimate or decide first is entirely up to you and will depend on the situation. If you first determine the number of resource units, you have a *Fixed Units* task. If you first estimate the duration you have a *Fixed Duration* task.

In any situation you will have to estimate the first variable, decide about the second and calculate the third. The result: you will know the date the task will be done and the cost of it.

---

[15] These metrics were taken from *Sizing Up Software* by Capers Jones in Scientific American of December 1998.

On the next pages we will discuss Fixed Work tasks and Fixed Duration tasks. The Fixed Units tasks are less common and we will postpone those to Chapter 8 Entering Assignments. You need Fixed Units mostly when you make changes to an assignment.

 If you don't intend to enter resources and assignments you will have to estimate the durations for all tasks. Project 2000 needs durations to create the Gantt Chart. If you will assign resources eventually, you can use work estimates. We will not assign resources in this chapter and will discuss this also in Chapter 8 Entering Assignments.

Preparing the Gantt Spreadsheet

ID	Task Name	Type	Duration	Work

↑
**Fixed Work,
Fixed Units, or
Fixed Duration**

Let us prepare the Gantt spreadsheet so we have the right fields to enter our estimates. The illustration shows which fields we will insert.

We need the following fields in the Gantt spreadsheet:
◆ **ID**
◆ **Task Name**
◆ **Type**: By setting the right task type you tell Project 2000 to leave the estimate you enter alone. For example, if you estimate that a task will take 10 person days, you enter 10 days in the Work field and you set the task type to Fixed Work. The tool may (re)calculate the duration or the resource units needed, but not the Work.
◆ **Duration**: for the Fixed Duration tasks
◆ **Work**: for the Fixed Work tasks

If you have the default **Entry** table displayed, we need to insert the fields **Type** and **Work**:

1. Choose **View, Gantt Chart**

2. Click anywhere in the column **Duration** and choose **Insert, Column**
    OR
    Right-click on the **Duration** column heading and choose **Insert, Column...**; the
    Column Definition dialog appears:

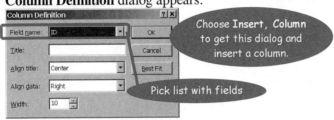

3. Select from the list **Field Name** ID ▼ the item **Type** and click OK.

4. Repeat steps 2 and 3 to insert another column **Work** before the column **Start**.

5. Make sure you have the right default task type selected in **Tools, Options, Schedule, Default Task Type**. This option determines the task type for new tasks you will create. Click OK. We are now ready to enter duration and work estimates.

 If you started with the wrong default task type, you can change all tasks at once by clicking on a column heading to select all tasks and clicking the **Task Information** tool 📋. Click the **Advanced** tab and select the right type from the list **Task type** and click OK.

Fixed Work Tasks

Once you determine the amount of work, you will often find that your next step will be to establish how many resources will do the job. When you know the work and the number of resource units, Project 2000 will derive the number of business days (duration). For now, we will only give you the steps for entering work estimates. In the chapter on assignments we will explain how to assign resources to tasks, see page 277. Then we can explain the steps of how to enter this example into MS Project.

Once you know the amount of work (10PDs), you sometimes know in how many business days it needs to be done. Let's say you have only 4 business days for the task (duration). From this, Project 2000 can derive the number of resources you need (2.5).

1. Enter the name of the task in the field **Task Name.**

2. Press ⌷Tab⌷; the cursor moves into the field **Type**. (If you press ⌷Enter⌷ the cursor will move down to the next task.)

3. Select from the list ⌷Fixed Units ▼⌷ the task type **Fixed Work**. Press ⌷Tab⌷ twice to enter the **Work** field. Notice that Project 2000 entered a default duration of **1 day?.**

4. Enter in the **Work** field ⌷0 hrs ⌷ the number of person hours you estimate the task will take. You only need to enter the number and Project 2000 will append "hrs". If the time unit is different, for example, when you want to enter three weeks, you have to type "3w". In that case, Project 2000 needs the time unit abbreviation as well. Valid abbreviations are: "m" for minutes, "h" for hours, "d" for days, "w" for weeks and "mo" for months.

5. Press ⌷Enter⌷ and then ⌷Home⌷ to position the cursor for the next task.

 The time unit **months** is new in Project 2000.

Fixed Duration Tasks

For Fixed Duration tasks you enter the duration first. A task such as *meeting* is a prime example of a fixed duration task, because you decide the duration upfront. Then you could decide how much effort you are willing to spend in the meeting and enter the work. Or you can decide who you will invite to the meeting and assign the number of units, and Project 2000 will calculate the total amount of work.

1. Enter the name of the task in the field **Task Name.**

2. Press ⌨Tab; the cursor moves into the field **Type**. (If you press ⌨Enter the cursor will move down to the next task.)

3. Select from the task type list `Fixed Units` ▾ **Fixed Duration**.

4. Enter in the **Duration** field `1 day?` ⬍ the number of business days you estimate the task will take. You only need to enter the number and Project 2000 will append *days*. If the time unit is different, for example, you want to enter *2 hours*, you have to type the time unit abbreviation as well: "m" for minutes, "h" for hours, "d" for days, "w" for weeks and "mo" for months.

5. Press ⌨Enter and then ⌨Home to position the cursor for the next task.

 Notice that an "m" will be interpreted as "minute" instead of "month".

Estimating: Difficulties and Techniques

Estimating is one of the most difficult project management skills to learn. The following factors make it difficult:

◆ **In which time unit to estimate?**
You have the choice to estimate the number of calendar days, business days or person days (hours). Each situation is different. Sometimes you know the time frame in

which the activity has to be ready (calendar days: deadline date), sometimes you know first how much effort it will take (person days: work).

◆ **What to include?**
What do your resources include in their estimates? Do they imagine in their estimate being able to work full-time on the task? Do they include personal time, like calls to their significant other? Do they include time spent in meetings to discuss or present deliverables? Do they include waiting times?

Waiting time is, for example, the time you have to wait to receive a permit. Many schedulers include these waiting times in their duration estimates. We propose to enter them as lags on dependencies instead. For a definition of lag and how to enter it, see page 175.

◆ **Unknown events**
In any project there are always many unknown events. For example, in a project to move a company the location is often unknown when the move is planned:

◇   How easy will it be to find a location?

◇   How long will it take to prepare the new location?

◆ **Unknown resources**
During the planning phase it is often unclear whether enough resources will be available, who will be available and if they will be available at the time they are needed.

◆ **Unknown experience and skill levels**
Even if you do know which resources you will have on your project, you may not know their experience and skill level. For estimating this creates an extra challenge, because the estimator should not only look at the job, but also at who will do the job in order to come up with an estimate. How much skill does the job require? What is the skill level the resource has?

◆ **Unknown learning curves**
Projects create products that are unique. Some say that because of the lack of repetition, the effect of learning curves is limited in projects. Still, I think, learning plays an important role:

◇   Because the project is new, participants have to be willing to learn.
R & D projects and Product Development projects are prime examples.

◇   There is some repetition in projects, for example: status reports, quality control, and timesheets. In implementation projects the same system is installed in many locations.

The learning curve theory is therefore applicable to projects and to duration estimates.

We will discuss each of these difficulties in more detail.

In Which Time Unit to Estimate?

There are two choices we need to make:

◆ Estimate in person days, business days or calendar days?

◆ Estimate in regular durations or elapsed durations?

Estimating in Person, Business or Calendar Days?

Do you estimate the number of person days, business days or calendar days?

◆ *Person Days*:
One person day is one person working one full day. The number of person days is the amount of *work* or *effort* needed on the task. Person day estimates are needed to calculate the cost.

◆ *Business Days*:
A business day is a working day. You need to know the number of business days in order to calculate the calendar days.

◆ *Calendar Days*:
You need the number of calendar days if you are asked to commit to a date. Calendar days are also known in MS Project as elapsed days.

Elapsed Durations

A working day has 8 hours for most of us; an elapsed day has 24 hours. An elapsed day is like a calendar day, as most people will understand 'one day'. Elapsed durations are used for tasks that go through the night and through the weekend like backing up a computer system or the drying of paint.

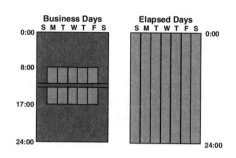

At food companies, new food products are shelved for months in order to find out, if the food preservation procedures are adequate. These months are elapsed months. At defense systems developers, a new monitor for a tank is kept in a shake and bake oven for, let's say, two days to test its ruggedness. The two days are elapsed days. Elapsed activities continue 24 hours around the clock.

Time unit	Enter normally as	Enter in elapsed time as
minutes	*m*	*em*
hours	*h*	*eh*
days	*d*	*ed*
weeks	*w*	*ew*
months	*mo*	*emo*

Instead of typing in "5d" to get 5 days, you have to type in "5ed" to get 5 elapsed days.

What to Include? Pure Work Time or Gross Work Time?

Pure   **Gross**

The term *Pure Work Time* [16] expresses an important concept very well. Pure work time is working 100% of your time with 100% focus on the task. Pure work time is 100% productive time without interruptions.

Gross Work Time, on the other hand, includes much time spent on other things than the tasks in the task list.

Gross work time could include:

◆ Personal time, for example:
  ◇ coffee breaks
  ◇ visits to the restroom, water fountain and coffee pot
  ◇ personal telephone calls
  ◇ TGIF[17], farewell and anniversary lunches for colleagues
  ◇ daydreaming

◆ Non-project tasks, for example:
  ◇ troubleshooting
  ◇ debugging existing software
  ◇ technical support to colleagues
  ◇ company meetings
  ◇ company functions

---

[16] I learned this term first from my former colleague Brian Petersen.

[17] TGIF stands for *Thanks Goodness It's Friday*

Do you, as the project manager, estimate in pure work time or in gross work time? Do your resources estimate in pure work time or in gross work time? Is it possible that they provide you with pure work time estimates, whereas you always interpret them as gross work time estimates? If that is the case, your resources will never meet their deadlines. It is important that everybody estimates consistently in either pure work time or gross work time. The calendar settings have to be set accordingly in Project 2000.

Only when it is done consistently, can you produce reliable schedules from these estimates. If everybody estimates in gross work time, you don't have to do anything special. Project 2000 has default working times from 8AM-12PM and from 1PM-5PM and is set up to receive gross work time estimates.

If you want to work with pure work time estimates, you have to decrease everybody's availability from 100% to lower than 100%. If you have found that people are productive 80% of their work time, you have to enter this as their availability. For how to do this, see page 248: Part-time Availability.

Unknown Events: The Rolling Wave Approach

When you are performing a project to relocate the office and you have yet to find the location, you cannot know how long it will take to remodel the new location. Perhaps only minor remodeling is necessary, or maybe you will spend a long time getting the location up to par. You should perhaps keep the estimate for this part of the project on the safe side by assuming you will have to remodel the new location a lot. You enter just one line item for the remodeling in the WBS and you enter the uncertain, but safe estimate.

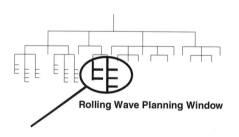

Rolling Wave Planning Window

This is called the *Rolling Wave* approach; you don't detail the plan until you know what to expect. In the Rolling Wave technique you use a planning window. In a project of a year you could use a planning window of one quarter. The planning window moves as time goes by and as soon as a deliverable falls inside the planning window, you break down the detail activities for the deliverable. This avoids having to redo large portions of the WBS.

Unknown Resources

If you don't know which resources you will get, you have to make assumptions for planning purposes. If you don't, you cannot finalize your schedule. The assumption you make is that you will get the resources needed when your schedule indicates you need them. Of course, it is a good idea to discuss your resource requirements with the resource manager, HR or executives to do a reality check on the assumption. Make the assumption explicit in the project plan and make it loud and clear, so no one's lack of memory will come to haunt you.

"C++ Programmer"

"Winston"
(C++ Programmer)

You enter the resources as generic resources in terms of roles, functions or positions. If you don't know whether you will get *Winston* on your team, you enter C^{++} *Programmer*. This simple technique will allow you to do your estimates, enter resources and enter the assignments as well. The latter will be explained in Chapter 8 Entering Assignments. You might consider keeping your estimates on the safe side in case you get the junior programmer.

Unknown Experience and Skill Levels

Even if you do know the name of the resource that will do the job, you still may not know how much experience the person has and at which skill level he or she should be classified.

If this is a major concern, use several resource categories such as *Junior Visual Basic Programmer* and *Senior Visual Basic Programmer*.

Unknown Learning Curves

We should consider two factors:

◆ Organizations create new and unique products through projects. As a consequence there will always be a lot of on-the-job learning.

◆ The number of repetitions in projects is considerably lower than in manufacturing operations. *Projects are never boring.*

The amount of learning and little repetition in projects together imply that resources hired on projects have to be fast learners. The ability to learn quickly is perhaps the most important characteristic of good project resources.

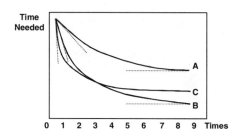

Fast learners (B and C in the illustration) have a learning curve that has a steep slope down. Fast learners can also end up with a faster time per deliverable than slow learners (compare the horizontal dotted lines for A and B). However, it is not a given that the fastest time per deliverable is lower for fast learners (compare the horizontal lines for B and C). Because of the little amount of repetition in projects, the initial learning rate seems to be more important than the eventual fastest time.

We recommend you hire people with a C-learning curve on your projects. For estimating, the learning curve can pose difficulties, the estimator should look not only at the job, but also at who will do the job in order to produce the estimate. How much repetition does the job have? Is the resource a slow or a fast learner? These factors complicate estimating and, again, you may have to make some assumptions as to the rate of learning of the resources. Don't forget to make these assumptions explicit in your project plan. Otherwise you may end up with slow resources and the blame for late delivery. If you don't document how you arrived at your estimates, you will not be able to learn from the discrepancies between actuals and plan.

Copying and Moving Data

Editing Fields of Multiple Tasks at Once

1. Select the tasks by clicking on the first task, hold down `Ctrl` and click on the next ones until they are all selected.

2. Click `📧` or hold down `Shift` and press `F2`; the **Multiple Task Information** box appears:

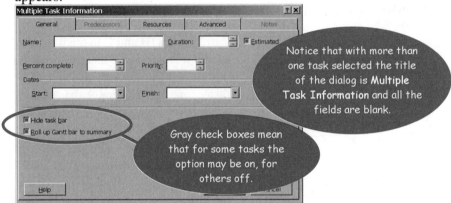

3. Make the changes needed on each tab.

4. Click `OK`.

The Multiple Task Information dialog can be used as a time saver for many purposes. Examples are:

◆ Setting the duration of all the milestones to 0 (zero) on the tab **General** and uncheck ☐ **Estimated** to make the question mark disappear.

◆ Changing the tasks from **Fixed Duration** to **Fixed Work** tasks on the **Advanced** tab in the field **Task Type**.

◆ Adding a resource to many tasks at once on the tab **Resources**.

◆ Assigning high *priority* to a group of tasks, so they will not likely be affected by resource leveling. Choose the tab **General**, and enter a number between 0 and 1000 in the field **Priority**.

Copying With Fill Down

1. Enter the value that you want to copy down in the top cell of the area into which you wish to copy the value.

2. Click and hold down on the top cell and drag over all adjacent cells to fill (if you bump the edge of the screen, it will take off like a rocket.)
    OR

     Hold down Shift and press ↓ to select all cells you wish to fill (use this because computers are too fast these days, or the applications are not slowed down enough.)
    OR

    Hold down Ctrl and click on all non-adjacent cells to fill with the value.

3. Choose **Edit, Fill, Down**.
    OR

    Hold down Ctrl and press D.

Examples in which you can use the fill down feature:
◆   Changing the constraint types for many tasks. To get rid of constraints change them to **As Soon As Possible**.
◆   Setting the **Level Assignment** field for all the detail recurring tasks to '*Yes*'.
◆   In the resource sheet you can fill down the department or the group for the resources.

Fill Up or Fill Down Using the Fill Handle

1. Enter the value you wish to fill into other cells in the top or the bottom cell of the area to fill into.

2. At the bottom right of the cell 1 day? ⟶ Fill handle

3. Point to the fill handle and when you see a cross-hair mouse pointer 1 day? you drag over the cells to be filled.

Copying or Moving Cells

When copying or moving cells you have to make sure that the receiving cells can accommodate the type of data you insert. MS Project will warn you if the cells cannot receive it.

Moving Cells

1. Select the cells and point to the border of the selected area, make sure the mouse pointer changes from a plus sign ⊕ to an arrow ↖.

2. Click, hold down and drag the cells to their new place.

 If you classify as "mouse-challenged" or as a "careless clicker", you should consider turning this cell drag and drop option off. You can do so by choosing **Tools, Options,** tab **Edit,** de-select ☐ **Allow Cell Drag and Drop**.

Copying Cells

1. Select the cells and point to the border of the selected area, make sure the mouse pointer changes from a plus sign ⊕ to an arrow ↖.

2. Hold down ⌈Ctrl⌉ and drag the cells to their place.

 You cannot use copy and paste to copy one cell and paste it into many other cells, like you can in Excel. It does not work in Project 2000.

Clearing Cells

Select the cells (not the locked first column) and choose **Edit, Clear, All**. This feature can also be used to selectively clear only the formatting, notes or hyperlinks of a task.

Copying or Moving the Data of a Column

1. Select the whole column by clicking on its column-heading.

2. Point to the border of the selected column in the sheet (not in the heading). Make sure the mouse pointer changes from a plus sign ⊕ to an arrow ↖.

3. Drag to move.
    OR
    Hold down ⌈Ctrl⌉ and drag to copy.

4. Release the mouse on the column in which you want the data.

Make sure the copy-to column can receive data of that type: dates can be copied into date columns, text into text, and numbers into numbers. If not, you will receive an error message from Project 2000.

Copying Between Projects

Copying Data Between Projects

1. Open the project to copy from.

2. Select the tasks or resources by dragging over the ID numbers (the first column with the gray color) to select the entire task or resource.

3. Choose the menu items **Edit**, **Copy** or click . The data is now temporarily stored in the clipboard.

4. Open the project to be copied to.

5. Select the row before which to insert the data and choose the menu items **Edit**, **Paste** or click [📋].

 You can also copy certain cells between projects instead of entire rows. If you do this you have to be careful to paste the data in a blank area of the sheet, otherwise existing data will be overridden. Choose **Edit, Undo** or click [↩] if an accident occurs.

Copying Objects Between Projects

1. Choose **Tools, Organizer**; the **Organizer** dialog appears:

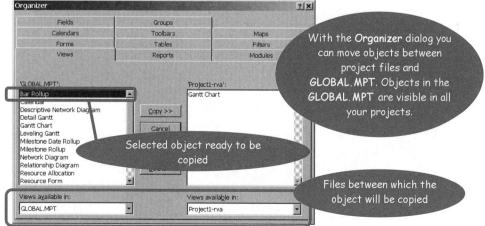

2. Click on the tab of the type of objects to transfer.

3. Select from the lists | GLOBAL.MPT ▾ | at the bottom of the dialog, the file from which to copy the object and the file to copy to.

4. Select the object and click | Copy >> | .

5. Click | Close | or | Cancel | when done.

The organizer allows you to copy objects to other project files (.MPP) or to the *global.mpt*. Any objects you put into this global template are visible in all your projects, unless they have the same name as other objects that are part of the project file.

Using the Organizer you can, for example:
◆   Make the Standard Project Calendar available to other people.
◆   Create a standard report and make it available to colleagues.
◆   Share views, tables and filters with other people.

Exercises

Relocation Project – Entering Estimates

Continue to work with your file *Relocation.MPP* or open the file
04 Entering Estimates.MPP in the subdirectory *Relocation Project* on the CD-ROM.

Insert the fields *Type*, *Duration* and *Work* in the order they appear in the column headings
of the table below and enter the data of the table into the Relocation project file. The tasks
with a zero duration will become milestones.

ID	Task Name	Type	Duration	Work
1.	*REQUIREMENTS*	*Fixed Duration* [18]		
2.	*research staff requirements*	*Fixed Work*		*2 d*
3.	*summarize requirements*	*Fixed Work*		*2 d*
4.	*LOCATION*	*Fixed Duration*		
5.	*select the realtor*	*Fixed Duration*	*4 d*	
6.	*visit the sites*	*Fixed Duration*	*1 d*	
7.	*evaluate the sites*	*Fixed Duration*	*1 d*	
8.	*meet to select the location*	*Fixed Duration*	*1 d*	
9.	*legal review*	*Fixed Duration*	*0.5 d*	
10.	*location selected*	*Fixed Duration*	*0 d*	
11.	*REMODELING CONTRACT*	*Fixed Duration*		
12.	*select the contractor*	*Fixed Duration*	*2 d*	
13.	*meet to discuss contract*	*Fixed Duration*	*1 d*	
14.	*revise the schedule*	*Fixed Duration*	*1 d*	
15.	*negotiate the contract*	*Fixed Duration*	*1 d*	
16.	*contractor contracted*	*Fixed Duration*	*0 d*	

---

[18] Notice that you cannot change the Type of a summary task; it is set by MS Project to
Fixed Duration. No Durations or Work numbers are provided for Summary Tasks, because these
are calculated by Project 2000.

ID	Task Name	Type	Duration	Work
17.	REMODELED LOCATION	Fixed Duration		
18.	relocate walls	Fixed Work	10 d	100 d
19.	electric wiring	Fixed Work	5 d	25 d
20.	paint	Fixed Work	2 d	8 d
21.	drying of paint	Fixed Duration	4ed [19]	
22.	install cabinetry	Fixed Work	5 d	40 d
23.	install LAN	Fixed Work		60 d
24.	lay carpet	Fixed Work	10 d	60 d
25.	facility remodeled	Fixed Duration	0 d	
26.	MOVE	Fixed Duration		
27.	select mover	Fixed Duration	2 d	
28.	pack	Fixed Duration	2 d	
29.	move	Fixed Duration	2 d	
30.	unpack	Fixed Duration	2 d	
31.	new location opened	Fixed Duration	0 d	

Compare your file with the solution file *05 Entering Dependencies.MPP* in the subdirectory *Relocation Project* on the CD-ROM.

---

[19] Notice the 'e' in '4ed'; this is an elapsed duration that continues through the night and weekend.

Case Study – Escalated Estimates

MILDEVICES is a manufacturer of military products. The company makes navigation and intelligence products. LCD screens and consoles are some of their major products. MILDEVICES has engineering and manufacturing staff. There is a project control office with 25 project management staff members and this office reports directly to the VP-Operations. The project control staff supports the engineers in realizing the projects.

Upper management typically initiates a new project. One executive becomes the project sponsor and finds an engineer he will appoint as the project manager. The project manager puts the budget together with his team and the budget is submitted for approval by senior management.

Executives typically cut the proposed budget because they are concerned with the bottom line of the company. The engineers find that the cuts are applied arbitrarily and often feel they end up with impossibly tight budgets. As a consequence, they start to increase their estimates in order to receive reasonable budgets. Senior management in turn reacts to this by cutting the proposed budgets even more. The new cuts are done in a way that makes even less sense to the engineers. As a result, the project managers now jack up their estimates even further and hide their padding in the estimates wherever they can. The openness and the mutual trust are gone between the executives and project managers.

One of the schedulers in the project office, Debbie, says this about these developments: "The numbers the engineers receive back from senior management are so ridiculously low that they just laugh at them". Inevitably, she says, budget overruns take place.

QUESTIONS:

1. What type of problem is this? Is it an organizational problem, a cultural problem, or a financial problem?

2. If a project manager asked you for advice, what would you advise to break this escalating spiral?

3. If an executive asked you for advice, what would you advise for breaking this escalating spiral?

Chapter 5 Entering Dependencies

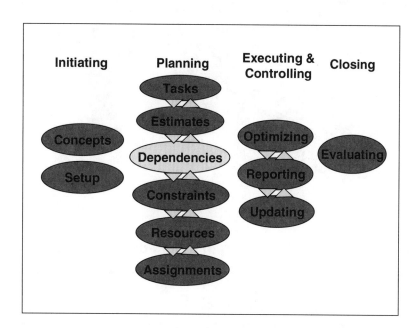

We have the tasks and the estimates entered into our project file and are ready to enter the dependencies, the links between the tasks.

After this chapter you will:

◆ know what dependencies are

◆ be able to set dependencies in the Gantt Chart

◆ be able to set dependencies in the Network Diagram

◆ be able to set multiple predecessors or successors on a task

◆ be able to check and edit dependencies

◆ be able to format the Network Diagram view in an attractive way.

Drowning in a Schedule

Nob is visibly annoyed as he boldly states: "The schedules don't help me! I stopped making them!"

Bob is alarmed by Nob's vigor. "Why is that, Nob?"

"Well, the schedule is only accurate after you've just finished it. One week later the schedule is out of date. As soon as a change happens the schedule is useless. And Bob, you know changes happen all the time in projects. Every day something changes!"

"Yeah, I know, in my projects things also change all the time, but I still manage to keep up with those changes."

Nob sighs in despair. "Well, I can't keep up with the changes. With every change I spend an hour updating my schedule. I don't have time for that. Not now ... when the project is running."

"One hour for each change? It takes me only ... 5 minutes for each one. Why do you spend so much time on keeping your schedule up to date?"

"When a change occurs, I have to adjust half my schedule every time!"

Bob is amazed and notes: "Each change only requires me to make one adjustment in my schedule. Are you using dependencies in your schedule?"

"What do you mean 'dependencies'?"

Dependencies

What are Dependencies?

A *dependency* is a relationship between the start or finish dates of two tasks that reflects

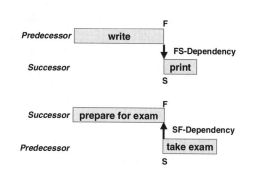

the cause and effect between them. The result of the first dependency shown in the illustration is that the finish date of the independent task *write* (predecessor) drives the start date of the dependent task *print* (successor). Whenever the finish date of *write* moves, the start date of *print* will move with it.

Many people think of dependencies as the chronological sequencing of tasks. If you think this, you may get stuck on the concept of dependencies. One person I met could not establish the difference between a successor and a predecessor. He thought the predecessor is always the task that is scheduled earlier. He held a chronological concept of dependencies. He became confused when he saw that successors are sometimes scheduled earlier than predecessors, like in the second example *prepare for exam* and *take exam*. As a result he never truly understood the difference between a predecessor and a successor. It is NOT a matter of chronology! The words *predecessor* and *successor* are somewhat misleading, because they imply chronology.

Dependencies are not about chronology, but about cause and effect. Think of the predecessor as the driving task (driver); the successor is the driven task (follower). The right question to ask yourself therefore is *"Which task drives the other task?"* in order to find the predecessor. We suggest you consider using the terms *driver* and *follower*, instead of predecessor and successor.

Why Should I Use Dependencies?

You may be used to entering start and finish dates. That is what most people did when they scheduled on paper. It is not necessary to indicate start and end dates when you work with Project 2000. We even strongly recommend NOT entering start and finish dates.

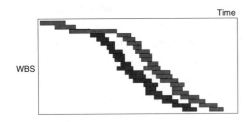

Instead, Project 2000 only needs to know what the cause and effect is between the tasks that have to be performed. Entering the logic between the tasks is also called *setting dependencies*. In the illustration you can see that the duration of the third task was revised and all the dependent tasks are immediately rescheduled as a result.

The main benefit of making all the dependencies between the tasks explicit is that when the duration or start date of one task changes, Project 2000 can recalculate the entire schedule for you. If you don't use dependencies you have to redo the entire chart yourself by hand. That is what Nob did in the story at the start of this chapter. This may seem acceptable when you still have the time during the planning phase, but it becomes impossible during the execution of the project. During execution too many things change and they change continuously. I have seen too often that early in the execution of the project the Gantt Charts were dumped in a drawer and never looked at again. A schedule without dependencies is just a nice chart, a snapshot of your project and no more than that. To create a useful model of your project that continues to predict the project finish date, you have to use dependencies.

Choosing the Options

Tab	Option
Schedule	☑ **Autolink inserted or moved tasks** With Autolink on, MS Project will set or break dependencies itself assuming that you want sequential dependencies for all tasks.
	[Set as Default] Sets the option above as the default setting for any new schedules you create. The existing schedules are not affected because this option is stored in the project files as you can read in the label of the section: **Scheduling Options for 'Project 1'**.

To access the options, choose **Tools, Options**.

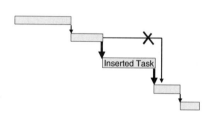

Autolink works within a series of sequentially dependent tasks. If you insert a task inside the series, Project 2000 will immediately incorporate it in the chain of dependencies. It breaks one dependency and sets two new ones (the fat arrows in the illustration). If you move a task, it closes the chain (cutting two dependencies and creating one new one) and it incorporates the task at the destination in the series of tasks (cutting one dependency and creating two new ones).

 This feature is very helpful during the planning phase of the project. During the execution of the project, however, it may be better to turn it off. Project 2000 makes its own decisions on which dependencies to set or break. To the uninformed scheduler they may seem arbitrary.

Types of Dependencies

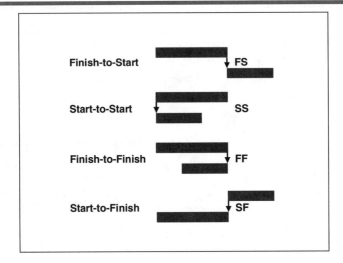

There are four types of dependencies, as shown in the illustration. Examples of each are:

◆ *Finish-to-Start* (*FS*)
Writing and then printing a report.

◆ *Start-to-Start* (*SS*)
The carpenters start three days after bricklayers started (Start-to-Start plus three days).

◆ *Finish-to-Finish* (*FF*)
After the writing is finished, the translation will be ready in two days.
(Finish-to-Finish plus two days).

◆ *Start-to-Finish* (*SF*)
Due to the fixed date of the exam, the start of the exam will force the preparation to end.

Absolute Lead or Lag Time

In a situation in which you want the successor to wait some time before it can start, you can add a *lag* to a dependency. This acts as if the dependency has a duration itself and it keeps the two task bars always apart by the amount of lag. For example, if you apply for a building permit, you often have to wait six weeks before you can start the construction.

This would be a Finish-to-Start dependency with a lag of six weeks between the tasks, *apply for permit* and *start construction*.

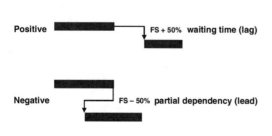

In a *partial dependency* the successor is dependent upon the partial completion of its predecessor. As a result, the task bars overlap each other in time. This is also called a *lead*. For example, if you write a report, you could finish the entire report before you send it to the editor. You could also send the first half and overlap the writing and editing. This could be a Finish-to-Start dependency between *write report* and *edit report* with a lead of three weeks. In Project 2000, you will enter leads as negative lags, so in this case you would enter FS-3W.

Note that while the lag and lead are shown here on the Finish-to-Start type of dependency they can be applied to the other types of dependencies as well.

Relative Lead or Lag Time

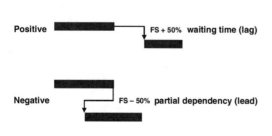

You can express the amount of lead or lag as a percentage of the duration of the predecessor. The task bars then take positions relative to each other. With this feature it is possible to have a successor start halfway through the duration of the predecessor and keep it on the halfway mark, regardless of how the duration of the predecessor is revised or changed. We needed this in the *write report* example, after the first half is written we send it to the editor.

An example from the food sector: the shelf life of new food products has to be tested, but these tests are long. Successors are often started at 50% of the duration of the predecessor when it looks as if the shelf life will be good. If the test turns unfavorable corrective actions are taken.

In construction projects, the electrical engineering design often starts when the civil engineering design is 60% complete.

Choosing the Right Type of Dependency

Sometimes when you are creating your project model, you may not be certain about the type of dependency to use. Of the examples in the illustration, the best one depends on the situation that is modeled. If the situation allows you to postpone the exam, when you are not prepared for it, the Finish-to-Start dependency is the best. An example is the PMP-exam[20] that can be postponed if you are not ready to take it. If you cannot postpone taking the exam, like a university exam, the Start-to-Finish is the best one. When the exam starts it will end the preparation. Typically, university students count backwards in preparing for an exam.

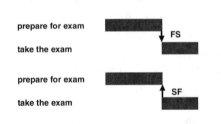

Which is the best model of the situation?

In forward scheduling you will use the FS-dependency most often. You could argue that when you schedule backwards the SF-dependency should be the dependency you use most often. After all, in backward scheduling, the finish date drives every task in the project.

 Project 2000 does not change the default dependency to SF when you switch to backward scheduling.

---

[20] PMP® stands for Project Management Professional, an accreditation by the Project Management Institute – PMI ®. See www.pmi.org for more information.

Steps for Choosing the Right Type of Dependency

Here is a process of four questions to choose the right dependency:

1. *Which task drives the other?*
   To determine which task is the predecessor, ask yourself: *"Which task drives the other?"* to find the driver (the independent task or predecessor). People often ask themselves: *"What should be scheduled first or earliest?"* This question asks for the chronology of tasks. Dependencies are not about chronology, but about cause and effect. We recommend you use the first question to find the predecessor.

2. *Does the start or the finish of the predecessor drive the other task?*
   This question helps to find the type of dependency you need**.**

3. *Does the predecessor drive the start or the finish of the successor?*
   Once you know the answer to this question, you know the type of dependency you need: Finish-to-Start (FS), Start-to-Start (SS), Finish-to-Finish (FF) or Start-to-Finish (SF).

4. *Should there be a lag or a lead on the dependency?*
   A lag delays the successor in time (further to the right in the time scale), whereas a lead schedules the successor earlier in time (further to the left in the time scale).

Categories of Dependencies

Different situations need different types of dependencies:

◆ *Decision Point Dependencies*

◆ *Hard and Soft Dependencies*

◆ *External Dependencies*

◆ *Resource Dependencies*

We will discuss each of these in more detail.

Decision Point Dependencies

Decision points are important nodes in the network of dependencies. (We discussed these on page 114.) They are like the central station for the railroads; many tracks are coming together and springing from it.

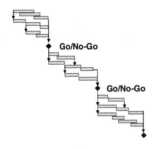

If you want to create decision points in your schedule, you have to make sure that all activities that rely upon the decision also have the decision as their predecessor.

What you will see in a schedule with decision points is several networks of dependencies linked together at the nodes, the decision points.

Hard and Soft Dependencies

Some tasks have to be done in an absolute sequence, others have a preferred sequence.

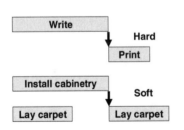

Hard or mandatory dependencies are dependencies that are absolutely necessary. Common sense dictates to create these dependencies. For example, the two activities, *write the report* and *print the report,* require a hard dependency. It does not make sense to schedule the printing in any other way than driven by the finish date of the writing.

Soft or discretionary dependencies are a matter of preference from a practical or personal point of view. For example, the two tasks *installing cabinetry* and *laying the carpet* are not necessarily dependent on each other. The project manager may prefer to set a dependency to make sure that the cabinetmakers do not spill glue and damage the new carpet.

Project 2000 does not have a special feature for creating soft dependencies. It will be easier to optimize the schedule if you remember where you created the soft dependencies. You could document the discretionary dependencies in the **Notes** field or in one of the extra **Text** fields.

External Dependencies

External dependencies are needed when there are impacts outside your control. You have an external dependency when you:

◆ receive goods or materials from a supplier
◆ require input from another project

In general, when you are dependent on an event that is beyond your control.

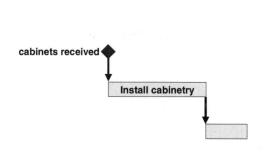

In the example in the illustration you could leave the milestone out when you schedule such an external dependency. But who will get blamed if you do leave it out and the cabinets arrive late? It would just show as a slipped start date on the task, *install cabinetry*, and the installers would receive the blame.

In the case of external dependencies, we recommend you insert an extra milestone for the event in your schedule with a Start-No-Earlier-Than schedule constraint. The constraint will keep the milestone diamond on the date you have agreed to. Then create dependencies from the milestone into your activities. (We will discuss constraints on page 218: Entering Constraints.)

The advantage is that if the shipment of cabinets arrives late, it is clear that this was beyond your control. If the milestone were omitted, it would look like that the installers started working late on their task. It is a simple technique that keeps the fingers pointed to the right people in the case of a dispute.

Resource Dependencies

This category is a special case that forces tasks to be sequenced because of work overloads. A resource dependency appears when two tasks compete for the same resource. If you cannot find other solutions, one of them has to be delayed in order to keep the workload reasonable for the resource. You could force the delay by setting an extra dependency. However, we don't think you should do that, because what happens if you reassign one task to Sam?

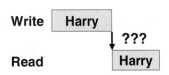

If one of the two tasks is re-assigned, the dependency should be broken as well, because it was created to keep the workloads reasonable. If you forget to break a resource dependency, you end up with a schedule that is sub-optimal. Breaking such a soft dependency is often forgotten.

We will deal with resource dependencies in more detail in Chapter 9 Optimizing the Schedule on page 299.

Entering Logic

Project 2000 offers a variety of ways to enter dependencies into the project file:

◆ In the Gantt Chart:
  ◇ Link tools
  ◇ dragging
  ◇ Task Information Form
  ◇ Task Form: predecessor and successor fields or ID-field

◆ In the Network Diagram:
  ◇ dragging
  ◇ Task Information Form

We will now discuss these different ways in more detail.

Entering Dependencies in the Gantt Chart

Using the Link Tool

To Set a Dependency

1. Select consecutive tasks by dragging over their names
   OR

   Select the predecessor first and hold down [Ctrl] and click on the successor. You can click on the task name or on its task bar.

2. Click [⊜] OR hold down [Ctrl] and press [F2]; the tasks are now Finish-to-Start dependent.

This method allows you to set Finish-to-Start dependencies only.

To Delete a Dependency Between two Tasks

1. Select the predecessor and the successor by dragging over their task names.
   OR

   Select the predecessor first and then hold down [Ctrl] and click on the successor. You can click on the task name or on the task bar.

2. Click [⊜] or hold down [Ctrl] + [Shift] and press [F2]

To Delete all Dependencies on a Task

Select the task and click [⊜].

You can easily delete all dependencies in the entire schedule if you select all tasks first by clicking on a column heading and then click [⊜].

Using the Mouse

To Draw Dependencies

1. If necessary, zoom in using to make the task bars wider.

2. Point to the center of the predecessor task bar; make sure you see a four-headed arrow mouse-pointer

3. Drag vertically toward the successor task bar and make sure the mouse pointer now looks like: ⊕. Release the mouse button inside the task bar of the successor. An arrow is set and the task bar of the successor moves out to just after the predecessor's task bar. A Finish-to-Start dependency is set:

This method allows you to set Finish-to-Start dependencies only.

 If you drag into the edge of the screen, the screen starts scrolling very fast in the Gantt Chart, it launches like a missile.

 If you drag horizontally you are rescheduling the task bar and most likely setting an undesirable schedule constraint!

To Edit or Delete the Dependency

1. Point with the tip of the mouse-pointer arrow to the dependency arrow you want to change.

2. Dependency arrows can overlap each other. So wait one second until the yellow feedback window pops up that confirms which dependency you have selected.

Task Link: Finish-to-Start (FS)   Lag: 0d
From: (ID 5) write
To: (ID 6) print

3. If you have the right dependency arrow selected, double-click on it.

4. Select the **Type** of the dependency using the list Finish-to-Start (FS) and change the **Lag** time.
OR
Click Delete to get rid of the dependency.

Using the Task Information Form

1. Select the successor.

2. Click or hold down Shift and press F2; the **Task Information** dialog appears:

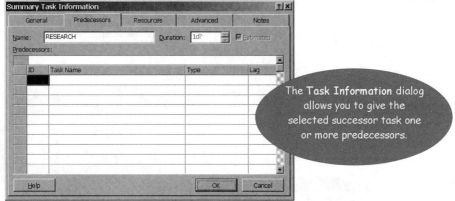

3. Click the **Predecessors** tab; the dialog should now look like above.

4. Click in the **Task Name** field and select the predecessor task from the list
.
OR
Enter the ID number in the **ID** field.

5. Select the type of dependency in the **Type** field and enter the lag or lead in the **Lag** field.

6. Click OK .

Using the Task Form

You may need the Task Form if the predecessor and successor are a screen or more apart.

1. In the Gantt Chart display the **Task Form** by choosing **Window, Split**.

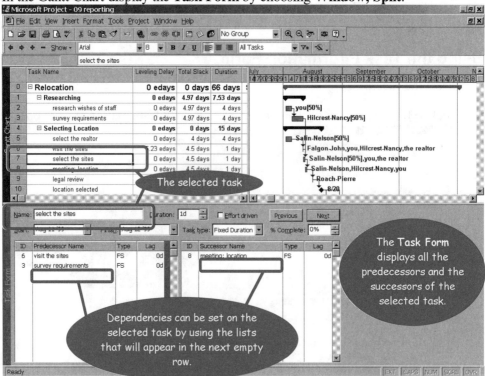

2. Click on the **Task Form** in the bottom and choose **Format, Details, Predecessors & Successors** to view the dependencies of the selected task.

3. Click in the field **Predecessor Name** or **Successor Name** and use the list
    [▼] to create the dependency.
    OR
    Type the ID number of the predecessor or successor in the **ID** field.

4. Set the type of dependency in the **Type** field and add a positive lag or negative lag (lead) in the **Lag** field, if necessary.

5. Click [OK   ].
    The data is entered into the project database only after the **OK** button is clicked.

Entering Dependencies in the Network Diagram

The Network Diagram

To apply the view, choose **View**, **Network Diagram**. The Network Diagram displays an overview of all the dependencies you have set; the dependencies are depicted as arrows.

By default, the **Network Diagram** displays the different types of tasks in differently shaped boxes:
◆ summary tasks in a parallelogram
◆ detail tasks in a rectangle
◆ milestones in a hexagon

The critical tasks have a red border instead of the (default) blue. These default types of boxes can be changed by choosing **Format, Box Styles**; see page 197.

Viewing the Network Diagram Toolbar

1. Right-click on any toolbar, the pop-up menu appears with all available toolbars.
    OR
    Choose **View, Toolbars**.

2. Choose **Network Diagram**; the toolbar is displayed:

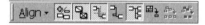

This toolbar makes many useful features directly accessible. For an explanation of each tool see page 524: Network Diagram Toolbar.

Displaying More Tasks on the Screen

If you have the window split, remove the split window by double-clicking the divider line between the top and bottom view using the mouse pointer ‡ or by choosing **Window, Remove Split**.

You can also get more task boxes by using **Zoom Out** with the 🔍 tool. However, the text becomes illegible when zoomed out too far, but if you point the mouse pointer to a task box a pop-up appears that allows you to read the task data. The screen tip that pops up looks like this:

print	
Start: Thu 4/6/00	ID: 6
Finish: Fri 4/7/00	Dur: 2 day:
Res:	

To zoom back in, click the plus tool 🔍.

Another method to display more task boxes, is to hide all the fields except the ID-number by clicking 🔲 on the **Network Diagram** toolbar or choosing **Format, Layout…**, ☑ **Hide all fields except ID**. Use the dialog that pops up when hovering the mouse pointer for a while over a task box, to see the task names.

A last method to display more task boxes gets rid of all the fields on a task box except the task name. Removing the fields makes the boxes a lot smaller. See the steps on page 193: Choosing the Fields in Each Box.

To Set Dependencies in the Network Diagram

1. Point to the center of the predecessor box and make sure the mouse pointer is a plus sign: ✛

2. Click the left mouse button, hold down and drag towards the box of the successor; the mouse pointer should change into a ⊕ . Even if the box is not visible you can drag against the side of the screen, which will start scrolling automatically. Unlike in the Gantt Chart, the screen does not scroll too fast in this (newer) view.

3. Release the mouse button in the center of the successor box; an arrow appears and the dependency is now set.

This method allows you to set Finish-to-Start dependencies only.

If you release the mouse button outside of the successor box, a new task is created! If this happened inadvertently, press [Delete] while the new task is still selected.

To Delete Dependencies in the Network Diagram

1. Point with the tip of the mouse pointer to the dependency arrow you want to delete, like this:

2. Double-click; the **Task Dependency** dialog appears:

    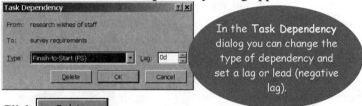

    In the **Task Dependency** dialog you can change the type of dependency and set a lag or lead (negative lag).

3. Click **Delete** .

4. All the dependent tasks are rescheduled and are moved to an earlier date under forward scheduling. They may have zipped all the way to the project start date. You should create a new dependency if they are scheduled too early.

Checking the Logic

The Network Diagram has an invisible grid like in a spreadsheet, except that the arrow keys take you only to cells that exist; the task boxes.

1. If you have automatic repositioning on, the boxes are re-arranged upon every change you make. It will be very difficult to check the logic in the network when the boxes jump all over the place. We recommend you turn it off by choosing **Format, Layout...,** the **Layout** dialog appears:

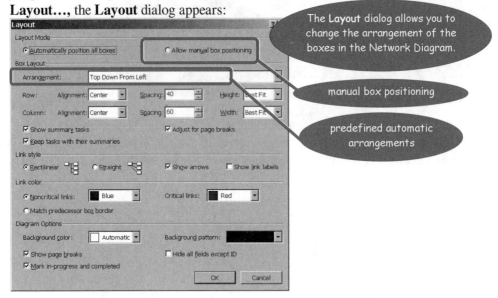

The **Layout** dialog allows you to change the arrangement of the boxes in the Network Diagram.

manual box positioning

predefined automatic arrangements

2. Select ⊙ **Allow manual box positioning** and click [OK]. To see if the logic of the dependencies makes sense, use the arrow keys to follow a chain. Click on the first task box in a chain and press → to follow the chain forward. When there is a split you can press the ↓ or ↑ to switch from one chain to the other
    OR
    press ← to go backward. Press the ↓ or ↑ to switch chains.

3. Use the methods discussed before to delete, add or modify dependencies, if necessary.

Checks on Dependencies

We discussed the techniques to enter dependencies. All the dependencies together are called the *network* or the *logic*. Now you need to check the network to determine if it will indeed give you the benefit you created it for. This benefit was that if you make one change, the rest of the schedule is automatically updated.

It will only do this if the network complies with the following checks:

Circular Dependency:

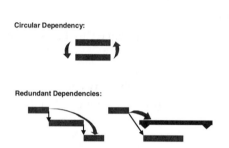

Redundant Dependencies:

- ◆ the logic makes sense
- ◆ all the detail tasks are incorporated in the network
- ◆ there are no "loose ends "
- ◆ there are no circular dependencies
- ◆ there are no redundant dependencies
- ◆ there are as many parallel paths as possible, if your project has a tight deadline

A "loose end" is a task that does not have a successor. In any project there should be only one loose end, the project end milestone (ignoring the summary tasks and recurring tasks). Schedulers often forget to give every task one or more successors, in particular in the following situations.

- ◆ People often forget to set a dependency on the finish of the predecessor in an SS-dependency. The finish must also be linked, otherwise the predecessor in an SS-dependency could still continue even though the project is already finished.

- ◆ People often forget to set a dependency into the start of the successor in an FF-dependency. Alternatively, the start date can be held in place by a constraint.

If you forget to set dependencies the schedule will not update itself with every change you make. More importantly, with an incomplete network you will not have a meaningful *Critical Path*. The Critical Path is the most widely used technique to manage the time of a project. We will explain it in more detail in Chapter 9 Optimizing the Schedule.

However, some detail tasks do not need a successor:

◆ *recurring tasks,* like status meetings
◆ *overhead tasks*, like project management or quality control. These are also known as *hammock tasks*, because their start and end date are driven by or hung up on other tasks.

All other tasks need to have at least one successor. If there are no logical links to other detail tasks, there should be a link to the project end milestone.

Certain tasks can only be linked to the project end milestone. Examples are:

◆ tasks to inform people or organizations (FYI-tasks)
◆ tasks that create entirely independent parts of a system, that can easily be assembled at the end

Redundant dependencies clutter the view unnecessary. It makes the network overly complicated. If the network is complicated people will not try to understand it and use it. Thus, the value of setting dependencies decreases.

Redundant dependencies can be:

◆ dependencies that leap-frog one another as is shown in the illustration, and
◆ dependencies that run in parallel on detail tasks and summary tasks as shown in the illustration. We recommend keeping the dependencies on the detail level and cutting the ones between the summary tasks.

Limitations of Dependencies

Here are some limitations on creating dependencies:

◆ **Only one link between two tasks**
It is impossible to set more than one link between two tasks. Thus you cannot hook up both the start and the finish of two tasks using an SS as well as an FF dependency.

◆ **No links on the parts of a split task bar**
You cannot set dependencies on the parts of a split task bar; you can only link to the start of the first part and from the finish of the last part.

◆ **You cannot link to the finish of a Summary Task**
You cannot set a FF- or SF-dependency to a summary task as the successor. The finish date of a summary task is always calculated. However, you can link FROM the finish of the summary task.

◆ **Percentage lags only on predecessor duration**
You cannot set a lag that takes a percentage of the duration of the successor task (the percentages are always taken on the predecessor). So you cannot create a dependency that drives, for example, the halfway point of a successor.

Logic on Summary Tasks

What are the advantages and disadvantages of setting dependencies on summary tasks?
Advantages:
◆ Setting dependencies on summary tasks is easier & quicker.
◆ It gives high-level logic that executives sometimes like to see.
◆ In certain situations you can do with one dependency on the summary task, instead of setting several dependencies on detail tasks when they start independently of each other. See illustration below:

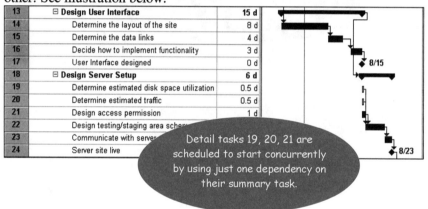

Detail tasks 19, 20, 21 are scheduled to start concurrently by using just one dependency on their summary task.

Disadvantages:
◆ On summary tasks you can only set rough high-level logic. High-level logic often does not allow you to create the tightest schedule possible.
◆ Not all types of dependencies can be used on summary tasks; you cannot link FF or SF to summary tasks.

◆ The *Critical Path* is more difficult to find when the chain runs over detail tasks AND summary tasks. When you follow the Critical Path, a critical detail task may not have any successor. It looks like the Critical Path stops and you may not realize that the Critical Path continues through a dependency on the summary task. (For a discussion on the Critical Path see page 305.) See illustration below:

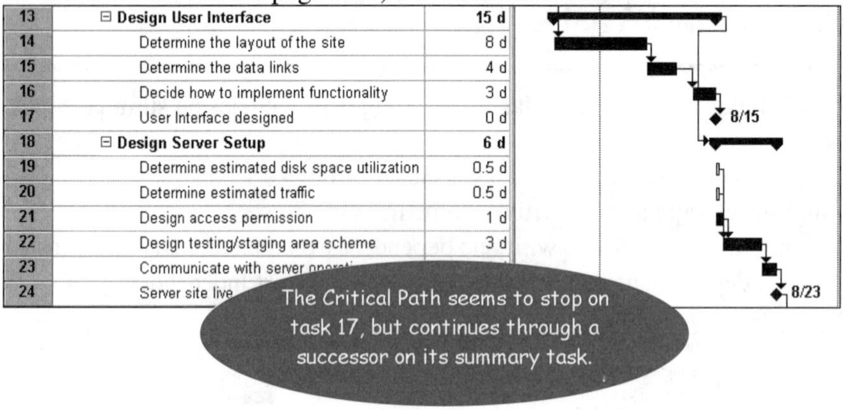

13	⊟ **Design User Interface**	**15 d**
14	Determine the layout of the site	8 d
15	Determine the data links	4 d
16	Decide how to implement functionality	3 d
17	User Interface designed	0 d
18	⊟ **Design Server Setup**	**6 d**
19	Determine estimated disk space utilization	0.5 d
20	Determine estimated traffic	0.5 d
21	Design access permission	1 d
22	Design testing/staging area scheme	3 d
23	Communicate with server opera...	
24	Server site live	

The Critical Path seems to stop on task 17, but continues through a successor on its summary task.

Printing the Network Diagram

Printing the Network Diagram can be helpful in communicating the flow of the logic to the stakeholders. Prior to printing, you can change the appearance of the view to suit your needs.

The Layout of the Boxes

You can customize which fields are shown, the border of the boxes and the font.

Choosing the Fields in Each Box

To show only the ID-field in the boxes, click the **Hide Fields** tool on the **Network Diagram** toolbar. By hovering for one second with the mouse pointer over the boxes, you will still be able to read the task name in the pop-up.

OR

Change the layout of the fields on the task boxes in such a way that only task names will show.

1. Choose the menu items **Format, Box Styles**.

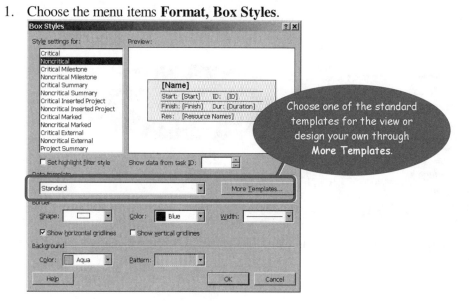

2. Click More Templates... , the **Data Templates** dialog opens:

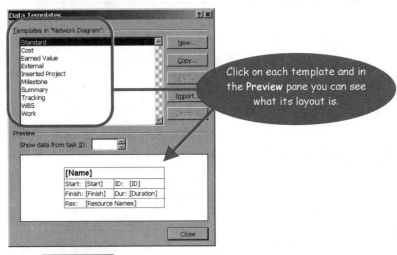

Click on each template and in the **Preview** pane you can see what its layout is.

3. Click New... , the **Data Template Definition** dialog opens:

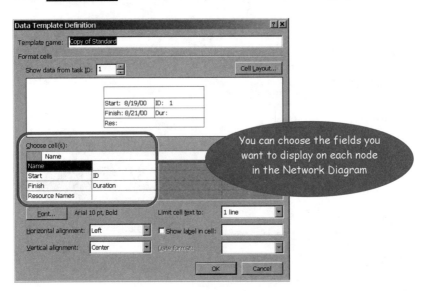

You can choose the fields you want to display on each node in the Network Diagram

4. Enter a name for this template in the field **Template Name** for example, *Task Names Only*.

5. Click 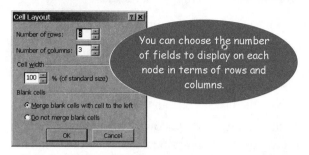, the **Cell Layout** dialog opens:

You can choose the number of fields to display on each node in terms of rows and columns.

6. Set the **Number of rows** and **Number of columns**. If you have long task names, set the **Cell width** percentage to greater than 100%. All the boxes will have the same width.

7. Click OK, you are now back in the **Data Template Definition** dialog.

8. In the table-like area below **Choose cell(s)** click on a cell in the grid; a list button appears:

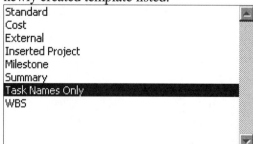

Use the list to pick a field.

9. Select from this list the field to display. You have now created a new layout template.

10. If you have long task names, set **Limit cell text to** more than one line.

11. Click OK, you are now back in the **Data Template** dialog; you can see the newly created template listed:

```
Standard
Cost
External
Inserted Project
Milestone
Summary
Task Names Only
WBS
```

12. Click Close, you are now back in the **Box Styles** dialog.

13. Now we have to apply this template to the different types of tasks. Select under **Style Settings For** all the different types of tasks by dragging over them.

14. Under **Data Template** use the list to select the data template you just created.

15. Click [OK], the **Network Diagram** view now shows boxes with only the task names. Many more boxes fit in one screen.

Instead of applying a data template to all the tasks, you can use a data template for specific types of tasks. To select specific task types hold down [Ctrl] and click in the **Format, Box Styles** dialog. If you select only the non-critical items it would look like:

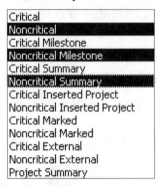

Changing the Border of the Boxes

You can use different border formats to indicate the status of a task, like not started, in progress, critical, completed.

1. Choose **Format, Box Styles,** the **Box Styles** dialog appears.

2. Under **Style Settings for** select the type of task for which to change the border. Under **Border** you can choose the **Shape, Color** and **Width**. The **Preview** area in the top right shows what it will look like.

3. If you have more than one data field in the boxes, you can choose to:
   ☑ **Show horizontal gridlines** and/or
   ☑ **Show vertical gridlines**.

4. Click [OK].

Changing the Font

1. Choose the menu items **Format, Box Styles,** the **Box Styles** dialog appears.

2. Click [More Templates...], the **Data Template** dialog opens.

3. Click [Edit...], the **Data Template Definition** dialog opens.

4. Click [Font...], and select the font type and size you need.

5. Click [OK], you are now back in the **Data Template Definition** dialog

6. Click [OK], you are now back in the **Data Template** dialog.

7. Click [Close], you are now back in the **Box Styles** dialog.

8. Click [OK], you should now see the new font applied.

The Layout of the Diagram

Showing the Type of Dependency on each Arrow

It is often helpful to see the type of dependency displayed for each relationship, like in the following snapshot:

Click **Show Link Labels** 🔲 on the **Network Diagram** toolbar.
OR

1. Choose **Format, Layout…**, the **Layout** dialog appears:

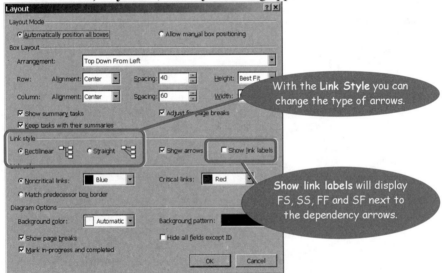

2. Under **Link Style** select ☑ **Show Link Labels**.

3. Click [OK], you will now see **FS** attached to each Finish-to-Start arrow, as well as **SS**, **FF** and **SF** to their respective arrows.

Changing the Type of Arrow

Click the ⊞ on the Network Diagram toolbar.
OR

1. Choose **Format, Layout…**, the **Layout** dialog appears.

2. In the **Link Style** section, choose the type of arrow.

3. Click OK .

Hiding the Summary Tasks

Summary tasks look like parallelograms in the **Network Diagram** view:

If you set all the logic between detail tasks, which is often the preferred method, you can hide all the summary tasks to remove clutter and save space.

Click ⊞ on the **Network Diagram** toolbar.

Collapsing and Expanding Summary Tasks

If you set dependencies between summary tasks you can focus on the high-level logic by collapsing the detail task boxes into the summary box.

The summary tasks can be collapsed to hide all the detail tasks that belong to the summary. You click the ⊟ at the top left of the box or you click the box and hold down Alt + Shift and press - .

They can be expanded again by clicking the ⊞ or hold down Alt + Shift and press + .

Note that all the dependencies of the collapsed tasks are hidden as well, including those that go into other summary tasks on the detail level.

Improving the Layout of the Boxes

Project 2000 attempts to arrange the boxes as well as it can. By default, the tasks are laid out from the top left to the bottom right. Project 2000 now has several layout arrangements to choose from. You can improve the layout by choosing a different arrangement, or you can move boxes manually.

1. Choose **Format, Layout…,** the **Layout** dialog appears:

    For automatic positioning you can select an arrangement from the list.

2. Make sure that under **Layout Mode,** ⊙ **Automatically position all boxes** is selected, otherwise you have to choose **Format, Layout Now** every time to see the effect of a different arrangement.

3. Under **Arrangement** use the list:

Top Down From Left

    to change the layout of the boxes.

4. Click [OK], the layout of the boxes has changed according to your choice. If the layout is not satisfactory, try other layout arrangements.

Notice that the boxes are never positioned on the page breaks with automatic positioning.

Improving the Layout of a Selection of Boxes

After you selected the arrangement you prefer most, you may still want to position boxes manually.

1. Select the boxes by dragging a lasso around them.
    OR

    Hold down Ctrl and click on them.

2. Click **Layout Selection Now** on the **Network Diagram** toolbar. The boxes are rearranged to the best Project 2000 can do.

Moving a Box Manually in the Network Diagram

1. Choose **Format, Layout…,** the **Layout** dialog appears:

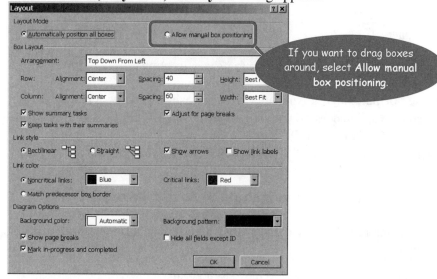

2. Select ⊙ **Allow manual box positioning**.

3. Click 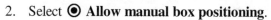 OK .

4. Point to the border of the box you want to move and make sure that the mouse pointer changes to a ⁺⤢.

5. Click and hold down and drag the box to its new location.

Moving a Group of Boxes Manually

1. First you have to select all boxes to move as a group. Click on the first box, hold down ⌨Ctrl and click on other boxes; the boxes are highlighted as a sign of being selected.
   OR
   Click and drag a lasso around all the boxes to select.
   OR
   Hold down ⌨Shift and click on the border of a summary task to select it and all its detail tasks.
   OR
   Hold down ⌨Shift and click on the border of a detail task to select its entire chain of successors.

2. Click and hold down on the border of one selected box and make sure you see the mouse pointer ⬦.

3. Click and hold down to drag the group to its new location.

 Do not choose **Format, Layout Now** after moving boxes manually; it rearranges the **Network Diagram** and undoes all your laborious moving. If it happened by accident, you can undo the mess by choosing **Edit, Undo** or click ↶ (before doing anything else). Use the tool **Layout Selection Now** ⬒ instead of **Format, Layout Now**.

Aligning the Manually Moved Boxes

You can select a number of boxes and then align all boxes with the earliest predecessor of all selected boxes.

1. First you have to select all boxes to move as a group.
   Drag a lasso around all the boxes to be selected.
   OR
   Click on the first box, hold down ⌨Ctrl and click on other boxes; the boxes are highlighted as a sign of being selected.

2. Click Align ▾ on the **Network Diagram** toolbar and choose how to align the selected boxes with the task that is earliest in the chain of tasks. The boxes should now be aligned.

Exercises

Review

For each of the following situations determine:
◆ Which is the predecessor and successor?
◆ What type of dependency do you need?
◆ Would you advise to add a lead or a lag to the dependency?

1. You gather the requirements (*gather requirements*) and then analyze them (*analyze requirements*).

2. You have to wait three weeks (*apply for permit*) to get a permit (*receive permit*).

3. Halfway through the system analysis (*perform system analysis*) we typically start the programming (*program*).

4. The concrete foundation has to be finished and dry (*pour foundation*) before the walls can be erected (*lay bricks*).

Relocation Project – Dependencies

Continue to work with your file *Relocation.MPP* or open the file
05 Entering Dependencies.MPP in the subdirectory *Relocation Project* on the CD-ROM.

Enter the following dependencies using the **Link** tool on the **Standard** toolbar:

1. The tasks *research staff requirements* and *summarize requirements* are sequentially dependent.

2. The tasks of the deliverable *LOCATION* are all sequentially dependent upon each other.

3. The tasks of the deliverable *REMODELING CONTRACT* are all sequentially dependent upon each other. The dependency between *select contractor* and *meet to discuss contract* has a lag of 5 days; it will take a time frame of 5 days (plus one day for the meeting) to get the participants to meet together.

4. The tasks *relocate walls* through *install cabinetry* of the deliverable *REMODELED LOCATION* are sequentially dependent upon each other.

5. The tasks of the deliverable *MOVE* are all sequentially dependent upon each other.

Enter the following dependencies by ⌜Ctrl⌝ + clicking to select the tasks and using the **Link** tool:

6. In the deliverable *REMODELED LOCATION* the tasks *install cabinetry* and *install LAN* can take place concurrently after the paint dries (*drying of paint*)

7. After the tasks *install cabinetry* and *install LAN* are finished, the carpet can be put in place (*lay carpet*).

8. After the carpet is laid (*lay carpet*) the milestone *facility remodeled* is accomplished.

You forgot to set the dependencies between the deliverables (phases). Change to the view **Network Diagram** and enter these dependencies:

9. The task *evaluate the sites* can start after *summarize requirements* is finished.

10. The task *select the contractor* can start after the milestone *location selected* is accomplished.

11. The task *select mover* can start after *location selected*.

12. The task *relocate walls* can start after the milestone *contractor contracted*.

13. After the milestone *facility remodeled* the task *pack* can start.

Compare your file with the solution file *06 Entering Constraints and Deadlines.MPP* in the sub-directory *Relocation Project* on the CD-ROM. Use the view **Network Diagram** to make the comparison.

Case Study CoalPower

CoalPower power station has approached you to do a 2-day introductory workshop in MS Project. CoalPower is a first-time client and it seems this 2-day contract will be their only need for training and consulting for a while, even though the organization is large and has multiple plants. The key players at CoalPower are:

- Andy: plant manager, you find out that he has some similar cultural heritage as you and find an easy basis for conversation with him. Andy sits in on the first part of the workshop you are conducting on site. He is only interested in the big picture of what MS Project can do for the organization. Andy is concerned about the frequent delays in the engineering projects, which you found out when you talked one-on-one during a lunch break.

- <u>Norm</u>: manager of the engineers who design and manage repair, maintenance and construction projects in the power station. You have had difficulties in negotiating with Norm. Norm told you, only after you had closed your consulting contract, that you have to travel an extra 250 miles to get to the site of the plant.

- <u>Dave and Harry</u> are managing the major maintenance projects like the replacement of the $2M turbine condensers. Replacing these condensers will stop the operations in the entire plant. They have been planning their projects mostly off the top of their heads. Norm is getting increasingly anxious about this and has told them, "If you get sick nobody knows what to do or how to do it. I need to see a detailed planning of your projects!"

- <u>Art</u> is the technical drawing expert. Art designs most of the small constructions and creates the technical drawings. Art is overworked and has, at any given time, 50 projects on his plate. Norm often criticizes him for not delivering the drawings when Norm wants them.

Questions:

1. What would you recommend to Dave and Harry?
   ◇ How will they benefit from scheduling their projects with MS Project?
   ◇ Will they be motivated to use the tool?
   ◇ What do you think of Norm's approach in forcing them to schedule their projects?
   ◇ How important are the dependencies in their schedule?

2. What would you recommend to Art?
   ◇ What is his main concern in his projects?
   ◇ How should he model his many projects in MS Project? Address in particular if he should use dependencies, and how.
   ◇ How will Art benefit from modeling his projects in MS Project?

Chapter 6 Entering Deadlines and Constraints

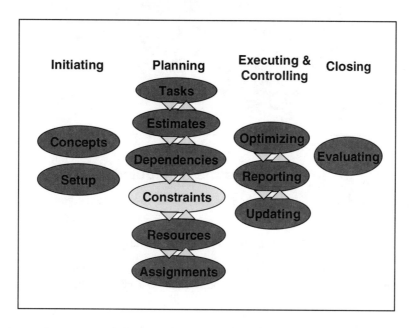

At this point we have entered the most important data into the schedule and we already have a Gantt Chart. There may be certain constraint dates that we may have to add to the model to make it more realistic. Also, we may want to capture deadlines to be able to monitor their achievement. Constraints and deadlines are the topics of this chapter. We will also discuss formatting and at the end of this chapter we will have a Gantt Chart that is ready for printing.

After this chapter you will:
◆ know the difference between constraints and deadlines
◆ know the different types of schedule constraints
◆ know in which situations to use constraints.
◆ be able to enter schedule constraints into the project model
◆ know the advantages and disadvantages of entering constraints
◆ know how to format and print the Gantt Chart

"I Nailed the Schedule."

Nob sits at his desk bent over his schedule. He seems to be stressed out and disappointed. He has given up.

Bob enters Nob's office. "What happened Nob? Are you having a bad day?"

Nob perks up and responds, "No, I am just tired. I was up late last night working on this blasted schedule. It takes me too much time. I thought I had it nailed before we started work on the first tasks."

"What takes you so much time?"

"Well, I make one change to update the schedule and the schedule never turns out the way I want it. I have to go through my entire schedule to make it right with every change I make. Last time, you told me that if I enter dependencies the schedule would be easier to maintain."

Bob is curious how the schedule is set up. "May I have a look at your schedule?"

"Of course, it's on my screen!"

Bob checks the indicators field and says, "Hey, I see you have a lot of schedule constraints in your schedule, why do you need that many?"

"Well, I didn't enter any of those!"

"You can easily end up with them if you enter start and finish dates on tasks, or if you drag the task bars."

What are Deadlines and Schedule Constraints?

A deadline is a date you committed to and a constraint is a restriction to the scheduling MS Project does.

It is possible to force tasks to be scheduled on certain dates, which is necessary for tasks like *attend meeting, attend conference* and *monitor seminar.* Fixing dates is a matter of putting a scheduling *constraint* on the task. You could consider a Must-Start-On constraint for the aforementioned tasks. A Must-Start-On is a hard constraint. Project 2000 cannot reschedule tasks with Must-constraints. Constraints affect the network of dependencies. The more constraints you create, the less freely your network will flow back and forth, when you enter changes.

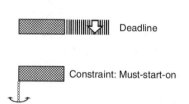 Deadline

Constraint: Must-start-on

The new feature of *Deadlines,* on the other hand, does not restrict the movement of the network of task bars. We recommend, therefore, that you enter dates you committed to as deadlines rather than as constraints. Visually, it is clearer when you are missing a deadline.

The deadline stays visible in the timescale as an arrow ⇩ , but does not influence the scheduling of task bars, like constraints do. When you want to track a deadline for a specific task, but you don't want to limit the scheduling by setting a constraint, you can set a deadline date for the task instead. Or you could consider setting a softer, one-sided constraint, like Finish-No-Later-Than.

Choosing the Options

Tab	Option
Schedule	**☑ Tasks will always honor their constraint dates** This option makes tasks obey their schedule constraints. We recommend you keep this option on because now you can model soft constraints using the Deadline feature, whereas you may have other hard constraints that you always want observed.
	Set as Default Sets the option above as the default setting for any new schedules you create. The existing schedules are not affected because this option is stored in the project files as you can see in the label of the section divider: **Scheduling Options for 'Project 1'**.

Scheduling Regimes

Before discussing the types of constraints, we need to discuss the basic scheduling regime you choose. The two choices are:

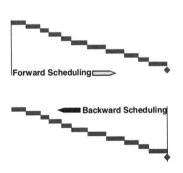

◆ *Scheduling forward* from the project start date. You do forward scheduling if you entered the project start date and want to find the expected finish date. Under forward scheduling all tasks are scheduled as soon as possible.

◆ *Scheduling backward* from the project finish date. You schedule backward if you entered the project finish date and want to find out when to start the project. Under backward scheduling all tasks are scheduled as late as possible.

You can see whether you are scheduling forward or backward by checking the **Project, Project Information** dialog in the list **Schedule from**.

Types of Constraints

The eight types of constraints are:

Tendencies:
◆ ASAP (As Soon As Possible, the default under Forward Scheduling)
◆ ALAP (As Late As Possible, the default under Backward Scheduling)

One sided constraints:
◆ SNET (Start No Earlier Than)
◆ FNET (Finish No Earlier Than)
◆ SNLT (Start No Later Than)
◆ FNLT (Finish No Later Than)

Rigid Constraints:
◆ MSO (Must Start On)
◆ MFO (Must Finish On)

Tendencies

Under the default, *forward scheduling*, Project 2000 uses As-Soon-As-Possible (ASAP) for all tasks. MS Project will pull the task bar as far to the left in the time scale as the network of predecessors allows. Even when the regime is ASAP, you can schedule certain tasks As-Late-As-Possible (ALAP). For example, *packing equipment* should be scheduled ALAP in a move project. ALAP task bars will tend to go to the right as much as the network of successors allows.

Under backward scheduling, all tasks are ALAP by default, but you can also change some tasks to ASAP. Even though ALAP and ASAP do not have a constraint date, they have a tremendous impact on the schedule and are in that sense "constraining".

One-Sided Constraints

This group of one-sided constraints limits the movement of task bars in only one direction:
◆ SNET and FNET constrain free movement of the task bars going to the left in the timescale, the task bars cannot go to the left of the No-Earlier-Than date.
◆ SNLT and FNLT constrain free movement of the task bars going to the right in the timescale, the task bars cannot go to the right of the No-Later-Than date.

Rigid Constraints

The last group of rigid constraints, MSO and MFO, fix the task bar entirely to the date indicated and deny any free movement.

Realize, though, that the task bar can still grow or shrink in size when you revise the estimate. This will make the other unconstrained end of the task bar move.

No-Earlier-Than Constraints

An example of a SNET constraint is when raw materials will not be delivered until a certain date; you can start the activity no-earlier-than the delivery date.

An example of FNET is when the day shift has to instruct the night shift, so they can finish no earlier than the night shift starts, even though they may be running ahead of schedule.

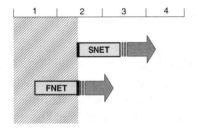

The No-Earlier-Than constraints are restricted in moving earlier in time (moving to the left in timescale views). They can be pushed to the right by the network without a limit. Under ASAP scheduling they will not be able to cause a schedule conflict, in other words, they are soft constraints under forward scheduling.

Under backward scheduling, the project finish date is hard. As you add dependencies you will see that the ALAP task bars will be pushed out to earlier (to the left in the timescale). They can be pushed to the left as far as the No-Earlier-Than date allows. If pushed any further Project 2000 will alarm you of a schedule conflict. No-Earlier-Than constraints are therefore said to be hard constraints under backward scheduling.

No-Later-Than Constraints

An example of a SNLT constraint might be the backing up of a computer system that can be moved later when people are working late, but it would have to start no later than, let's say, midnight in order to be finished on time. An example of FNLT is when you

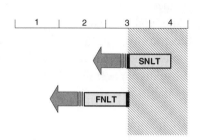

committed to deliver a report no later than March 13th.

The No-Later-Than constraints are restricted from moving beyond the date specified (moving to the right in a timescale view). They can be pulled to the left by the network up to the start date of the project. Under ALAP scheduling they will not be able to cause a schedule conflict, in other words, they are soft under backward scheduling.

Under forward scheduling, the project start date is hard. As you add dependencies, you will see that the ASAP task bars will be pushed out to later (to the right in the timescale). They can be pushed as far as the No-Later-Than constraint date allows. If pushed any further, Project 2000 will warn you of a schedule conflict. No-Later-Than constraints are, therefore, said to be hard constraints under forward scheduling.

Must Constraints

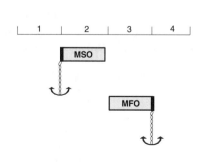

An example of an MSO constraint is when you hold an important meeting that Must-Start-On January 9th at 9:00 AM.

An example of an MFO constraint is when you have a contractual date by which you must have moved out of an office space.

Both MSO and MFO constraints are always hard constraints under forward and backward scheduling. Where you use an

MSO constraint, the start will always be on the date indicated. With an MFO constraint the finish will always be on the date specified. MSO and MFO constraints can easily cause schedule conflicts under both forward and backward scheduling.

In Which Situations do you Need Constraints?

Deadlines do not need a lot of maintenance while the project is running, but constraints do. Every time you have a major change in your schedule, you may either have to update all the constraint dates that are affected, or you will have to solve the schedule conflicts. If a task does not have any constraints, its dependencies push it into place. We recommend, therefore, that you enter only the constraints that are absolutely necessary. You can enter many deadlines into your schedule without any disadvantages.

 Constraints should NOT be used for temporary availability of resources. A better place to indicate temporary availability is through availability profiles. We will discuss these on page 247: Resource Availability.

Constraints can be set for:
◆ External dependencies
On page 179, we discussed that an external dependency should be entered as an extra milestone and the milestone should be held in place by a Start-No-Earlier-Than constraint.
◆ Weather restrictions
You have to get road construction done before the rain or winter season starts. Outdoor construction activities can only start before or after the winter.
 There is a new feature in Project 2000 that allows you to schedule this without using constraints, see page 131: Using Task Calendars. Task Calendars create a more dynamic model.
◆ Meetings, presentations, training or, in general, tasks with a group of people involved. In order to get a group together, you have to set a date, otherwise it will not happen. When the date is agreed upon, a constraint should be set so Project 2000 does not move it off its date. Often you will use Must-Start-On or Must-Finish-On here.
◆ Certain milestones, see below.

Milestones and Constraints

On page 114, we discussed the types of milestones. Here we will determine if we need a constraint and which type of constraint to use. The type of constraint will depend on the hardness of the milestone. The hardness of a milestone is the resistance you will experience when you try to move its date. For soft dates you can use the *Deadline* feature instead of constraints. For harder dates use the feature of *schedule constraints*. The harder the date, the harder the constraint should be.

The types of milestones are listed here from soft to hard:

◆ *Decision points*
These are important points at which decisions are made about the remainder of the project. Decisions are normally not made when there is a lack of pertinent information; the decision milestone date is often allowed to float freely in the schedule. The decision can be:
◇ Go/No-Go: which can end a project
◇ Go-Left/Go-Right: in which the how-to or direction is determined for the rest of the project.
If there is a target date or a deadline for the decision point, we recommend using the new Deadline feature that we will discuss hereafter.

◆ *Target dates*
These are soft deadlines that are inserted to break up a long series of tasks. They focus the efforts on finishing a component of a deliverable. The project manager decides with the team where to insert these target dates. Teams need several target dates in order to meet the deadline of the deliverable; they are interim evaluation points. Target dates function as reminders, and should keep everyone focused and on track. In this case, we recommend the use of the Deadline feature and no constraints

◆ *Do-or-Die Dates*
These are hard deadlines, often contractual dates, by which you are committed to hand over a deliverable. These dates should be clear in the schedule at all times. We recommend you enter these into the schedule as deadlines as much as possible in order to keep the schedule dynamic. However, if a deadline is a hard contractual date, you could add a Finish-No-later-Than (FNLT) schedule constraint. This allows it to float up to the constraint date.

◆ *Deliveries*
Subcontractor deliveries can be scheduled using external dependencies as we

discussed on page 179. The delivery date you agreed upon should be entered as an event with a Start-No-Earlier-Than (SNET) constraint.

◆ *Ceremonies*
Ceremonies are short official events. If the duration of the ceremony is negligible, it can be entered as a milestone with a zero-duration. An example might be the official opening of a new plant. The date of a ceremony is often hard, because ceremonies are often public. The schedule needs a Must-Start-On (MSO) constraint for these milestone events. If the ceremony has a duration, it is no longer a milestone, but a task and will still need a constraint.

◆ *Project End Date*
This is the delivery date for the project product. Meeting the project end date is always a challenge in project management. All the chains of dependencies come together in the project end milestone. A Must-Finish-On (MFO) or a Finish-No-Later-Than constraint is often set on the project end date. You will immediately receive a scheduling conflict message when the project end date is in jeopardy.

In Project 2000 there is a new feature, called **Deadlines,** that reminds you of the date agreed upon without constraining the schedule. This is a feature we recommend strongly over using schedule constraints. The more constraints you have, the more time you will spend on your schedule. You will have to maintain it during project execution when you don't have much time. The fewer constraints you have the more dynamic your schedule will be.

Deadlines

Entering Deadlines

1. Choose **View, Gantt Chart**.
2. Click on the task for which you want to set a deadline.

3. Click or hold down ⓈShift and press F2; the **Task Information** dialog appears:

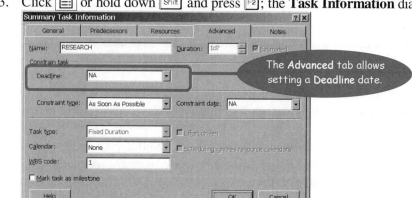

The **Advanced** tab allows setting a **Deadline** date.

4. Click the tab **Advanced**.

5. Under **Constrain task**, type the deadline date in the **Deadline** field or use the pull-down calendar to click on a date.

6. Click [OK], you will now see an arrow ⇩ in the timescale that represents the deadline date.

If you have to be done before November 1ˢᵗ, you have to enter October 31ˢᵗ as the deadline date. The deadline will be scheduled at the end of the day on the date you enter. If you enter November 1ˢᵗ as the deadline date, the task will be done by 5PM on November 1ˢᵗ.

Managing Deadlines

You will not get automatic warning messages from Project 2000 if deadlines are not met. What you do get is an exclamation icon ◆ in the **Indicators** column.

Also, if you use the list of filters |All Tasks ▼| on the format toolbar and apply the filter **Tasks with Deadlines**, you can quickly filter out and see which deadlines are slipping.

Constraints

Entering Constraints

You can set constraint dates in a variety of ways:

◆ Dragging task bars: this method will allow you to set SNET constraints only (under forward scheduling).

◆ Entering dates: You can enter a start date that will set a SNET constraint, or you can enter a finish date that will set a FNET constraint (under forward scheduling).

◆ Using the task fields of **Constraint Type** and **Constraint Date**, you can select the type of constraint from a pick list.

◆ Using the **Task Information** box on the **Advanced** page tab.

As is often the case in MS Project, you can enter constraints in several different ways. The first two ways are easy and quick but do require you to know which constraints Project 2000 will set. We recommend using the last two ways.

Setting Constraints by Dragging Task Bars Horizontally

1. Point to the middle of the task bar; make sure you see a four-headed arrow: ✥.

2. Click and hold to drag the bar horizontally to where you want it scheduled. Make sure you see a horizontal two-headed arrow, like this: ▮▮▮◀�‖▶▮▮▯ .

3. Look at the yellow pop-up to see what the new dates will be:

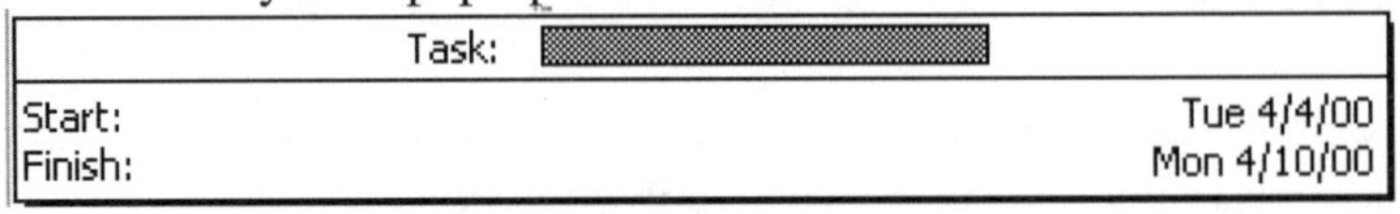

Task: ▮▮▮▮▮▮▮▮▮▮▮▮▮▮▮	
Start:	Tue 4/4/00
Finish:	Mon 4/10/00

4. Release the mouse when the task bar is scheduled on the date you want. It has a **Start-No-Earlier-Than** constraint on it to keep it in its new place. (Under backward scheduling it will be a **Finish-No-Later-Than** constraint.)

 If you drag vertically, you are creating dependencies!

Setting Constraints by Entering Dates

In the field **Start** you can pick a date from the drop-down calendar. By default, this creates a SNET constraint on the task under forward scheduling, and it creates a SNLT constraint under backward scheduling.

In the field **Finish** you can pick a date from the drop-down calendar. By default, this creates a FNET constraint on the task under forward scheduling, but it creates a FNLT constraint under backward scheduling.

Many people use the **Start** and **Finish** fields to schedule all their tasks. Most do not intend to create constraints, but are unaware that MS Project is setting them. Their schedules become rigid and require a lot of work to maintain. If dependencies are used instead, the schedules require a lot less maintenance. We recommend you do not use these fields at all for data entry. In addition, using them will require too much memorizing of what type of constraint will be set.

Setting Constraints Using the Task Fields

1. Insert the field **Constraint Type** by clicking in the column before you wish to insert and choosing **Insert, Column**. The **Column Definition** dialog appears:

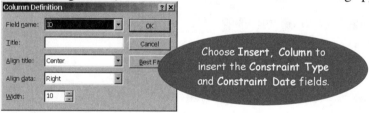

2. Select from the list **Field Name:** `ID ▼` the item **Constraint Type**.

3. Click `OK`.

4. Repeat these steps to insert the field **Constraint Date** as well.

5. You can now enter any type of constraint in the Gantt spreadsheet by selecting the type from the list in the field **Constraint Type** `Start No Earlier Than ▼` and picking the date from the drop-down calendar in **Constraint Date** `Tue 4/4/00 ▼`.

Setting Constraints Using the Task Information Box

1. Select the task.

2. Click 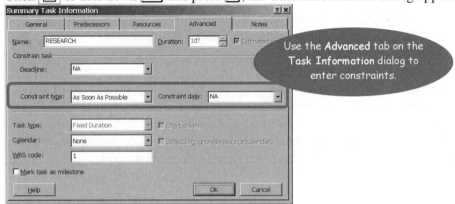 or hold down Shift and press F2; the **Task Information** dialog appears.

    Use the **Advanced** tab on the **Task Information** dialog to enter constraints.

3. Click the tab **Advanced** and under **Constrain Task:**

    Select the type from the list: 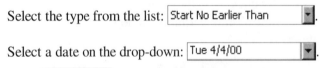 Start No Earlier Than.

    Select a date on the drop-down: Tue 4/4/00.

4. Click OK.

To Check all the Scheduling Constraints

1. In the Gantt Chart choose the menu items **View, Table: <name of current table>**,
    More Tables; the **More Tables** dialog appears:

    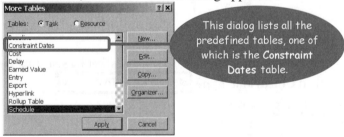

    This dialog lists all the predefined tables, one of which is the **Constraint Dates** table.

2. Select the **Constraint Dates** table in the list.

3. Click [Apply] you can now see the fields **Constraint Type** and **Constraint Dates** to check all constraints on the tasks.

If you have to be done before November 1st, you have to enter October 31st as the constraint date. The constraint is scheduled by default at the end of the day on the date you enter. If you enter November 1st as the constraint date, the task will be done by 5PM on November 1st.

To Delete Constraints

You can delete constraints one by one, but if you want to delete them fast, you could use the fill-down feature. This is useful if you entered dates in the **Start** and **Finish** fields without wanting the constraints that came with it.

1. Apply the **Constraint Dates** table as per the previous series of steps.

2. Enter the constraint type you want to fill-down in the top cell.
    To delete constraints select:
    As Soon As Possible under forward scheduling
    As Late As Possible under backward scheduling

3. Click on this top cell and hold down to drag down over all the cells into which you want to copy the constraint.

4. Choose **Edit, Fill, Down** or hold down [Ctrl] and press [D].

Limitations of Constraints

◆   Maximum 1 constraint per task
    Sometimes it would be nice to set two constraints on a task when the task has to be done in its 'window of opportunity'. For an example, do a test when a specialized lab is available. You cannot do this with constraints, because you can only set one constraint on a task.
    But you can use a new Project 2000 feature that allows you to create a calendar for a task and apply it to the task using the field **Task Calendar**. We discussed this on page 131: Using Task Calendars.

◆   Only SNET and FNLT constraints on summary tasks

Printing the Gantt View

With the Wizard tool you can choose format options for the *Gantt Chart* by answering to prompts.

To Adjust the Text Styles

Text styles can be applied to certain task types. The dialog is similar to the **Format, Font** dialog except that the font dialog is used for formatting tasks that are selected.

1. Choose **Format, Text Styles…**, the **Text Styles** dialog appears:

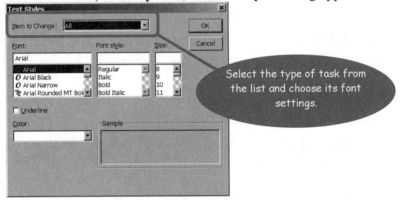

Select the type of task from the list and choose its font settings.

2. From the list at the top, select the **Item to Change:** All. Then select the format using **Font, Font style, Size** and **Color**.

3. Click OK.

If you select the item **All**, all the text will be affected, even the text styles you had set previously.

To Wrap Task Names Around

You can double the height of all rows.

1. Select the entire sheet by clicking on the table selector at the intersection of the row and column headings in the top left corner of the spreadsheet:

2. Point to one of the row dividers in the row headings (that is normally the ID-column); make sure you see the double-headed arrow mouse pointer .

3. Drag the divider down to at least double the row height. Project 2000 will automatically wrap the text onto the second line. It wraps the text in the fields: **Task Name, Notes** and the extra text fields (**Text1, Text2,** etc.).

 You will have also doubled the number of pages in your printout.

 In Project 2000, you can now wrap the text in one single row. In previous releases, you could only double the row height of all or none.

To Adjust the Column Width

Double-click on the heading of the column to adjust; the **Column Definition** dialog shows up. Click [**Best Fit**]; the column width automatically takes the appropriate width for all tasks in the project.
OR
Point to the divider in-between two column headings. Make sure you see a double-headed mouse pointer and double click: [Task Name ↔ Duration].

The width of the column is now wide enough to accommodate the widest text in the field for the entire project.

To Position the Divider on a Column Split

Put the divider between the spreadsheet and the Gantt Chart exactly on the border of a column by double clicking anywhere on the divider using the mouse pointer ↔.

To View the Whole Project Timescale

1. Choose **View, Zoom**; the **Zoom** dialog appears:

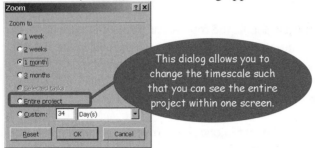

This dialog allows you to change the timescale such that you can see the entire project within one screen.

2. Select ⦿ **Entire Project**.

3. Click OK .

To Format the Timescale

Click 🔍 to zoom out until you can see all the task bars. If you went too far you can use the 🔍 tool to zoom back in on the details.

Or, if you want to customize the timescale to your exact preference:

1. Double click on the timescale itself

    OR

    Choose the menu items **Format, Timescale**; the **Timescale** dialog appears:

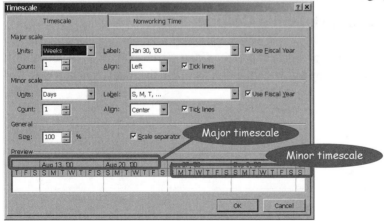

Major timescale

Minor timescale

2. Choose the settings for the **Major scale** (top half of the timescale) and the **Minor scale** (bottom half).

3. Click [OK].

To Format the Task Bars

1. Double-click anywhere in the background of the time scale area.
   OR
   Choose **Format, Bar Styles**, the **Bar Styles** dialog appears:

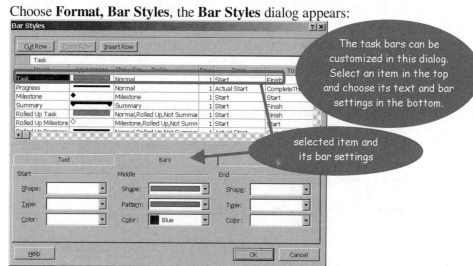

The task bars can be customized in this dialog. Select an item in the top and choose its text and bar settings in the bottom.

selected item and its bar settings

2. In the list select the type of task for which you want to change the appearance:

Name	Appearance	Show For ... Tasks
Task		Normal
Split	....	Normal, Split
Progress		Normal
Milestone	◆	Milestone
Summary		Summary
Project Summary		Project Summary

3. Choose your settings for the selected task type at the bottom of the page tabs **Text** and **Bars**.

4. Click [OK].

Some remarks about this dialog box:

◆ Project 2000 first creates in the Gantt Chart the task bar listed at the top, and then draws the second task bar over top, if they overlap. The order in which the items are listed is, therefore, important. Later ones lay over top of earlier ones.

◆ Under **Show For ... Tasks** you can use the listed items. You can also type in the word **Not** in front of each item to create an exception for that type of task. "**Not Summary**" means format the task bars as specified except for summary tasks.

◆ In the bottom half, on the tab **Text,** you can add text to the task bars. In the default Gantt Chart you will find the following:

  ◇ **Resource Names** are put to the right of the detail task bars.

  ◇ The **Start** dates are shown next to the milestone diamonds.

To Show Milestone Diamonds on Summary Task Bars

1. Select the milestone tasks by ⌨Ctrl and click.

2. Click 📋 , the **Task Information** dialog appears and click the tab **General**.

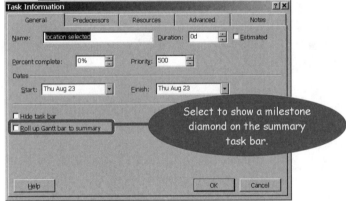

3. Select ☑ **Roll up Gantt Bar to summary**.

4. Select the summary task and make sure that in the same dialog the option
    ☑ **Show rolled up Gantt bars** is selected:

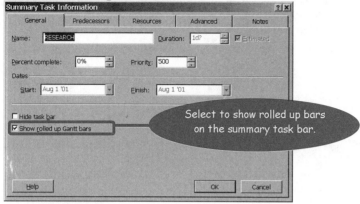

5. Click **OK**.

To Adjust the Page Setup

Setting the Page Orientation

1. Choose **File, Page Setup**, the **Page Setup** dialog appears and click the tab **Page**:

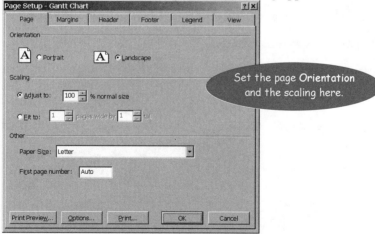

2. Select ⦿ **Portrait** or ⦿ **Landscape**.

3. Click **OK**.

Setting the Margins

1. Choose **File, Page Setup**, the **Page Setup** dialog appears and click the tab **Margins**:

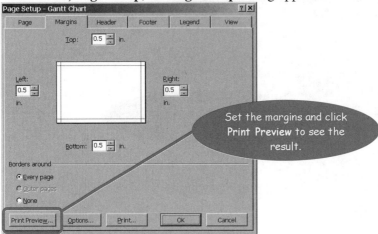

2. Set the margins you need.

3. Click OK .

Creating a Header, Footer or Legend

1. Choose **File, Page Setup**, the **Page Setup** dialog appears. Click the tab **Header**, **Footer** or **Legend**:

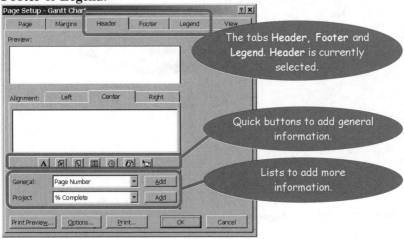

2. Under **Alignment** click the tab **Left, Center** or **Right** and position the cursor inside the text box where you want to add a reference to project data.

3. Select a reference from the **General** list at the bottom and click [Add]. The reference is added. Add as many text references as needed; each refers to data entered in the **File, Properties** and the **Project, Project Information** dialogs.

4. Using the list **Project fields** at the bottom you can insert project-level information, like the **Baseline Finish** and forecast **Finish** or the **Baseline Cost** and forecast **Cost**.

5. Click a button:

Button	For
A	the font, size and style. In order to format the text in the header select the text first and then click **A**.
[#]	page number
[+]	total number of pages
[date]	date: the system date
[time]	time: the system time
[path]	the path and filename
[image]	This button takes you into a dialog for inserting a graphic image into a header, footer or legend. It is often used to insert the project logo.

7. Click [OK] or [Print Preview...].

Exercises

Relocation Project – Constraints and Deadlines

1. Continue to work with your file *Relocation.MPP* or open the file
   06 Entering Constraints and Deadlines.MPP in the sub-directory *Relocation Project*
   on the CD-ROM.

2. Set deadlines on the milestones:

ID	Milestone	Deadline Date
10	location selected	Aug. 20
16	contractor contracted	Aug. 30
25	facility remodeled	Oct. 25
31	new location opened	Oct. 31

3. Enter the following constraints:

ID	Task	Constraint
8	meet to select the location	Start-No-Earlier-Than August 22nd
28	pack	As-Late-As-Possible

   The CEO, *Mr. Salin,* is out of the country until *August 22.* Task *Pack* should be
   scheduled *As-Late-As-Possible*, otherwise the equipment may be packed days before
   the actual move takes place over the weekend. You want the employees to be packed
   as late as possible just before the weekend.

4. Compare your file with the solution file *07 Entering Resources.MPP* in the
   sub-directory *Relocation Project* on the CD-ROM.

5. Save your file for the next exercise.

Relocation Project – Printing the Gantt Chart

With the tasks, estimates, dependencies and constraints entered we now have all the data to print a Gantt Chart.

1. Continue to work with the file from the previous exercise.

2. Format the timescale of the Gantt Chart in the following way:

	Major Scale	**Minor Scale**
Units	Months	Days
Count	1	7
Label	Jan '00	1,2,...52
Align	Center	Center
Enlarge	100 %	

3. Format the Header, Footer and Legend of the Gantt Chart in the following way:

Page Tab	Section	Set to	Font
Header	Center	&[View] &[Project Title] [Date]	Arial, Bold, 20
Footer	Left	&[Manager] &[Company]	Arial, Regular, 8
	Right	&[Date]	Arial, Regular, 8
Legend	Legend on	⦿ None	

4. Compare your file with a printout of the solution file *07 Entering Resources.MPP* in the sub-directory *Relocation Project* on the CD-ROM.

Chapter 7 Entering Resources

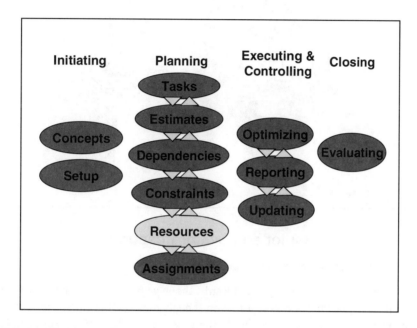

With the Tasks, Estimates, Dependencies and Constraints entered we basically have a Gantt Chart that is a dynamic model of our project. You could stop here if resources, their workloads and costs are less of a concern for you. If you do expect, however, that resources will affect your schedule, you may have to add them to the model and assign them to tasks.

After this chapter you will:

◆ know about the different types of resources: human resources, facilities, machines and materials

◆ be able to enter each type of resource into the project

◆ know how to enter temporary, part-time, full-time and overtime availability

◆ be able to create resource calendars

◆ know how to create a resource report

Junior and Senior Resources

Nob is sitting at his desk. Bob drops by and asks: "Hey Nob, how is it going?"

Nob answers angrily, "Upper management wants the impossible again. They want me to finalize the planning on this new project, even though they can't promise me that I can get Harry to do the engineering and Mary to do the supervising. How can I finalize a plan without knowing who I have on my team?"

Bob takes a chair and sits down. "I know it is difficult. I had a similar project and we had to produce estimates on cost and finish date. We entered *Senior Mechanical Engineer* instead of *Harry* into the schedule and we wrote explicitly in the proposal that the estimates were based on the availability of a senior engineer."

"What if you end up with a junior?"

"You immediately issue a change request."

Nob is still confused: "Yes, but I still need to find a contractor. How can I cost a project without having quotes from the contractor?"

"That is a bit more complicated," answers Bob. "But what I would do if I were you, is call around to contractors and ask for a very preliminary verbal quote. You add some safety to it and you make it clear in the project proposal that the estimate is a rough, order-of-magnitude estimate."

What is a Resource?

Resources are people, facilities, machines or materials used to create the project product. Each activity needs one or more resources.

There are also responsible people. A resource and responsible person differ in that:
◆ the responsible person does not necessarily spend time and effort on the project like resources do
◆ resources also include material resources
◆ people are made responsible for deliverables; whereas resources are normally assigned to activities

Project 2000 accommodates defining resources in the **Resource Sheet** and assigning resources in the **Gantt Chart** view. We will discuss assigning in the next chapter.

Responsible people are assigned to deliverables. Each deliverable needs a responsible person. Deliverables are summary tasks and if you assign a person to summary tasks the assignment will create effort for the responsible person. If you want to indicate responsibilities in your schedule without effort, you could best accomplish this by assigning the responsible people to the milestones. Since milestones have a zero-duration and therefore no effort, it is better to assign responsibilities by assigning to milestones. Responsibilities can also be created using extra fields, like **Text1**. Rename the field name by using **Tools, Customize, Fields**.

When to add a Resource?

A resource should only be defined as a resource if it may increase the duration or the cost of the project. If you enter resources and you allow them to affect the scheduling of tasks, you have created a *resource-limited schedule* [21], also known as a *resource-constrained schedule*.

Resources that could increase the duration of the project are most often human resources, however, all the others (facilities, machines and materials) could lengthen the project as

---

[21] See the glossary of the PMBOK® Guide, 2000 Edition

well. Human resources will often increase the project duration when they are assigned to many tasks and become over-allocated. An example might be experts or busy executives. A resource that is easy to replace will not likely affect the schedule. Materials that have to arrive from afar also affect the schedule.

For managing the cost of the project, you have to define all the people, facilities, machines and materials that have a significant cost associated with them in the resource sheet. For example, if you need outside legal advice, you will pay large enough amounts to need capturing them in your budget. Realize that Project 2000 is not meant to be accounting software. MS Project is a modeling tool in which you have to stay away from the details i.e., small expenses. Furthermore, project managers can afford to ignore dollars and decimals, but accountants can't! Lastly, project managers need only be concerned with expenses that have to be paid from the project budget. Resources you won't pay for from your budget can be left out of the schedule. If you use a boardroom that is paid for by the corporation, you would not add it as a resource to the resource sheet. On the other hand, if you will be paying the rental on a training room from your project budget, you should add the training room as a resource to the resource sheet.

Choosing the Options

Choose **Tools, Options** and click on the tab where you want to change settings.

Tab	Option
General	☑ **Automatically add new resources and tasks** This allows entering a new resource, on the fly, wherever and whenever you need a new resource without going to the resource sheet first.
	Default Standard Rate By entering a rate you can decrease the typing you need to do. If the standard rate is set to $50/hr, you don't need to enter a rate for any resource that is $50/hr.
	Default Overtime Rate By entering a rate you can decrease the typing you need to do.

Tab	Option
	Set as Default This sets the options above as the default setting for any new schedules you create. The existing schedules are not affected because these options are stored in the project file (as you can see in the section divider label **General Options for 'Project 1'**).
Schedule	**Show Assignment units as a: Percentage** or **Decimals** Units of resources can be expressed in percentage or decimals in the **Max. Units** field (availability) and in the assignment units field (workload). This option is generic and applies to all your projects, existing and new. For example: you have a resource, which is available half-time to your project. This option gives you the choice to enter this as *50%* (percentage) or as *0.5* (decimals) in the **Max. Units** field. For part-time resources, percentages seem to work better. Let's consider a situation in which you have 3 carpenters available to your project. You could enter them as a group and enter *300%* (percentage) or *3* (decimals). For consolidated resources the decimals seem easier to understand. If you have both part-timers and group resources in your project, you will still have to choose either percentage or decimal for all resources.

Types of Resources

Important questions for each type of resource are:
◆ Should the resource add to the total amount of work in the project?
◆ Should the resource be included in workload leveling?

We will discuss these questions for each type of resource:

◆ **Human resources** are people whose efforts should add up in the *Work* field. The total amount of work should be reasonable, which means it is within or close to their availability. If there are over-allocations, their workloads should be leveled. Human resources generate cost and should be given a standard rate and, if applicable, an overtime rate and cost-per-use rate. They have a time-related cost and the rate needs to be appended with "/h" (per hour) or "/w" (per week).

◆ **Facilities** should not add to the total amount of effort in the field **Work**. We, therefore, have to make them **Material** resources. Facilities do add to the cost and need a standard rate, and perhaps a cost-per-use rate.
If you enter facilities as material resources, MS Project cannot prevent the facility from double reservations by leveling its 'workload'. You would not want two meetings held in one room at the same time. You have to keep an eye on the reservation of the facility yourself. You could, of course, choose to enter the facility as a **Work** resource, but this will start adding its 'effort' to the amount of **Work** in the project, which is not desirable.

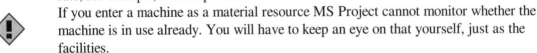

◆ **Machines** should not add to the amount of **Work** and should be entered as **Material** resources as well. Machines need a standard rate. They can also have a cost-per-use rate, for example, for setup costs.
If you enter a machine as a material resource MS Project cannot monitor whether the machine is in use already. You will have to keep an eye on that yourself, just as the facilities.

◆ **Material** resources are consumable resources. They should not add to the amount of **Work**. Materials do not need to be leveled. Materials do cost money, but have a unit-related cost only. The unit cost should be entered in the **Std. Rate** field.

What if you Don't Know who you will get?

In the planning phase, you often don't know exactly who is going to do the task. This chapter started with the story of Nob, who was wondering how he could finalize his planning if he did not know whom he would have on his team. It stopped him from finalizing his planning. If you know you are going to need a programmer, you can enter this resource, for the time being, under the generic name *programmer* in the resource sheet. If you need more precision in your model, you can create junior and senior generic resources, such as *junior programmer* and *senior programmer*.

Not knowing the exact names of the individuals should not stop you from planning the project. As soon as you know the name of the individual, you can overtype the generic resource with the name of the individual. MS Project will transfer all the assignments from the generic resource to the individual.

Change the View to Enter Resources

1. Choose **View, Resource Sheet**.

2. Check if the table **Entry** is active:
   choose **View, Table: <name of current table>, Entry**.

Resource Fields

You will find the following fields in the Resource Sheet:

Indicator
This field will display indicators for a variety of situations. If a resource is over-allocated this column will show an ◈ icon.

Resource Name
This is where you enter the name of the resource. We recommend using the format *last name – first name,* if you have more than one page of resources. Notice the use of a dash (-); you cannot use the comma (,) because it is used as separator for multiple entries in fields (also called the *list separator* in Project 2000).
What you type in this field will show up in the lists used for assigning resources. Only the entries in this field will show in those lists. It is therefore imperative that you make the resource names easy to recognize and unique in this field. If you have more than one *John*

Smith, you cannot discriminate between them when you are assigning resources. In the resource sheet you can look at other fields like **Group** to find out who is who.

Type
The type of resource can be **Work** (default) or **Material**. Work resources are people. Material resources are facilities, equipment and materials. An example of a material resource is *desktop computers*.

Material Label
The label you type in (for a material resource only!) will show up in several other views and reports. For example, the label *desktop computers* will show on the y-axis in the Resource Graph view to indicate the number of units used over time. In the timescale of the Gantt Chart it will show up to the right of the task bars.

Initials
Initials instead of the name are useful in assigning resources to a task. In previous versions of MS Project this field was very useful because you had to assign by typing the name or the initials of the resource, but nowadays you can point and click to assign.

Group
The group is the name of the department to which the resource belongs. If you fill in these group names, you can filter on, or group by, all the tasks for the department. And, better still, with the new group feature you can group the resources together into their respective groups and see totals for work and cost.

Max. Units (Maximum Units)
This is the maximum or total number of resource units available, which is 100% for a full-time resource and 50% for a half-time resource. For a consolidated resource it is the number of team members in the team. For material resources you don't need to enter availability.

Std. Rate (Standard Rate)
Enter the standard rate for regular work in this field. For example, if you enter "10.50/h", it means the person earns $10.50 per hour. For material resources you don't need to add a time unit; it will be calculated per unit of material.

If you type	you will see	which means
m	min	minutes
h	hr	hours
d	day	days
w	wk	weeks
mo	mon	months
y	yr	years

Ovt. Rate (Overtime Rate)

Enter the rate for overtime work in this field. Do this only if you will pay for overtime work instead of compensating by giving time off. Project 2000 expects you to indicate separately how many hours are worked in overtime on each assignment; those hours will be charged against the overtime rate. Material resources cannot have an overtime rate.

Cost/Use (Cost-per-Use or Per-Use-Cost)

Enter the rate that has to be paid every time the resource is used in this field. It can be an up-front fee, for example for a bulldozer. If you need a bulldozer transported to your site this may cost $200 before it does any work. The cost-per-use will be incurred on every task to which the resource is assigned. The cost is calculated as the Cost/Use rate times the number of units assigned.

Accrue At

Select Start, End, or Prorated to indicate when the costs are incurred. Tab to the **Accrue at** field and click the pull-down button ▼ that appears when you are in the field to get a list. Select one of the following options:

Accrue at	Incurs the Cost	Example
Start	As soon as the task starts.	actors
Prorated	The cost is incurred as the task progresses; the cost goes up with the **% Complete**.	employees
End	As soon as the task finishes.	consultants

Base Calendar

Select a calendar from the list. The *base calendar* specifies the working hours and working days for the resource. Material resources cannot have a base calendar.

Code

Type an alphanumeric code, such as an accounting code. This is used to charge the expenses for the resource to a particular cost account. It can be useful for the financial department. Often the tasks, and not the resources, will be coded to charge to the cost accounts.

Entering Resources

You can enter the resources into the resource sheet in two ways:

◆ Downloading the resources from the Mailing List

◆ Keying in the resources manually

Downloading the Resources From the Mailing List

If you are using MS Outlook for your contact information and address list, you may be able to download the resource names easily from that list. This will prevent you having to type all of them. MS Outlook even has powerful import features in the menu items **File, Import and Export ...**. If you keep your addresses in another contact management application or database, you should be able to import them into MS Outlook. Then you can use the following steps to transfer the resource names into MS Project.

1. Display the toolbar by making a right click on any toolbar and clicking on **Resource Management.** The Resource Management toolbar is displayed:

2. Click [image] (**Address Book**); the **Choose Profile** dialog may appear in which you have to indicate which user profile you want to use on the computer system. The user profiles make it possible to have more than person taking turns on the computer, enabling each to use their own preferences and setup.

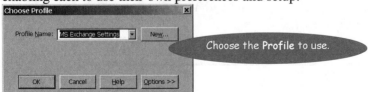

Choose the **Profile** to use.

3. Click [OK]; the **Select Resources** dialog appears:

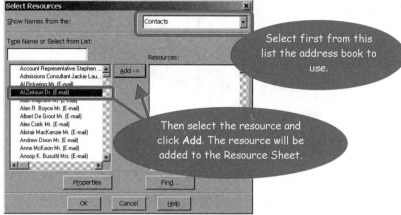

4. Select the address list from the **Show Names from the:**
Contacts ; the names of the resources are now shown in the list
on the left. (If no address lists are shown, you have to add the **Personal Address
Book** or the **Outlook Address Book** to the profile. In MS Outlook you can do this by
choosing **Tools, Services**.)

5. Type in the first character(s) of the name of the person to add in the field
Type name or select from list; the list scrolls immediately to the person. Press the
arrow keys ⬇ and ⬆ to highlight the resource exactly, if needed.

6. Press [Enter] or click [Add ->]; the resource is now added to the list **Resources** on the
right. This list of people will be transferred into the resource sheet of MS Project.

7. Repeat the last two steps for all resources you would like to add.

8. Click [OK]; the resources are now added to the end of the resource list. You
can always go back into the address list to pick up more resource names.

9. You will still have to add the other types of resources: facility, machine and material.
You can do this with the next steps.

Keying in the Resources Manually

1. Customize the table first:
   ◇ Delete all columns you will not need by clicking on their column heading and
     pressing [Delete].

◇ Insert new fields you will need by making a right click on the column heading; a pop-up menu appears. Choose **Insert Column**; the **Column Definition** dialog appears:

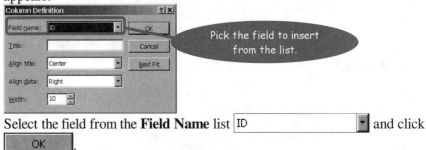

Select the field from the **Field Name** list ID and click OK .

2. Enter the name of the resource in the field **Resource Name** and press:

Enter to go down (to the next row), or

Tab to go right (to the next column).

3. If the resource is a material resource (facilities, machines or materials) change the **Type** from **Work** to **Material** and enter the base unit of the material into the field **Material Label**, for example, *brick*.

If you change the type of the resource you will loose any rates you may have typed in for the resource. This is because **Work** resources require a time-related rate, like $50/h, whereas the **Material** resources need a per-unit cost, like $150/door.

4. Enter the availability in the field **Max. Units**

5. Enter the cost rates into the fields **Std. Rate, Ovt. Rate** and **Cost/Use**.

Another easy way to enter data is by dragging over all cells in which you want to enter resource information. Multiple cells are selected with one cell still white; the input cell. Enter the data in this input cell and use the Tab key to make it go to the next cell until you have filled all.

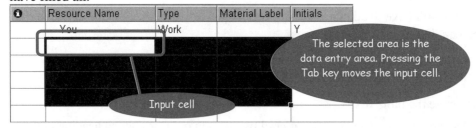

Resource Calendars

A resource calendar is a calendar that is specific for an individual. You can enter

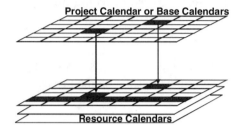

Project Calendar or Base Calendars

Resource Calendars

individual working times and vacations in a resource calendar. There is a resource calendar available for each resource, but you do not need to modify any unless you wish to do so. All resource calendars will have the settings that you entered on the project calendar, see page 95: Creating the Project Calendar.

If someone takes an individual holiday, tasks assigned to him or her will be delayed until the resource is back. The resource has

an impact on the schedule; it causes the duration of the project to increase. This type of situation is important to model in Project 2000. A poorly timed vacation can easily jeopardize precious deadlines. To edit a resource calendar follow these steps:

1. Choose **Tools, Change Working Time…**; the **Change Working Time** dialog appears:

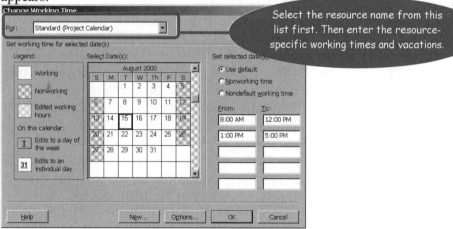

Select the resource name from this list first. Then enter the resource-specific working times and vacations.

2. Select the resource for which to set the calendar in the list

For: | Standard (Project Calendar) ▼

3. Change the work hours by selecting the **M** through the **F,** 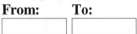 and then typing the working time in the boxes:
    From: To:

4. To set an individual holiday, highlight the days (you can select multiple days by holding down ⌨Ctrl and clicking or dragging) and select ⦿ **Nonworking time.**

5. Click ▮ OK ▮.

 You can even change holidays from the Standard (Project Calendar) back to working days. If you want to change the exception back to the original setting on the Project Calendar you have to select ⦿ **Use Default.**

 There is a new task-related field, **Ignore Resource Calendar** that is by default set to *No* for all tasks. This field determines if Project 2000 will use the resource calendar when scheduling assignments. The field is useful when the task also has a Task Calendar. With the new field you can resolve if the Resource Calendar or the Task Calendar determines the scheduling of the task. The field should have *No* or *Yes* respectively.

 In previous versions of MS Project, Fixed Duration tasks used to ignore the resource calendars completely. In Project 2000 the Fixed Duration tasks will look at the resource calendars, but may split the task bar when one of the resources is not available.

The working hours on resource calendars can become very intricate and require a lot of data-entry, such as resources working day shifts and night shifts in alternating weeks. You have to ask yourself if you would prefer to manage these shift resources as a consolidated resource instead of individual resources. Your schedule might otherwise become maintenance-hungry. In projects, shift work is less prevalent than in the ongoing operations of a company.

Resource Availability

The availability of resources is very diverse from one resource to another. The different types are:

◆ *Temporary*
Somebody can be "loaned" to a project for only one month.

◆ *Varying availability*
A resource who is available full-time one month, but half-time the next month, has varying availability.

◆ *Part-time*
A person who works fewer hours a day or fewer days a week.

◆ *Full-time*
Project 2000 sees a full-time person as one who works 40 hours a week and 5 days a week. This is the default work week, and diversions from this are exceptions.

◆ *Overtime*
If the deadline is in jeopardy, resources can be asked to work overtime to compensate for a lack of progress.

◆ *Consolidated resources*
Consolidated resources are multiple resources that are not entered into the schedule as individuals but as one group.

On the next pages we will discuss how each of these resources could be entered into Project 2000. In many cases you will have to edit the resource calendar.

Temporary and Varying Availability

If a resource is available only during a certain period you can enter this *availability* in the **Resource Information** dialog 📇 on the tab **General**. An example of temporary availability is when a specialized test lab is only available for a project team in the month of May.

In Project 2000 you can easily model varying availability. You can set up an entire profile of availability, such as 80% in April, 50% in May, 100% in June, etc. On the same **General** tab under **Resource Availability,** you can enter the availability profile:

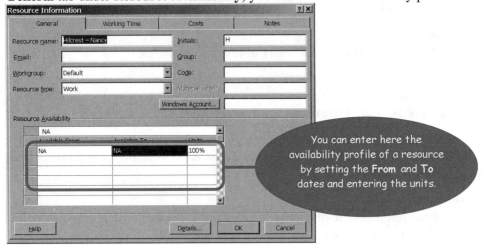

You can enter here the availability profile of a resource by setting the **From** and **To** dates and entering the units.

Part-time Availability

Part-time resources can be:

◆ People who work, for example, 4 hours each workday. These should be entered with the **Max. Units** set to 4h/8h x 100% = 50% in the resource sheet.
OR
The working-time hours on the resource calendar should be set to only four hours per day. For example, the working hours could be set to 1PM-5PM.

◆ People who work four out of five weekdays; enter these into the schedule by marking a weekday as a non-working day on their resource calendar
(**Tools, Change Working Time**).

When someone is working on multiple projects you may have them working only part-time on your project.

A resource can also be assigned to work part-time on a task, which we will discuss in Chapter 8 Entering Assignments.

Full-time Availability

People who work full-time need to have their **Max. Units** set to 100%.

Their working hours as set in the resource calendar should correspond with the number of **Hours per Day** and **Hours per Week** settings in the **Tools, Options, Calendar**. For example, if the hours per day in **Tools, Options** is set to 7.5 hours/day, the calendar should show for example 8AM - 12PM and 1PM - 4:30PM (double-click on the resource and click on the tab **Working Time**).

Overtime Availability

Overtime work is work outside the regular work hours as indicated on the Project Calendar.

 In the initial planning phase of the project, you would normally not plan overtime, unless the project is extremely time-constrained. The overtime feature is more useful during the execution phase when we may try to compensate for slippages.

Overtime can be entered in several different ways depending on what you pay the resource for it and what the overtime rate is:

◆ If the resource is not paid for overtime, but is compensated with time off, there are several ways in which you can model this:

◇ You can enter the overtime by increasing the **Max. Units** in the resource sheet to greater than 100%. This is the quick and easy way to do this, and the resource will be working the overtime during the entire project. OR

◇ To be somewhat more precise you could use the **Resource Information** dialog 🗐, tab **General**; in **Resource Availability** you could specify overtime for a period in which the resource works more than 100%. OR

     ◇ Increase the working time on the resource calendar. For example: somebody works 20 % overtime in one week, and in the second week the overtime is compensated in time off. OR

     ◇ Enter the overtime by changing holidays or weekend days on the resource calendar to working days. Later on, weekdays are set to non-working days to compensate for time.

◆ If the resource is paid for overtime at the regular rate, you only need to accept certain over-allocations. All the hours are charged at the standard rate.

◆ If the resource is paid for overtime hours at a higher rate, you have to enter all the hours worked in overtime separately. You enter them on the Task Form in the Gantt Chart, see below.

Entering Overtime Hours at the Overtime Rate

1. Choose **View, Resource Sheet** and enter the overtime rate in the field **Ovt. Rate**.

2. Choose **View, Gantt Chart**.

3. Choose **Window, Split** to display the **Task Form**.

4. Click on the **Task Form** to make it active.

5. Choose **Format, Details, Resource Work** to display the field **Ovt. Work**. The view should now look like:

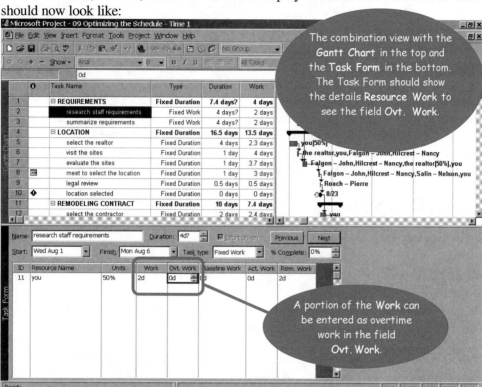

> The combination view with the *Gantt Chart* in the top and the **Task Form** in the bottom. The Task Form should show the details *Resource Work* to see the field *Ovt. Work*.

> A portion of the **Work** can be entered as overtime work in the field *Ovt. Work*.

6. For each assignment you now indicate in the **Ovt. Work** field how many of the hours in the field **Work** will be worked in overtime.

7. Click [OK] when done with an assignment.

Realize that the number of overtime hours has to be reasonable relative to the total number of hours **Work**. If an assignment is 10 hours, you could ask for 2 hours in overtime and finish the task in one business day. If the assignment is 20 hours, you cannot expect a resource to work 8 hours and then 12 hours in overtime to finish within one day. Project 2000 would schedule this as one 20-hour work day.

Consolidated Resources

Consolidated resources are pooled resources, not individuals. A group of people is entered as one consolidated resource. The maximum units are set to the number of full-time equivalent individuals who are part of the consolidated resource.

Consolidating resources only makes sense if the resources can substitute for each other. If you have experienced and novice resources you could create two consolidated resources: junior and senior. For example, if you find that the experience level among programmers varies widely, create a group of junior and a group of senior programmers. MS Project is a modeling tool in which you only capture the most significant parameters.

Cost Management

Cost Situations

Economists distinguish variable cost and fixed cost. Variable cost can vary with time needed, units consumed or number of uses.

Labor cost is a time-related human resource cost. Facilities can also have time-related costs like rent or lease expenses. Machines can have:
◆ time-related cost such as rent,
◆ unit-related cost such as a newspaper print machine for which it is the cost of paper per newspaper, or
◆ use-related cost such as the setup cost of the printing machine

Fixed costs can be related to resources or to tasks. Resource-related fixed cost can be entered in the **Cost/Use** field. An example of resource-related fixed cost is the upfront cost for transporting a bulldozer to the construction site. Examples of task-related fixed costs are: expenses for licenses, patents, and any fixed-price contracts.

A resource can have more than one type of cost associated with it. For example, a bulldozer can have a per use fee of $200 for transportation in addition to an hourly rate of $300. In this case you can enter the per-use fee in the **Cost/Use** field and the hourly rate in the **Std. Rate** (standard rate) field.

Apart from the cost variations the cost rates themselves can change over time, this is known as *rate profile*. In MS Project you can capture the rate-profile in the *Cost Rate Table* feature.

Entering Human Resource Costs

If you hire, for example, a programmer at $300/day, you can enter this in the resource sheet.

1. Choose **View, Resource Sheet**.

2. Enter the name of the resource in **Resource Name**.

3. Leave the **Type** of the resource to the default setting of **Work**.

4. Enter the rate in the field **Std. Rate**; for the programmer you would enter *$300/d*.

5. Enter the other cost rates **Ovt. Rate** and **Cost/Use**, if they are applicable.

6. Enter the **Accrue At**; the timing of the cost, for which you choose at the **Start**, **Prorated** or **End.** Prorated is accrued as the task progresses for which Project 2000 will look at the **% Complete**. In the timescale, the end is the right side of the task bar and that is when the costs will be incurred. The Cost/Use is always incurred at the start of the task.

7. Assign the human resources to the tasks, which we will discuss in the next chapter.

In the snapshot is shown how the prorated accrual is incurred proportionally to the **% Work Complete**:

> The **% Work Complete** of 50% creates $600 **Actual Cost** of $1,200 total **Cost**.

Resource Name	Accrue At	% Work Complete	Work	Details	S	M	T	W	T
1 ⊟ programmer	Prorated	50%	32 hrs	Cost		$300.00	$300.00	$300.00	$300.00
				Act. Cost		$300.00	$300.00		
code module		50%	32 hrs	Cost		$300.00	$300.00	$300.00	$300.00
				Act. Cost		$300.00	$300.00		

The time-related cost for facilities, like rental and lease, should be entered as material costs.

Entering Material Costs

The cost of materials should be incorporated into the project model if they are significant enough to keep track of and if they will be paid from your project budget.

1. Choose **View, Resource Sheet**.

2. Enter the name of the resource in **Resource Name**.

3. In the field **Type** [Work ▼]; select **Material** from the list.

4. Enter a **Material Label** that will show up in the Resource Graph and other views and reports, to remind viewers that this resource is a material resource. Enter it in plural, for example '*bricks*' when you typically assign more than one unit.

5. In the **Std. Rate** field you enter the unit cost for this resource. Notice that you don't need to enter the /h or /d for material resources. For the bricks we could enter, for example *$0.75*. The overtime rate field is neither available nor needed for material resources. You can fill in a **Cost/Use** as well, for the bricks this could be the cost of transportation to the site, let's say *$400.00*.

6. Enter the **Accrue At**; the timing of the cost, for which you choose at the **Start, Prorated** or **End.** Prorated is accrued as the task progresses for which Project 2000 will look at the **% Complete**. Materials are often accrued at the start, facility and machines are often prorated. The Cost/Use is always incurred at the start of the task.

7. Assign the number of material resources to the tasks that are needed. We will discuss this in the next chapter.

In the snapshot is shown how the accrual for material costs will work. The 1000 bricks cost $2 each. The training room rental costs $400.

A material cost accrued at the start of the task.

	Resource Name	Accrue At	Work	Details	Apr 9, '00 S	M	T	W	T
1	⊟ bricks	Start	1,000	Cost		$2,000.00	$0.00	$0.00	$0.00
				Act. Cost					
	lay bricks		1,000	Cost		$2,000.00	$0.00	$0.00	$0.00
				Act. Cost					
2	⊟ training room	End	1	Cost		$0.00	$400.00		
				Act. Cost					
	train students		1	Cost		$0.00	$400.00		
				Act. Cost					

A facility cost of $400 accrued at the end of the task.

Entering Time-related Cost for Facilities and Machines

This is the most difficult resource situation to enter into Project 2000. The use of facilities and machines should not add to the **Work** of the project. This would lead to the conclusion that they have to be entered as **Material** resources. But for material resources you cannot have time-related cost calculated automatically by Project 2000 depending on the duration of the task. You can only enter unit- or use-related cost. If you pay a fixed amount for every use of a training room, you enter that cost in the **Cost/Use** field.

The only way to model time-related cost in Project 2000 is by entering the resource as a **Work** resource. Enter the daily or monthly rent in the **Std. Rate** field. This will also make it possible to keep the 'workload' leveled for the training room, in other words, to prevent double booking of these resources. But this way adds the 'work' of the facility to the total work of the project, which is not desirable. You can find the total amount of 'work' for the facility in the resource sheet by viewing the field **Work**; you could then subtract this amount.

As you can see, there is no one best way to enter the time-related cost for facilities or machines, and you have to choose what fits best in your situation.

Entering Varying Cost Rates

1. Varying cost rates can be filled in the cost rate table in the **Resource Information** dialog. Click and the **Resource Information** dialog appears, then click the tab **Costs**.

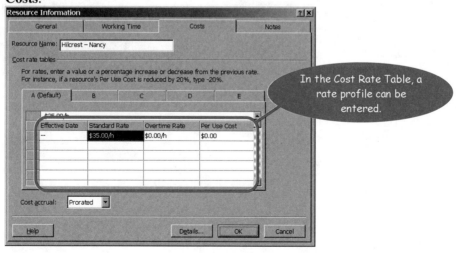

2. Enter the **Effective Date** and enter the rates that will apply after that date.

3. Repeat the previous step for as many times as the rate changes over time.

4. Click [OK]; Project 2000 will calculate with the appropriate rate depending on when the task is scheduled in time.

In Project 2000 you can now create rate profiles for all the different types of costs: **Standard Rate**, **Overtime Rate** and **Per-Use-Cost**.

Entering Fixed Cost in the Gantt Chart

The fixed cost has to be filled in as a task-related cost on the Gantt Chart in the column **Fixed Cost.**

1. Insert the column **Fixed Cost** or apply the table **Cost**.

2. Enter the fixed cost in the field **Fixed Cost**. Also indicate when the fixed cost will be accrued in the field **Fixed Cost Accrual.** Your choices are at the **Start, Prorated** during the task or at the **End** of the task.

3. Project 2000 will then calculate the total cost for the task in the field **Cost** as:
    Cost = Fixed Cost + (work costs) + (material costs)
    See the next snapshot of the Task Usage view for an illustration of this formula. The total cost of $3,800 on the task *lay bricks* consists of *fixed cost $600*, material cost *$2,000* for the bricks and labor cost *$1,200* for the work of the brick layers:

	Task Name	Fixed Cost	Cost	Duration	Work
1	⊟ lay bricks	$600.00	$3,800.00	5 days	40 hrs
	bricks		$2,000.00		1,000
	brick layers		$1,200.00		40 hrs

The **Cost** for the task is the total of **Fixed Cost**, material cost and labor cost.

 Notice that if you enter any cost directly into the **Cost** field, the cost is immediately interpreted as **Fixed Cost** and transferred into that field.

Printing the Resource Sheet

Customizing the Table

1. Choose **View, Table: Entry, More Tables**; the **More Tables** dialog box appears:

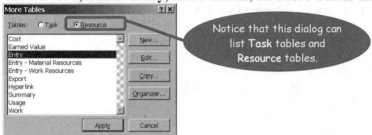

Notice that this dialog can list **Task** tables and **Resource** tables.

2. Select ⦿ **Resource** to display the list of resource-related tables. Select a table that is close to what you need and click [Copy...]; the **Table Definition** dialog appears:

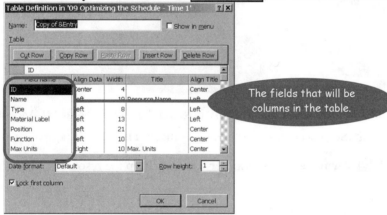

The fields that will be columns in the table.

3. Change the name for the new table to a more descriptive name.

4. To add this table to the menu, check ☑ **Show in Menu**.

5. To delete a field from the table, click on it and click [Delete Row].

6. To add a field to the table, click on the row before which to insert it and click [Insert Row], and select the field from the list [＿＿＿＿ ▾].

7. Click [OK].

The extra columns used (**Text1, Text2, .. Number1,.. Flag1,..**) can be permanently renamed by choosing **Tools, Customize, Fields.** This feature allows you to create new fields for resources like *Position*, or *Telephone Number*.

Sorting Resources Alphabetically

Choose **Project, Sort** and one of the predefined sorting orders, such as **By Cost, By Name** or **By ID**.
OR
to sort on other fields:

1. Choose **Project, Sort, Sort By….** The **Sort** dialog appears:

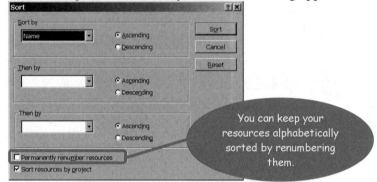

2. Then choose the first sort key in the **Sort By** box and the sorting order ⊙ **Ascending** or ⊙ **Descending**. Set a second key to break ties under **Then By,** if necessary.

3. You can check ☑ **Permanently Renumber** option to keep the resources sorted in the chosen order.

4. Click [**Sort**] to effectuate the sorting.

Formatting the Text

1. Click on the menu items **Format**, **Text Styles;** the **Text Styles** dialog appears:

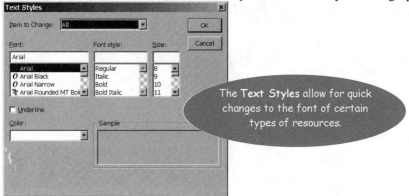

The **Text Styles** allow for quick changes to the font of certain types of resources.

2. Choose under **Item to Change** the **Over-allocated resources** and notice that by default these critical resources are displayed in red.

3. Choose a color, font and appearance for the items and click OK .

Formatting the Gridlines

1. Choose **Format, Gridlines...** and choose the options. The **Gridlines** dialog appears:

Gridlines can be added or removed.

2. Select the **Line to change**, and then the **Type** of line for this item, its **Color** and the **At Interval**.

3. Click OK .

Choosing the Page Setup

1. Choose **File, Page Setup...**; the **Page Setup** dialog appears:

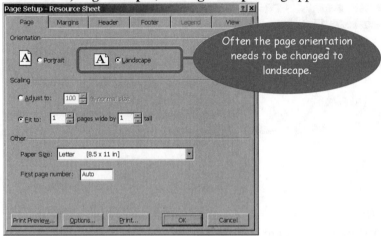

2. Select the appropriate tab. On the tab **Page** you can change the page orientation **Portrait** or **Landscape**. To insert headers, footers or a legend, please review the instructions on page 419: Choose the Page Setup Settings.

3. You can select the **Scaling** option to fit the report on a certain number of pages.

4. Choose the other options needed and click Print Preview... or Print... .

Preview the Resource Spreadsheet

Choose **File**, **Print Preview** or click .the **Print Preview** screen appears:

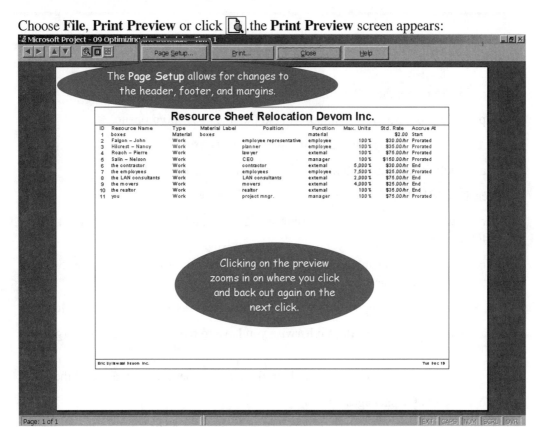

Exercises

Review A

Is it possible to model the following situations in MS Project? If so, how?

1. Up-front fee of $500 for a bulldozer. And the rate is $1000/d onsite.

2. A consultant charging $400/d until January 1st, then $450/d.

3. Car rental: for the first 100 km no charge then $0.45/km.

4. Penalty of $1000/d for delivering late.

5. Harry, who works as a Business Analyst at $500/d and, as a Systems Analyst for $400/d.

6. Volume discounts for materials; for example, if you buy one door it costs $150, if you buy 10 doors they cost $90 each.

7. A freelancer who typically works on the weekend and delivers the work on Monday.

8. Pay an invoice within 30 days otherwise you have to pay a late payment charge of 10%.

9. Overtime hours accumulated throughout the year and paid for at the end of the year.

10. Courier costs for packages

11. Low and high season hotel room rates. (For example, in New York the hotel rates double in December.)

Chapter 7 Entering Resources

Review B

Which of the following resources should have its workload leveled in MS Project? (Enter a check mark in the appropriate cell.) Explain.

Resource	Always Leveled	Never Leveled
1. expert		
2. computer		
3. mortar		
4. boardroom		

Relocation Project – Entering Resources

Continue to work with your file *Relocation.MPP* or open the file *07 Entering Resources.MPP* in the sub-directory *Relocation Project* on the CD-ROM.

Below you will find the resources that will be needed in the Relocation project. Notice that there are generic resources in the list, like *movers*. You found their rates by telephoning around. There is no **Cost/Use** for these resources.

Resource Name	Type	Material Label	Position	Function	Max. Units	Std. Rate	Accrue at
you [22]	*Work*		*project mngr.*	*manager*	*1*	*$75/h*	*Pro-rated*
Salin – Nelson	*Work*		*CEO*	*manager*	*1*	*$150/h*	*Pro-rated*
Falgon – John	*Work*		*employee represen-tative*	*employee*	*1*	*$30/h*	*Pro-rated*

---

[22] This is you, yourself. Please, fill in your own name instead of *you*.

PAGE 263

Resource Name	Type	Material Label	Position	Function	Max. Units	Std. Rate	Accrue at
Hilcrest – Nancy	Work		planner	employee	1	$35/h	Pro-rated
Roach – Pierre	Work		lawyer	external	1	$75/h	Pro-rated
the employees	Work		emplo-yees	employee	75	$25/h	Pro-rated
the contractor	Work		contrac-tor	external	50	$30/h	End
the realtor	Work		realtor	external	1	$35/h	End
the movers	Work		movers	external	40	$25/h	End
the LAN consultants	Work		LAN consul-tants	external	20	$75/h	End
boxes	mat-erial	boxes		material		$2	Start

1. Customize the table of the resource sheet view as shown in the table above. The field *Position* and *Function* are not standard fields in MS Project. You can use the field **Text1** and **Text2** and permanently rename them to *Position* and *Function* respectively using the feature **Tools, Customize, Fields**.

2. Enter the resources in the table above. Use the **Fill Down** feature for the columns *Function* and *Accrue at*.

3. Sort the list of resources on resource *Name* as the first sorting key and on *Function* as the second sorting key. Select the option to permanently renumber the resources.

4. You decided you are going to work nine hours per day during August to kick-start the project, starting half an hour earlier (7:30) and ending an hour later (17:30).

5. *Nancy Hilcrest* will go on a one-week holiday in the third full week of August.

6. You realize that due to the project requirements the disruption to normal company operations should be minimal, the move will have to take place over the weekend. Set, for the *Movers*, all the weekdays to non-working days and the weekend days to

8 hours per day. Compare your file with the solution file *08 Entering Assignments.MPP* in the sub-directory *Relocation Project* on the CD-ROM. Save your file for the next exercise.

Relocation Project – Printing the Resource Sheet

1. Continue to work with the file from the previous exercise.

2. Apply the following **Text Styles**:

Item to Change	Font	Size	Arial
All	*Arial*	*10*	*Regular*
Row & Column Titles	*Arial*	*10*	*Bold*

3. Enter the following **Page Setup** settings:

Page Tab	Section	Set to	Font
Page	*Orientation*	*Landscape*	
	Scaling	*Fit to: 1 page wide by 1 tall*	
Margins	*top,bottom,left,right*	*1 Inch*	
	Borders Around	*every page*	
Header	*Center*	*&[View] &[Project Title]*	*Arial Bold 20*
Footer	*Left*	*&[Manager] &[Company]*	
	Right	*&[Date]*	*Arial Regular 8*

4. Apply the following **Gridlines**:

Line to Change	Normal – Type
Sheet Rows	*Blank (at top of list)*
Sheet Columns	*Blank (at top of list)*
Title Vertical	*Blank (at top of list)*
Title Horizontal	*Blank (at top of list)*

5. Compare your file with a print-out of the solution file *08 Entering Assignments.MPP* in the sub-directory *Relocation Project* on the CD-ROM.

Troubleshooting

1. Open the file *LastNameFirstName.MPP* in the sub-directory *Troubleshooting* on the CD-ROM. Enter your first name in the resource sheet, and then enter your last name. Questions:

   ◇ Why does the first name show up in two fields?

   ◇ Why does the second entry override the first one?

2. Try entering the resource *Smith, Harry*. Why does Project 2000 not allow you to do that?

Chapter 8 Entering Assignments

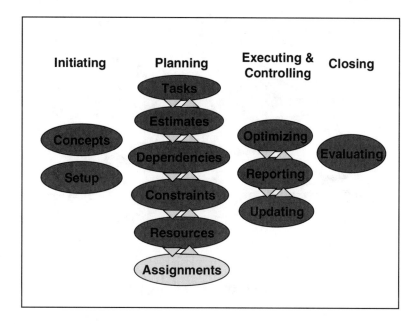

The assignments are the last type of data to enter into our project model. After this chapter we will have a complete model of our project, but most likely the model will not meet all the time and budgetary constraints we have entered into it. We will address that in the next chapter on optimizing.

After this chapter you will:

◆ know the difference between Fixed Duration, Fixed Units and Fixed Work tasks

◆ be able to enter each type of task into MS Project

◆ know how to assign resources to tasks using the Assign Resources dialog or the Task Form

◆ be able to assign resources to work part-time on tasks

◆ know how to make changes to assignments

◆ know how to create a report of the assignments

Leave the Best Alone

"Hey Nob, how did your project go?"

"Not very well, Bob, some tasks slipped near the end of our project and it wrecked our deadlines."

"Didn't you have some buffer time left?"

"Well, we did … but for some reason we didn't make the deadline even though we added resources to the team."

"You added resources and you still didn't make the deadline?"

"No, what happened is that the new resources needed to be trained on the job and our best people had to be taken off their daily crunching to get them up to speed."

"Well, Nob, we learned something from that experience…."

What is an Assignment?

An assignment is a combination of one task and one resource. The assignment reflects who will do the task.

In the example given, *Ed* is assigned to *Write Report* and *Mary* is assigned to *Print Report.*

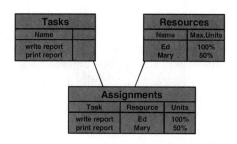

Each of the three entities, tasks, resources and assignments has its own specific fields. Some fields look alike but are in fact different. Tasks have **Start** and **Finish** dates, and each assignment has its own **Start** and **Finish** dates. There is a resource field maximum units (**Max. Units**) and there is an assignment field **Units**.

The **Max. Units** of a resource reflect the maximum availability of the resource to the project. For one full-time person the **Max. Units** would be 100%. The availability can also be less than 100% for part-time resources. For consolidated resources it represents how many individuals the group has. We discussed resource availability in the previous chapter. In the illustration *Ed* is *100%* available, whereas *Mary* is only *50%* available.

The assignment-related field **Units** reflects:
◆ whether a person works full-time or part-time on the task, or
◆ how many individuals in a consolidated resource are needed on the task.

One resource unit is one person working full-time. For a *full-time assignment* fill in 100% in the field **Units** on the Task Form. In the illustration *Ed* will work full-time on *write report.*

If you enter less than 100% you are asking the resource to work part of her available time on the task. You have assigned the resource to the task *part-time*. To create a part-time assignment, fill in a percentage as the units for the resource. In the illustration *Mary* will work *50%* of full-time availability on the task *print report*, which equals her maximum availability to the project.

The units assigned can be changed quickly on the **Assign Resources** dialog.

Full-time or Part-time Assignment

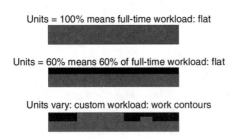

Units = 100% means full-time workload: flat

Units = 60% means 60% of full-time workload: flat

Units vary: custom workload: work contours

In both the full-time and part-time assignment, the work of the resource will be spread evenly across the duration of the task. The work is said to be flat.

You can vary the workload over the task duration and Project 2000 calls this a *work contour*. There are pre-defined work contours, but you can also create your own spread of work over a task:

◆ You can apply one of the pre-defined work contours using the **Assignment Information** dialog. If you double-click on an assignment in either the **Task Usage** or the **Resource Usage** view, the **Assignment Information** dialog will be displayed. You can then select a pre-defined contour from the list **Work contour**.

◆ You can even fill in, on a day-by-day basis, how many hours you need from the resource on a task. You can enter the needed hours directly into the **Task Usage** view. This detail is seldom needed in the planning of projects. Also, if you do decide to plan your project to this level of detail, you will spend a lot of time maintaining your schedule, particularly when you enter the required hours on a day-by-day basis. For this reason, we do not recommend this.

Choosing the Options

The assignment-related options are shown in the table below. Before creating assignments consider the most appropriate settings for these options.

Tab	Option
Schedule	**Show assignments units as a:** `Percentage ▾` **Percentage** is the best choice when you have part-time resources; if there are consolidated resources **Decimal** is better. This option is a generic option that is stored in the *global.mpt*.
	Duration is entered in: `Days ▾` Choose the default time unit and save time entering data.
	Work is entered in: `Hours ▾` Choose the default time unit and save time entering data.
	Default task type: `Fixed Units ▾` Choose the type of tasks you will use most. This option is meant to be a timesaver.
	☐ **New Tasks are effort driven** This option can lead to Project 2000 changing assignment data; for now, we recommend you turn it off.
	`Set as Default` Sets the options above (except the first one) as the default settings for any new schedules you create. The existing schedules are not affected because these options are stored in the project file. You can read this from the label of the section divider that says **Scheduling Options for 'Project 1'**.

Types of Detail Tasks

For each assignment there are three variables:

◆ Duration is the length of a task expressed in business days.

◆ Units are the percentage of a resource or the number of resources assigned to a task. For a full-time resource it would be 100%, for a half-time resource 50%, for two resources 200%. (You can change it to be shown in decimal numbers via **Tools, Options, Schedule**.)

◆ Work is the amount of effort expressed in person days. A person day is one person working one day full-time.

MS Project uses the following formula for the assignments: *Duration x Units = Work*

	Duration	* Units	= Work
Fixed Duration meeting	2 h	8	16 h
Fixed Units budget	6 h	1	6 h
Fixed Work write report	5 h	2	10 h

There are three kinds of detail tasks: *Fixed Duration*, *Fixed Units* and *Fixed Work* tasks. As their names indicate, each of these three types fixes one of the three variables in the formula. If you enter the fixed variable and a second one, it will calculate the third. If you have a task *meeting* with a fixed duration of 2 business hours, and you invite 8 people to the meeting, Project 2000 will calculate 16 person hours of work. Another example: a task *write report* with 10 person hours of fixed work, could be worked on by two people and Project 2000 will then calculate a duration of 5 business hours. Most of your tasks will be either Fixed Duration or Fixed Work. The Fixed Units task type is useful when you want to make changes to the assignment while keeping the units the same.

The formula does not apply to assignments with a work contour (effort patterned over the duration of the task). Nor does it apply to tasks with multiple assignments that are uneven; where one assignment is longer than another.

The following table suggests the uses of the task types:

Type of task	Use in situations like:
Fixed Duration	♦ If the duration does not decrease when human resources are added, such as backing up a computer system. ♦ Tasks that always have many resources assigned, such as meetings and trainings. ♦ When the deadline is so tight that it determines the durations of the tasks and you have to make it work within that time. ♦ When workload is not the project managers' problem e.g., for external resources, such as subcontractors and consultants.
Fixed Units (default)	When you cannot get more resources to do the work, for example you only have two internal resources. There are not many pure Fixed Units tasks in practice, but this task type has an important role when changing assignment values. We will discuss this on page 286: Changing an Assignment.
Fixed Work	When the effort required is the easiest to estimate or the first thing you estimate. This is often the case. For example, you estimate that painting a family home takes 12 person days of effort or that coding a module in a software application will take 20 person hours.

Estimating and the Types of Tasks

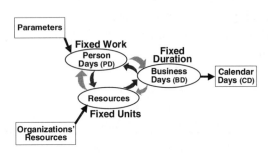

We discussed the process of estimating already in Chapter 4 Entering Estimates. We can now determine the type for each task in the WBS. Some tasks will be treated as Fixed Work tasks, others as Fixed Duration or perhaps Fixed Units tasks. It is important to be aware of the task type when assigning resources, because each type of task makes Project 2000 calculate differently. For example, Project 2000 will never recalculate the duration on a fixed-duration task, but if you add a second resource, it will double the total work on the task. We will therefore insert the column **Type**, so we can see at any point what type of task it is. You may also want to insert the field **Effort Driven** because you want to keep this field to *No* (except for Fixed Work tasks). Insert the field **Work** as well. The layout of columns we recommend is as shown:

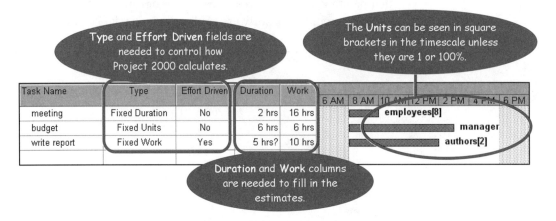

We can now see all three variables of the formula: *Duration x Units = Work*
where *Units* can be seen in the timescale. The resources assigned and the number of units assigned show to the right of the task bars. If there are multiple resources assigned, you have to add up the units.

You could insert the column **Resource Names** as well. This field displays the number of resources used in square brackets after the name of the resource; however, the column is often too narrow.

Designing the View for Assigning Resources

1. Choose **View, Gantt Chart**.

2. Choose **View, Table <current table name>, Entry,** the **Entry** table is applied that has the columns: ❶ , **Task Name, Duration, Start, Finish, Predecessors** and **Resource Names,** respectively.

3. We will insert the column **Type** before the column **Duration**. Right-click on the column **Duration** and choose **Insert Column...** from the pop-up menu; the **Column Definition** dialog appears:

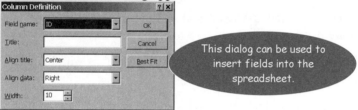

4. Select from the list **Field Name** ID ▾ the column **Type** and click OK .

5. Repeat the steps 3 and 4 for the fields **Effort Driven** and **Work** and insert them in the order as indicated in the snapshot below. Optionally, you could insert **Resource Names** as well, or just look at the assignments and units in the timescale.

Task Name	Type	Effort Driven	Duration	Work	6 AM	8 AM	10 AM	12 PM	2 PM	4 PM	6 PM
meeting	Fixed Duration	No	2 hrs	16 hrs		employees[8]					
budget	Fixed Units	No	6 hrs	6 hrs					manager		
write report	Fixed Work	Yes	5 hrs?	10 hrs				authors[2]			

Entering a Fixed Duration Task

It will take 10 PDs

Person Days (PD)

training of 1 day

resources

10 people will attend

When the duration is fixed, changes in the assignments do not affect it. Examples of *fixed duration tasks* are *training session* and *meeting*. The duration of a meeting or training session is typically decided and will not vary (much) with the number of participants. In the illustration, we see a training of 1 day fixed duration. If 10 people attend, the total work will be calculated as 10 person days.

1. In the Gantt spreadsheet enter the task name and set the task **Type** to **Fixed Duration**. Enter the duration.

2. Enter the work estimate in the field **Work** or assign the resources with the units required; we will discuss how on the next pages.

3. MS Project will have calculated the third variable in the formula $D \times U = W$ (where D=Duration, U=Units and W=Work).

MS Project schedules fixed duration tasks with more than one person assigned sometimes with a split task bar when one of the resources is not available when the others are. This looks strange on a task such as a *meeting*, because the split task bar suggests there will be two meetings. You can solve this by changing the task **Type** to **Fixed Work**.

Entering a Fixed Work Task

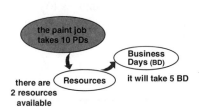

Fixed work tasks are very common. A task is a fixed work task if the first thing you estimate is the amount of effort (work). Once you fix the work, MS Project will calculate either the duration or the necessary number of resources. In the illustration we see the paint job is estimated to take 10 person days. If two people do this job, it will take 5 business days.

1. In the Gantt spreadsheet enter the task name and set the task **Type** to **Fixed Work**. Enter the total work on the task in the field **Work**.

2. Enter the available duration or assign the resources with the units required; we will discuss how on the next pages.

3. MS Project will have calculated the third variable in the formula $D \times U = W$ (where D=Duration, U=Units and W=Work).

Entering a Fixed Units Task

For fixed units tasks you know the number of available resources for the task. You want the duration or total work to be calculated by Project 2000. The illustration shows an example in which there are 2 resources available for the job. You know it normally takes 10 person days of work. The resulting duration is 5 business days.

1. In the Gantt spreadsheet enter the task name and set the task **Type** to **Fixed Units.** Enter the duration, or the work, of the task.

2. Assign the resource with the units needed; we will discuss how on the next pages.

3. MS Project will have calculated the third variable in the formula $D \times U = W$ (where D=Duration, U=Units and W=Work).

The **Fixed Units** task type is mostly used when you want to make changes to the task or its assignments. The fixed units task type allows you to keep the assigned units the same when you change the work or the duration.

Overview Assigning

The following are the many different ways you can assign resources to tasks. The methods are listed from simple to sophisticated.

◆ **Task Sheet** view: you can assign at max units only.

◆ **Assign Resources** dialog box. You can assign resource units or work.

◆ **Task Information** dialog box.
   ◇ You can assign units or work.
   ◇ You can create multiple assignments in once.

◆ **Task Form** view.
   ◇ You can assign units and work.
   ◇ You can create multiple assignments in once.

◆ **Task Usage** or **Resource Usage** view.
   You can assign work "day-by-day" and create variable workloads. Only in the **Task Usage** or **Resource Usage** view can you enter workload that varies over the duration of the task. In all other situations, you create a flat workload when assigning. Generally, flat workloads are a good enough approximation of the true workload. If it isn't, you should consider breaking up the tasks into smaller tasks or using the work contour feature. Predefined *work contours* allow you to spread the work across the task duration in a certain pattern.

There are many ways to apply resources to tasks. The more sophisticated the method, the more detail it allows you to enter about the assignment. It is important to enter only as much detail as you need, because all data needs to be maintained for the life of the project. During project execution, you will have little time to maintain the schedule.

We will discuss two methods in more detail: **Assign Resources** dialog, and the **Task Form** view. The Assign Resources dialog allows you to drag resources onto tasks and is fast. The Task Form allows you to enter the units and the work for one or more resources at a time and is flexible. Together these two methods will give you the speed AND the flexibility you may need.

Assign Using the Assign Resources Dialog

Assigning Resources by Dragging

1. Click 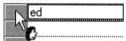; the **Assign Resources** floating dialog appears:

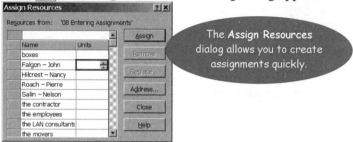

The **Assign Resources** dialog allows you to create assignments quickly.

2. Click on the resource to assign.

3. Point to the resource selector ▢; the mouse pointer now has a person's head attached:

4. Click, drag and drop the resource onto the task you want to assign to. The resource is now assigned; it has a check mark in front of its name. It also shows in the field **Resource Names** and to the right of the task bar in the timescale.

When you drag resources onto tasks, Project 2000 assigns:

◆ individual resources to their maximum availability (**Max. Units**)

◆ only one unit of consolidated resources

Assigning Multiple Resources to Multiple Tasks

1. Click 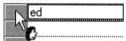; the **Assign Resources** floating dialog appears.

2. Select the tasks to assign by dragging over them.
   OR

   Select by holding down Ctrl and clicking on them, if you want to randomly select tasks.

3. Select the resources you want to assign by holding down `Ctrl` and clicking on their resource selector ☐ in the **Assign Resources** dialog:

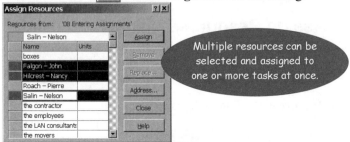

Multiple resources can be selected and assigned to one or more tasks at once.

4. Click ☐ **Assign** ; a check mark appears in the resource selector: ☑.

To Enter the Units on an Assignment

1. Select the task(s).

2. Click ☐; the **Assign Resources** dialog appears.

3. Enter the percentage of the resource or the number of resources you need in the field **Units**. The units should be entered as a percentage or as decimals, depending on the setting in **Tools, Options, Schedule, Show assignments units as**.

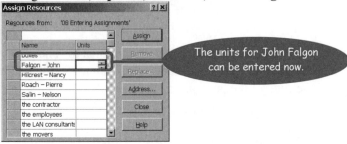

The units for John Falgon can be entered now.

4. Click ☐ **Assign** .

 If you change an assignment, Project 2000 may (re)calculate the work if it is a **Fixed Duration** task, or the duration if it is a **Fixed Work** task.

 The **Units** field asks for units to be entered but you can even enter the work in this field and Project 2000 will calculate the units required. If you want to do so, you have to make sure you include the time unit, as in *5d*, to make it clear that Project 2000 should interpret your entry as work instead of units.

To Delete an Assignment

1. Display the **Assign Resources** dialog by clicking .

2. Select the resource that is assigned. The check marks ✓ in front of the resource
    names indicate which resources are assigned to the selected task(s):

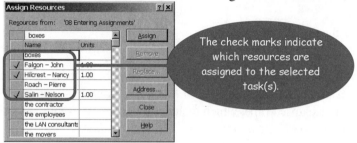

The check marks indicate which resources are assigned to the selected task(s).

3. Click on an assigned resource and change the number assigned in the field **Units**.

4. Click Remove .

Assign Using the Task Form

Fields on the Task Form

◆ *Name*
A descriptive title for the task.

◆ *Duration*
How long the task will take. Type a number followed by an abbreviation indicating the time period. For example, *4d* means *4 days of 8 hours*. Duration is working time only by default, or can be elapsed time, which includes holidays, weekends, vacations, and nights (*4ed* means *4 days of 24 hours*).

◆ *Effort Driven*
Effort driven will keep the total amount of work constant while adding or removing resources. This option only kicks in after entering the assignments the first time. Work will be redistributed among the resources (keeping the relative workloads the same). Fixed work tasks are always effort driven.

◆ *Start*
MS Project automatically calculates the start date based on task dependencies. If you type a date, MS Project sets a Start-No-Earlier-Than constraint date for the task, which forces MS Project to schedule the task on or after that date. We don't recommend entering dates because the constraints make the model less dynamic.

◆ *Finish*
MS Project calculates the finish date based on the start date plus the total duration. If you type a date, MS Project sets a Finish-No-Earlier-Than constraint for the task. We don't recommend entering dates.

◆ *Task Type*
Detail tasks come in three kinds: Fixed Duration tasks, Fixed Units tasks, and Fixed Work tasks.

◆ *% Complete*
A percentage showing how much of the task duration is completed. We will discuss this in the Chapter 11 Updating the Schedule.

To Assign

1. In the Gantt Chart, choose **Window, Split**.
   OR
   Double-click on the sliding window handle at the bottom right of the screen to display
   the Task Form:

   the sliding window handle

2. On the Task Form we need to see at least the fields: **Resource Name**, **Units** and
   Work. To display these click on the Task Form and choose **Format, Details,
   Resource Work**.
   OR
   Right-click on the task form and choose **Resource Work**. The Task Form now looks
   like:

   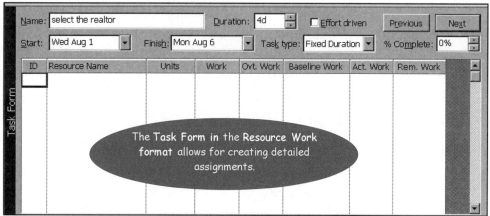

   The **Task Form** in the **Resource Work**
   format allows for creating detailed
   assignments.

3. On the Task Form click in the field **Resource Name** and a list button will appear:

   If you click on the list button, the
   list of resources is displayed.

4. Click the list button and select a resource from the list that appears. Fill in the **Units**
   (the percentage of a full-time equivalent resource) and/or the **Work** (person hours of
   effort needed). You can assign more than one resource at a time, which is easy to do
   on this form.

5. Click OK .

To Delete an Assignment

1. On the **Task Form**, select the assigned resource.

2. Click on the resource to remove and press Delete .

3. Click OK .

Entering Multiple Uneven Assignments

If there are multiple assignments on a task, often one of the assignments drives the duration of the task. The assignment that takes the longest to complete will drive the duration of the task. Example: if three painters, *Joe*, *Frank* and *Mary*, are assigned to paint a house and *Joe* will work ten days and *Frank* only the first six days and *Mary* the last five days, the duration will be ten days. *Joe* determines the duration of the paint job.

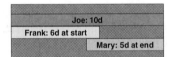

1. In the Gantt Chart, display the Task Form by choosing **Window, Split**.

2. To enter multiple uneven assignments, set the task **Type** to **Fixed Units** on the Task Form.

3. Select the resources from the **Resource Name** list: [▼] and enter the different amounts of **Work** for each assigned resource.

4. Click OK ; you can see the result of the uneven assignments by choosing **View, Task Usage**.

Task Name	Details	Dec 31, 00							Jan 7, 01					
		S	M	T	W	T	F	S	S	M	T	W	T	F
⊟ write	Work		16h	16h	16h	16h	16h			24h	16h	16h	16h	16h
Joe	Work		8h	8h	8h	8h	8h			8h	8h	8h	8h	8h
Frank	Work		8h	8h	8h	8h	8h			8h				
Mary	Work		0h	0h	0h	0h	0h			8h	8h	8h	8h	8h

Mary's assignment is scheduled on the last 5 days of the task duration.

Typically, the resources with the least work finish early, unless you change their assignment start date. In the illustration *Mary* drives the task finish date as much as *Joe*.

The formula $D \times U = W$ does not apply on a task with multiple uneven assignments.

We don't recommend you create more than one assignment with different start dates on a task. The project schedule will stay simpler if you split the task into more tasks, one for each assignment. Where people need to get together as a group, you can create a short meeting task. In the example given, the meeting could take place on day six.

Assigning to Recurring Tasks

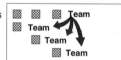

If you assign a resource on the summary *recurring task* the assignments are immediately transferred to the detail tasks. This is done automatically, compliments of Project 2000.

You should only assign to recurring tasks, such as status meetings, if the efforts for these meetings are not included in the task estimates of the resources.

You could assign in situations such as:

◆ the meetings are lengthy and therefore require considerable effort (work) of the resources, or

◆ you require attendance at the meetings and you want to show them in the to-do lists.

Changing an Assignment

Before you change any of the three variables in the formula $D \times U = W$, you should always think <u>first</u> about the task type you need for that change. With every change, Project 2000 will recalculate a value and it may not recalculate the one you want, if you don't think about the task type first.

Changes that will trigger a recalculation are, among others:
◆ changing the duration (D) of a task by entering a new duration or by stretching the task bar with the mouse.
◆ adding a resource to a task, units (U) were changed
◆ changing the work (W) of a task or of one of its assignments.

The **Type** of the task and the **Effort Driven** attribute determine how MS Project will react. The steps to change an assignment are:

1. Choose and set the task **Type** first. You can determine the appropriate task type by asking yourself: *Which value do I want to keep the same?* For example, if you want to keep the duration the same, you should set the **Type** to **Fixed Duration**.

2. Ensure **Effort Driven** is set to *Yes* only for **Fixed Work** tasks.

3. Then make the change on the assignment you wanted to make.

By choosing a **Type** for a task, you fix one of its three values in the formula. Changing the fixed value itself is tricky because then it is hard to predict what MS Project will recalculate. If you reconsider the type of the task first, you will always be able to predict what MS Project will do. To find the appropriate type you need for the change, ask yourself again: *Which value in the formula do I want to keep the same?* The answer to this question will tell you which task type you need. For example, if you want to keep the number of resource units the same, you need **Fixed Units**. If you want to keep the duration the same you need **Fixed Duration**. If you want to keep the total amount of work on the task the same, you need **Fixed Work**. The task Type is not something you set once and never look at again. You continue to monitor it in order to control how Project 2000 calculates.

Here is an example of how this works. Assume you have a fixed units task *write* of 4 days duration. The task has one resource assigned and you want to add a second resource.

This will show in Project 2000 as:

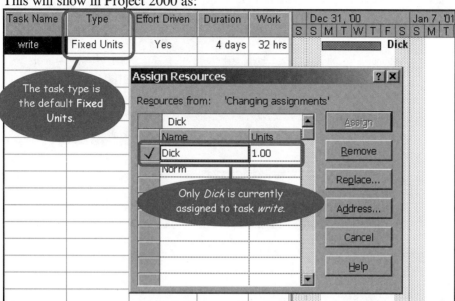

Task Name	Type	Effort Driven	Duration	Work
write	Fixed Units	Yes	4 days	32 hrs

The task type is the default **Fixed Units**.

Assign Resources

Resources from: 'Changing assignments'

Dick

Name	Units
✓ Dick	1.00
Norm	

Only *Dick* is currently assigned to task *write*.

Assign
Remove
Replace...
Address...
Cancel
Help

If you have underestimated the work, you want Project 2000 to increase the work when you add the resource. You want the duration to stay the same. First you change the task **Type** to *Fixed Duration*, and **Effort Driven** to *No*, then you add the second resource.

The work has doubled from *32 hrs* to *64 hrs* as is shown in the next snapshot:

Task Name	Type	Effort Driven	Duration	Work	Dec 31, 00 / Jan 7, 01
write	Fixed Duration	No	4 days	64 hrs	Dick,Norm

*Work has doubled from 32 to 64 hrs, because the task **Type** is **Fixed Duration**.*

Assign Resources

Resources from: 'Changing assi...

Norm	
Name	Units
✓ Dick	1.00
✓ Norm	1.00

Norm is added to task.

Remove

Replace...

Address...

Close

Help

If you want to add a resource to a **Fixed Duration** task the work goes up, but if you add a resource to a **Fixed Work** task the duration will go down.

Often you will find that you want to keep the assigned units the same on a task while changing the duration or the work. In this case you will need the **Fixed Units** task type. This task type is very useful when making changes. It is more a transitional task type, after using it you normally set the task type back to **Fixed Duration** or **Fixed Work**.

For example: if you change the work on a **Fixed Units** task, Project 2000 will recalculate the duration. For example, the Duration = 10 days, Units = 1 (fixed), Work = 10 days. If you change the work to 5 days, Project 2000 will decrease the duration from 10 to 5 days; one person can deliver five person days of effort (work) in five business days (duration).

Never change the fixed value itself. Project 2000 is harder to predict when you change the fixed value itself. Always set the appropriate task type first, before changing the fixed value itself.

When there are multiple assignments, one (or more) of the assignments can drive the duration of the task. Before you can make a change, you should find out which assignment(s) drive(s) the duration of the task. Consider changing that assignment instead.

 Notice that when you apply the task type **Fixed Work** the attribute *Effort Driven* is turned on by Project 2000. When you change to a different task type again the **Effort Driven** attribute sticks. This may create unexpected recalculations, if you don't deactivate again. You can display the task-related field **Effort Driven** and toggle it to *No*. Effort-driven tasks act similar to Fixed Work tasks and are redundant.

 To replace a resource for another one use the **Assign Resources** dialog 🖼️, select the assigned resource and click Replace... . Select the new one and click OK .

Printing the Assignments

The **Task Usage** view shows all the assignments in detail. Choose **View, Task Usage** to apply it. This view shows all assignments below the tasks.

#	O	Task Name	Work	Details	T	W	T	F	S	S	M	T	W	T	F	S
1		⊟ REQUIREMENTS	4 d	Work		0.57d	0.6d	0.6d			0.53d	0.5d	0.5d	0.5d	0.2d	
2		⊟ research staff requirements	2 d	Work		0.57d	0.6d	0.6d			0.23d					
		you	2 d	Work		0.57d	0.6d	0.6d			0.23d					
3		⊟ summarize requirements	2 d	Work							0.3d	0.5d	0.5d	0.5d	0.2d	
		Hilcrest – Nancy	2 d	Work							0.3d	0.5d	0.5d	0.5d	0.2d	
4		⊟ LOCATION	13.5 d	Work		0.57d	0.6d	0.6d			0.67d	3.87d			2.23d	
5		⊟ select the realtor	2.3 d	Work		0.57d	0.6d	0.6d			0.53d					
		you	2.3 d	Work		0.57d	0.6d	0.6d			0.53d					
6		⊟ visit the sites	4 d	Work							0.13d	3.87d				
		Falgon – John	1 d	Work							0d	1d				
		Hilcrest – Nancy	1 d	Work							0d	1d				
		the realtor	1 d	Work							0d	1d				
		you	1 d	Work							0.13d	0.87d				
7		⊟ evaluate the sites	3.7 d	Work											2.23d	
		Falgon – John	1 d	Work											0.6d	
		Hilcrest – Nancy															
		the realtor															
		you															
8	🔲	⊟ meet to select the locati														
		Falgon – John															
		Hilcrest – Nancy															
		Salin – Nelson															
		you															
9		⊟ legal review															
		Roach – Pierre															
10	◆	location selected	0 d	Work												
11		⊟ REMODELING CONTRACT	7.4 d	Work												
12		⊟ select the contractor	2.4 d	Work												
		you	2.4 d	Work												
13		⊟ meet to discuss contract	3 d	Work												

The italic resource names below the task are its assignments. If you double-click on them the **Assignment Information** dialog appears.

In the timescale you can exactly see how Project 2000 scheduled the work assigned.

To show the assignments below each resource, choose **View**, **Resource Usage**:

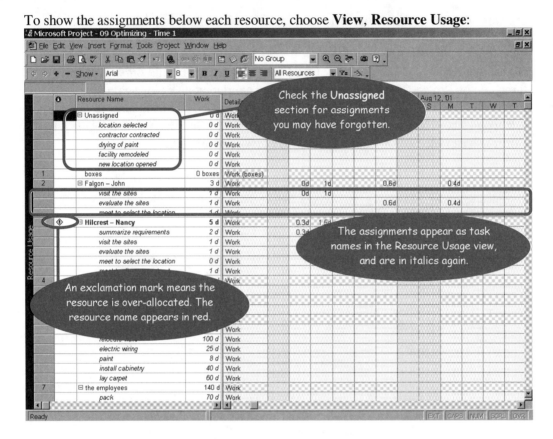

If you don't see the numbers in the timescale, select a task (or resource) and click **Go to selected task** . To change the time unit, use the **Zoom In** or the **Zoom Out** tools.

Alternatively, there are assignment reports available.

1. Choose **View, Reports**, the **Reports** dialog appears:

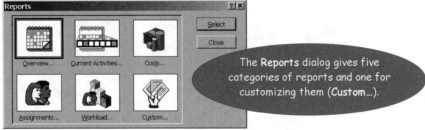

2. Double-click the button **Assignments…** , the **Assignment Reports** dialog appears:

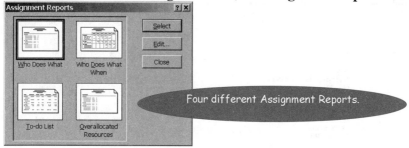

Four different Assignment Reports.

3. You can choose from:

◇ **Who Does What**
This report is similar to the Resource Usage view; the assignments are listed below the tasks.

◇ **Who Does What When**
The work on each task is shown spread over time.

◇ **To-Do List**
You will be prompted to select a resource and the report shows all the tasks with their start and finish times.

◇ **Overallocated Resources**
This report shows only the resources that are over-allocated with all their assignments (including the ones that cause the over-allocation).

Here is an example of a **To-Do List** report:

To Do List as of Sat Dec 23
Relocation Devom Inc.
Eric Uyttewaal

ID		Task Name	Type	Duration
Week of July 29				
2		research staff requirements	Fixed Work	4 days?
5		select the realtor	Fixed Duration	4 days
Week of August 5				
2		research staff requirements	Fixed Work	4 days?
5		select the realtor	Fixed Duration	4 days
6		visit the sites	Fixed Duration	1 day
7		evaluate the sites	Fixed Duration	1 day
Week of August 12				
7		evaluate the sites	Fixed Duration	1 day
Week of August 19				
8		meet to select the location	Fixed Duration	1 day
12		select the contractor	Fixed Duration	2 days
27		select mover	Fixed Duration	2 days
Week of August 26				
12		select the contractor	Fixed Duration	2 days
27		select mover	Fixed Duration	2 days
Week of September 2				
13		meet to discuss contract	Fixed Duration	1 day
14		revise the schedule	Fixed Duration	1 day
15		negotiate the contract	Fixed Duration	1 day

Exercises

Review A

Read the following situations and determine if you will make the first estimate in person days work (PD), in business day duration (BD) or in elapsed day duration (ED). Explain why and indicate which type of task: Fixed Duration (FD), Fixed Units (FU) or Fixed Work (FW) you recommend.

1. Writing a report of ten pages that normally takes one person four hours per page to produce.

2. One load to be transported over a distance of 4000 miles with one driver.

3. One package that has to be flown over a distance of over 4000 miles. It has to be there in two working days.

4. Painting a house and, as the painter, you are asked for a fixed price quote and the earliest end date.

5. Painting a building and, as the contractor, you give the painter a maximum of two weeks to complete the job in your schedule.

6. Backing up a computer system before the conversion to a new operating system. Once started, the backing up requires little supervision.

7. A meeting with a presentation to all employees.

Review B

A resource is writing two different documents concurrently and you cannot plan when he is working on one or the other. How would you model this situation in Project 2000, and, in particular, which assignments would you make?

Relocation Project – Entering Assignments

Continue to work with your file *Relocation.MPP* or open the file
08 Entering Assignments.MPP in the sub-directory *Relocation Project* on the CD-ROM.

Enter the assignments as shown in the table below. First, add the fields **Type, Duration**
and **Work** to the Gantt Chart view in such a way that the view matches the WBS column
headings in the table below.

Remember that MS Project uses the formula: *Duration x Units = Work*. We recommend
the following steps for entering assignments:

◆ Enter the **Type** of the task first, then enter the fixed value in the field: **Duration** or
Work.

◆ Enter the second value.

◆ Let MS Project calculate the third value in the formula. Notice, that in the table
below, for each detail task one of the three variables is not provided. MS Project will
calculate it.

Think about the easiest way to enter each assignment: using the **Task Information** dialog
box, the **Assign Resources** or the **Task Form**. Only the **Fixed Work** tasks are **Effort
Driven**.

WBS				ASSIGNMENTS	
Task Name	Type	Dur.	Work	Resources	Units
REQUIREMENTS	*Fixed Duration*				
research staff requirements	*Fixed Work*		2d	*you*	0.5
summarize requirements	*Fixed Work*		2d	*Hilcrest*	0.5
LOCATION	*Fixed Duration*				
select the realtor	*Fixed Duration*	4 d		*you*	0.5
visit the sites	*Fixed Duration*	1 d		*Falgon* *Hilcrest* *the realtor* *you*	1 1 1 1

WBS				ASSIGNMENTS	
Task Name	Type	Dur.	Work	Resources	Units
evaluate the sites	*Fixed Duration*	*1 d*		*Falgon*	*1*
				Hilcrest	*1*
				the realtor	*0.5*
				you	*1*
meet to select the location	*Fixed Duration*	*1 d*		*Falgon*	*1*
				Hilcrest	*1*
				Salin	*1*
				you	*1*
legal review	*Fixed Duration*	*0.5 d*		*Roach*	*1*
REMODELING CONTRACT	*Fixed Duration*				
select the contractor	*Fixed Duration*	*2 d*		*you*	*1*
meet to discuss contract	*Fixed Duration*	*1 d*		*the contractor*	*1*
				Hilcrest	*1*
				you	*1*
revise the schedule	*Fixed Duration*	*1 d*		*you*	*1*
negotiate the contract	*Fixed Duration*	*1 d*		*you*	*1*
REMODELED LOCATION	*Fixed Duration*				
relocate walls	*Fixed Work*	*10 d*	*100 d*	*the contractor* [23]	
electric wiring	*Fixed Work*	*5 d*	*25 d*	*the contractor*	
paint	*Fixed Work*	*2 d*	*8 d*	*the contractor*	
drying of paint	*Fixed Duration*	*4 ed*			
install cabinetry	*Fixed Work*	*5 d*	*40 d*	*the contractor*	
install LAN	*Fixed Work*		*60 d*	*the LAN consultants*	*5*
lay carpet	*Fixed Work*	*10 d*	*60 d*	*the contractor*	
MOVE	*Fixed Duration*				

[23] Notice that the Duration and Work are both filled in already; MS Project just needs to know who will be assigned. MS Project will then calculate the number of units needed from the resource; you don't need to fill the units in.

WBS				ASSIGNMENTS	
Task Name	**Type**	**Dur.**	**Work**	**Resources**	**Units**
select mover	*Fixed Duration*	*2 d*		*you*	*1*
pack	*Fixed Duration*	*2 d*		*the employees* *boxes*	*35* *400*
move	*Fixed Duration*	*2 d*		*the movers*	*10*
unpack	*Fixed Duration*	*2 d*		*the employees*	*35*

Compare your file with the solution file *09 Optimizing – Time 1.MPP* in the sub-directory *Relocation Project* on the CD-ROM. Notice that the project is missing its November 1st deadline. We will need to optimize the schedule.

Relocation Project – Changing Assignments

Continue to work with your file *Relocation.MPP* or open the file *09 Optimizing – Time 1.MPP* in the sub-directory *Relocation Project* on the CD-ROM.

How should you go about making the following changes to the assignments? You may need to change the **Type** of the task first. The task *install LAN* currently has a duration of 6 days, 10 consultants working on it and 60 days of work.

1. You would like to know how long the task *install LAN* would take if the *LAN consultants* would work with 10 consultants instead of 5?
    You should get a duration of 6 days. Keep this change.

2. You want to know how many consultants are needed if you want *install LAN* to be done in 3 days.
    You should find that 20 *LAN consultants* are needed. Keep this change.

3. You think you over-estimated the work; and you will need only 30 days instead of 60 days and you want to keep the duration 3 days. What is the number of consultants needed now?
    You should find 10 consultants are needed. Keep this change.

4. You want to keep the number of consultants to 10, but you want to change the duration from 3 to 6 days. How much work is now on the task?
    You should end up with 60 days of work, which brings us back to where we were at the start of this exercise after exploring the various scenarios.

Troubleshooting

1. Open the **Assign Resources** dialog and try to close MS Project by choosing **File, Exit**. Can you do this? Why?

Chapter 9 Optimizing the Schedule

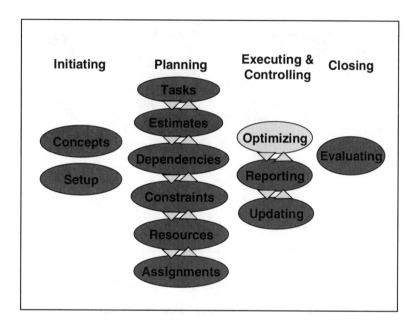

After entering the schedule data we now have a dynamic model of our project that tells us whether the project is feasible as we envisioned it. In most situations the schedule will show that the duration is too long, or the cost is too high or the workloads are unreasonable. In some cases, all are off. With a dynamic model we can now explore different scenarios to find the best solution. We can optimize for time, for time and cost or for time, cost and resource availability.

After this chapter you will:
- be able to optimize the project for time
  - ◇ be able to display the Critical Path
  - ◇ be able to solve a fragmented Critical Path
  - ◇ be able to apply several methods to shorten the project
- be able to optimize the project for time and cost
- be able to optimize the project for time, cost and resource availability
  - ◇ know how to level the workloads of the resources
  - ◇ be able to find and shorten the Resource-Critical Path
- be able to track the impact of changes to the schedule

Crashing Into the Deadline

Nob sits down to lunch with Bob. Nob is curious. "How did you make that impossible project work?"

"Well, it wasn't all that impossible ... we did meet the tight deadline!"

"Everybody thought you were putting your career on the line by taking on that project!"

"Everybody ... including me! We had to use every trick in the book to make it work!"

"So, what's your secret?"

Bob explains: "We attended a workshop in which the instructor challenged us to work in teams and crashing a schedule as much as we reasonably could. I learned that if you apply all methods, you often find more time in your schedule than you think you will."

"Where did you find that time? Did you add resources? Was your cost still within budget?"

"Our cost was only slightly over. Instead of adding more resources, we brainstormed long and hard about which tasks we could do in parallel. We overlapped tasks as much as we could using partial dependencies and we got rid of waiting times... that was really all we did! These methods are called 'fast-tracking'. It's a matter of working smarter instead of harder."

The Pulling Forces

Scope
Quality
Time
Procurement — Project — Cost
Communications
Resources
Risk

Adapted from
PMBOK® Guide 2000
Exposure Draft

Optimizing a schedule is the true art of scheduling. When optimizing you have to consider the project in all its aspects. The Project Management Institute has identified the dimensions by which projects need to be optimized in its Guide to the Project Management Body of Knowledge (PMBOK® Guide).[24] A change in one area often impacts another. On each project eight forces are at work and project managers have to consider all of them in an integrated fashion. The PMBOK calls this Project Integration Management. Project 2000 provides sufficient features for most, but not all, eight areas:

◆ **Quality**
The quality of deliverables must be according to the specifications and expectations of the client. You can schedule quality activities in Project 2000, but the tool does not provide a full-fledged quality management system. However, quality can and should always be considered while optimizing.

◆ **Scope**
The scope of a project can be captured using the WBS. It contains the deliverables to be produced and the activities can be derived from them. Project 2000 is an excellent tool for managing scope.

◆ **Time**
Deadlines can be scheduled and managed very well in Project 2000.

◆ **Cost**
You can manage resource and material expenses with Project 2000 so they stay within the restrictions of your budget.

---

[24] The 2000 Edition of the PMBOK® Guide.

◆ **Resources**

The workloads have to stay within the availability of the human resources. You can do resource leveling with Project 2000. Although, one issue we will have to deal with is when you level resource workloads, the Critical Path can become fragmented. We will discuss the new concept of a Resource Critical Path.

◆ **Risk**

Risk management activities can be scheduled in Project 2000, but it does not have features for Risk Management Planning, Risk Identification, Qualitative Risk Analysis, Quantitative Risk Analysis, Risk Response Planning and Risk Monitoring and Control[25]. Project 2000 does allow you to introduce some probability into the schedule with PERT, but does not provide full-fledged Monte Carlo simulation capabilities. There are add-on tools that can complement Project 2000. We will discuss simulation as a technique.

◆ **Communications**

You can create a variety of reports in Project 2000, but the software is not a complete document configuration management system. Such a system is needed for project communication management in complex projects. Project Central enhances the communications features of Project 2000 tremendously.

◆ **Procurement**

Project 2000 is not a contract management system; a separate system is needed for managing procurement in projects.

Improving one aspect often impacts the others. When the impact is negative you are trading off between the dimensions. For example, if you hire more resources to meet a tight deadline, the impact may be positive on time, but negative on cost. Sometimes, you can find methods that are positive in more than one respect and neutral in others. These are the methods to find and apply first. We will make several suggestions.

---

[25] The new breakdown of the Project Risk Management knowledge area in the PMBOK® Guide, 2000 Edition.

Overview Optimizing Schedules

In all optimizing approaches we will include the consideration of Quality and Scope. Because these two dimensions do not differentiate the approaches, we have not included the words Quality or Scope in the name of each approach. We will discuss three optimizing approaches:

◆ **Optimizing for Time**

This approach is also known as *'optimizing under the assumption of unlimited resources'*. The other approaches will not assume that you have access to unlimited resources. You have access to unlimited resources if you can hire and fire (or release) any resource you need and if cost is not of primary concern. You need only consider the forces: quality, scope and time. Under this assumption, you can use the Critical Path Method (CPM). Many industries have been using CPM for decades. Typically, the construction and consulting industries apply CPM. Many others find this optimization too narrow.

◆ **Optimizing for Time and Cost**

If you can possibly find more money to solve quality, scope or time problems, you should apply this approach. You could use money to buy better raw materials, to rent better equipment or to pay penalties for late delivery. If you use the extra money to hire more people, or rent more facilities or equipment, you should use the next approach.

◆ **Optimizing for Time, Cost and Resources**

If you must also consider the availability and the capacity of the resources to arrive at a feasible schedule of your project, you should use this approach. You are making trade-off decisions between quality, scope, time, cost, and resource availability. For example, a decision to pay extra to get more overtime. If you treat resources as scarce you will have to look at their availability and their workload. The first thing you do is level the workloads. Leveling often disjoints the Critical Path and we cannot simply use CPM any longer. The approach we will suggest is called the *Resource-Critical Path*.

As you can see, we are adding a dimension every time and the optimizations will become more complex as we go along. Including five out of the eight dimensions is the most complex optimization we will discuss in this book.

Choosing the Options

The following options are relevant for all optimizing approaches:

Tools	Option
Tools, Options, View	☑ **Show Summary Tasks** and ☑ **Project Summary Task** The project summary task is inserted at the top of the task list and summarizes the entire project because everything is indented beneath it. The project summary task is useful when optimizing because it displays the total cost and duration of the project. Existing schedules are not affected because this option is stored in the project file, as you can see from the label of this section **Outline Options for 'Project 1'.**
	Set as Default Sets the options chosen as the default settings for any new file you create. Existing files are not affected.
Tools, Options, Calculation	**Tasks are Critical if Slack is less than or equal to** 0 This field creates a threshold for making tasks critical or not. Normally, this option is set to zero, which means that Project 2000 shows the task with zero slack, or with a negative slack as critical and colored red. This option is also stored in the project file.
Tools, Resource Leveling	Under **Leveling calculations:** ◉ **Manual** Automatic leveling continuously levels the workloads. Project 2000 accomplishes this by delaying tasks. In time or cost optimizations there is no need to level the workloads. This option is a generic option that takes effect in all your project files. If you switch the option to **Manual**, you could delete any traces of leveling left in the task field **Leveling Delay** by choosing **Tools, Resource Leveling,** Clear Leveling... .

Optimizing for Time

Scope

Quality

Time

Procurement ⟨⟩ Project ⟩ Cost

Communications

Risk

Resources

Adapted from
PMBOK® Guide 2000
Exposure Draft

The dimensions that we will consider in this type of optimization are quality, scope and time.

When you use the Critical Path you are essentially doing a time optimization. The technique for this type of optimization is the Critical Path Method (CPM). Many project managers have gotten used to considering cost and resource availability while crashing the Critical Path. We will not do that. We will discuss the CPM method here in its original form and discuss including other factors in the other approaches.

Techniques

◆ **The Critical Path Method (CPM)**
The CPM is a beautiful product of human logic. The beauty lies in the fact that it really helps project managers meet their deadlines by highlighting the tasks that are most likely to affect the project deadline.
Finding and highlighting the Critical Path in your schedule is known as the *Critical Path Method*. A critical task does not have buffer time, or slack, and any delay experienced on a critical task will slip your project end date. The CPM uses one duration estimate for each task.

◆ **The PERT Method**
Program Evaluation and Review Technique (PERT) technique is a more sophisticated application of the CPM. Instead of one duration estimate for each task, the PERT uses three estimates for each task: Optimistic (O), Realistic (R) and Pessimistic (P). These durations are converted to one duration with the following formula: Expected Duration = (O + 4 x R + P) / 6. After the expected durations have been calculated, CPM can again be applied to the schedule.

Project 2000 has a toolbar **PERT Analysis** that enables you to apply the PERT-method to your schedule. Right-click on a toolbar and choose **PERT Analysis**. Click the **PERT Entry Sheet** tool and enter the estimates. Then click the

Calculate PERT tool to have Project 2000 calculate the expected durations in the **Duration** field.

◆ **Simulation of the Schedule**
Another way to make probability visible is by subjecting the schedule to Monte Carlo Simulation. This type of simulation creates many versions of the same schedule based on the probability ranges you provide for the estimates. The simulation software then calculates averages over all the versions. For more on Monte Carlo Simulation, see page 333.

We will elaborate on CPM and Simulation.

The Critical Path Method (CPM)

Finding the Critical Path in your network of dependencies is determining how long your project will take. The concept of the Critical Path is fairly simple. Observe the situation in the illustration. It is a simple authoring project: *outline* the document, *write* the text, *edit* the text, while somebody else *makes graphics*. When the text and the graphics are ready, the *format* can be done and the project is finished. All arrows are Finish-to-Start dependencies. Before we discuss the Critical Path theory, you should ask yourself the question: *What is the minimum duration for this project*?

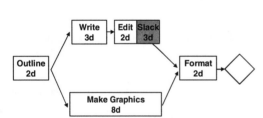

It does not take a rocket scientist to find that the duration for this project is 12 days. If you found the right answer, you understand the concept. You can find the Critical Path by comparing two parallel paths. You add the durations and the lags on each path and compare the totals. The longest one is the Critical Path. You continue comparing the parallel paths until you have checked them all and found the Critical Path for the project.

Parallel chains make a network of which all but one have slack. Sometimes a few chains are equally as critical. Slack exists on a chain of tasks when it is performed in parallel with another chain that takes more time. The longest chain in the network is the Critical Path. The Critical Path determines the minimum duration of the project. The duration that is feasible for the project may be longer when resources are over-allocated.

Over-allocations may force tasks to be delayed. Only when there are many parallel paths is it a challenge to find the Critical Path in the network.

Let's have a look at how Project 2000 goes about finding the Critical Path. It makes a forward pass and a backward pass through the network and then calculates the slack on each task.

Forward Pass

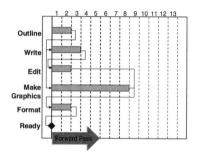

Project 2000 starts with the first task, looks at its duration, and calculates the earliest date it can be ready. This is the **Early Finish** date. The *outline* will be ready at the end of day 2. It will then continue determining the **Early Start** date of its successor(s). *Write* and *make graphics* are the successors; they can start on day 3. The early start date of the successors will be the same as the early finish date of *outline*, unless other dependencies into the successor cause it to start later. Project 2000 continues to calculate the early finish for *write* and *make graphics*.

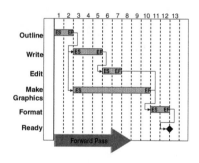

On the forward pass MS Project calculates two dates for each task: the early start (ES) and the early finish (EF) date. The result of this forward pass is shown in the second illustration.

In the illustration, *Format* cannot start until both *edit* and *make graphics* are finished and the earliest start date for *Format* is therefore day 11. Project 2000 continues through the last task in the chain. The software now knows what the earliest finish date is for the project, in the example – day 12.

Backward Pass

Project 2000 then goes backward through the network starting at the project end date to calculate the late finish dates for the tasks. The **Late Finish** date is the latest date a task should be finished in order to meet the project end date. By subtracting the duration of the task, MS Project then calculates the late start date. The **Late Start** date means the latest date you can start working on the task to have it finish by its late finish date. For *Format,* this is day 11, the same as its early date. We then continue with the late finish dates of the predecessors. *Edit* can finish, at the latest, on day 10 and the project will still end on the same date. *Edit* has a late finish date that is three days later than its early finish date. *Edit* has slack.

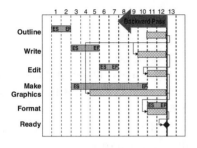

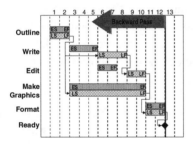

If a task has more than one successor, like *Outline*, Project 2000 takes all successors into consideration. The earliest successor determines the late finish date of the task, in this case day 2 (*Make Graphics*), not day 5 (*Write*). So, the latest finish for making the *outline* is determined by the late start date of *Make Graphics*, and not the late start date of *Write*.

Calculating Slack

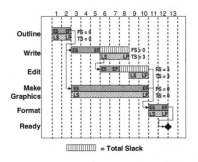

||||||||||| = Total Slack

Total slack is the amount of time you can delay a task without affecting the project end date. The Total Slack (TS) of a task is the difference of the **Late Finish** date minus the **Early Finish** date:

$$TS = LF - EF$$

It tells how much a task can slip before delaying the whole project. For example, the task *write* has three days of total slack. If the author calls you and tells you he fell sick, you will ask immediately "*Do you think you will be better within 3 days?*" If he says no, you know you should find somebody else. You can't permit the project to slip. If he says yes, you may still have a problem because the editor will now receive the text later, which might cause conflicts in her planning.

Where the late finish date is equal to the early finish date there is no slack; the task is by definition on the Critical Path. A task can be delayed for as much Total Slack as it has. Beyond that, it will delay the project as a whole.

Tasks with a *negative slack* are tasks that are late; they don't meet the project deadline or constraint dates set in the schedule.

The *Free Slack* (FS) is the difference of the **Early Start** of the task's successor minus the **Early Finish** date of the task itself:

$$FS = ES_{successor} - EF$$

If there are multiple successors, the earliest one has to be taken. Creating the *outline* of the document has two successors in the example and is most constrained by the early start of *Make Graphics*. As a result it does not have Free Slack. The Free Slack tells you how much you can slip the task before it affects any of its successors. The Free Slack is always less than or equal to the Total Slack. The difference between Total Slack and Free Slack manifests itself in the task *Write*; it has no Free Slack but 3 days of Total Slack. It can use the Free Slack of its successor *Edit*.

Project 2000 generates all the dates discussed and you can find these dates in the task fields **Early Start**, **Early Finish**, **Late Start** and **Late Finish**.

The Critical Path

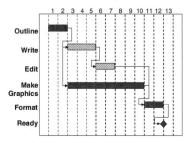

The Critical Path can now be found by finding the tasks that do not have Total Slack. In the example the tasks *Outline*, *Make Graphics* and *Format* do not have Total Slack and are the tasks on the Critical Path. Project 2000 can easily highlight the Critical Path for us. It can highlight the Critical Path in red. We need to see the Critical Path to find the tasks by which we can find time in our schedule and improve our chances to finish on time.

Constraints and Negative Slack

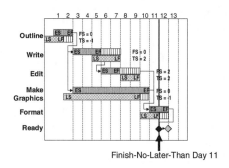

Finish-No-Later-Than Day 11

When you enter constraints into the schedule, the amounts of slack change. For example, a Finish-No-Later-Than constraint affects the backward pass (late dates), not the forward pass (early dates) and the total slack numbers change as a result.

In the example project we will introduce a hard constraint that is one day before the early finish date. The illustration shows how this constraint changes the total slack in the project. On the backward pass the latest finish dates are determined. These dates take constraints like Finish-No-Later-Than into account. The forward pass determines the early dates, regardless of constraints.

In the illustration you can see that the slack turns negative when the latest dates are before the earliest dates. The critical tasks now have –1 day slack. Project 2000 notices this as a scheduling conflict and will warn you with a dialog like this:

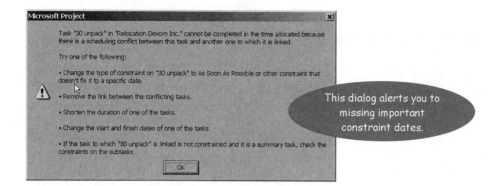

As you can see, Project 2000 gives concrete advice as to how to solve conflicts. The constraints that can cause scheduling conflicts, or negative slack, are the ones that can put pressure on the network. In *forward scheduling* these are:

◆ Must-Finish-On
◆ Must-Start-On
◆ Finish-No-Later-Than
◆ Start-No-Later-Than

In *backward scheduling*, the following constraints can cause negative slack:

◆ Must-Finish-On
◆ Must-Start-On
◆ Start-No-Earlier-Than
◆ Finish-No-Earlier-Than

Because constraints do affect the calculation of slack, you should use them as sparsely as possible without compromising the quality of the model of the project. We recommend entering constraints for true deadlines, only the Do-or-Die dates. If they are target dates, we recommend you use the feature of Deadlines as discussed on page 216.

Steps to Optimize for Time

1. Highlight the Critical Path
2. Sort the tasks based on duration
3. Find the longest critical task
4. Make a change on it
5. Consider impacts on quality, scope and time
6. Decide whether you want to keep the change
7. Repeat steps 3 to 7

The rationale behind these steps is that you first have to find the critical tasks. You should highlight the Critical Path in red so you can easily see whether a task is critical or not.

Then find out which of the critical tasks have the longest durations by doing a sort. The longest tasks hold the possibilities for the biggest gains. In other words: *Don't sweat the small stuff!* Focus on the long ones first with which you can achieve the largest gains.

After that, you have to come up with a way to do the work faster. We will suggest methods and explain them. Before you decide to go on to the next longest critical task, you have to establish whether it helped you enough, or if the trade-offs on quality or scope were too high a price to pay.

Steps to Optimize for Time

1. *Highlight the Critical Path*
2. Sort the tasks based on duration
3. Find the longest critical task
4. Make a change on it
5. Consider impacts on quality, scope and time
6. Decide if you want to keep the change
7. Repeat steps 3 to 7

The explanation of all the steps will take quite a few pages. To show where we are, we will use a graphic. The graphic to the left indicates the first step of *Highlight the Critical Path*:

Highlighting the Critical Path

1. Click the **GanttChartWizard** ; a series of dialog boxes follow.

2. Press Next > , select ◉ **Critical Path**; the sample box on the left now shows some task bars in red.

3. Click Finish , and Format It ; the task bars of the critical tasks on the Critical Path are now colored red.

You can color the text of the task names red as well:

1. Choose **Format, Text Styles**

2. Select red from the list **Item to Change** All ▼ the item **Critical Tasks**.

3. Select red from the list **Color**.

4. Click OK .

Display the Column Total Slack

By default, Project 2000 shows tasks as critical if their *total slack* is less than or equal to zero.

1. Insert the column *total slack* in the Gantt spreadsheet by making a right-click on a column heading and choosing **Insert Column**; the **Insert Column** dialog appears:

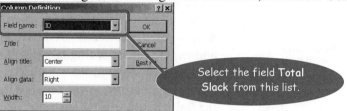

Select the field **Total Slack** from this list.

2. From the list **Field name** ID select the item **Total Slack.**

3. Click OK; the field is now displayed.

4. Drag the sliding door ▶◀, the divider between the spreadsheet and the timescale, to the right place to accommodate the new field in the view.

The total slack explains why some tasks are critical (total slack less than or equal to zero) and other ones are not (total slack greater than zero). If the total slack is negative, you are missing the project deadline.

What you will often see is that the Critical Path is not a complete chain of tasks that stretches from the project start date to the project end date. You likely will see a fragmented Critical Path.

A Fragmented Critical Path

Normally, the Critical Path provides a complete explanation of what happens between the project start and finish date. However, the Critical Path looks fragmented more often than not and does not provide a complete explanation of the duration of the project. If you

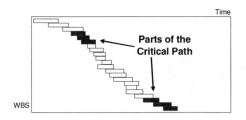

shorten a non-critical task, it will not make the project shorter. If you cannot see the Critical Path, optimizing becomes a painful process of trial and error. You have to address the causes of fragmentation first. You typically want to see a complete Critical Path of tasks from the start date to the finish date of the project. This sequence of tasks explains the project duration. We will explore how to make a complete chain of critical tasks appear.

Causes of a Fragmented Critical Path

The Critical Path can become fragmented for several reasons.
◆ Unavailability of Resources
◆ Schedule Constraints and Deadlines
◆ Elapsed Durations
◆ Task Calendars
◆ Workload Leveling.

We will discuss each of these reasons and what to do about them in more detail.

Unavailability of Resources

In the illustrated example, the move has to take place on a weekend, and the workweek of the movers is changed such that only the Saturday and the Sunday are working days. The result is that Project 2000 will always schedule the *move* in the weekend. Depending on when the predecessors of the move are done, this could cause slack to be created. When slack is created, the Critical Path will only start after the *move* and be fragmented.

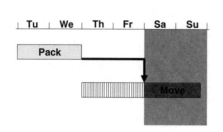

Is this real slack? Real slack is time that can be used as a buffer. In this case, the slack is real because delaying *pack* to Friday does not impact the project. In this situation, delaying would even be desirable because people may not be productive when they are all packed up and ready to go. This could be accomplished by making the schedule constraint As-Late-As-Possible on the **Task Information Form** for the task *Pack*. If we were to do this, the slack just moves over to the predecessors of *Pack*.

Because slack now exists on the most Critical Path, we have to raise the threshold for critical tasks.

Raising the Threshold for Critical Tasks

1. Choose **View, Gantt Chart**.

2. Insert the column **Total Slack** by making a right-click on a column heading and choosing **Insert Column**. Select the column from the list
Field Name ID ▾ and click OK . You should now have the column inserted in the Gantt Chart.

3. Check to see that you have tasks similar to *Pack* in your project. Look at what the total slack is for that task. In our example, *Pack* has two days of slack and we would raise the threshold for critical tasks to two days in our example.

4. Choose **Tools, Options,** tab **Calculation**. Increase the field **Tasks are Critical if Slack is less than or equal to:** 0 ▲▼ to the value you found in step 3.

5. Click OK ; the Critical Path has probably now extended. If not, you will have to check on the other possible causes for a fragmented Critical Path.

Schedule Constraints and Deadlines

We have already seen that constraints can cause negative slack, but they can also cause positive slack, or buffers. Deadlines also affect the slack calculation in a similar fashion as constraints do.

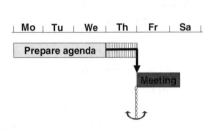

Let's say you have tasks like *Prepare agenda* and *Meeting* in your schedule. Typically, meetings, presentations and gatherings occur on a specific date and should be entered with a schedule constraint like Must-Start-On. As soon as you start entering fixed dates, slack can be created on the predecessors of the task. The Critical Path starts to look disjointed; only the task *Meeting* will be indicated as critical, because *Prepare agenda* has slack.

This is the second reason why we recommend you use as few schedule constraints as possible without compromising the quality of the model of your project. In this situation, constraints make it more difficult to find the Critical Path. The constraints that can cause positive slack in *forward scheduling* are:

◆ Must-Finish-On
◆ Must-Start-On
◆ Start-No-Earlier-Than
◆ Finish-No-Earlier-Than

In *backward scheduling* these constraints are:

◆ Must-Finish-On
◆ Must-Start-On
◆ Start-No-Later-Than
◆ Finish-No-Later-Than

Again, we have to ask ourselves: *Is this real slack?* In this case the slack is real because slipping the task *Prepare agenda* does not impact the project, unless it slips more than a day. We have to solve this, again, by raising the threshold for critical tasks, as discussed in the previous situation.

Elapsed Durations

An elapsed duration is expressed in calendar days as opposed to business days. A task

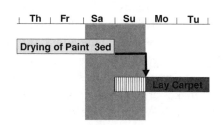

with an elapsed duration that ends during non-working time creates slack on its successor if they are regular tasks that start on the next business day. In the illustration, you can see that the task *Lay Carpet* is scheduled to start on the Monday (because it has resources assigned). This creates one day of slack on *Drying of Paint* with a duration of 3 elapsed days (3ed).

Once more we have to ask ourselves: *Is this real slack?* The slack is real here, because the *Drying of Paint* could continue for another day without impacting the project. Again, we have to solve this by raising the threshold for critical tasks, as discussed before.

Task Calendars

The new feature, Task Calendars, can fragment the Critical Path. If the *design* task can be ready long before the weather is good enough to start construction, the *design* task will

have slack and therefore will not be seen as critical. The task *construct* and its successors will be critical.

Just as in the previous situations, the slack is real slack and the only way to create a complete path of the most critical tasks is by raising the threshold for criticality. What you will find is the most critical path in your schedule that explains the project duration.

Workload Leveling

Consider the illustration showing two tasks *Write* and *Read* that can be done independently of each other. You have assigned one resource that is over-loaded. You

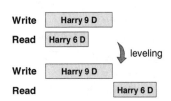

decide to level the workload to make the schedule more realistic. In some instances you cannot solve the over-allocations in any other way than by delaying a task. As you delay a task, you create slack on another task that competed for the same resource. Slack makes critical tasks non-critical. The Critical Path evaporates before your eyes.

One last time, we have to ask ourselves: *Is this slack real?* In this case, the answer is *No*. The slack is NOT real slack because any delay DOES impact the project. If Harry needs more time on *Write*, his other task *Read* will slip. How are we going to solve this one?

Harry is assigned full-time to both tasks. Clearly, he cannot do both at the same time. Cloning Harry is not an accepted project management practice yet (hopefully, it never will be, even though this could make life much easier for project managers).

Re-assigning one of the tasks to other resources is not an option either when there are no other resources. Therefore, we often have to delay one of the two tasks, but when we delay one, we create slack on the other task. This slack is not real. If you use it, you will slip the project end date. If you slip the task *Write,* it will drive the task *Read* further out. Normally, you can use slack to buffer the impact of unforeseen events, but not in this case. Both tasks are resource-critical even though the current Critical Path algorithm suggests that only the task *Read* is critical. The CPM algorithm only looks at dependencies when it calculates the early and late dates; it does not take resource workloads into account.

We may have conveniently forgotten that CPM assumes that resources are available in unlimited quantities. However, this is applicable in only a few organizations that can easily and quickly hire (and release) extra resources, thus rendering them unlimited.

Should we add Logical Dependencies?

Some people suggest you should add dependencies to level out the workloads of the resources. You could model resource dependencies as logical dependencies. This works well until you start changing the assignments. If you substitute the resource on one of the tasks, you have a schedule that could be shorter than it actually is, because of a dependency that has become obsolete! Adding logic to level workloads in order to keep a Critical Path is a static solution that has a short life. We recommend you keep your schedule dynamic. There is a different method for optimizing in this situation. We will explain it in more detail on page 343: Optimizing for Time, Cost and Resources.

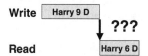

Many schedulers apply the Critical Path theory in such a way that they keep the resource workloads down by creating extra dependencies. They know the schedule would not be feasible if they didn't use extra dependencies. If you belong to this category, I would like to invite you to consider a new method instead of extra dependencies. We will discuss the Resource-Critical Path method in the section Optimizing for Time, Cost and Resources starting on page 343.

Sorting on Duration

Steps to Optimize for Time

1. Highlight the Critical Path
2. *Sort the tasks based on duration*
3. *Find the longest critical task*
4. Make a change on it
5. Consider impacts on quality, scope and time
6. Decide if you want to keep the change
7. Repeat steps 3 to 7

Now we have highlighted the Critical Path, the next thing to do is to find those tasks where we can gain the most time. We can find those by sorting on duration.

The sort is just meant to find the long critical tasks. We will reset the sort order as soon as we find them.

You may have to apply the sort again when you want to find the next longest critical tasks.

1. In the Gantt Chart, choose **Project, Sort, Sort by…**; the **Sort** dialog appears:

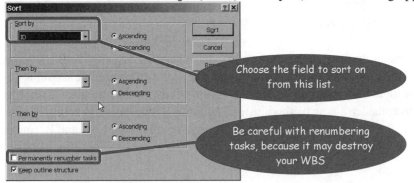

Choose the field to sort on from this list.

Be careful with renumbering tasks, because it may destroy your WBS

2. Select from the list **Sort by** ID ▾ the item **duration** and set the sort order to ⦿ **Descending**.

 3. Do not renumber the tasks and uncheck ☐ **Permanently renumber tasks**. If all tasks are renumbered you will likely have a catastrophe on your hands, because you will lose the structure of the WBS.

4. Make sure you sort the task and not the families of summary tasks; uncheck ☐ **Keep outline structure**.

5. Click ▓ Sort ▓. The longest tasks are now at the top of the screen. The ones that are long and critical are the prime candidates for optimization.

After you have identified the tasks to focus on first, you can revert to the original sort order by choosing **Project, Sort, by ID.**

Inserting a Project Summary Task

If a task is inserted at the top of the list and all the tasks below it are indented, MS Project will summarize the whole project in its fields **Start, Finish, Duration** and **Cost**. This task is the project summary task. It will show us the duration of the project before we start making changes. In order to make what-if analyses, you need to see the possible impact of any idea you try out. Take note of the current duration, work and cost of the project before making a change.

1. Choose **Tools, Options**; the **Options** dialog appears.

2. Click the tab **View**:

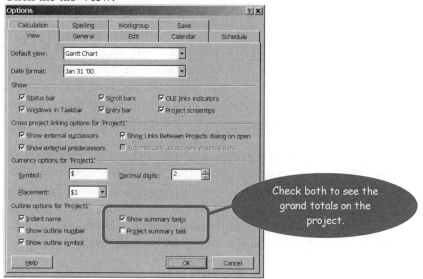

Check both to see the grand totals on the project.

3. Under **Outline Options** check both ☑ **Show Summary Tasks** and ☑ **Project Summary Task**.

4. Click ⬚ OK ⬚ ; the project summary task now shows total duration and total cost for the project. The task name of the project summary task is the **Title** of the project that can be found in **File, Properties,** tab **Summary**. If no title is filled in, the filename will stand in for it. We recommend, however, using the project title as the task name for the project summary task.

Shortening the Duration of the Project

Shortening the Critical Path

When the project has to finish earlier than the schedule shows, the Critical Path has to be shortened. Any change has to be evaluated against the impact on at least the three driving forces: the quality of the deliverables, the scope and the duration of the project. We could even consider the cost although we are not obliged to do so, because we assumed having unlimited resources.

Steps to Optimize for Time

1. Highlight the Critical Path
2. Sort the tasks based on duration
3. Find the longest critical task
4. ***Make a change on it***
5. Consider impacts on quality, scope and time
6. Decide if you want to keep the change
7. Repeat steps 3 to 7

The best solutions are those that make the quality (Q) go up ($\uparrow$), the scope (S) go up ($\uparrow$) and the time (T) go down ($\downarrow$). Unfortunately, there are no such ideal solutions. The next table only provides indications as to what the effect could be of each action in a typical project. You have to determine the effects in your own project. If a question mark (?) is shown, you have to look at your specific situation to determine the effect of the measurement. A zero (0) means that there is no expected impact.

The table provides ideas on how to improve the schedule. The actions are ranked in overall effectiveness; the most effective ones first. The first two methods are called *fast-tracking* and they overlap activities. Fast-tracking is working smarter instead of harder. When you add resources instead, you choose to work harder. Adding resources is called *crashing*. You will find this method at the bottom of the list because you are increasing the cost of the project. Crashing is trading off time and money.

We recommend you start by finding the critical tasks with the longest duration. Then explore whether the first two methods of fast-tracking can be applied to those long tasks, then focus on the next-longest task, etcetera. After having exhausted the fast-tracking on all tasks, you go to the next action in the table. (Q=Quality, S=Scope and T=Time)

	Action	For	Q	S	T
1.	Change sequential dependencies into partial dependencies (fast-tracking)	critical tasks	0	0	↓
2.	Create parallel paths from a sequential path (fast-tracking)	critical tasks	?	0	↓
3.	Change schedule constraints	critical tasks	0	0	↓
4.	Shorten lags (waiting periods)	critical tasks	0	0	↓
5.	Split task bars around Must-Start-On tasks	critical tasks	0	0	↓
6.	Split long tasks into many shorter ones	critical tasks	0	0	↓
7.	Decrease estimates	critical tasks	↓	↓	↓
8.	Reduce the scope or delete tasks	critical tasks	↓	↓	↓
9.	Add resources (*crashing*)	critical tasks	?	?	↓

Changing Sequential into Partial Dependencies

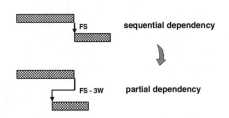

sequential dependency

partial dependency

There are four types of dependencies that can be combined with a positive lag time (waiting time/gap) or negative lag time (overlap/lead). The illustration shows a Finish-to-Start dependency with an overlap of 3 weeks (*lead* or negative *lag* of -3w): FS-3w. The overlap can be entered in an absolute number of days or weeks, like -3w. It can also be entered as a percentage of the duration of the predecessor.

1. In the timescale of the Gantt Chart, point with the tip of the mouse pointer to the arrow of the dependency and double-click. The **Task Dependency** box appears:

You can easily change a sequential into a partial dependency by making the **lag** negative.

2. Select from the list **Type:** Finish-to-Start (FS) ▼ the kind of dependency. Choose **Start-to-Start** or **Finish-to-Finish** to overlap tasks. Or leave the type **Finish-to-Start** and enter a negative **lag** (lead).

3. Type in the **lag** in time units, like *-3W* or in a percentage of the duration of the predecessor, like *-50%*. A positive lag moves task bars to the right in the timescale of the Gantt Chart. If you type a negative number, the tasks will move to the left. In a **Finish-to-Start** dependency, you will overlap the predecessor for the lag you specify. For **Start-to-Start** or **Finish-to-Finish** dependencies, enter zero or a positive lag to create partial dependencies.

4. Click OK ; you should now see the overlap you wanted between the two task bars in the timescale.

Creating Parallel Paths

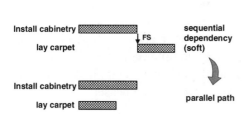

sequential
dependency
(soft)

parallel path

You can create a parallel path from a soft dependency. Hard, or mandatory, dependencies should not be cut. If the tasks are critical, the gain of time can be large.

In the illustrated example the carpet layers will have to work neatly and put plastic over the new carpet where it is laid.

1. In the Gantt Chart point with the tip of the mouse pointer to the arrow of the dependency and double click on the arrow; the **Task Dependency** dialog appears.

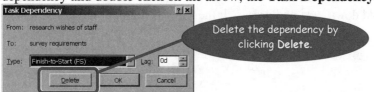

2. Verify whether the right dependency is shown and click ⬚ Delete .

3. Click ⬚ OK ; the dependency is removed. You may need a new link coming from the predecessor, because it could be a loose end in the network now. You may also need a new link into the successor, because it may have jumped all the way back to the project start date.

Changing Schedule Constraints

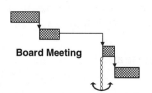

Board Meeting

Your project needs authorizations to proceed for certain matters. If these decisions are made in board meetings or steering group meetings on the last Thursday of each month, it slows down the project progress immensely.

If you lobby hard, you could perhaps achieve a more expedient authorization procedure and take some 'anchors' out of your schedule.

1. Select the task with the constraint.

2. Click [📋] or hold down [Shift] and press [F2]; the **Task Information** dialog appears.

3. Click the **Advanced** tab:

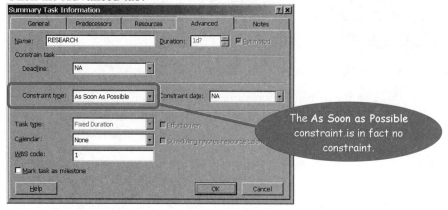

4. Under **Constrain Task** change the **Constraint type** to **As Soon as Possible**.
    OR
    Change the **Constraint date**.

5. Click [OK].

Shorten Lag

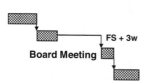

Board Meeting

FS + 3w

If you have any lag between critical tasks you could possibly reduce it now that you are armed with the argument that the lag is on the Critical Path. For example, if you have to wait for a board's decision, and you typically have to wait three weeks before the board convenes, you could perhaps lobby to make it an executive decision instead of a board decision.

1. In the Gantt Chart point with the tip of the mouse pointer to the arrow of the dependency.

2. Double-click on the arrow. The **Task Dependency** dialog appears:

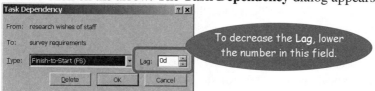

To decrease the Lag, lower the number in this field.

3. Verify whether the right dependency is shown and decrease the amount of **Lag**.

4. Click [OK].

Split Task Bars Around a Short Must-Start-On Task

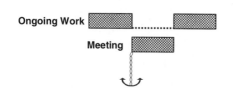

Ongoing Work

Meeting

If you have a meeting or training to attend, you have to drop your regular work. The meeting or training takes place on an agreed upon and fixed date. You can model these by using schedule constraints, like Must-Start-On. In the illustration, your ongoing task cannot be completed before the meeting, and could be scheduled entirely after the meeting, but splitting it around the meeting gives the tightest schedule.

To split a task bar:

1. Click the **Split Tasks** tool 🔲; a yellow pop-up appears and the mouse pointer now looks like: I⊩

2. Point to a task bar and click and drag where you want the split to occur. A part of the task bar splits off and in the yellow pop-up you are shown what the new start and finish date of the part will be when you release the mouse. The pop-up looks like:

Task: ▓▓▓▓▓▓▓▓▓▓	
Start:	Wed 4/5/00
Finish:	Sat 4/8/00

3. Drag it to where you want to schedule it and release the mouse button; the task bar is now split in two parts. Notice that the two parts are connected by dots:
    ▓▓▓▓▓▓▓......▓▓▓▓

Even though this feature works well at first sight, we do not recommend using it during the planning phase of the project. The network may reschedule the task. The split inside the task bar should move accordingly to keep it scheduled around the short task, but it does not move automatically. You will have to adjust your schedule manually every time changes happen. That's why we don't recommend it.

A better approach is to create a task calendar for those tasks that might be affected. On the task calendar you indicate non-working time for the duration of the short Must-Start-On task. To find out how to do this, see page 131: Creating a new Task Calendar.

Alternatively, you could allow the over-allocation to occur for the resource and then level the workloads using the **Tools, Resource Leveling** option, ☑ **Leveling can create splits in remaining work.** In this case the resource leveling will create a split and when you level again, it will move the split as needed.

Lastly, you could ignore the over-allocation, assuming that the resources will work overtime.

Split Tasks with a Long Duration

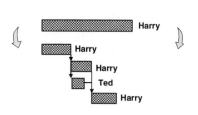

Breaking a long task into smaller tasks gives Project 2000 more possibilities to optimize. The benefit is immediate if you can assign portions of the task to other non-critical and perhaps cheaper resources. The easiest way to break up a task is by changing it into a summary task and adding detail tasks to it.

In most cases you don't need to split task bars if you split the task into subtasks instead. For example, electricians wire a building, but after the inspection they have to come back to install the cover plates. You could show this as one task with a split task bar, but it would be better if you split it into the two tasks: *pull cables* and *install cover plates.* Now you can set dependencies between the tasks. If you have a choice between task-splitting and bar-splitting, we recommend you split the task rather than its bar.

Decrease Estimates

Often when you get closer to the tasks at hand you can provide a more precise estimate. Sometimes, you will find you overestimated and can do it faster. Sometimes, you find better and quicker ways to do it. In both cases you can sharpen the estimate and cut off some of the duration. This may happen at the expense of the quality or the scope of the project.

Reduce the Scope or Delete Tasks

Reducing the scope is a matter of deleting deliverables. If there were deliverables qualified as nice-to-have, these would be good candidates. Not delivering on what you promised may be dangerous from a contractual point of view, not to mention to your reputation.

Alternatively, you could focus on the level below deliverables and find tasks to delete. Sometimes you can find activities in the realm of nice-if-we-get-around-to-it. These are the candidates to cut. This may happen at the expense of the quality of the deliverables.

Deleting tasks is as easy as selecting them and pressing ⌫. However, if you have set the baseline already, you should consider keeping the baseline data, only deleting the dependencies and the scheduled values: **Work, Cost, Fixed Cost**. Leave the fields **Baseline Work** and **Baseline Cost** alone to maintain the integrity of the baseline.

Add Resources

Often people start by asking for more resources when they start to feel the heat of their deadlines. If you do so, you choose to work harder instead of smarter and it will cost you more money. I have often observed that when new resources arrive, the best resources are taken off their jobs to train the new ones. This causes the slippage to increase instead of decrease. Therefore, I titled the story at the start of the previous chapter *Leave the Best Alone!*

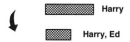

How many people can you add to tasks? While optimizing on time only, we could in theory add an unlimited number. In practice there are, of course, limits. If you add too many people, eventually nothing will get done. Even though we have assumed we have unlimited resources, it does not seem reasonable to add more than the maximum units that are filled in on the resource sheet. Make sure you use the task type **Fixed Work** before adding resources. This will make sure the duration decreases when you add them.

Consider Impacts on Quality, Scope and Time

Steps to Optimize for Time

1. Highlight the Critical Path
2. Sort the tasks based on duration
3. Find the longest critical task
4. Make a change on it
5. *Consider impacts on quality, scope and time*
6. *Decide if you want to keep the change*
7. Repeat steps 3 - 7

As the next step, you will have to make an evaluation of the impact on Quality, Scope and Time for the change you made. The impact on Time can be concluded from the project summary task. To see the project summary task you have to jump to the top of the project. Instead, you can also use the statistics dialog. You can display it by choosing **Project, Project Information, Statistics...** . You will save some clicks if you display the Tracking toolbar:

1. Right-click on any toolbar and choose **Tracking** from the pop-up menu. The Tracking toolbar is displayed:

2. The dialog is now available with one click on the **Project Statistics** tool.

You can now see how much time you have gained, and whether it is worth the sacrifices you made on the scope of the project or the quality of the deliverables. You then continue to repeat steps 3 to 7 in the process of optimizing until you have solved the scheduling conflict.

This concludes our discussion of the Critical Path Method.

Monte Carlo Simulation

Once you have optimized the Critical Path you should ask yourself: *How much time contingency should I reserve in order to protect the project deadline?* Monte Carlo Simulation can help you determine that.

What is Monte Carlo Simulation?

The best-known simulation technique is *Monte Carlo Simulation*. You specify, for tasks that are hard to predict (or for each task, if you want), the lower and upper limit of an estimate and you choose a probability curve between those limits. The simulating software then generates estimates for all the tasks using these parameters. It uses number

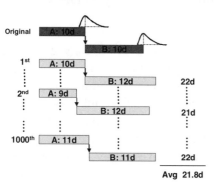

generators that produce estimates that comply with the range and the distribution curve you have chosen for the estimate. It creates the first version of the entire schedule and calculates the Critical Path. In the illustration, the *original* schedule is shown as well as the *1ˢᵗ*, the *2ⁿᵈ* and the *1000ᵗʰ* version created by the software.

The simulation software continues to create versions of the schedule and will create as many as you want. Simulations often create up to a thousand versions of the schedule. In each version it calculates the Critical Path of the schedule. The simulation software will then calculate averages and forecast end dates. It calculates the probabilities for a range of finish dates.

Before we delve into its complexity, let me first try to convince you why using Monte Carlo simulation is necessary.

Why do we Need it?

Simulation of Sequential Paths

If you ask many different people for an estimate on a task, you can plot the estimated duration on the x-axis against the number of times you hear it on the y-axis. The result will be a distribution curve that depicts the probability of a range of finish dates. It will look like the curve in the illustration. The estimate that you hear most often is the mode, which is why the mode is shown under the top of the curve. The median divides the surface under the curve in two equal parts; there are as many estimates to the left as to the right of it. The mean is the mathematical average of all estimates you collect.

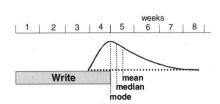

If you do this a few times, you will find that the resulting curve is often skewed to the right. In other words, durations tend to stretch rather than shrink. You probably knew that already if you have been a project manager for some time. Even if you don't have project management experience, it probably makes sense. What the skewed curve means is that it is more likely the duration of the task will increase a week than that it will decrease a week. In other words, it happens more often that tasks take longer than that they shrink.

However, the Critical Path consists of many tasks. It could be that you overran a task duration early in the schedule. This overrun can be compensated by later under-runs. The overall effect of the skewing of estimates is therefore not that dramatic, nevertheless, you can safely make the statement that schedules made with single estimates per task are often optimistic.

Parallel paths cause a more dramatic impact.

Simulation of Parallel Paths

It can be shown that parallel paths do affect the probability of the project end date. Where paths come together, the chance decreases that the milestone will be achieved with every path that is added leading to the milestone. In the example, the chance for on-time delivery is exactly 81%. If one path is early the other may be late and vice versa. When two paths both have to be finished, you have to multiply the chances: 90% x 90% = 81%.

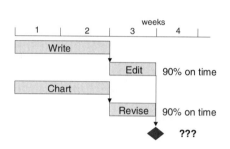

You can see that the more parallel paths you have in your schedule the more time risk you will experience. This phenomenon is known as *path-convergence* or *merge-bias*. The aggregated effect of many merging paths of different lengths is very difficult to predict. The more parallel paths you see in your schedule, the more you will need to simulate the schedule.

The paths make it unlikely that your end date, as shown by your MS Project schedule, will be met. That is why we developed the habit of padding our schedule. You need to do simulation in order to find the aggregated effect of the skew. You could use simulation to find how much padding you will need in your schedule.

Project 2000 does not have simulation capabilities, but there are good add-ons on the market with which you can simulate MS Project schedules. One add-on is Risk+ [26] and another is @Risk for MS Project [27]

---

[26] Made by C/S Solutions, see www.cs-solutions.com

[27] Made by Palisade Corporation, see www.palisade.com

Output of Monte Carlo Simulation

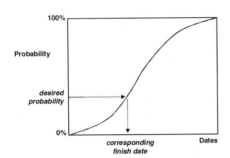

An s-curve can then be created that shows projected finish dates against the probability to meet the date. The benefit is that you can see the chance that your project is complete by a certain date. Alternatively, you can choose the level of probability you feel comfortable with, and derive the project finish date. You can quote this date with confidence; it can be met.

You also know the size of the time buffer you need in your project. If you read from the s-curve that, for a 90% probability, you need to add three weeks as a buffer, you should do it.

Assumptions of the Critical Path Method

In Summary: the Critical Path theory is based on three assumptions:
◆ Assumption 1: estimates are normally distributed
◆ Assumption 2: there is no merge-bias or path-convergence
◆ Assumption 3: you have unlimited resources available

We have already seen that assumption 1 does not hold true, but we can determine the magnitude of its effect by applying PERT or by using simulation.

As for assumption 2, we have proven that merge-bias and path-convergence do exist. This effect often causes the largest slippages in projects. Simulation is the only technique that can make the compounded effect visible. Applying the Critical Path method is good as long as you simulate it as well. Many overruns can be foreseen and quantified when simulation is applied to schedules.

Assumption 3 is more difficult to deal with. Both the CPM and the PERT techniques assume that resources are available in unlimited quantities. This assumption holds true, if workloads are not your problem. For example:
◆ If you intend to subcontract the work and if the resources are readily available, workload is not an issue. The resource allocation is the problem of the contractor.
◆ For a contractor who can hire resources easily in the quantity and of the expertise he needs, workload is not a problem either.
Workloads are not your concern in these cases and the assumption can stand.

The assumption to have unlimited resources available seems unrealistic in this day and age. In this era of global competition, many organizations cannot afford to supply unlimited resources; neither can they afford not to track the usage of their resources. Today, one percent difference in the bottom-line can be the difference between a viable and a non-viable company in the global market.

If you are managing the workload of your own scarce internal resources, workload is your concern. In that case both the CPM and the PERT techniques are of limited value. You need a new technique to optimize your schedule. Extra resources can be bought with money. We will first introduce cost in the optimization, and then we will add the limited availability of resources.

Optimizing for Time and Cost

Scope

Quality

Time

Procurement

Project

Cost

Communications

Resources

Risk

Adapted from
PMBOK® Guide 2000
Exposure Draft

When you optimize for time and cost, you should simultaneously consider the dimensions Scope, Time and Cost (and keep Quality in the back of your mind). Here we are adding the dimension of cost in our quest for the optimal schedule.

Any project manager with a budget should at least apply this type of optimization, or the next one on optimizing for time, cost and resources.

Steps to Optimize for Time and Cost

Steps to Optimize for Time and Cost

1. Highlight the Critical Path
2. Sort the tasks on **Cost**
3. Find the **most expensive** task
4. Make a change on it
5. Consider impacts on quality, scope, time and **cost**
6. Decide if you want to keep the change
7. Repeat steps 3 - 7

The steps for optimizing on time and cost are very similar to the steps for optimizing on time. The differences are bolded in the illustration. Because you should not lose sight of the time dimension of the project, you still have to find the Critical Path first. Then you sort on cost to find the most expensive tasks. You develop ideas as to how you might bring the cost down without compromising on the time, scope or quality. Enter the change and check the results to see whether you want to keep the change.

We will discuss how to accomplish some of these steps in Project 2000.

Sorting on Cost

To find the tasks on which we can make significant savings, we should sort the tasks on cost.

1. Choose **View, Gantt Chart**.

2. Choose **Project, Sort, Sort by...**; the **Sort** dialog appears:

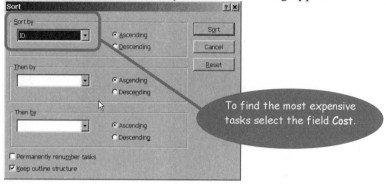

To find the most expensive tasks select the field *Cost*.

3. In the **Sort By** list box, select **Cost** and set the sort order to ⦿ **Descending**.

4. Do not renumber the tasks; uncheck:
   ☐ **Permanently renumber tasks** and
   ☐ **Keep outline structure**

5. Click [**Sort**]; the tasks are now fully sorted and you can easily find the tasks where you can make significant savings.

6. Reset the original sort order by choosing **Project, Sort, Sort by ID**.

Lowering the Cost of a Project

The best measurements are those that make the quality (Q) go up (↑), the scope (S) go up (↑), the time (T) go down (↓), and the cost (C) go down (↓). Unfortunately, there are no such ideal measurements. However, we will give you ideas about what you can do. The following table shows actions to lower the cost (C) and their likely impact on quality (Q), scope (S) and time (T). If a question mark (?) is shown, you need to look at your specific situation to determine the effect of the measurement. A zero (0) means that there is no expected impact.

	Action	**For**	**Q**	**S**	**T**	**C**
1	Find cheaper contracts	External contractors, consultants	0	?	?	↓
2	Reassign to cheaper resources	Expensive resources	↓	?	?	↓
3	Prevent overtime work	Resources with a higher overtime rate	0	0	↑	↓
4	Smooth the workloads	Resources with erratic workloads	?	?	?	↓
5	Break up a long task and reassign portions to cheaper resources	Long tasks	0	0	↓	↓
6	Decrease the estimate	Any tasks with labor costs	0	0	↓	↓
7	Reduce the scope or delete tasks	Any tasks with costs involved	↓	↓	↓	↓

The actions are listed in order of overall effectiveness. You should start at the top and work your way down the table. If you need to bring down the duration of your project as well, use the Optimizing for Time methods as well as we discussed on pages 322 and following.

If you are to manage the cash flow of your project as well, another measure might be to re-negotiate when the costs accrue, and change the resource field **Accrue at** accordingly. Changing the timing of the expenses to the end of the tasks will improve your cash flow.

Finding Cheaper Contracts

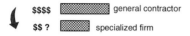

$$$$ ▨▨▨▨ general contractor

$$? ▨▨▨ specialized firm

The question you should ask yourself is: *Do I always solicit for more than one bid or proposal?* If the answer is *No* then this method may create significant savings. After all, contractors and consultants are quick to find out whether they are in a competitive situation, or not. Research whether there are specialized firms who are quicker or better at their trade than other suppliers.

1. Create the new resource in the resource sheet; choose **View, Resource Sheet**. For the how-to, see page 242: Entering Resources.

2. Choose **View, Gantt Chart** where we will change the assignments to the new resource.

3. Select the task, click ; the **Assign Resources** dialog appears:

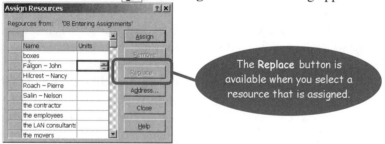

The **Replace** button is available when you select a resource that is assigned.

4. Click on the resource to replace.

5. Click **Replace...**; the **Replace Resource** dialog appears on top of the **Assign Resources** dialog:

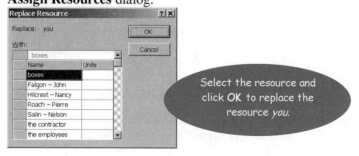

Select the resource and click **OK** to replace the resource *you*.

6.   Click on the substitute resource and click [OK]; the resource is now replaced on the task.

If you want to use the Task Form, see page 373: Replacing Critical Resources.

Reassigning to Cheaper Resources

We discussed above how to replace one resource with another.

Preventing Overtime Work

Preventing overtime work will only bring down the cost if you would actually pay a higher rate for the overtime work done. For how to decrease overtime, please refer to the section on how to create it in the first place, see page 377: Assigning Overtime Hours. Of course, if you reduce overtime, you may be extending your project duration. You can only do that if saving cost is more important than finishing as early as possible.

Smoothing the Workloads

In the illustrated example, you could raise the question: *If the cost for Ed's workload after smoothing is $30,000; what was the true cost before?* If a resource has an erratic workload, the resource may have days or weeks when he is not needed. The resource may have different work for which he will be paid from other funds than your project budget. If this is not the case, the project manager will likely keep the resource around,

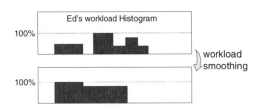

particularly if his skill set is scarce. The project manager then assumes the cost for the idle time. The answer to the question raised will then be that, before smoothing, the actual cost is higher. The project budget does not show this cost, because it only shows the cost of the assignments. If you smooth the workload you will decrease the hidden cost of the project. Because the cost was hidden in the first place, you will not see the cost of the project change.

Reducing the Scope or Deleting Tasks

We discussed this method previously, on page 330. Remember that the integrity of the original baseline may be compromised when re-baselining after deleting tasks.

Optimizing for Time, Cost and Resources

Scope

Quality

Time

Procurement

Project

Cost

Communications

Resources

Risk

Adapted from:
PMBOK® Guide 2000
Exposure Draft

We are now adding the dimension of resources to the ones we already monitor: Quality, Scope, Time and Cost. The resource dimension includes the workload of the resources relative to their availability. This dimension may trade off with:

◆ Cost, when you have to pay for extra resources.

◆ Time, when you cannot solve over-allocations in any other way than delaying tasks.

The optimization becomes more complex, but if we manage to handle this complexity we will have confidence that the project is feasible as far as the resources are concerned.

Steps to Optimize for Time, Cost and Resources

Steps to Optimize for Time, Cost and Resources

1. **Check the workloads and level them**
2. Highlight the **Resource Critical Path (RCP)**
3. Find the **most critical resource**
4. Make a change on it
5. Consider impacts on quality, scope, time, cost and **resources**
6. Decide whether you want to keep the change
7. Repeat steps 3 - 7

As the steps show, the first thing we have to do is check:

◆ whether the workloads are within the availability of the human resources, and

◆ whether the work is within the capacity of the equipment.

Then we will need to find the Resource-Critical Path (RCP), which is different from the Critical Path. Once you have found the RCP, optimization is very similar to methods we used with the Critical Path Method. The differences with the optimizations previously discussed are bolded in the box. There are quite a few pages on this optimization approach so we will show where we are using this box.

Workload Leveling

The first step in optimizing for time, cost and resources is checking the workloads. If there are over-allocations they need to be leveled.

We will discuss how to do this by hand or automatically with the help of Project 2000. If you level your schedule you will often insert delays for certain tasks. These delays will influence the calculation of the Critical Path. We will discuss that as well.

The Work Field

The field **Work** in the Gantt spreadsheet is not the same as the field **Work** in the

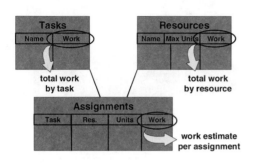

Resource Sheet, nor is it the same as the field **Work** on the Task Form.

In the Gantt Chart, **Work** is the total work of all resources on the task.

In the resource sheet, **Work** is the total work in the project for the resource. For material resources, it is the total number of units used in the project. For facilities and machines, the total is not very meaningful; it represents the number of times the facility or machine is used.

On the Task Form you can see the assignment-related **Work** field, which displays the work of one resource on a particular task.

Checking the Workloads: Resource Graph

1. Choose **View**, **Resource Graph**.
    OR
    Click **Resource Graph** on the view bar at the left.

2. Hold down Alt and press Home to make the timescale jump to the start of the project.

3. Use the Zoom out ⊖ and Zoom in ⊕ tools to adjust the timescale.

4. Press Page Down to go to the next resource.
    OR

    Press Page Up to go to a previous resource.

The *Resource Graph* is also known as the *Resource Histogram* [28].

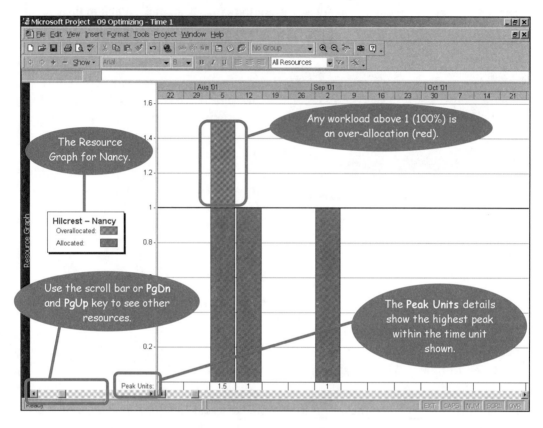

 The Resource Graph shows, by default, the **Peak Units,** which is the highest bar during the time period shown. **Peak Units** presents an inflated picture of the real work. Choose **Format, Details, Work** to get a more realistic view of the workloads.

---

[28] See the PMBOK® Guide, 2000 Edition.

Manual Leveling

There are many ways in which you can level the workloads by hand without using the **Automatic Leveling** or **Level Now** feature of Project 2000:

◆ Re-assigning tasks from critical resources to non-critical resources.

◆ Fine-tuning the number of units assigned to the tasks involved in the over-allocation. For example, you could keep two tasks scheduled in parallel, if you decrease the involvement of the resource to 50%.

◆ Taking resources off a task.
Sometimes you can do this when more than one person is already working on the task. Or as soon as you know who will really pull the cart.

◆ Contracting work out to subcontractors.
One definition of subcontractors is that they are people who solve your work overloads in exchange for money.

◆ Lowering quality standards to lower work estimates, which decrease the workload. You can often cut corners in the nice-to-have requirements.

◆ Changing dependencies. Decreasing overlaps between tasks that are done by the same resource. In the special case in which you have a team of people going from one city to another to install a system, consider setting extra dependencies. This solidifies the order in which locations are rolled out and it keeps the workloads of the teams reasonable.

◆ Allocating the best resources to the critical tasks first.

◆ Matching people to their tasks better such that the best person does the job and time is gained.

◆ Assigning overtime. Even though this does not solve the over-allocation, it shows that the problem is dealt with.

◆ Moving vacations until after the deadline.

◆ Splitting long tasks into many shorter ones and reassigning them to non-critical resources. Splitting tasks increases the number of puzzle possibilities.

◆ Splitting task bars and fitting workloads into a tight and smooth resource histogram.

◆ Delaying tasks: Slip one of the tasks that compete for the same resource. If you decide to delay one task, choose the task that has the most slack and the least number of resources assigned. If you delay a task with many resources assigned, you may cause many new over-allocations.

MS Project cannot replace you as a manager. It can neither re-assign tasks, nor change the units of an assignment. These measures are often better than delaying tasks. Project 2000 will only delay task bars or split them. It can only apply the last two methods listed, and it cannot do any of the other methods to level the workloads. We have to conclude that if you want the tightest schedule possible, you will have to level the workloads by hand.

Apply the Resource Allocation View

Click ▦ on the **Resource Management** toolbar.

OR

1. Choose **View, More Views...**; the **More Views** dialog appears:

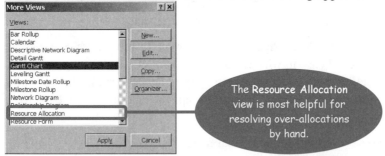

The **Resource Allocation** view is most helpful for resolving over-allocations by hand.

2. Select the **Resource Allocation** view and click [Apply]; a combined view appears with the **Resource Usage** view in the top pane and the **Leveling Gantt** in the bottom pane. The top pane shows the over-allocated resources and the bottom pane helps in resolving them.

3. Display a useful toolbar by right-clicking on any toolbar and choosing **Resource Management**.

Manual Leveling

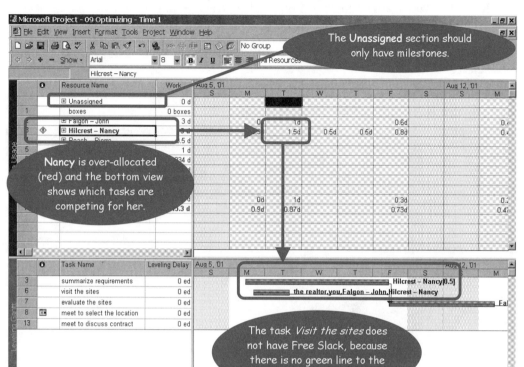

The **Unassigned** section should only have milestones.

Nancy is over-allocated (red) and the bottom view shows which tasks are competing for her.

The task *Visit the sites* does not have Free Slack, because there is no green line to the right of its task bar.

1. Check to see if you forgot any assignments. At the top, the heading **Unassigned** contains the unassigned tasks. Click on the button ⊞ to the left of it to see them, click ⊟ to hide them. Typically, only the milestones should be listed here.

2. Hide all assignments in the top pane by clicking on any column heading and clicking **Hide Subtasks** ⊟.

3. The over-allocated resources are shown in red. Check the **Indicators ⊙** column; it gives leveling advice. You will receive advice if you leave your mouse pointer over the icon ◈. If you are advised to level on a day-by-day basis, then zoom the time scale in until you see the days.

4. Scroll to the start of the project by dragging the scroll box on the horizontal scrollbar of the timescale to the far left. (Unfortunately pressing $\boxed{\text{Alt}}$ + $\boxed{\text{Home}}$ does not work in this view.)

5. Go to the first over-allocation by clicking on **Go To Next Overallocation** ![icon] on the **Resource Management** toolbar. Project 2000 searches day-by-day to find the next over-allocation. It does not stick to the selected resource.

6. Resolve the over-allocations one by one by applying one of the methods we discussed before.

In the next illustration, you can see how the over-allocation is solved by delaying one of the tasks that was competing for the same resource:

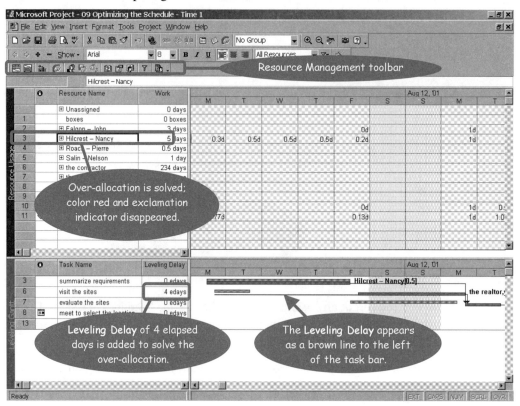

The bottom view can still be improved by displaying a line for the total slack as well. Adding a colored line for the total slack to each task bar can do this. Click in the bottom pane and choose **Format, Bar Styles**.

Insert a new line above the (free) slack line and use similar settings except the color (use light green) and under **To**, choose **Total Slack** from the list.

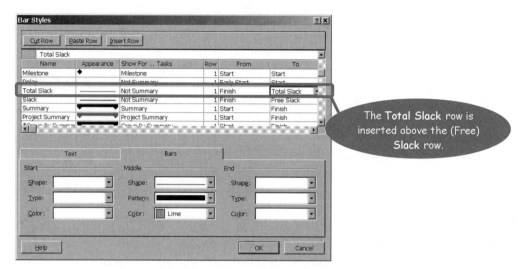

The **Total Slack** row is inserted above the (Free) **Slack** row.

As a result, the shorter free slack line will appear on top of the total slack line. Now you can see how far you can delay tasks without affecting the next constraint date or the project end date.

If a task does not have enough free slack to solve over-allocations, you can use its total slack to solve the work overload.

Automatic Leveling Scenarios

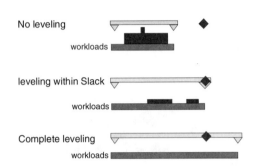

There are three scenarios you can develop with Project 2000. You can switch back and forth between them. Each scenario provides some useful information. In the illustration, you can see all three. The dark workloads are the over-allocations. The more the workloads are leveled, the less the over-allocations. Without doing anything you currently have the first one.

◆ **No leveling**

If you look at Gantt Charts, you can often see several tasks scheduled concurrently. Where two concurrent tasks have the same resources assigned, the workloads can be too big. If there are no over-allocations you will not need to level, only the task durations and dependencies drive the duration of the project. This scenario answers the question: *What workload will resources have when their workload is not leveled?* This scenario shows the minimum duration for the project.

◆ **Leveling within the slack of the project**

If you create a milestone at the proposed target date, you can level within the slack the target date creates. This scenario answers the question: *What workload will critical resources have while meeting the project target date?* This shows how many extra resources should be hired in order to meet this target date.

◆ **Complete leveling**

This answers: *What is the end date of the project if the workloads of all resources are entirely leveled?* This shows a comfortable deadline for the project. This is the date we recommend you first quote to your client.

No Leveling or Clearing the Leveling

1. If you have leveled workloads before, the field **Leveling Delay** will have entries. (You can insert this field by choosing **Insert, Column**.)

2. You can only clear the leveling if you are in one of the task views. Change to a task view, if necessary.

3. To remove the leveling delay, choose **Tools, Resource Leveling**; the **Resource Leveling** dialog appears:

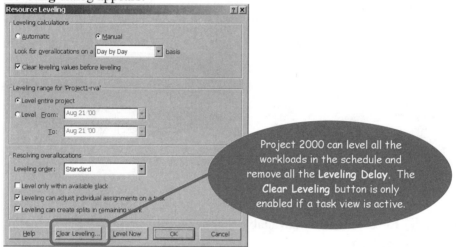

Project 2000 can level all the workloads in the schedule and remove all the **Leveling Delay**. The **Clear Leveling** button is only enabled if a task view is active.

4. Select ⦿ **Manual** and click ; the **Clear Leveling** dialog appears:

5. Select ⦿ **Entire Project** and click ▢ OK ▢; you are now back in the task view. The numbers in the field **Leveling Delay** should be zero.

Leveling Within the Slack of the Project

1. Make sure you have a project finish milestone by which all dependencies come together. The project milestone should have a **Must-Finish-On** constraint on the proposed deadline date.

2. Choose **Tools, Resource Leveling...**; the **Resource Leveling** dialog appears:

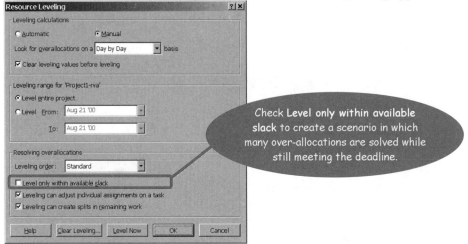

3. Check ☑ **Level only within available Slack**.

4. Click **Level Now**.

5. Click **OK**.

6. Check the workloads of the resources; often there are some over-allocations left.

If the workloads of the resources are too high to meet the deadline, then other methods have to be applied to make the workloads reasonable, see the methods we discussed on page 349: Manual Leveling.

Complete Leveling

1. Insert the column **Leveling Delay** in the Gantt spreadsheet by right-clicking on the column heading **Duration**, choose **Insert Column** and choose the field **Leveling Delay** from the list. This field allows us to see the result of the leveling.

2. Choose **Tools, Resource Leveling…**; the **Resource Leveling** dialog appears:

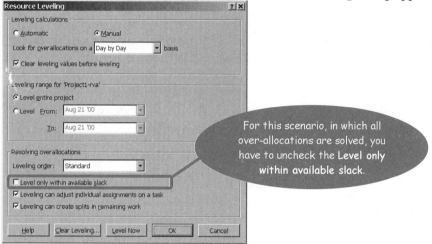

For this scenario, in which all over-allocations are solved, you have to uncheck the **Level only within available slack**.

3. Choose the precision of the leveling by selecting in the range of **Minute by Minute** to **Month by Month**. A double workload on Monday, but a total workload of 35 hours in a week, does constitute an overload on a day-by-day basis, but not on a week-by-week basis. The setting is about the granularity of leveling. We recommend **Day by Day** or **Week by Week** for most projects.

4. Check ☑ **Clear Leveling values before leveling** if you want to clear the field **Leveling delay** of old leveling values. Uncheck it if you want Project 2000 to add to the leveling delays incrementally.

5. Select ⊙ **Level entire project**.

6. Uncheck ☐ **Level only within available Slack**, otherwise Project 2000 may not solve all over-allocations.

7. Check ☑ **Leveling can adjust individual assignments** if you want to find the shortest, leveled schedule. If you have more than one person assigned to a task, this option will treat all as individual assignments rather than as a task for which the

whole group has to be available. If you use this, you can still override this option for certain tasks by entering *No* in the task field **Level Assignments**.

8. Check ☑ **Leveling can create splits in remaining work** if you want to allow Project 2000 to split task bars. It may generate a tighter schedule. The drawback is that the schedule becomes fragmented. If you want to exclude certain tasks from being split use the task field **Leveling can split**.
   Fixed Duration tasks will not be split by Project 2000 because this will increase their duration.

9. Click ⬛ Level Now . MS Project delayed certain tasks. In the column **Leveling Delay** you can see which tasks have been delayed and by how long.

How can you predict which task will be postponed when resources are over-allocated? This is hard unless you assign priority levels in the column **Priority** or on the view **Task Details Form**. MS Project will not delay the task with higher priority when you level using the leveling setting **Priority, Standard**.

The schedule is now realistic in the sense that the resources can do and finish the work assigned to them. Check the end date in the **Finish** column of the project summary task; it has likely slipped.

Please note that recurring detail tasks are not included in the leveling process, because Project 2000 sets the field **Level Assignments** to *No*. If you assigned resources to the recurring summary task and leveled the workloads fully, you may still see over-allocations. The over-allocations occur during the duration of the tasks. To work around this, fill down *Yes* in the field **Level Assignments** for all recurring detail tasks and level the workloads again.

Influencing Automatic Leveling

When you ask Project 2000 to level your schedule, it will try to choose intelligently which tasks to delay. It looks at the amount of slack on both tasks that compete for the same resource and delays the one task that has the most. It does not always delay the task you prefer. Project 2000 offers three choices to influence which tasks are delayed. Below are some suggestions on when to use each:

◆ **ID**
   Project 2000 will level tasks based upon their ID numbers. It will give the priority to the task higher up in the list of tasks. Use this setting to prioritize projects in a

consolidated file. Put your highest priority projects at the top of the list and then level your consolidated schedule.

◆ **Standard**
This is the default setting and is used for regular leveling. Under the standard leveling the task with the most slack will be delayed.

◆ **Priority, Standard**
When you are not entirely happy with MS Projects' leveling, you can enter a priority number for each task in the field **Priority**. In this way, you can influence which task is delayed in the leveling.

Another way to influence the leveling is by excluding certain resources from leveling. We discussed this on page 357: Excluding Resources From Leveling.

Excluding Resources From Leveling

Human resources can do more than one task at a time, also known as multi-tasking. Whether this increases productivity is a separate discussion. The type of leveling you need is filling the workload up to the limit of availability. I call this percentage leveling. You can exclude human resources by entering *No* in the resource field **Can Level**. Typically, you would exclude external resources from leveling because the workload of subcontractors is most often not your problem.

	Type	Leveling
Human	Work	percentage
Facilities	Material	yes/no
Machines	Material	yes/no
Materials	Material	exclude

In general, facilities and machines are occupied or not, and mostly need a yes/no type of leveling. Unfortunately, Project 2000 does not have facilities and machines as separate types of resources, nor does it have features for yes/no leveling. You will have to create a reservation system for boardrooms and training rooms outside of Project 2000.

Materials are consumables and don't need leveling. You can exclude materials by setting the resource field **Can Level** to *No*.

How Leveling affects the Critical Path

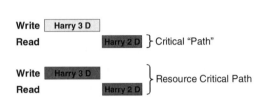

In the example illustrated, the two tasks are writing a report and reading a document. The tasks are not dependent on each other; Harry can choose to do them in any order. Before leveling is done, the Critical Path is the task *write*. After leveling, *read* is the only task seen as critical. Don't worry, there is nothing wrong with your software, this is how the Critical Path algorithm works and is supposed to work. The Critical Path assumes you have access to unlimited resources.

In Project 2000 the data look as follows:

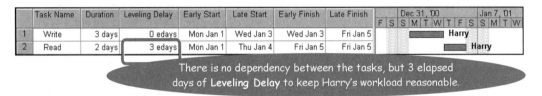

	Task Name	Duration	Leveling Delay	Early Start	Late Start	Early Finish	Late Finish
1	Write	3 days	0 edays	Mon Jan 1	Wed Jan 3	Wed Jan 3	Fri Jan 5
2	Read	2 days	3 edays	Mon Jan 1	Thu Jan 4	Fri Jan 5	Fri Jan 5

There is no dependency between the tasks, but 3 elapsed days of **Leveling Delay** to keep Harry's workload reasonable.

Let me prove this by applying the mathematics of the algorithm to the two tasks after leveling.

◆ On the forward pass, the Early Start for *write* is day 1 and the Early Finish is day 3 given the duration of 3 days. For *read* the Early Start is day 1; remember there is no dependency between the tasks, and the Early Finish is at the end of day 5, given the delayed start date of day 4.

◆ On the backward pass, the Late Finish for *read* is also day 5, the Late Start, therefore, is day 4. *Write* has to be finished on the project finish date; the Late Finish date is day 5. Remember, there is no dependency between the two. It has to start, at the latest, on day 3 to meet this date.

Total Slack can be calculated by subtracting the Early Finish date from the Late Finish date. The total slack of the task *read* is 5 - 5 = 0 days; the task is critical and highlighted in red. The total slack for *write* is 5 - 3 = 2 days; the task is not seen as critical by the algorithm, even though common sense dictates that there really is no slack on the task *write*, because it competes for the same resource, *Harry*. And if the task *write* takes longer *read* will be moved out. This example demonstrates the weakness of the Critical Path algorithm; it does not take resource dependencies into account.

The leveling of tasks can make the total slack indicator of a task meaningless and thus the Critical Path as well. Tasks with slack may in fact be driving the project end date, as is the case with the task *write* in the example above. If *write* is slipped it will move *read* with it.

The Critical Path theory assumes having access to unlimited resources. That is not the current reality any longer for many organizations that are competing in the global marketplace. Resources are often stretched to their limits. An organization that does not optimize the usage of its resources will soon notice this in their bottom line. In other words, many organizations find themselves having to level the workloads of their resources, and upon doing so, the Critical Path becomes useless; it evaporates before their eyes.

Critical Path or Resource-Critical Path?

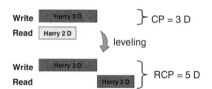

We need a new type of Critical Path that takes logical dependencies as well as resource dependencies into account. Such a path is called the *Resource-Critical Path*.

The question is raised: *What should you monitor, the Critical Path (CP) or the Resource-Critical Path (RCP)?* The answer is obvious from the previous examples; one should try to find the RCP. It is more helpful in a leveled schedule.

The Resource-Critical Path (RCP)

Let us first define this new concept of the RCP. It is the sequence of tasks that determines the project end date while taking logical and resource dependencies into account[29]. As you notice the definition has not changed very much from the Critical Path definition. However, other definitions of the Critical Path like *the sequence of tasks without slack* do not apply to the RCP, because resource-critical tasks can have slack. In the example above, the task *Write* has slack but still drives the project end date and is therefore as critical as *Read.* Both are Resource Critical Tasks however because the same resource does them.

The Resource-Critical Path, in other words, is the chain of tasks that drives the project end date while taking into account that resources have limited availability. When you have few resources, you should focus on the RCP instead of the CP.

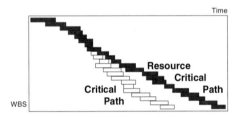

You can see in the illustration that the RCP often includes some early critical tasks and then tasks that are delayed because of leveling. Those tasks now drive the project end date. *Resource-critical tasks* are tasks that, when delayed, slip the project end date.

I would like to introduce an acronym here to help you remember this fundamental message, the acronym is **ERIC** (**E**ach **R**esource **I**mplies **C**riticality). In a leveled schedule, any resource can be so limited in availability and/or so much needed, that it could drive the project finish date. Therefore **E**ach **R**esource **I**mplies **C**riticality, or **ERIC** [30].

---

[29] See my article in the magazine *PM Network*, December 1999, PMI: *Take the Path that is Really Critical.*

[30] Hey, that's my first name!

Finding the Resource-Critical Path

Steps to Optimize for Time, Cost and Resources
1. Check the workloads and level workloads
2. **Highlight the Resource Critical Path (RCP)**
3. **Find the most critical resource**
4. Make a change on it
5. Consider impacts on quality, scope, time, cost and resources
6. Decide if you want to keep the change
7. Repeat steps 3 to 7

Finding and highlighting the RCP requires some work. Below you will see a process that will help in identifying the resource critical tasks. The idea behind the process shown is that any task that is pushed beyond its late finish date on the Critical Path schedule, likely is a resource-critical task[31].

These are the process steps:
1. Clear any leveling
2. Copy the **Late Finish** dates into **Date1**
3. Level the workloads
4. Copy the **Finish** dates into **Date2**
5. Filter on tasks with **Date2** is greater than or equal to **Date1**
6. Sort on **Finish** date

The steps to take in Project 2000 are:

1. Choose **View, Gantt Chart**.

2. Clear any leveling by choosing **Tools, Resource Leveling** and click Clear Leveling... .

3. Copy the **Late Finish** dates into the field **Date1**,
   right-click on a column heading and choose **Insert Column**; the dialog appears with which you can insert the columns **Late Finish** and **Date1**.
   Right-click on the **Late Finish** column heading and choose **Copy Cell**, right-click on the **Date1** column heading and choose **Paste**. The **Late Finish** dates are now copied into the spare date field.

---

[31] I learned this method from Lunny Sunshine of Artemis, www.artemispm.com

4. Level the workloads: choose **Tools**, **Resource Leveling** and click Level Now.

5. Copy the **Finish** dates into **Date2** using similar steps as under step 3.

6. Filter on tasks where **Date2** is greater than or equal to **Date1**.
   Choose **Project, Filtered for <name of current filter>, More Filters**. Click
   New... and enter the settings as shown in the following snapshot:

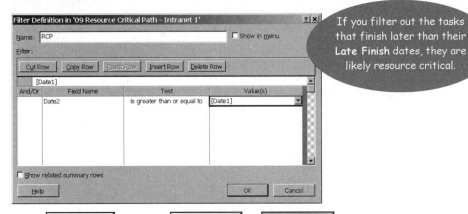

If you filter out the tasks that finish later than their **Late Finish** dates, they are likely resource critical.

7. Click OK and then Apply or Highlight; if you choose the latter, all the resource-critical tasks will have blue text. If you want to change the color to red, choose **Format, Text Styles** and set the appropriate settings.

8. Sort by the **Finish** date; choose **Project, Sort, By Finish Date**. The Resource-Critical Path is now shown as a waterfall of task bars from the beginning to the end of the project as we are used to seeing with the regular Critical Path.

This process has some shortcomings:

◆ Often more tasks are identified as resource-critical than there really are.

◆ There are exceptional situations in which a resource-critical task is not found. This will show up as a hole in the resource-critical path.

The method previously explained provides a good approximation of the RCP. But in order to overcome the shortcomings we will have to do some tweaking. We have to get rid of the extra tasks the algorithm filters out and we have to mark the tasks it forgot.

Highlighting the Resource-Critical Path

We recommend you use the field **Marked** to tag the tasks that are truly resource-critical. Then we will color the tasks you marked red to make the Resource-Critical Path appear as the good, old Critical Path did.

1. Insert the field **Marked** in the Gantt Chart.

2. We will display the critical tasks as red task bars. Click the **GanttChartWizard** ; a series of dialogs follows.

3. When given the option, select ⦿ **Critical Path**; the sample box shows critical task bars in red.

4. Click `Finish` and `Format It`; the task bars on the Critical Path are now colored red.

5. We have to modify what the **GanttChartWizard** did by choosing **Format, Bar Styles...** We will make two small changes so that all normal tasks have a blue task bar, except for tasks that are marked red. Set the following settings:

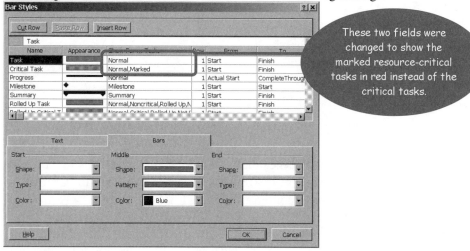

These two fields were changed to show the marked resource-critical tasks in red instead of the critical tasks.

6. You can now color task bars red if you change their field **Marked** to **Yes**. Tasks that are resource-critical have either a logical dependency or a resource dependency with other tasks. A logical dependency, as you know, is shown as an arrow between the task bars. A resource dependency is when two tasks are competing for the same resource; you will see in the timescale that the same resource is assigned to both tasks. For an explanation of the concept, see page 180.

    Resource-critical tasks can be identified easiest if you start with the project end milestone and walk the path of tasks backward. You look for dependency arrows or resources that are shared between the tasks.

To the un-initiated the schedule looks as if the regular Critical Path is shown, except that it is the Resource-Critical Path. The RCP really drives the project end date. When people are not familiar with the concept of the RCP, you could present this as your "Critical Path".

To the best of my knowledge, a robust algorithm to find the RCP has yet to be developed. For the time being we will have to find it manually. I hereby challenge you to develop the RCP algorithm that can be implemented in scheduling software, so we will be able to find it automatically.

Why Should I Care About the Resource-Critical Path?

There are five reasons why it is worthwhile to take the effort to find the RCP in your schedule. The reasons are:

◆ the RCP drives the Project End Date
◆ the RCP reveals the Critical Resource(s)
◆ the RCP allows finding domino-effects
◆ the RCP allows workload smoothing
◆ the RCP helps to do fast-tracking smarter

We will discuss each of these reasons.

The RCP Drives the Project End Date

Typically, somewhere along the Critical Path the resources start to constrain the schedule more than the dependencies. If the RCP stretches further, it overtakes the Critical Path. If that is the case, the RCP drives the project end date.

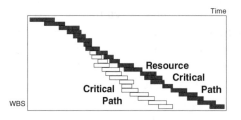

As you can see in the illustration, the white tasks constitute the regular Critical Path, but the leveling delayed some of the white tasks. The result of the leveling is shown as black tasks. The RCP is the combination of the critical tasks early in the schedule and all the resource-critical tasks later on. If you slip any of these tasks, the project will finish later.

Can we give the Critical Path Method a well-deserved retirement? The answer is no, because the Critical Path is still part of the RCP and often at the beginning of it. At the start of the project, resources often are not very busy and the logical sequence of tasks drives the schedule. As resources become very busy, they may start to drive the schedule instead of dependencies.

The RCP reveals the Critical Resource(s)

The RCP shows who the critical resources are. It also shows when the resources are critical. It is important to know who the resource is that determines the speed of the progress. Only if the project manager knows who it is, can he pay special attention to providing a work environment for this resource that is free of interruptions and disruptions.

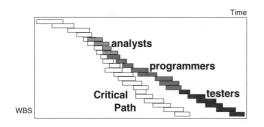

The RCP puts the focus back where it belongs. Managers are employees that perform through others. The RCP shows project managers which resources they should pay attention to. The RCP allows project managers to focus on people instead of tasks.

The RCP Allows Finding Domino Effects

If you make one change to a schedule, you may trigger a disastrous domino effect. *Have you ever had an avalanche of changes happen to you after you made one small change?*

Let me explain by using the illustration. What I show in this chart is that when *John* became sick, his task slipped. When he was ready to hand it off to *Mary* she had gone on holiday, so her task slipped even more. When she returned and ready with her task, *Gord* was temporarily re-assigned to another project, but he will return in three weeks. You decided not to wait for the return of *Gord* and you assign a new person. But the new person will need one

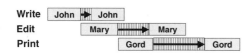

week of introduction and training, and so forth and so on. The result of one little slip can cause big delays because of resource dependencies rather than of task dependencies.

The RCP makes the most important resource dependencies visible. If you make the relationships between the resources visible, you can make changes to the schedule in a more educated fashion. You will not realize you are causing an avalanche of changes if you only monitor the conventional Critical Path.

The RCP Allows Workload Smoothing

There often is a huge amount of cost involved with erratic workloads. Please refer to the illustration. How much does Ed's workload cost before and after the leveling? He has periods in which he can twiddle his thumbs, and there are other periods in which he is overloaded (and may be wishing for another job). I often see companies burning out their critical resources, especially in IT projects. If a critical resource burns out, the individual and the organization are severely hurt. For organizations, this often has expensive consequences in terms of looking unprofessional, sick leave, lost contracts, and the cost of finding new, highly specialized people.

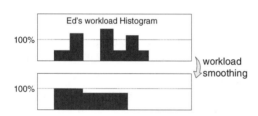

The Resource-Critical Path keeps an eye on the workloads continuously, because they drive it. The RCP, therefore, allows you to monitor and manage workloads better. The real cost of a smooth workload is often less than the cost of an erratic one.

The RCP Helps you to Fast-track Smarter

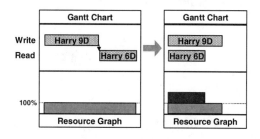

When crashing your schedule, you may be creating workload problems when you only focus on the Critical Path. You may work a long time to find a shorter schedule and just when you think you have a better schedule, you may realize you have changed time problems into workload problems. The schedule is now infeasible. If you ignore the resources you may create short, but infeasible schedules.

What is the Nature of the Beast?

To explore the nature of the RCP, I will present four different situations:
- ◆ Each resource has its RCP
- ◆ The RCP with multiple critical resources
- ◆ When multiple resources are assigned
- ◆ Logical dependencies and resource dependencies

Scheduling software will have to find the right Resource-Critical Path in all four situations before one can reasonably state that an RCP-algorithm has been found and the challenge is met.

Each Resource has its own RCP

In the example, the schedule is leveled every time for only one of the resources. This creates as many RCPs as there are resources. Ed and Di are both critical resources, but when leveled, Di pushes the end date out further than Ed. When shortening Di's RCP, you will arrive at a point after which Ed is more critical than Di. At that point, you have to shift your focus to Ed's workload instead of Di's. A similar thing can happen when crashing the good old Critical Path; another path can take over from the one we are working on any time. If you used the Critical Path Technique, you are probably familiar with that phenomenon.

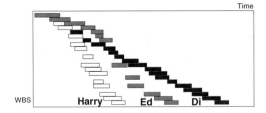

Another characteristic is that if there are hand-off points between resources, the RCP may be pushed out further than you would expect simply based on each individuals' resource-critical paths. The hand-off points run over a logical dependency. The logical dependencies link the chains of resource dependencies together.

The RCP With Multiple Critical Resources

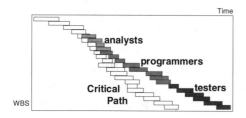

Several different resources typically drive the Resource-Critical Path. In the prototype software project the analysts drive the front end of the schedule, the programmers the middle, and the testers the back end. Every time there is a hand-off to the next resource there is a logical dependency. Logical dependencies connect the chains of resource dependent tasks.

When Multiple Resources are Assigned

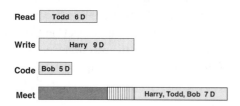

Consider one last example that will pose another challenge for the algorithm that can find the RCP. The illustrated example has resources assigned full-time to the tasks shown and multiple resources on the last task. The algorithm has to pick the right resource as the critical one, in this case, *Harry*.

Logical Dependencies and Resource Dependencies

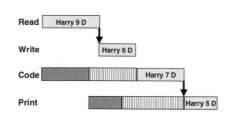

Leveling has delayed the tasks *Code* and *Print*. The difficulty in this situation is that there is no hard dependency between *Write* and *Code*, only a resource dependency. An algorithm that identifies the RCP has to be able to handle a combination of logical dependencies and resource dependencies.

Methods to Optimize on Time, Cost and Resources

As you can see we are now finally at the step to make a change. When the project has to finish earlier than the current schedule, it has to be shortened. The best measurements are those that make the quality (Q) go up (↑), the scope (S) go up (↑), the time (T) go down (↓), the cost (C) go down (↓), and the need for resources (R) go down (↓). Unfortunately, there are no such ideal measurements. The next table provides indications as to what the effect could be of each action in a typical project. You have to establish the impacts in your own project.

Steps to Optimize for Time, Cost and Resources

1. Check the workloads and level them
2. Highlight the RCP
3. Find the most critical resource
4. *Make a change on it*
5. Consider impacts on quality, scope, time, cost and resources
6. Decide whether you want to keep the change
7. Repeat steps 3 - 7

The methods discussed on pages 322 and following are repeated in the table because they are also valid in situations with limited resources. The difference is that these methods will now only work on resource-critical tasks instead of critical tasks. The actions are ranked in overall effectiveness. Because we now have limited resources we should also assess each method and its impact on the over-allocations in the project. Where I filled in a question mark (?) in the resources column (R), you have to check on new over-allocations after applying the measure. Where a zero (0) is shown, no impact is expected.

The table provides ideas as to how to improve the schedule. The actions are ranked in overall effectiveness. We recommend you start with finding the longest resource-critical tasks. Then explore whether the first two fast-tracking methods can be applied to those long tasks. After having exhausted the fast-tracking on all tasks, go to the next action proposed in the table.

The methods that make changes to assignments (actions 7 through 13) work for all tasks types except fixed duration tasks.
(Q=Quality, S=Scope, T=Time, C=Cost, R=Resources)

	Action	For	Q	S	T	C	R
1.	Change sequential dependencies into partial dependencies (fast-tracking)	resource-critical tasks	0	0	↓	0	?
2.	Create parallel paths from a sequential path (fast-tracking)	resource-critical tasks	?	0	↓	0	?
3.	Change schedule constraints	resource-critical tasks	0	0	↓	0	?
4.	Shorten lags (waiting periods)	resource-critical tasks	0	0	↓	0	?
5.	Split task bars around a Must-Start-On task	resource-critical tasks	0	0	↓	0	?
6.	Split long tasks into many shorter ones	resource-critical tasks	0	0	↓	↓	?
7.	Decrease estimates	resource-critical tasks	↓	↓	↓	↓	↓
8.	Reduce the scope or delete tasks	resource-critical tasks	↓	↓	↓	↓	↓
9.	Replace critical resources by non-critical resources	resource-critical tasks	↓	?	↓	?	↓
10.	Add non-critical resources	resource-critical tasks	0	0	↓	↑	?
11.	Postpone vacation of critical resources to after the deadline	resource-critical tasks	0	0	↓	↑	0
12.	Increase assignment units to full-time assignments for critical resources	resource-critical tasks	0	0	↓	0	?
13.	Assign overtime hours to critical resources	resource-critical tasks	↓	0	↓	↑	0

Fast-tracking with the RCP

Fast-tracking is making changes to dependencies in such a way that more tasks are scheduled concurrently. When you create overlaps, workloads are moved around as well and it is likely that you are creating over-allocations. If you apply these methods, you have to be careful not to create new over-allocations, which would render the fast-tracking useless. The best and easiest method, under unlimited resources, has to be applied here with greater care. The good news is that the RCP will often show which tasks will cause new over-allocations when fast-tracking.

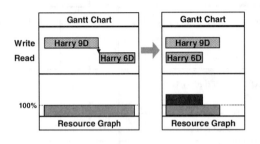

The fast-tracking efforts have to be focused on overlapping tasks that are done by different resources. For example, when you remodel an office floor, the tasks of carpenters and electricians can overlap each other as long as the carpenters start a few days ahead and finish a few days earlier.

We have discussed the first eight measures on pages 310 and following. We will discuss the remainder.

Replacing Critical Resources

If you replace a critical resource with a non-critical resource more tasks could possibly be scheduled in parallel.

In the illustration, Ted replaces Harry on the second task and this task can now be done in parallel with the first. The gain in time equals the duration of the second task.

1. In the Gantt Chart select a resource-critical task on which you can replace a critical resource.

2. Choose **Window, Split** to display the Task Form at the bottom.

3. Click on the name of the critical resource on the Task Form and use the list [_____] ⏷ to select the substitute resource.

4. Click [OK].

Or if you prefer using the **Assign Resources** dialog instead, follow the steps:

1. Click **Assign Resources** ; the **Assign Resources** floating dialog appears:

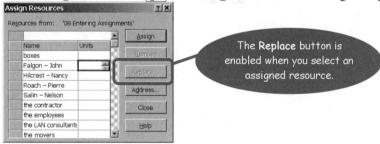

The **Replace** button is enabled when you select an assigned resource.

2. Click on the critical resource in the **Assign Resources** dialog.

3. Click [Replace...]; the **Replace Resource** dialog overlays the Assign Resources dialog.

4. Click on the resource to replace with and click [OK].

Level your schedule again and if the duration of the project is less then keep it; otherwise return to the previous version by closing without saving.

Adding Non-critical Resources

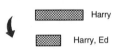

Two resources can normally finish a task faster than one resource. When you add a resource the duration will decrease, but it will only decrease if you have the right task type applied to the task before adding the resource. When you add a resource to a fixed work task the amount of work is now performed by two resources and could be done twice as fast.

1. Select a resource-critical task.

2. Choose **Window, Split** to pull up the **Task Form** in the bottom of the screen and determine which resource drives the duration of the task.

3. Select from the list **Task type** Fixed Units ▼ the type **Fixed Work**; this makes sure Project 2000 will shorten the duration when we add a resource.

4. Assign another resource and click OK ; the duration should have decreased.

Postponing Vacations

If you can convince your resource to postpone a vacation until after a critical deadline, you may be able to meet it.

In the illustration, you see the deadline depicted as a diamond. The vacation happened to be planned just before the deadline. If it can be moved the deadline can be met.

1. Choose **Tools, Change Working Time...**; the **Change Working Time** dialog appears:

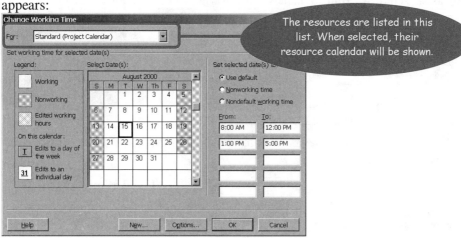

The resources are listed in this list. When selected, their resource calendar will be shown.

2. Under **For:** Standard (Project Calendar) ▼ select the resource.

3. Move the vacation for this resource to later dates, preferably after the deadline.

4. Click OK .

Increasing Assignment Units

When you notice that a half-time resource is working on critical tasks, you can finish the task earlier if you can get the resource to temporarily work full-time.

Again, the right task type has to be applied in Project 2000 if you want to see the duration decrease. The task type has to be fixed work. If the work is 10 person days and Harry works full-time instead of half-time on it, he will finish the task twice as fast.

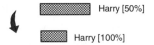

1. Select a resource critical task.

2. Choose **Window, Split** to display the **Task Form** in the bottom:

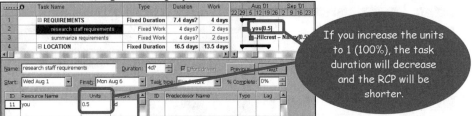

If you increase the units to 1 (100%), the task duration will decrease and the RCP will be shorter.

3. Determine which assignment drives the duration of the task if there is more than one resource assigned to the task.

4. Select from the list **Task type** Fixed Units ▼ the type **Fixed Work**; and click OK . This makes sure Project 2000 will shorten the duration when you increase the resource units.

5. Increase the resource units on a task so the resource works full-time on the critical task.

6. Click OK ; the duration should be decreased.

Assigning Overtime Hours

If you can get a resource to put in overtime, the critical tasks can often be finished earlier. Two situations can arise:

Harry: 40h

Harry: 30h + 10h overtime

- ◆ If overtime will not be charged, then change the resource calendar of that particular resource. You can increase the working hours or change holidays to working days. You can compensate by giving the resource time off later.
- ◆ If the overtime will be charged to the project at a higher overtime rate, then overtime should be entered in the overtime field on the Task Form. See below.

Entering Overtime Work at an Overtime Rate

1. Select a resource-critical task.

2. Pull up the **Task Form** in the bottom pane and choose **Format, Detail, Resource Work** to display the **Ovt. Work** field. The form should now look like this:

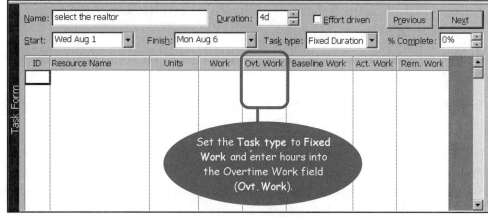

Set the **Task type** to **Fixed Work** and enter hours into the Overtime Work field (Ovt. Work).

3. Set the **Task type** to **Fixed Work** and click [OK].

4. Determine which resource drives the duration of the task and enter the hours to be worked in overtime in the field **Ovt. Work**.

5. Click [OK]; MS Project has scheduled the overtime hours outside regular working time and automatically recalculated the new duration.

Do not lower the original work estimate; MS Project subtracts overtime from the original estimate itself before calculating the new duration.

Consider the Impacts

After making changes, you have to consider impacts on Quality, Scope, Time Cost and Resources. For Quality and Scope you will have to evaluate the impact yourself. The impact on Time and Cost can be concluded from the statistics info box.

Steps to Optimize for Time, Cost and Resources

1. Check the workloads and level them
2. Highlight the RCP
3. Find the most critical resource
4. Make a change on it
5. **Consider impacts on quality, scope, time, cost and resources**
6. **Decide whether you want to keep the change**
7. Repeat steps 3 - 7

You can display the statistics dialog by choosing **Project, Project Information,** [Statistics...].

You will save some clicks if you display the **Tracking** toolbar:

1. Right-click on any toolbar and choose **Tracking** from the pop-up menu. The Tracking toolbar is displayed: [-√- ⇥ ⇥ ◄ 0ˣ 25ˣ 50ˣ 75ˣ 100ˣ ☰ 🖳 ▾]

2. The dialog is now available with one click on the **Project Statistics** tool [-√-]; the first tool on the toolbar.

You can now see how much time you have gained, and whether it is worth any sacrifices you may have made on the scope of the project or the quality of the deliverables.

Whenever you make a change to a resource-critical task, the workloads may move or change. You can check to see if this created new over-allocations by displaying the Resource Usage view. You may have to level the schedule again and determine once more what the new Resource-Critical Path is.

Often it is easiest to unmark all resource-critical tasks first. Then mark each task that you find to be resource-critical again. To unmark all, click on the column heading **Marked** and choose **Edit, Fill, Down**.

Optimizing on Time, Cost and Resources is a lot of work and practitioners would be greatly helped if the RCP could be found automatically[32].

---

[32] The company Prochain Solutions Inc. (www.prochain.com) sells add-on software, Prochain, that can extract the Resource-Critical Path from an MS Project schedule. They call this the *Critical Chain.*

Exercises

Review

1. How would you schedule *ordering materials* and *receiving materials* with an order time of three weeks? Would you use a Finish-to-Start dependency with a three-week lag? Or would you split the task bar for three weeks? Explain your answer.

2. A project is experiencing a lack of progress during execution. How would you schedule which resources are asked to make up with overtime for which they will not get paid? Detail the steps to take in MS Project.

Relocation Project – Understanding the Gantt Chart

Open the file *09 Optimizing – Time 1.MPP* in the sub-directory *Relocation Project* on the CD-ROM. Display the field **Total Slack** in the spreadsheet of the Gantt Chart.

1. Why does the Negative Slack decrease from -5.5 days on task 2 *research staff requirements* to -4.9 days on task 3 *summarize requirements*. (For the same reason the slack decreases from task 5 to 6.) Hint: the assignments are 50%.

2. Why does the negative slack decrease from -11.5 days on task 13 *meet to discuss contract* to -7.5 days on task 14 *revise the schedule*? Hint: Nancy is on holiday in the third full week in August.

3. Why does the negative slack increase from -7.5 days on task 20 *paint* to -9 days on task 23 *install LAN*? Hint: there is a task with an elapsed duration between them.

4. Why does the negative slack increase from -9 days on task 25 *facility remodeled* to -10 days on task *move*? Hint: there is a deadline on task 25.

5. Why does the negative slack decrease from -10 days on task *move* to -9 days on task *unpack*? Hint: the movers only work on the weekend.

Relocation Project – Shorten the Duration

This exercise is to try the Optimizing for Time approach.

1. Open the file *09 Optimizing – Time 1.MPP* in the subdirectory *Relocation Project* on the CD-ROM. Currently, the forecasted finish date is *November 15th*, but your CEO insists that the office should be moved by November 1st.

2. Display the Critical Path in your schedule. Make sure you understand all the total slack numbers on each task. If you do not understand the total slack numbers, first do the previous exercise *Understanding the Gantt Chart*.

3. The objective in this exercise is to bring down the duration (time) of the project as much as is reasonably possible. Use the methods that were discussed in this chapter to get ideas. Come up with your own ways to bring down the duration of the project as much as you can. Try them out and see how much time they save. Try to:

    ◇ make the project end date as early as possible, OR

    ◇ if you have a Must-Finish-On constraint on the project end milestone, make the **Total Slack** as large as possible on the project end milestone *new location opened*.

4. Try your ideas out and see if they work. If you keep a change make a note of it, in order to compare your measures against the solution.

5. Prepare to defend the changes you made in the schedule to the other students.

6. Compare your results against the ideas we will discuss in the next exercise.

Relocation Project – Ideas for Shortening the Duration

This exercise is to try the Optimizing for Time approach.

To illustrate how a schedule can be optimized, we will provide a complete optimization that will bring the project duration down to less than half the original duration! A similar reduction can be achieved in many projects by applying all the techniques discussed in this chapter.

1. Open the file *09 Optimizing – Time 2.MPP* in the sub-directory *Relocation Project* on the CD-ROM. The current duration of the project is 73 days.

2. When sorting the tasks on duration, it shows that the tasks *drying of paint, install LAN, relocate walls* and *lay carpet* are the longest tasks. All of these tasks are critical and seem to be a good starting point to find time in the schedule.

3. Enter the following changes to shorten the Relocation Project:

    a. Create an overlap in the dependency on *relocate walls*, so that *electric wiring* is done mostly in parallel with relocating the walls. Overlap *relocate walls* and *electric wiring* with an FF+1d dependency. The electricians can start on a wall as soon as the carpenters have it up. What is the duration of the project now?

    b. Cut the dependency between *lay carpet* and *install cabinetry* and cut the dependency between *lay carpet* and *install LAN*. Instead, make *lay carpet* dependent on *drying of paint*. Create new dependencies from *install cabinetry* and *install LAN* to *facility remodeled* to get rid of the loose ends in the network. You can lay carpet in parallel with installing cabinets and installing the LAN. What is the duration of the project now?

    c. Notice that the Critical Path is fragmented at this point. We have to make sure that we continue making changes to critical tasks only. Make the necessary changes to the schedule in such a way that you see the most critical path in the schedule again. Change the type of dependency between *electric wiring* and *paint* to FF+1d. The painters can start on a wall as soon as the electricians finish one. What is the duration of the project now? Why did the duration not come down?

    d. Change the type of dependency between *paint* and *drying of paint* to FF+1d. The paint starts drying as soon as the first wall is painted. What is the duration of the project now?

    e. Change the type of dependency between *facility remodeled* and *pack* into FF. The packing should ideally be ready when the facility is ready. What is the duration of the project now?

f. Cut the dependency between *location selected* and *select the contractor* and make *select the contractor* dependent on *evaluate the sites.* Create a new dependency between *location selected* and *meet to discuss contract.* You can select the contractor when you have an idea which location will be chosen. Notice that the duration of the task is changed by Project 2000 because of Nancy's holiday. We will make sure that at the end of the exercise it is set back to one day. What is the duration of the project now?

g. Get rid of the Start-No-Earlier-Than constraint on task 8 *meet to select the location* and arrange for a conference call or internet meeting with the CEO who is abroad. What is the duration of the project now?

h. Overlap *summarize requirements* and *research staff requirements* FF+1d. You can start summarizing as soon as you receive some completed questionnaires. What is the duration of the project now?   Why did the duration not come down?

i. Get rid of the lag on the dependency between task 12 *select the contractor* and task 13 *meet to discuss contract.* Make sure that you give an early warning of five days to the participants you expect in the meeting, so the five-day timeframe for calling the meeting is not needed anymore. What is the duration of the project now?

j. Change the task *install LAN* into a summary task by adding the following sub-tasks:
    install LAN cables (20 d of Fixed Work, predecessor *relocate walls),*
    install LAN hardware (20 d of Fixed Work, predecessor *install LAN cables),* and
    install LAN operating system (20 d of Fixed Work, predecessor *install LAN hardware,* successor *facility remodeled).*
    Keep the resource units on 5 units for all sub-tasks; remove the *LAN consultants* from the summary task. Cut the dependencies between *drying of paint* and *install LAN,* and between *install LAN* and *facility remodeled.* The result is a more refined and shorter schedule. What is the duration of the project now?

k. Increase the resource units of the *contractor* on the task *lay carpet* from 6 to 12. This decreases the duration of *lay carpet* to 5 days, which is now done entirely in parallel with *install cabinetry.* What is the duration of the project now?

l. You decide to ask the *LAN consultants* to work with 8 consultants instead of 5. Change all assignments of the *LAN consultants* to 8 units on the sub-tasks of *install LAN.* This will reduce the duration of the sub-tasks to 2.5 days. What is the duration of the project now?

m. The duration of the task *meet to discuss contract* was changed by Project 2000. Set its duration back to 1 day making sure that the total work on the task is 3 days and that Nancy Hilcrest can attend the meeting on the scheduled date. What is the duration of the project now?

4. Check the duration of the project; the duration should now be 34 days. We have reduced the duration from 73 to 34 days! This is a reduction to <u>less than half</u> of the original duration while most changes are quite defendable. You have seen here an example of how you can find time in your project schedule if you have created a dynamic model of your project in the first place. Could you apply similar methods in your own project schedule?

5. Are there trade-offs made against the scope or quality in this project? What are they? Are you going to undo some proposed changes? Why?

6. If you found a different final duration, find the differences between your file and the solution file *09 Optimizing – Time 3.MPP* in the sub-directory *Relocation Project* on the CD-ROM.

Relocation Project – Lowering the Cost

This exercise is to try the Optimizing for Time and Cost approach.

1. Open the file *09 Optimizing – Time Cost 1.MPP* in the sub-directory *Relocation Project* on the CD-ROM.

2. The objective now is to bring down the cost of the project while maintaining or decreasing the duration. Use the methods that were discussed in this chapter to get ideas. Come up with your own ways to bring down the cost of the project as far as you can. Try them out and see how much money they save.

3. Log each change and the total cost of the project after each change you keep.

4. Prepare to defend the changes you made to the other students.

5. Compare your results against the ideas that we will discuss in the next exercise.

Relocation Project – Ideas for Lowering the Cost

This exercise is to try the Optimizing for Time and Cost approach.

Open the file *09 Optimizing – Time Cost 2.MPP* in the sub-directory *Relocation Project* on the CD-ROM.

You found some new resources:

Name	Type	Position	Function	Max. Units	Std. Rate	Accrue at
Carpeteers	*Work*	*contractor*	*external*	*20*	*$140/d*	*End*
cablers	*Work*	*contractor*	*external*	*5*	*$40/h*	*End*
students	*Work*	*contractor*	*external*	*5*	*$80/d*	*End*

You find a specialized carpet company *Carpeteers* that is willing to do the job. Create this new resource: *Carpeteers*. Carpeteers estimates the work to total 30 person days and they will do it with 10 employees. Re-assign the task *lay carpet* to the new resource *Carpeteers*:

1. What is the current cost of the project?
   What is the current cost for the task *lay carpet*?
   What is the current duration of the project?

2. Re-assign the task to Carpeteers.
   What is the new forecasted cost for *lay carpet*?
   How much did we save on this task?

3. What is the new total cost for the project?

4. What is the new total duration of the project? Why is it lower?

5. What consequences does this change have for the scope and the quality of the project? Why?

6. Would you keep the re-assignment to *Carpeteers*?

7. Enter the following further changes to lower the cost of the Relocation Project:

   a. Delete the task *revise the schedule;* it is a nice-to-have task. How much is the total cost now?

b. Delete the task *select the Realtor* and hire the one you know. Is there a possible trade-off in doing this? How much is the total cost now?

c. Delete the task *select the contractor* and hire the one you know. Add a new dependency to keep the original logic. Is there a possible trade-off in doing this? How much is the total cost now? Note that the duration of the task *meet to discuss contract* is increased. Make sure its duration is set back to 1 day at the end of this exercise.

d. Make the task *install LAN* a summary task by adding the following sub-tasks: *install LAN cables (20 d of Fixed Work,* predecessor *relocate walls),* *install LAN hardware (20 d of Fixed Work,* predecessor *install LAN cables),* and *install LAN operating system (20 d of Fixed Work,* predecessor *install LAN hardware).* Keep the resource units on 5 units for all sub-tasks; remove the *LAN consultants* from the summary task. Cut the dependencies between *drying of paint* and *install LAN,* and between *install LAN* and *facility remodeled.* You ask the LAN-consultants to use cheaper resources to do the cabling of the LAN. They offer you specialized *Cablers* as shown in the table in the introduction of the question. Re-assign the task *install LAN cables* to the cheaper resource *Cablers.* How much is the total cost now?

e. You ask the contractor to come up with sharper estimates to save cost, and he can provide students who can help the carpenters in relocating the walls. He proposes to replace half of the carpenters with *students* as per the table. Are there possible trade-offs on time, scope or quality? How much is the total cost now?

f. In your search to save cost you decide that the 70 employees should pack all their stuff in one day instead of two days. Are there possible trade-offs on time, scope or quality? How much is the total cost now?

g. Set the duration of *meet to discuss contract* back to 1 day.

8. What is the forecasted cost for the project now?
The cost should now be $96,962.50, down from $128,793.75. If you found a different answer, find the differences with the solution file *09 Optimizing – Time Cost 3.MPP* in the sub-directory *Relocation Project* on the CD-ROM.

9. What is the forecasted duration for the project now?

10. Are there trade-offs in the scope or quality? What are they? Are you going to keep the changes proposed? Why?

Relocation Project – Leveling Manually

This exercise is to try the Optimizing for Time, Cost and Resources approach by leveling the workloads manually.

1. Open the file *09 Optimizing – Time Cost Resources 1.MPP* in the sub-directory *Relocation Project* on the CD-ROM.

2. Set **Tools, Resource Leveling...** to ⦿ **Manual leveling**.

3. Which view do you recommend to check the over-allocations?

4. Which resources are over-allocated?

5. You find that a few resources are over-allocated: *Nancy Hilcrest* and you yourself. What changes would you recommend to level the workloads manually?

6. Compare your file with the solution file *09 Optimizing – Time Cost Resources 2.MPP* in the sub-directory *Relocation Project* on the CD-ROM.

Relocation Project – Leveling Automatically

This exercise is to try the Optimizing for Time, Cost and Resources approach by leveling the workloads automatically.

1. Open the file *09 Optimizing – Time Cost Resources 3.MPP* in the sub-directory *Relocation Project* on the CD-ROM.

2. What is the current duration of the project?

3. Use automatic leveling to resolve all the over-allocations. Which view do you recommend for analyzing the results of automatic resource leveling?

4. Which field does MS Project change when leveling automatically?

5. Has MS Project increased the duration of the project? Why?

6. Are there any trade-offs in scope or quality? Would you keep the solution proposed by Project 2000? Why?

7. Compare your file with the solution file *09 Optimizing – Time Cost Resources 4.MPP* in the subdirectory *Relocation Project* on the CD-ROM.

Intranet Project – Shorten the Duration

This exercise is to try the Optimizing for Time, Cost and Resources approach using the Resource-Critical Path (RCP).

1. Open the file *09 Optimizing – Time Cost Resources 5 – Intranet Project.MPP* in the sub-directory *Relocation Project* on the CD-ROM [33].

2. How many resources do you need by month?

3. Would you level this file manually? Why?

4. What is the current duration of the project?

5. Level the workloads automatically, what is the duration now?

6. Check the Critical Path in the schedule; does it make sense?

7. Mark the RCP by entering **Yes** in the field **Marked** for each task you identify as resource-critical.

8. In the dialog **Format, Bar Styles** change the settings so they show a blue bar for all **Normal** tasks (critical and non-critical) and a red task bar for all **Normal, Marked** tasks (instead of for **Critical** tasks). You should now see red task bars for all tasks on the RCP in the schedule. Compare your file against the file *09 Optimizing – Time Cost Resources 6 – Intranet Project.MPP* in the sub-directory *Relocation Project* on the CD-ROM; the files should look the same.

9. The objective now is to bring down the duration of the project as much as possible (time), while maintaining or lowering the cost and keeping the workload reasonable (resources). Bring down the duration by shortening the RCP. Log each change and the resulting total duration of the project for each change you decide to keep.

10. Prepare to defend the changes you made to the other students.

11. Compare your results against the ideas that we will discuss in the next exercise.

---

[33] We will use a different file here because we have seen in the previous exercise that the workload leveling did not affect the project end date. In other words, the Critical Path is identical to the Resource-Critical Path in the Relocation Project.

Intranet Project – Ideas for Shortening the Duration

This exercise is to try the Optimizing for Time, Cost and Resources approach using the Resource-Critical Path.

1. Open the file *09 Optimizing – Time Cost Resources 6 – Intranet Project.MPP* in the sub-directory *Relocation Project* on the CD-ROM.

2. What is the current duration of this project schedule?

3. The challenge is to find methods to decrease the duration of the project that do not cost more and that do not cause new work overloads. You have to focus on the resource-critical tasks on the Resource-Critical Path (RCP). The following changes are examples of such measures:

    ◊   It is somewhat peculiar that the project manager is on the RCP. We should be able to take him/her off the RCP. A project manager should, in general, never be on the Critical Path except in very small projects in which he/she does tasks as a resource as well. Cut the dependency between task 8 *define specific functionality* and task 9 *define risks and risk management approach*. Give the task *Define risks and risk management approach* a new predecessor task 4 *Define user requirements*. Give *Define specific functionality* a new successor task 11 *Brief web development team*. Are tasks 9 and 10 still resource-critical? Are there new work overloads? If so, level the workloads again. Determine the new RCP. What is the duration and cost of the project now?

    ◊   The roll-out manager is doing his planning on the RCP. That type of task should not be on the RCP. Cut the dependency between task 31 *Integrate into website* and task 46 *Determine roll-out schedule*. Make task 46 *Determine roll-out schedule* dependent on task 24 *Server site live*. Are tasks 46 to 49 still resource-critical? Are there new work overloads? If so, level the workloads again. Determine the new RCP. What is the duration and cost of the project now?

    ◊   You see that the longest resource-critical tasks are tasks 29 *Development* and 30 *Develop any custom functionality*. They take one third of the schedule. If you can find an extra Web designer for task 30 *Develop any custom functionality*, you can schedule those two tasks in parallel. You request the resource manager for an extra designer and you will have one for that one task. Create a new resource *Web Designer 2* with the same rate as the first designer and assign him/her to task 30 *Develop any custom functionality*. Set a new dependency between task 28 *Determine development tool* and 30 *Develop any custom functionality*. Are there new work overloads? If so, level the workloads again. Determine the new

RCP. What is the duration and cost of the project now? Is task 30 still resource-critical?

4. We started with a schedule of 67 days that was not levelled. We then levelled and ended up with 116 days. We then shortened the schedule again to 83 days without increasing the cost and without work overloads. Does the current RCP make sense? Why?

5. Compare your file with the solution file *09 Optimizing – Time Cost Resources 7 – Intranet Project.MPP* in the sub-directory *Relocation Project* on the CD-ROM.

Case Study Multinational – IT

The client is the IT department of a large multinational. Recently, the organization made the corporate decision to use MS Project for all their projects. They used ABT's Project Workbench before. They still work very much as they did when they had Project Workbench; they like to enter actual hours worked and remaining hours. They have a separate timesheet system that reports actual hours worked by project or by category over many projects (e.g., 'maintenance').

Managers in the IT department are using the MS Project schedules as checklists. Many of them get frustrated using the scheduling features of MS Project and revert to using MS Excel instead. When this was acknowledged, the client decided to organize basic training in MS Project using a local training provider. Since the training, one year ago, the situation has not improved a lot, and many people are still using Excel. The ones who use MS Project are not taking advantage of all the features of the application.

In interviews with several users you find that they experience the following problems:
◆ Double data entry of actual hours into the timesheet system and into the project scheduler.
◆ IT executives impose tight deadlines using cost-payback arguments to successfully defend these challenging project deadlines. Your clients, the IT project managers, told you, "We have not been able to prove that these deadlines were not feasible."
◆ The organization has a matrix structure; many resources are working part-time on the project and are shared across several projects. There are many over-allocations and, in fact, so many that they were advised by ABT consultants to use AutoSchedule (automatic resource leveling) after which they should try to shorten the schedule.
◆ They experience ripple effects between projects; a change in one project can have impacts on other schedules.
◆ Most projects are independent projects and do not have cross-project dependencies.

◆ The training did not train participants on how to apply MS Project to their own real-life projects.

There is a need for more guidance for the Project Managers to lower the threshold using the more beneficial features of MS Project.

QUESTIONS

1. Which feature of MS Project should be used to address the ripple effect across projects?

2. What optimization method do you recommend in this situation? Why?

3. Will they then be able to prove that the imposed deadlines are not feasible?

4. What would you recommend in order to:

    ◇ get more project managers to use MS Project?

    ◇ get the project managers to use more features of MS Project?

Troubleshooting

1. Open the file *Sure-Critical.MPP* from the *Troubleshooting* subdirectory on the CD-ROM. Why are only the tasks 3, 4, 5 and 6 shown as critical and not 1 and 2?

2. Open the file *Why-Overload.MPP* from the *Troubleshooting* subdirectory on the CD-ROM. Why is the resource *You* over-allocated in the week of Sept. 2-9?

Chapter 10 Reporting

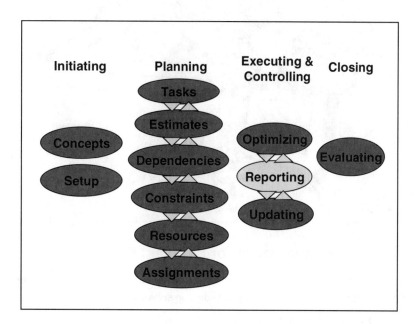

After this chapter you will:

◆ know the standard reports of Project 2000

◆ be able to customize a standard report

◆ be able to customize views for reporting:
   ◇ create a custom table
   ◇ create your own filters
   ◇ create new groupings

◆ know how to create some useful and hard-to-get-at printouts

◆ know how to copy custom objects between projects

◆ be able to print your schedule:
   ◇ be able to check the spelling in your project
   ◇ know how to set up a printer
   ◇ know how to set page breaks manually

Status Report or Forecast Report?

As an experienced project manager, Bob checks in with Nob whom he has just promoted to team leader. Bob asks Nob, "Have you updated your schedule?"

"Yeah, I put all the actuals in it!"

"And does it impact the end date for your deliverable?"

"No, the date is still the same, I can show you on the screen..."

"It looks good except for this one task ... it seems to slip."

"Yeah, the actual progress reported to me was disappointing. I entered it into the schedule." explains Nob.

"So they are progressing slowly. Did you ask them how many more days they need?"

"Yeah, Fred thinks it will be another five days."

"You forgot to enter that new forecast into your schedule!"

Nob wonders, "Do you think it makes a difference? I'll enter it and we will see." A minute later he exclaims: "Oh my gosh, the whole chain of tasks turned immediately red!"

Bob adds, "And the deadline date is not met any longer! What are we going to do about it? What you gave me is a status report, I need a forecast report."

Project Communications Management

Creating One-page Printouts … Always!

This title may seem pretentious if you are juggling a schedule with thousands of tasks. Regardless of the size of the project, you can always surprise your managers and clients with one-page reports. There is a simple technique to do this and it will make your executives happy, if not euphoric. Executives typically don't have the time to dig through pages and pages of schedule. They expect you to provide concise information by creating one-page reports. A one-page report can only show the major milestones. That is all you need if all the milestones are on schedule and the budgets are feasible. Where a milestone is off its baseline, you provide a second one-page report that provides an explanation for the discrepancy. In the illustration, you can see in the milestone chart that there is a slippage on the *Roofing* milestone. In the bottom one-page report the detailed cause of the slippage is shown. With a few one-page reports you should be able to give an adequate status and a forecast report for a project of any size.

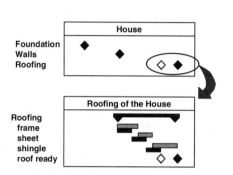

In a similar fashion, you can create a one-page high-level cost report, if there are discrepancies you can show another one-page report with the explanation for the differences.

You will have to master the filters feature of Project 2000 to accomplish this. Before we delve into that, let us ponder the fundamental question: whether or not to show your time buffer.

Hiding your Time Buffer?

When we optimized the schedule in the previous chapter, you may have found a healthy amount of slack. The dilemma of whether to hide the slack or not can be one of the most difficult choices. Your choice should depend on several factors concerning upper management:

◆ What is the dominant pulling force in the project?
   Is the project driven by time, cost, quality or availability of resources? If time is the dominant force, everybody will be scrutinizing your schedule to find slack. The more people who look for it, the less chance you will succeed in keeping it hidden.

◆ What is the interest of upper management?
   Do they have a strong business interest in speeding up your project as much as they can? In many software and hardware projects, the sole focus is to be the first one to market. If that is the case, you will not likely succeed in keeping the time buffer for yourself.

◆ How mature is upper management in terms of project management?
   Do they think that, as the project manager, you should own some slack to meet the deadlines or do they prefer to own the slack themselves? It is generally accepted project management practice that the project manager who is responsible for meeting deadlines owns slack in her project. Greedy upper management may try to confiscate your slack.

◆ How mature is the organization in project management?
   The organization may be very centralized. If that is the case, you will likely lose visible slack. Project management thrives well in a decentralized organization. In these organizations, upper management establishes a contract with the project manager, first through a project charter and next through the project plan. These formal documents should clearly spell out the rules of the game. If your organization doesn't use these project documents, or if they don't use them in a formal way, you risk losing slack you make visible.

Similar questions can be asked when it comes to the client:

◆ What is the dominant pulling force in the project?
◆ What is the interest of the client? Do they want the project product as soon as possible or is low cost more important?
◆ How mature is the client in terms of project management?
◆ How mature is the client organization in project management?

◆ What is the type of contract with the client?
In dealing with the client it is important to be aware of the type of contract that is established. If it is a time and materials contract, the client will be looking over your shoulder. If the contract is fixed-price, you will probably want to hide your time buffer from the client as well as your profit margin.

The big drawback for project managers of hiding time buffers is that it creates a culture of secrecy. If the different levels of management stop communicating openly with each other, the situation may worsen over time. Ideally, the time and money buffers should be on the table instead of under the table. If a project manager habitually hides slack and an executive happens to find out, the executive may start cutting time off future schedules for this project manager. The project manager will then in turn hide even more slack in hard-to-find places. The executive may start slashing the schedules more and arbitrarily. The situation deteriorates. I have been witness to organizations that continuously play this game, instead of conducting projects in an open, professional manner. If you think you can defend the slack in your project successfully, we recommend you try that. Openness is greatly preferred over a culture of secrecy that can create a vicious downward spiral.

If at any point upper management or the client tries to snatch your buffer, insist that with the buffer they also assume the accountability for meeting the agreed upon deadlines. Only if the stakeholders allow the project manager to own a reasonable amount of slack, can she carry responsibility for meeting deadlines.

Methods to Hide the Time Buffer

If you are in a situation in which it is impossible to show a time buffer, you have to hide it in your schedule. The following are methods to hide a buffer. Most of them are the opposite of the optimizing methods we discussed in the previous chapter. They are ranked in ascending likelihood that they will stay hidden from examining eyes:

1. **Overestimating lags**
Lags are gaps between task bars of dependent tasks. Lags are used to model time that is out of your control, as when you are waiting to receive a construction permit. It is smart to estimate these lags on the (very) safe side. They can be noticed in the Gantt Chart. For the how-to, see page 182: To Edit or Delete the Dependency.

2. **Insert extra holidays in the project calendar**
You can insert extra common holidays in the project calendar. The task bars that span these days will stretch. This can be noticed in the Gantt Chart. For the how-to, see

page 98: Entering the Holidays. For a more sophisticated use of calendars, see below under inserting extra holidays for your critical resources.

3. **Decrease the working hours on the project calendar**
   This is frequently applied. Managers know that resources are not productive eight hours a day even though their workday is eight hours. On the project calendar you start the business day later or finish it earlier. For the how-to, see page 97: Entering the Working Hours.

4. **Ignore the benefits of learning curves**
   If you have repetitive activities in your schedule, you will likely benefit from the decreasing learning time in every repeat. Your estimate should be lower with every repeat. If you ignore this effect of the learning curve, you are in fact keeping a buffer in your schedule. See: Chapter 4 Entering Estimates.

5. **Introduce ramp-up and wind-down factors**
   If your resources are involved in more than one project at a time, your resources will be less productive because of setting up and closing down work on a task. You can include these in your estimates. See: Chapter 4 Entering Estimates.

6. **Introduce distraction factors for high-focus tasks**
   Certain tasks require your full focus, but the world around you will not stop spinning. Writing text is an example in which most people need to be able to concentrate fully. Increase the estimate on these tasks with a distraction factor. See: Chapter 4 Entering Estimates.

7. **Introduce extra revision cycles**
   Every revision cycle has two tasks: revise and modify. For writing, you could add tasks like *edit* and *re-write*. You might even get away with another cycle of *re-edit* and *re-re-write*, but you may want to call it something else. For the how-to of inserting tasks, see page 128: Inserting Multiple Tasks.

8. **Keep maximum units of resources low**
   In a resource-constrained schedule you can influence the forecasted project end date by changing the availability of resources (**Max. Units**). If you are not entirely sure of how many you will receive, you can create some slack if you keep them on the safe and low side. For the how-to, see page 252: Consolidated Resources.

9. **Assign one scarce expert to more tasks than needed**
   If one expert is in great demand, he will likely drive the deadlines. If you assign him

to more tasks than strictly needed he will drive out the deadline even further, thus creating slack. It is hard to argue with using the best expert on tasks. For the how-to, see page 278: Overview Assigning.

10. Create extra inconspicuous tasks

One of my students once confided that he always creates a task *Find alternative resources* in the task list wherever slightly appropriate. I won't mention his name so as not to spoil the fun for him. Other good ones that are hard to argue with are *Apply quality check* or *Update the project plan*. See page 128: Inserting Multiple Tasks.

11. Padding the duration and work estimates

One project manager once shared his wisdom with me that *To Pad or Not To Pad* is similar to the Shakespearian *To Be or Not To Be.* You are entering into a culture of secrecy, however. See: Chapter 4 Entering Estimates.

12. Set extra soft dependencies

Soft dependencies are dependencies that are not absolutely needed, but that can be defended with an argument such as: "*We prefer to do it like this, because it has the following advantage ...*". For the how-to, see page 180: Entering Logic.

13. Be pessimistic about material delivery dates

When you are dependent upon receiving a shipment before you can do your work, create a delivery milestone on a date that is later than the date you were promised by the supplier. For the how-to, see page 179: External Dependencies.

14. Insert extra holidays for your critical resources

Determine who the most critical resources in your schedule are and insert extra holidays on their resource calendar. This cannot be seen easily on the Gantt Chart and can be quite effective. For the how-to, see page 245.

15. Don't use overtime yet

If you know you can count on your resources working some overtime, don't enter it in the schedule yet in the planning phase. Whenever your team members work a weekend, the two days will be pure gain. For the how-to, see page 377: Assigning Overtime Hours.

As you may have noticed, all these methods boil down to not fully optimizing your schedule. If you don't use all the methods of optimization or if you don't apply them to their fullest, you may keep a buffer in your schedule. We recommend you try to optimize your schedule to the maximum first, to be sure about the real amount of buffer you have.

How to Defend Visible Buffers

As we stated before, it is highly preferable if you keep the buffer you own visible in your schedule. It is the professional thing to do, because it is generally accepted project management practice that when upper management asks a project manager to commit to a deadline, it allows him to own the buffer. A simple way to defend a buffer is to create a separate line item for it in the task list, instead of leaving it as an undefined, gaping hole in your schedule. Call the line item *Time Contingency Reserve*, which is a technical term that may impress some to such a degree that they let you keep it. Assign yourself as the resource, so it adds a buffer of effort and cost as well and it becomes clear you own it. Make sure this line item is dependent on the last tasks and make the project end milestone its sole successor.

There is another, entirely scientific, method that will prove you need a reasonable amount of slack in your schedule: Monte Carlo simulation. We discussed this on page 333: Monte Carlo Simulation. You can use simulation to create a probability curve of project end dates. When you have the curve you can then decide which probability you feel comfortable with and find out what end date results. This dictates how much buffer you should create. Or you could ask upper management with what level of confidence they feel comfortable and quote a date accordingly.

Communication Vehicles in Project 2000

I will subsequently use the word *printout* instead of the more common word *report,* because *report* refers to the report feature in MS Project. To publish your schedule you can either print a report or print a view. In Project 2000 you now have a third option and that is to publish your schedule on a website through Project Central.

◆ **Reports**
There are several different standard reports available in MS Project in the **View, Reports...** menu. All reports are table-like with precise, numeric information. Reports have one feature called **Show Totals** that cannot be reproduced using Views. Furthermore, there are some printouts you can only create using the reports feature:

◇ **Project Summary**: gives statistics on the entire project. You can find it in the section **Overview**.

◇ **Project Calendar**: prints the holidays and working hours. You can find it in the section **Overview** listed as **Working Days**.

◇ **Resource Calendars**: prints the resource-specific calendars that can be included in any resource report. To include the resource calendar information, choose one

of the **Assignment** reports and click , on the tab **Details** check
☑ **Calendar**.

◆ **Views**

Printing a view shows on paper whatever you created on the screen: (WYSIWYG –
What You See Is What You Get). MS Project is very user-friendly in this respect.
You can print any view from the menu except for all the forms (Task Form, Resource
Form and Relationships Diagram). You cannot print the bottom view of a split
combination view either. Only with Views you can:

◇ print the graphical charts like Gantt Chart, Network Diagram and Resource
Graph on paper,

◇ apply the new feature of groupings

◆ **Project Central**

Project Central is a new feature in Project 2000. It is a separate companion
application shipped with Project 2000. It allows you to communicate via a website
and is therefore the way of the future. Project Central is not only a communication
tool, it facilitates collaboration and delegation as well. We will discuss Project
Central in the next chapter.

In this chapter, we will discuss the paper printing reports and views.

Printing a Report

To print a report, first select the report category you want and then select a specific report to view in the print preview window.

You can choose one of the standard reports from the following categories:

◆ **Overview**
Overview reports show information over the entire project duration, including summary tasks, critical tasks, project milestones, cost and schedule information.

◆ **Current Activities**
Current Activity reports show a variety of task information, such as tasks that are not started, in progress, completed, or behind schedule.

◆ **Costs**
Cost reports show budgets for all tasks over the entire project duration; time-phased budget, tasks and resources that are over budget; earned-value information for all tasks.

◆ **Assignments**
Assignment reports show assignments for all resources over the entire project duration; or assignments for only the resources you specify, assignments displayed by week; and resources that are over-allocated.

◆ **Workload**
Workload reports show task usage or resource usage information.

Then there is an extra category called **Custom,** which allows you to create a new report or to customize or copy any of the existing reports discussed above.

Previewing Reports

1. Choose **View, Reports...**; the **Reports** dialog appears:

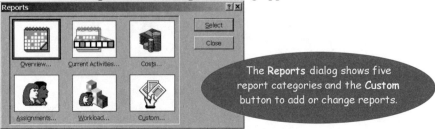

The **Reports** dialog shows five report categories and the **Custom** button to add or change reports.

2. Double-click on a report category, if you double-click the **Overview** reports; the **Overview Reports** dialog appears:

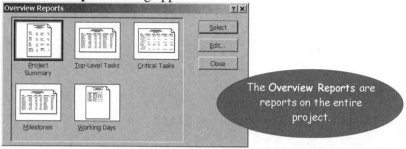

The **Overview Reports** are reports on the entire project.

3. Some printouts cannot be produced in other ways, such as the **Project Summary** report. If you double-click on it, you will see the report in print preview:

The **Project Summary** report shows total Duration, Work and Cost, as well dates.

Relocation Devom Inc.
Devom Inc.
Eric Uyttewaal
as of Thu Jan 4

Dates

Start:	Wed Aug 1	Finish:	Tue Nov 13
Baseline Start:	NA	Baseline Finish:	NA
Actual Start:	NA	Actual Finish:	NA
Start Variance:	0 days	Finish Variance:	0 days

Duration

Scheduled:	73 days?	Remaining:	73 days?
Baseline:	0 days?	Actual:	0 days
Variance:	73 days?	Percent Complete:	0%

Work

Scheduled:	4,803 days	Remaining:	4,803 days
Baseline:	0 days	Actual:	0 days
Variance:	4,803 days	Percent Complete:	0%

Costs

Scheduled:	$128,793.75	Remaining:	$128,793.75
Baseline:	$0.00	Actual:	$0.00
Variance:	$128,793.75		

Task Status

		Resource Status	
Tasks not yet started:	31	Work Resources:	9
Tasks in progress:	0	Overallocated Work Resources:	1
Tasks completed:	0	Material Resources:	1
Total Tasks:	31	Total Resources:	11

4. You will get an error message if you don't have a printer set up on your computer. You can set one up through Windows; choose **Start, Settings, Printers, Add Printer**.

5. The mouse pointer has changed to 🔍 and by clicking on the preview you can zoom in on the details and with another click you will zoom out again.

6. To change the margins, header, or footer, click **Page Setup...** at the top of the screen.

7. To print the report, click **Print...** .
   To return without printing, click **Close** .

To Customize a Report

1. Choose **View, Reports...**; the **Reports** dialog appears:

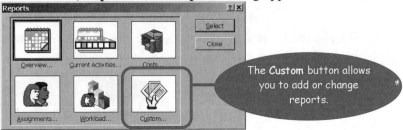

The **Custom** button allows you to add or change reports.

2. Double-click on the **Custom...** category ; the **Custom Reports** dialog appears:

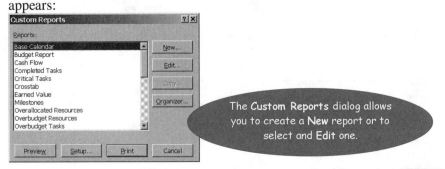

The **Custom Reports** dialog allows you to create a **New** report or to select and **Edit** one.

3. Select a report from the list that is closest to what you want and click **Copy...** to copy and edit the report, leaving its original intact
   OR

   click **Edit...** to edit the report itself. (Some reports cannot be edited, for example the **Base Calendar** report)

If you selected a task report, the **Task Report** dialog appears:

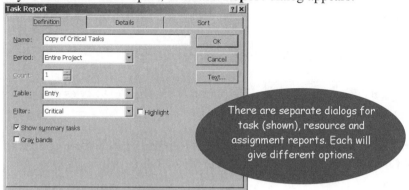

4. Enter a descriptive name for your report under
   Name: [   ].
   Depending on what type of report you choose, the dialog provides the appropriate choices. See for an explanation of them below these steps.

5. Click [OK] when done.

6. Click [Preview] to display the report in print preview.

7. If it looks good, click [Print...] and the **Print** dialog appears.

8. Click [OK] to print it.

Report Customization Options

We will discuss the most common options for customizing reports:

◆ **Definition** tab:
Choose the table and the filter.
Check ☑ **Gray bands**: to print gray bands separating individual tasks or resources, which will improve the readability.

◆ **Details** tab:
Choose the data to include in the report. If you are editing a task-related report you can include certain task fields. In resource reports, you can include resource fields. In either resource or task reports you can include assignments.
Check ☑ **Border Around Details** to print borders around the details you include in the report.

Check ☑ **Show totals** for any fields that should be added up; the totals are shown at the bottom of the report.

◆ **Sort** tab
Specify a sort order for the records in the report.

On all tabs you can click [Te_x_t...]. This button opens the **Text Styles** dialog in which you can choose the fonts and their sizes for the report.

Over the years I have found that **Views** rather than **Reports** provide more options to create the right printout. In the rest of the chapter we will discuss using **Views**.

Printing a View

The view can be changed in many ways depending on the need for information. These are the steps to tailor the printout to your needs:

1. Design a new **Table**, which columns do you want?
2. Design a new **Filter**, which tasks or resources to show?
3. Create a new **Group**.
4. Create a new **View** that applies the newly created **Table, Filter** and **Group**.
5. Sort the records.
6. Apply any formats such as time scale, text styles, bar styles.
7. Choose the **Page Setup** settings.

A view applies a table, a filter and a group, and contains many layout settings:
- ◆ the sorting order through the menu items **Project, Sort**,
- ◆ any formats applied through the **Format** menu item,
- ◆ all page setup settings from the **File, Page Setup** dialog, and
- ◆ any objects inserted.

That is why we recommend creating a new view before doing the sort, format and page setup. All are stored in a single **View** object. The **Table, Filter** and **Group** also exist as separate objects in the **Tools, Organizer**. If you want to create a new view, for example an *Executive Overview*, you could create a table and call it *Executive Overview*, a filter called *Executive Overview* and a group called *Executive Overview*. When you apply the view it will apply all its components. If you name them all the same, it is clear that they belong together. This helps when you want to give the view to somebody else; in the Organizer you can easily see which objects the view uses.

You could even start the name of the objects by an * (asterix) or an _ (underscore) to sort your objects at the top of the list. Or you could use an acronym to indicate they are customized for your organization, at the International Institute for Learning, we use IIL.

New views can be created using a *single view* or two views (top and bottom view). The latter is called a *combination view*. Combination views are useful for analyzing projects, because what you select in the top view is always shown in more detail in the bottom view.

Tables

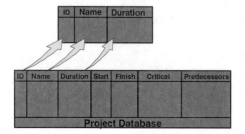

A table is a selection of fields from the project database and their order. A table does not contain project data; it is a layout only. MS Project is different from other applications because tables in, for example, Word or Excel contain data. In the illustration, you can see that the table only displays the fields *ID, Name* and *Duration* of all the fields present in the Project 2000 database.

Using an Existing Table

1. Make sure you are in one of the table views; a table view looks like a table on the **View Bar** at the left side of the screen. There are also views that look like fill-in forms; they do not use a table. The Network Diagram and the Resource Graph do not use tables either.

2. Choose **View, Table <name of current table>** and choose the table you want to apply. The current table (if listed) has a check mark in front of it.
    OR

    Right-click on the **Select All** area [   ] where the row headings intersect with the column headings. A pop-up menu appears from which you can choose the table to apply.

3. The layout of columns is now replaced by a new layout as per the definition of the table object you applied.

Designing a new Table

Instead of changing the **Entry** table constantly, there are advantages creating a new table object for each reporting need you have. In this way you will not have to re-invent the wheel every time.

1. Choose **View, Table <name of current table>, More Tables…**; the **More Tables** dialog appears:

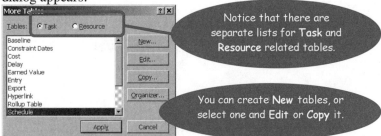

Notice that there are separate lists for **Task** and **Resource** related tables.

You can create **New** tables, or select one and **Edit** or **Copy** it.

2. To list the task tables, select ⊙ **Task**, for resource tables select ⊙ **Resource**.

3. Select the table that is closest to what you want in the **Tables** box and click
   Copy… to create a duplicate with which to work. The **Table Definition** dialog appears:

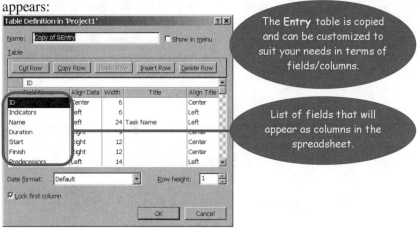

The **Entry** table is copied and can be customized to suit your needs in terms of fields/columns.

List of fields that will appear as columns in the spreadsheet.

4. In the **Name** box, type a new name for the table.

5. To delete a field in the table, click the row to delete, and click Delete Row .
   To insert a new field in the table, click the row before which you want the new field and click Insert Row .
   To replace a field at once, click it and select the new field from the list.

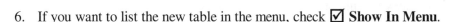

6. If you want to list the new table in the menu, check ☑ **Show In Menu**.

7. If you want to lock the first field, check ☑ **Lock First Column**. There are advantages to having a locked first column; it allows you to select an entire task or resource record in the database and the locked title will not scroll off the screen. The

data cannot be edited in the locked column, which is just fine for ID numbers that are maintained by MS Project anyway.

8. Click [OK]; you are now back in the **More Tables** dialog.

9. To apply the table and return to your project, click [Apply].

Filters

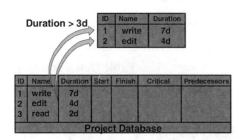

A *filter* selects and displays records from the project database that meet a criterion you set. You can filter tasks or resources. Project 2000 allows you to create a criterion that selects within any field in the database. The filter does not contain the project data, it is just the screen applied to the project database. As you can see in the illustration, the tasks with a duration greater than three days are filtered from the database.

 A filter does not display any tasks that are collapsed under their summary task. If you ever wonder why the filter does not display certain tasks, they were probably collapsed. Expand all summary tasks first, using the [**Show** ▾] tool, before applying a filter.

Applying an Existing Filter

1. Choose **Project, Filtered for <name of current filter>**.
    OR
    Click the [▾] of the tool [All Tasks ▾] on the standard toolbar; the list with filters rolls down.

2. Select a filter from the list. Only the records that meet the criterion are now displayed.

As with tables, there are advantages to creating a new table object for each reporting need you have. In this way you will not re-create it every time.

Designing a new Filter

1. Choose **Project, Filtered for <name of current filter>, More Filters**; the **More Filters** dialog appears:

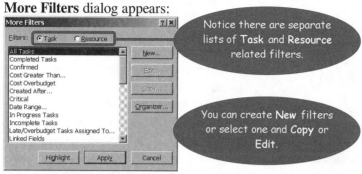

Notice there are separate lists of **Task** and **Resource** related filters.

You can create **New** filters or select one and **Copy** or **Edit**.

2. Click on a filter that is close to what you want and click 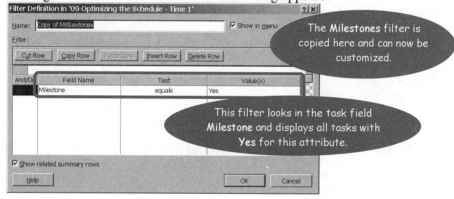 ; this will keep the original in tact. The **Filter Definition** dialog appears:

The **Milestones** filter is copied here and can now be customized.

This filter looks in the task field **Milestone** and displays all tasks with **Yes** for this attribute.

3. Enter a name for the filter; keep it the same as the table you created.

4. To list the new filter in the menu check ☑ **Show In Menu**.

5. Change the filter definition:
   select the field to filter on from the list under **Field Name**
   select the comparison from the list under **Test**
   type in a literal value under **Value(s)** or choose another field to compare to from the list.

6. Click 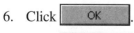 .

7. Click  .

Groups

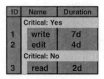

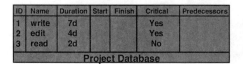

Project Database

Groups are categories that allow you to reorder the task list. When you apply a grouping, the original structure of the WBS will be temporarily hidden and the new grouping will be displayed. In the illustration, you can see that the tasks are categorized on the attribute *Critical* in two groups of *Yes* and *No*. The attribute *Critical* is a task-related yes/no field. When you apply **No Group** again, the grouping will disappear and the Work Breakdown Structure will re-appear.

 This new grouping feature gives Project 2000 the power of a relational database.

 Notice that if an item falls in more than one group the item is repeated. For example, if you assigned two resources to a task and then grouped the tasks by resource, the task will show up for both resources.

Applying an Existing Grouping

1. Choose **Project, Group by: <name of current group>**.
   OR
   Click ▾ of the list `No Group` ▾ on the standard toolbar; the list with different groupings rolls down.

2. Select a group from the list; the records are sorted and displayed within their groups.

As with tables and filters, there are advantages to creating a new group object for each reporting need you have. In this way you will not re-create it every time.

Designing a new Grouping

1. Choose **Project, Group by: <name of current group>, More Groups…**; the **More Groups** dialog appears:

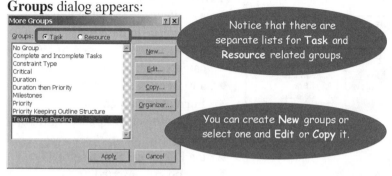

Notice that there are separate lists for **Task** and **Resource** related groups.

You can create **New** groups or select one and **Edit** or **Copy** it.

2. Click on a group that is close to what you want and click Copy…; this will keep the original in tact. The **Group Definition** dialog appears:

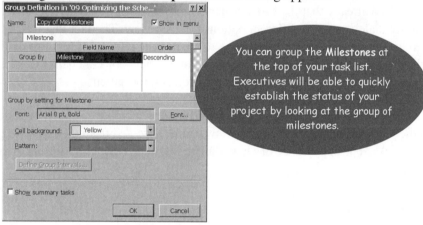

You can group the **Milestones** at the top of your task list. Executives will be able to quickly establish the status of your project by looking at the group of milestones.

3. Enter a name for the group; keep it the same as the name of the table you created.

4. To list the new group in the menu check ☑ **Show In Menu**.

5. Change the group definition:
   select the field to group by from the list under **Field Name**
   select **Descending** or **Ascending** from the list under **Order**.

6. Click OK; you are now back in the **More Groups** dialog.

7. Click Apply.

Views

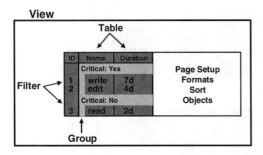

A view contains:
- ◆ a reference to the table it uses
- ◆ a reference to the filter it applies
- ◆ a reference to the group by which it categorizes the data
- ◆ any formats applied through the **Format** menu item
- ◆ the sorting order applied via **Project, Sort**
- ◆ the **File, Page Setup** settings
- ◆ any objects inserted

Perhaps you noticed already that the **Format** menu looks different in each view. Also, the **File, Page Setup** dialog contains different options for each view. The fact that the menus change depending on the view can be confusing to the occasional user of MS Project. The reason for the changes is that the settings are stored in the view object. Thanks to it, the view provides a steady display and printout of the project information.

It is a good idea to create a new view for each reporting need you have. The view can also be added to the **View** menu. If you do so the view can be accessed from then on with two simple mouse clicks. The appearance of views can be fine-tuned using the sorting and the format menus.

Creating a new View

1. Choose **View, More Views…**; the **More Views** dialog appears:

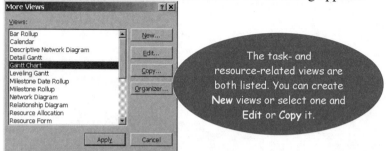

The task- and resource-related views are both listed. You can create **New** views or select one and **Edit** or **Copy** it.

2. Choose the view that is closest to what you want and click **Copy…**.
OR
Click **New…**; the **Define New View** dialog appears that allows you to choose between creating a single or a combination view. We will create a single view.
Click **OK**.

3. The **View Definition** dialog appears:

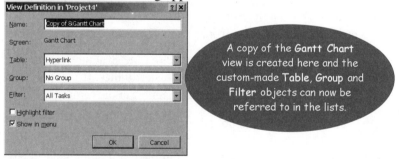

A copy of the **Gantt Chart** view is created here and the custom-made **Table**, **Group** and **Filter** objects can now be referred to in the lists.

4. Fill in the name for the new view and select the **Table**, the **Group** and the **Filter** from the lists provided. It helps if all the components of the view have the same name to make it obvious they all belong together. You can still return to the definition dialogs to rename them.

5. If you want this report to show in the menu check ☑ **Show in menu**.

6. Click **OK**; you are now back in the **More Views** dialog.

7. Click **Apply**.

Sort the Records

Choose **Project, Sort**; choose one of the listed sort orders; the sort will be applied
immediately
OR

1. If you want to customize the sort order, make sure you are in a task view to sort tasks
    and in a resource view to sort resources. Choose **Project, Sort, Sort by...**; the **Sort**
    dialog appears:

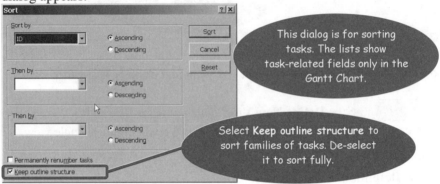

2. Select the first sort order key from the **Sort by** list, if you think you will need a
    second sort key to break the ties, select it from the list **Then by**.

3. An important choice is whether you want to keep the outline structure or not. If you
    do keep it, Project 2000 will only sort the summary task families. If you don't keep it,
    Project 2000 will do a complete and continuous sort ignoring the families.

4. Click [Sort] and the sort will be applied.

 The sort order is stored in the view object in which you applied it. Each view can have a
different sort order.

 Be careful with using ☑ **Permanently renumber tasks**; you may lose your carefully
crafted outline structure of the Work Breakdown Structure. You can use **Undo** [↰] to set
it straight or close your file without saving.

Apply any Formats

The **Format** menu supplies many possibilities to improve the appearance of the printout. All the changes you make through the format menu will be stored in the view object you have on the screen when you make the change.

The format menu items change when you apply another view. When you realize that each view has its own format menu, you will understand that MS Project is a bigger tool than you first thought.

We reviewed the different format options when we discussed printing each view:
◆ the Gantt Chart, please see page 222: Printing the Gantt View.
◆ the Network Diagram, please see page 193: Printing the Network Diagram.
◆ the Resource Spreadsheet, please see page 257: Printing the Resource Sheet.

I will summarize the important choices here:

◆ What text and bar formats do you want?
You can customize the text and bars for individual tasks you select, using the menu items **Format, Font** or **Bar**. Or you can do it faster by applying a style to each different type of task by choosing **Format, Text Styles** or **Bar Styles**. We recommend you use the styles first before overriding them for single tasks.

◆ Which date formats do you want in the spreadsheet and in the timescale?
First of all, choose the default date format for all date fields in Project 2000, by choosing **Tools, Options**, tab **View, Date Format**. If you want to change the date order (e.g., from mmddyy to ddmmyy) you have to go the **Control Panel, Regional Settings** (Windows 98) or **Regional Options** (Windows 2000).
To override the default date format in the spreadsheet, choose **View, Table <name of current table>, More Tables**, click Edit... and select it from the list **Date Format** at the bottom.
To override the default date format in the timescale, choose **Format, Layout** and select the format from the list **Date Format**.

◆ Do you want to show dependencies in the Gantt Chart or Tracking Gantt? Make your choice using **Format, Layout, Links**. You can also choose between straight or hooked arrows.

◆ Do you want to roll up detail task bars onto their summary task bars in the Gantt Chart? A regular summary task bar looks like ▼━━━━▼ , as you know. A rolled up summary task bar looks like:

▼▛━▌━▼ with detail task bars rolled up, or

▼━━◆◆▼ with milestones rolled up on it. You have to choose between:

◇ No rolling up (default)

◇ Rolling up certain hand-picked detail task bars.
Hand-pick the task bars by selecting them, clicking the **Task Information** tool ▦ and checking ☑ **Show rolled up Gantt bars**

◇ Rolling up all detail task bars when their summary tasks are collapsed.
Choose **Format, Layout, ☑ Always roll up Gantt bars**.

◆ What fields do you want to show in the **Task Usage** and **Resource Usage** views? You can select fields other than the default **Work** field. Choose **Format, Details** or, better yet, right-click in the yellow of the timescale and a menu will pop up that allows you to quickly pick one listed or other ones through the menu item **Detail Styles…** .

◆ In the Resource Graph view you can also choose to graph other details than the default **Peak Units** by choosing **Format, Details**. Notice that the peak units will give an inflated impression of the workloads when you zoom the timescale out from days to weeks to months. Peak units inflate because MS Project takes the highest bar within a period to summarize the entire period. You should consider changing to **Work** for a more realistic depiction of the expected workload over time.

Choose the Page Setup Settings

The page setup settings are stored in the view object you have on the screen when you choose **File, Page Setup**.

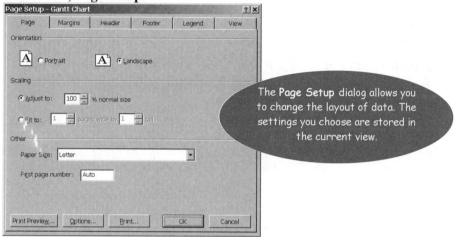

The **Page Setup** dialog allows you to change the layout of data. The settings you choose are stored in the current view.

As with the formatting, we will only summarize the important options in the **File, Page Setup** dialog, since we discussed many of them already in previous chapters:

◆ **Page** tab:

   ◇ **Orientation**: for most projects it is best to choose ⊙ **Landscape**. This will allow you to keep the entire timescale on one page and prevent you from having to tape the pages together.

   ◇ The **Scaling** options will only be available when your printer can handle them; the range is from 10% to 500%.

◆ **Header, Footer, legend** tab:
Choose the position first: **Left, Center** or **Right**. You can type in any header text or use the lists **General** or **Project Fields** to select the type of information. Clicking ▐ Add ▌ will add a cryptic code for it in the header. These codes refer to entries you made in the **File, Properties** dialog. If you make changes there, all headers will be updated automatically. The font size is small by default for a header, to increase it select the text by dragging over it and clicking ▐ A ▌. The **Font** dialog appears in which you choose the font, style and size.

◆ **View** tab:
The important options here are:

◇   ☐ **Print first** `3` ⬍ **columns on all pages**; you should not have to use this option when you only print one page wide. I have always been able to print only one page wide in even the largest schedules of thousands of tasks. You could use the landscape page orientation.

◇   ☑ **Print Notes**; this will create a separate page with notes by task. The task IDs are used to relate the notes to the tasks.

◇   ☑ **Fit timescale to end of page** is useful only when your timescale does not stretch to the right hand side of the page. This option will stretch it. Note that it does not shrink the timescale; it only stretches.

Copying Views Between Projects

Once you have created a view object, you can use it in other projects or share it with other people. You can even put it in your *global.mpt* and use it in all your other project files.

1. Choose **Tools, Organizer...**; the **Organizer** dialog appears:

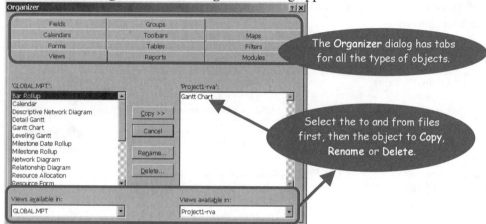

2. Activate the tab **Views** as the type of object to copy.

3. Using the lists at the bottom of the dialog, on the left select the file from which to copy the object and on the right the file to copy to.

4. In the list on the left, select the view object to copy and click .

5. Click the tab **Tables** and copy the table that the view uses.

6. Click the tab **Filters** and copy the filter object that the view uses as well.

7. Click the tab **Groups** and copy the group object that the view uses as well.

8. Click **Close**, or click **Cancel** if you did not transfer an object.

 It is a lot easier to see which objects are the components of a view if they all have the same name. That's why we recommended to keep the names the same.

The organizer allows you to copy objects into the *global.mpt* file. Any objects you put into this global template are visible in all your projects, unless there is already an object in the project file that has the same name.

Examples of Useful or Hard-to-Get-At Printouts

Responsibilities by Department

With the new *Group* feature, it is easy to communicate lists of responsibilities by department. For each resource you can enter the department in which each person works and you can create responsibility lists by department. The image below shows part of such a printout:

	Resource Name	Work	Details	Aug	Sep	Oct	Nov
	⊟ **Group: No Value**	**0 days**	Work				
	⊞ Unassigned	0 days	Work				
	⊟ **Group: employee**	**148 days**	Work				
2	⊟ Falgon – John	3 days	Work	3d			
	visit the sites	1 day	Work	1d			
	evaluate the sites	1 day	Work	1d			
	meet to select the location	1 day	Work	1d			
3	⊞ Hilcrest – Nancy	5 days	Work	5d			
7	⊞ the employees	140 days	Work				140d
	⊟ **Group: external**	**316 days**	Work				
4	⊞ Roach – Pierre	0.5 days	Work	0.5d			
6	⊞ the contractor	234 days	Work	1d	133d	94d	6d
8	⊞ the LAN consultants	60 days	Work			60d	
9	⊞ the movers	20 days	Work				20d
10	⊞ the realtor	1.5 days	Work	1.5d			
	⊟ **Group: ma...**	...ys	Work				
5	⊞ Salin – Nelson	1 day	Work	1d			
11		.3 days	Work	14.43d	0.87d		
	⊟ **Group: material**		Work				
1		0 boxes	Work (				

Annotations on the image: "Effort needed by department, by resource, and by assignment"; "Third Level: assignments"; "Second level: resources"; "First level: departments"

To Enter the Departments

1. Choose **View, Resource Sheet**.

2. Enter the department in which each person works in the field **Group**.

To Create a Responsibilities by Department Printout

1. Choose **View, Resource Usage**.

2. Select from the list [No Group ▼] on the **Standard** toolbar the item
   Resource Group; the result will show three outline levels:

   ◇ the first level shows the resource groups i.e., departments

   ◇ the second level shows all resources working in each department

   ◇ the third level shows all the assignments for each resource

Workload Histogram for Individuals and Groups

Workload histogram is synonymous with *Resource Graph* in MS Project. When you enter
the group or department the resource works in, you can create interesting workload
histograms. You can create a graph that compares the workload of an individual with the
total work for the group (department). The snapshot below shows the total work of the
LAN consultants relative to the total workload of all the *external* resources filtered out
using the **Group...** filter:

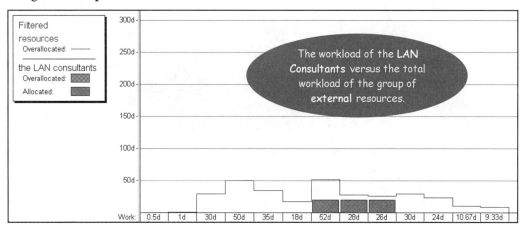

1. Enter the department in the **Group** field for each resource as we did for the previous
   sample printout.

2. Choose **View, Resource Graph**.

3. Press [Page Down] until you see the graph of the individual for whom you want to compare the
   workload to the total workload of the department or group.

4. Choose **Format, Details, Work**; this exchanges the **Peak Units** for total **Work** numbers.

5. Choose **Format, Bar Styles**; the **Bar Styles** dialog appears:

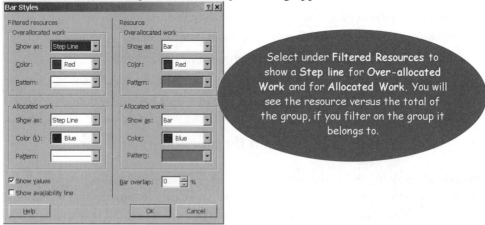

6. Select the settings as shown in the snapshot above and click [OK]; the view now shows stepped bars for the workload of the resource and a red line for the total work in the project.

7. Make sure you have filled in the resource related field *Group* in the resource sheet. Then select the filter **Group...** from the list |All Tasks ▼| on the **Formatting** toolbar; the **Group** dialog appears:

8. Enter the name of the group the resource belongs to in the field **Group Name** and click [OK]; now you see the workload of the resource relative to the total workload of the department the person belongs to.

9. Create the header and footer in the **File, Page Setup** dialog.

10. Print the report by choosing **File, Print**.

 Note that, unfortunately, you cannot change the y-axis, MS Project often creates a y-axis that is too long.

To-Do Lists in the Calendar View

To-Do Lists by Resource

The calendar view does not show many tasks within one day. When we first discussed this view on page 70, we stated that the calendar view is particularly suited for creating to-do lists by resource. There are several reasons for this:

◆ Typically a resource has only one or two tasks on any given day. Two tasks can easily be displayed in the calendar view.

◆ Not all people understand Gantt Charts, but most people can read calendars. To-do lists in the calendar view are often easier to understand than in the Gantt Chart.

◆ You can show the resource-specific holidays and vacation days in this view.

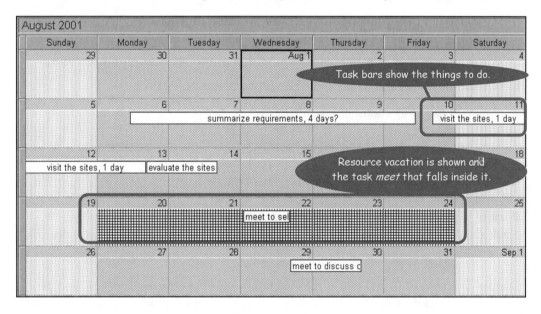

Creating a To-Do List for a Resource

1. Choose **View, Calendar**.

2. Select from the filter list All Tasks ▾ on the **Formatting** toolbar, the **Using Resource...** filter; the **Using Resource** dialog appears:

3. Select from the list **Show tasks using** [▼] the resource for which to create the to-do list.

4. To create the shading for vacation time. Choose **Format, Timescale...**; the **Timescale** dialog appears:

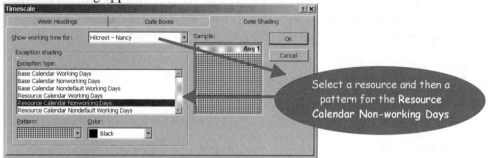

5. Click the tab **Date Shading**. Under **Show working time for** select the resource of this to-do list and choose the appropriate pattern and color settings.

   Click [OK]. The view now shows the non-working days for the resource.

6. Create the header and footer in the **File, Page Setup** dialog.

7. Print the report by choosing **File, Print**.

To Adjust the Row Heights and Column Widths

Choose **View, Zoom** to adjust the row heights of the days.
OR
Point to the horizontal divider between the weeks; the mouse pointer changes into ⬍.
Click and drag the divider down to increase the height of all rows. Drag it up to decrease the height.

Double-click the right-hand side of the column dividers between the days to adjust the column such that the data fits in it. You can also drag them, but this amounts to trial and error.

To Change the Timescale

Double-click on the timescale; the **Timescale** dialog appears:

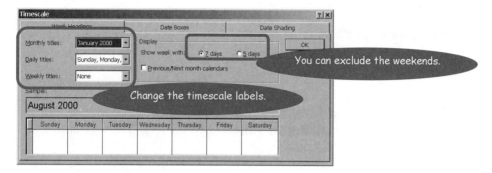

On the page tab **Week headings** you can:
◆ Change the titles shown for the months, weeks and days.
◆ Select to **Show week with** ◉ **5 days** as opposed to the default 7 days.

To Format the View

In **Format, Bar Styles** you can:
◆ Choose the appearance of the different types of tasks.
◆ Add text labels inside the task bars by selecting the labels in the field **Field(s)**. You can even add multiple labels, like: **Name, Resource Name**, but you will find that the text is cut off to fit inside the bar.
◆ When the text gets too long use ☑ **Wrap text in bars**.

To Improve the Layout of the Task Bars

1. Choose **Format, Layout…**; the **Layout** dialog appears:

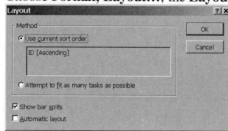

2. Under **Method** you can select different layout arrangements for the task bars:

◉ **Use current sort order** will list the task bars based upon the active sorting.

◉ **Attempt to fit as many tasks as possible** tries to optimize the use of space by displaying more than one bar horizontally.

3. If you check ☑ **Automatic layout** the task bars will be rearranged every time the sort order changes or tasks are inserted or deleted.

Printouts That Include the Notes

The **Notes** field can hold a lot of text; there is virtually no limit to it. You may need to capture a lot of text:

◆ To create a WBS dictionary, a narrative description of the major deliverables in the WBS.

◆ To capture checklist items or reminders.

To include the notes in your printouts, you have two options:

◆ Print all the notes together on a separate notes page using a View, or

◆ Print the notes in between the tasks they relate to using a Report

Below you see an example of the former:

WBS Dictionary Relocation Devom Inc.

1   REQUIREMENTS
The requirements deliverable includes:
- researching the wishes of all the staff through a questionnaire by email
- the results should be summarized
In order to achieve an 80% satisfaction rate by the personnel it is important to find out about their requirements.

4   LOCATION
The Location deliverable is the new location with the following requirements:
- the location should have a capacity of up to 150 work spaces.
- the location should be accessible for disabled people
- the location should have parking facilities for at least 50 cars
- the location should have modern work cubicles and an open workspace
The deliverable is the physical location and the contract with the landlord or leaseholder. The corporate lawyer should review the contract.

11   REMODELING CONTRACT
The deliverable Remodeling Contract is the contract with the general contractor to renovate the office space to meet the needs and requirements of the workforce. At least two different contactors should be asked for a bid.

17   REMODELED LOCATION
The deliverable Remodeled Location is the finished new location ready to be moved into. All the activities of the general contractor should be included in this deliverable.

26   MOVE
The deliverable Move is the physical transfer of equipment, materials and archives to the new location. The employees will have to pack their own files and materials. The move will have to take place on a weekend to minimize the interuption of normal operations and to minimize the cost of unproductive employees.

Print a View With a Separate Notes Page

1. In the Gantt Chart choose **File, Page Setup**; the **Page Setup** dialog appears:

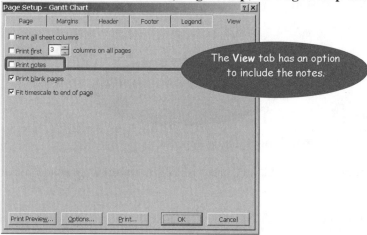

The **View** tab has an option to include the notes.

2. Click the tab **View**.

3. Check ☑ **Print Notes**.

4. Click Print Preview... , Print... or OK .

Print a Report With Notes in Between the Tasks

1. Choose **View, Reports;** the **Reports** dialog appears:

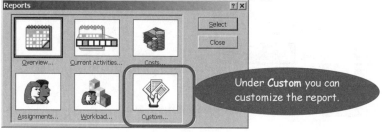

Under **Custom** you can customize the report.

2. Double-click on **Custom** ; the **Custom Report** dialog appears.

3. Scroll down the list and select **Task**:

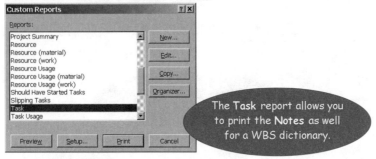

The **Task** report allows you to print the **Notes** as well for a WBS dictionary.

4. Click **Edit...** ; the **Task Report** dialog appears.

5. Click the tab **Definition,** if needed, and select ☑ **Show summary tasks** to include the deliverables.

6. Click the tab **Details** and select ☑ **Notes**; the notes will now appear on the print-out.

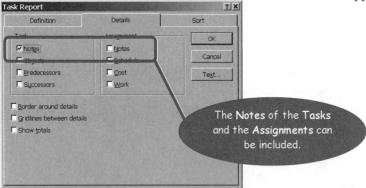

The **Notes** of the **Tasks** and the **Assignments** can be included.

7. Click **OK** and click **Preview** ; you can see the notes in between the tasks. Click **Print...** .

8. Click **Close** three times to go back to the view.

Printout of the Time-phased Budget

If your financial department asks you as the project manager to predict how much money your project needs over time, you should print a time-phased budget. You have two options:

◆ Time-phased budget by task or deliverable; use the **Task Usage** View, or
◆ Time-phased budget by resource; use the **Resource Usage** View.

Below you see an example of the former with expenses of each deliverable by month:

	Task Name	Cost	Details	Qtr 3, 2001			Qtr 4, 2001		
				Jul	Aug	Sep	Oct	Nov	Dec
1	⊞ REQUIREMENTS	$1,650.00	Cost		$1,650.00				
4	⊞ LOCATION	$6,093.75	Cost		$6,093.75				
11	⊞ REMODELING CONTRACT	$3,525.00	Cost		$3,037.50	$487.50			
17	⊞ REMODELED LOCATION	$86,175.00	Cost			$29,925.00	$42,750.00	$13,500.00	
26	⊞ MOVE	$31,350.00	Cost		$1,350.00			$30,000.00	
			Cost						

1. Choose **View, Task Usage** or **Resource Usage**.

2. Click **Go to selected Tasks** 📑 to scroll the numbers in view; you will see the effort required spread over time with the details **Work** displayed by default.

3. Choose **Format, Details, Cost**; notice the check mark in front of **Work**; the work details are currently shown in the chart.
   OR
   Right-click in the yellow column where the word **Work** is repeated, and choose from the pop-up menu **Cost**.

4. Choose **Format, Details, Work** to turn this field off; notice there is now a checkmark in front of **Cost**.
   OR
   Right-click in the yellow column where the word **Work** is repeated, and choose from the pop-up menu **Work**.

5. Adjust the level of detail of the outline structure you want to show in the printout. Click on any column heading and click ⌐ **Show** ▾ ⌐; choose the appropriate level of detail. In the example, only deliverables are shown.

6. Adjust the timescale to show the time unit your financial department would like to see in the printout by using **Zoom in** 🔍 and **Zoom out** 🔍.

7. Create the header and footer in the **File, Page Setup** dialog.

8. Print the report by choosing **File, Print**.

Printing

We will discuss some last things to do and settings to choose before sending the schedule to the printer.

Specify Columns to Spell-Check

1. Prevent MS Project from halting at any abbreviation or code. You can do this by **Tools, Options...,** click tab **Spelling**.

2. Choose or type **Yes** for those columns you want to check.

3. Select ☑ **Ignore words in UPPERCASE** and
   ☑ **Ignore Words with Numbers** to decrease the halting at abbreviations.

4. Click OK .

To Check the Spelling in the Schedule

1. Choose **Tools, Spelling**.

2. When the spelling checker displays a misspelled word in the **Not In Dictionary** field you can:

   ◇ Click Ignore to ignore the misspelled word.

   ◇ Type the correction in the **Change To** field and click Change .

   ◇ Click Add to add the word to the user dictionary.

Inserting Page Breaks Manually

1. Select the task or resource to push onto the next page.

2. Choose **Insert, Page Break;** a dashed line will appear that represents the page break.

3. Choose **File, Print** and check ☑ **Manual page breaks** to make the breaks appear in the printout.

 The page breaks set in the table also insert breaks in the report based on the same table. Therefore, use them only when really needed.

Inserting the Project Logo Into the Header

1. Choose **File, Page Setup**.

2. Click the tab **Header**.

3. Click **Insert picture** ; the **Insert Picture** dialog appears:

4. Navigate through your directory system and select the image file with the logo of your project.

5. Click [Insert]; the logo is now displayed in the header.

6. If the logo image is too big you can click on it to make selection handles appear around the image. Point to a corner selection handle and drag to resize the picture.

The Timescale is Too Short or Too Long

The timescale often has to be adjusted because it may spill over onto the second page and you would like to shorten it. Or the timescale occupies only a small part of the page and you would like to stretch it.

To Shorten the Timescale

1. Choose **Format, Timescale**.

2. In the section **General**, decrease the **Size** percentage, which will shorten the timescale.

To Stretch the Timescale

1.   Choose **File, Page Setup**.

2.   Click the tab View and check ☑ **Fit timescale to end of page**.
     This will stretch the timescale to fill the page.

Print Preview

Use Print Preview to check the header, footer, legend, margins and the timescale before printing, or check the position of the boxes on a network diagram.

1.   Apply the view you want to print.

2.   Click [🔍] or choose **File, Print Preview**:

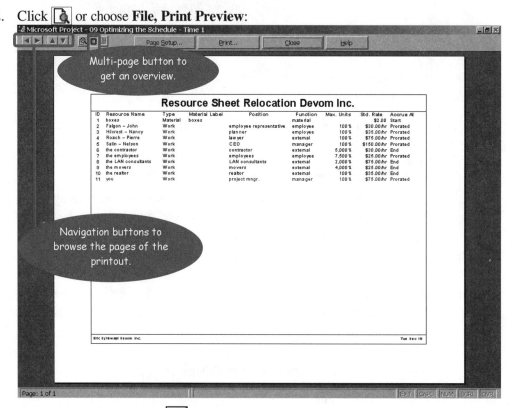

3.   Use the multi-page button [⊞] to get an overview over all the printed pages, and then click on one of the pages to zoom back into.

4.   Click on the print preview where you would like to zoom in. Click again to zoom out.

5. To change the margins, header, footer, or legend text, click | Page Setup... |.

6. To print the view, click | Print... |.
   To return without printing, click | Close |.

Printing the Current View

Click 🖨 to send the schedule directly to the printer.
OR
Choose the print options using these steps:

1. Choose **File, Print**; the **Print** dialog appears:

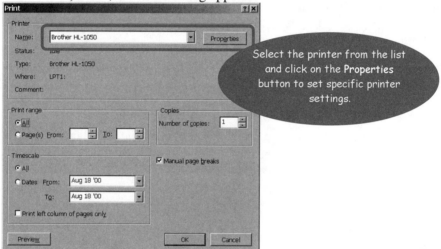

2. Select a printer in the **Name** list.

3. Click | Properties | to select the options available for the printer, such as paper source and orientation. Note that the choices you make here apply to all applications. Click | OK | when finished to go back to the **Print** dialog.

4. Select from the options available for your printer; see below for an explanation.

5. Click | OK | to start the printing or click | Close | to return to your project without printing.

 Colors you may have used are automatically replaced by hatching patterns on a black and white printer.

Print Options

◆ **Print Range**

Select ⊙ **All** to print the entire project.

OR

Type the first and last pages to print in the **Page(s) From** and **To** fields.

◆ ☑ **Manual Page Breaks**

Select to use the manually set page breaks. Clear to use automatic page breaks set by Project 2000.

◆ **Timescale** if you are printing a view with a timescale (Gantt Chart, Task Usage, Resource Graph, and Resource Usage view), the Timescale box is active:

from project start date to finish date use ⊙ **All**

for a particular period select ⊙ **Dates From To**.

Sending a Project File to Colleagues

1. Choose **File, Send To, Mail Recipient.** The MPP-file will be attached to the email. The **Choose Profile** dialog may appear, select a user profile and click OK . The new email message dialog appears:

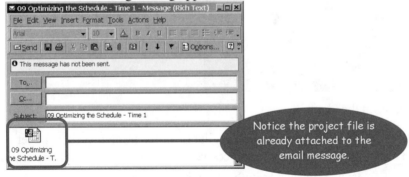

Notice the project file is already attached to the email message.

2. Fill in the **To** and the **CC** fields and send the message.

Instead, you can use the **File, Send To, Routing Recipient** feature to send the schedule to a chain of people, each of whom will receive the schedule for review.

If you don't want your colleagues to change your project file, you should create a Portable Document File (PDF) from it using Adobe Acrobat.[34] Adobe Acrobat sets itself up as if it were a printer, so you can create PDF-files simply by choosing **File, Print**.

---

[34] See www.adobe.com

Review Exercises

Can you print the following? Would you do this through a Report or through a View?

Can you print?	Yes/No	Report or View
1. Gantt Chart		
2. Project Calendar		
3. Resource Calendar		
4. Project Statistics (as shown in the **Project, Project Information,** Statistics... dialog)		
5. Cash Outflow report		
6. Notes		

Relocation Project – Reporting an Executive Overview

1. Open the file *10 Reporting 1.MPP* in the sub-directory *Relocation Project* on the CD-ROM. We will create a custom view that provides executives with a high-level overview of the project.

2. Create a new task table named *Executive Overview.* Use the columns **ID, Name, Duration** and **Cost**.

3. Create a new filter *Executive Overview* to display milestones and their summary Tasks.

4. Create a new view *Executive Overview* that is shown in the menu. Make sure that when you apply the view *Executive Overview*, the corresponding table and filter are both applied.

5. Apply the following **Timescale** settings:

	Major Scale	**Minor Scale**
Units	*Months*	*Weeks*
Count	*1*	*1*
Label	*January*	*1,2,...52*
Align	*Center*	*Center*
Enlarge	*100*	

6. Apply the following **Page Setup** settings:

Page Tab	**Section**	**Set to**
Page	*Orientation*	*Portrait*
	Scaling	*Fit to: 1 page wide by 1 tall*
Margins	*top,bottom,left,right*	*0.5 inch*
	Borders Around	*none*
Header	*Center*	*&[View] &[Project Title]*
	Arial, Bold, 20	
Footer	*Left*	*&[Manager] &[Company]*
	Center	*none; delete the default entry*
	Right	*&[Date]*
Legend	*Legend on*	*none*
View		☑ *Print all Sheet Columns*
		☑ *Fit Timescale to end of Page*

7. Compare your file with the view *Executive Overview* of the solution file *10 Reporting 2.MPP* in the sub-directory *Relocation Project* on the CD-ROM.

Relocation Project – Reporting Cost by Function

1. Open the file *10 Reporting 2.MPP* in the sub-directory *Relocation Project* on the CD-ROM.

2. Create a table *Cost by Function* that shows the fields **Resource Name**, **Position**, **Function** and **Cost**.

3. Create a grouping *Cost by Function* such that you can easily read the total cost by function category of the project.

4. Create a new resource sheet view named *Cost by Function* that is shown in the menu. The view should apply the corresponding table and grouping.

5. Set the **Page Setup** settings as per the following table:

Page Tab	Section	Set to
Page	*Orientation*	*Portrait*
	Scaling	*Fit to: 1 page wide by 1 tall*
Margins	*top,bottom,left,right*	*1 inch*
	Borders Around	*every page*
Header	*Center* *Arial, Bold, 20*	*&[View] &[Project Title]*
Footer	*Left*	*&[Manager] &[Company]*
	Center	*none; delete the default entry*
	Right	*&[Date]*

6. Compare your file with the solution file *11 Updating the Schedule 1.MPP* in the sub-directory *Relocation Project* on the CD-ROM.

Chapter 11 Updating the Schedule

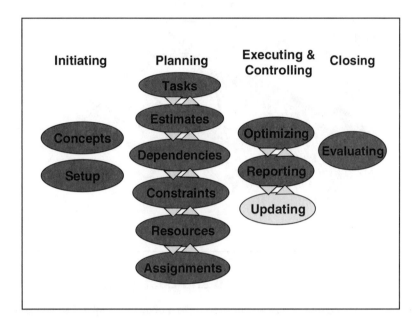

After this chapter you will:

◆ be able to set the baseline

◆ be able to view and track the progress

◆ be able to update your schedule

   ◇ on the task level

   ◇ on the assignment level using paper timesheets, email timesheets or web timesheets (Project Central)

◆ know how to communicate the status of the project

◆ be able to optimize the schedule again to compensate for slippages

Scope Creep and Lost Sleep

Nob enters Bob's office and drops, exhausted, into a chair. He sighs, "It happened again, ... we are late and over budget!"

Bob turns his chair and asks, "How did that happen?"

Nob looks defeated while he answers. "Everything was fine until my boss wanted an extra feature..."

"An extra feature sounds like out-of-scope work," Bob immediately notes.

Nob responds slowly. "Yeah, as the project manager I would like to say: hey ... this is a scope change, you can't expect us to just add this feature to our list. But, when your boss starts breathing down your neck and insists on it, it is hard to say no."

"Didn't he give you extra time and money for the extra work?" Bob asks in amazement.

"No, a new requirement was all we got."

Bob feels sorry for Nob, but probes further anyway. "Wasn't it obvious that the requirement was out of scope?"

"To me it was..."

Overview of Updating

Executing a project is often a more chaotic experience than anticipated in the project plan. The progress can run behind or ahead of the baseline. When it runs behind the schedule often has to be optimized again to manage slippages. When a task is delayed, corrections to the schedule have to be made in order to meet the deadline. Unexpected expenses, or sudden budget cuts may have to be compensated for. Optimizing methods are important when you plan a project, but even more so when you execute a project.

The process steps for updating schedules can be summarized as follows:

◆ Baseline: set it once for the entire schedule and maintain it.

◆ Choose the update strategy
  ◇ Tasks update
  ◇ Assignments update

◆ Prepare for the update
  ◇ set the **Tools, Options**
  ◇ display the right view and toolbar
  ◇ set the **Status Date**

◆ Update: enter the actual values and remaining estimates.

Normally, you would set the baseline only once. Only in exceptional circumstances, such as a strike, should you re-baseline. If you do re-baseline you should only do it for the tasks affected. If deliverables or tasks are deleted or added <u>after</u> the baseline has been set, the baseline has to be updated e.g., when errors in the schedule turn up unexpectedly or when the scope of the project changes. It is <u>not</u> a good idea to reset the baseline often, because comparison to it becomes less and less valuable.

The Baseline

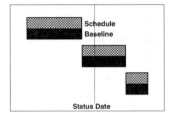

The baseline is a frozen copy of the final approved schedule. The *baseline schedule* is the target to aim for. The baseline should remain the same throughout the project, unless there are formal scope changes approved. In those cases, the baseline will need maintenance. In the illustration, you can see that each task bar is split into two parts. The top part is the current schedule – the dynamic model of the project. The bottom part is the static baseline to compare against.

Viewing the Baseline

1. Choose **View, Gantt Chart**.

2. Click on the menu items **View, Table <name of current table>, More Tables**.

3. Choose the table **Baseline** in the list.

4. Click [Apply].

Notice that the fields in the baseline date columns show **NA** when the baseline is not set for the tasks.

You can replace the baseline dates with new current schedule dates. Copying the current schedule into the baseline fields again overwrites all the dates, cost, and work information in the baseline fields.

There are ten interim schedules (Start1/Finish1 through Start10/Finish10), which are extra sets of start and finish date fields. In each of these you can store a version of your plan you would like to keep. You can copy a set into any other set at any time.

 Be aware that the interim schedules, unlike the baseline, only contain the start and finish dates, and hold no duration, work or cost data.

Setting the Baseline

1. If you want to set planned information for certain tasks, select the tasks.

2. Choose **Tools, Tracking, Save Baseline**.

3. Select ⦿ **Save Baseline**.

4. To set the baseline for all tasks, select ⦿ **Entire Project**
    OR
    to set it for selected tasks only, select ⦿ **Selected Tasks**.

5. Click [OK], the original schedule is saved in the **Baseline** fields for comparison.

If you add tasks later on, MS Project will prompt you to set the baseline for these tasks upon closing the file. You can have MS Project baseline the new tasks.

Maintaining the Baseline

Situations in which you need to maintain the baseline are:
◆ formal scope changes: added scope or deleted scope
◆ extenuating circumstances: e.g. strike, economic recession
◆ acts of God: fire, flood, tornado, hurricane …

As soon as you add tasks to your WBS, the PlanningWizard notices that the baseline is incomplete and will prompt you to update the baseline upon closing the file with the following dialog (unless you disabled the PlanningWizard in **Tools, Options**, tab **General**):

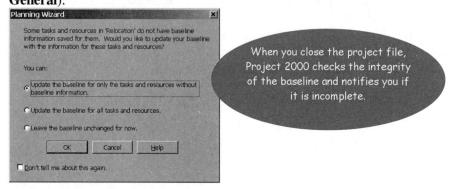

You have to be careful selecting the second option ⊙ **Update the baseline for all tasks and resources**. This will reset the entire baseline schedule, including those parts that were not affected by the scope change.

You can also update your baseline schedule manually:

1. Select the tasks affected by the scope change.

2. Choose **Tools, Tracking, Save Baseline**.

3. Select the option **For: ⊙ Selected tasks**.

4. Click OK .

The tasks that you selected now have a new baseline, but you may have to update the baseline for summary tasks on all higher levels in the outline structure using the same steps.

The snapshot shows a discrepancy on the summary task:

	Task Name	Duration	Baseline Dur.	Baseline Start	Baseline Finish	Aug 01	Sep 01
						29 5 12 19 26	2 9 16 23 30
1	⊟ REQUIREMENTS	11.4 days	7.4 days	Wed Aug 1	Fri Aug 10		
2	research staff requirem	4 days	4 days	Wed Aug 1	Mon Aug 6	you[0.5]	
3	new inserted task	4 days	0 days	NA	NA		
4	summarize requiremen	4 days	4 days	Mon Aug 6	Fri Aug 10	Hilcrest – Nancy[0.5]	

The inserted task of the scope change is highlighted. You can see that the *Duration* of the summary task *Requirements* is updated to *11.4 days*, but the *Baseline Duration* remained *7.4 days*. Even after setting a baseline for this new task.

Notice also that the durations of the detail tasks do not add up to the duration of the summary task. Durations rarely add up, but in this case it is caused by longer working hours for resource *you* that makes the total (*11.4 days*) less than the sum (4+4+4=12 days).

Choosing the Reporting Period

As we discussed on page 118, ten reporting periods usually gives the client enough possibilities to take corrective actions. What does this mean for our projects? The table below shows what it means for projects of different lengths.

Project Duration	Reporting Period
1 month	weekly
3 months	monthly
1 year	bi-monthly
5 years	quarterly / bi-annually

You don't want too many reporting periods because each progress report takes time and effort to prepare and may make the overhead cost of project management too heavy a burden for the project budget. You don't want too few reporting periods because your project may be spinning out of control without you knowing it. The client will often prescribe the reporting period, taking away the choice.

Showing Progress

Graphically

The progress can best be seen in the **Tracking Gantt** view. This view shows the task bars

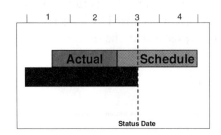

Status Date

as in the illustration. The blue scheduled task will slowly but surely be filled in with solid blue to indicate how much progress has been made. Ideally, the solid blue runs up to the Status Date, as the task progresses as scheduled.

The black baseline allows us to analyze slippages. In the illustration, you can see that the task started 0.5 week later than scheduled and is also progressing 0.5 week slower. Therefore, the total schedule variance is 1 week.

Mathematically

You can express progress in terms of the duration progress at the task level. As long as you keep revising the **Remaining Duration** with your latest estimates, the duration will be recalculated, and Project 2000 will calculate the **% Complete.** The % Complete will be a useful indicator of progress on tasks.

$$\% \text{ Complete} = \frac{\text{Actual Duration}}{\text{Duration}}$$

$$\% \text{ Work Complete} = \frac{\text{Actual Work}}{\text{Work}}$$

You can also update the work on the level of assignments. Similarly, if you keep revising the **Remaining Work**, the total work will be recalculated. Project 2000 will calculate the **% Work Complete**, which will be a useful progress indicator.

Updating Strategies

The strategy of updating the tasks is easy and quick. You only have to enter actual dates and durations, and in most cases, you can do that with the mouse. When you update the tasks, MS Project can calculate and update the assignments automatically. It makes the broad assumption that the planned hours are worked directly proportional to the percent complete. This method is less precise than entering actual hours worked (updating assignments), but in most situations it's precise enough. Updating assignments requires more work from you and your team during busy project execution.

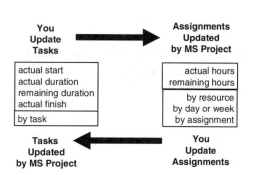

For a tasks update, the options need to be set differently than for an assignments update.

Tasks Update

Preparing to Update Tasks

Here are the things you need to do before updating the tasks:

◆ Choose the **Tools, Options**

◆ Collect the actual and remaining forecast data

◆ Prepare the view:
  ◇ Change the view to **Tracking Gantt**
  ◇ Apply the **Tracking Table**
  ◇ Display the **Tracking Toolbar**

◆ Set the **Status Date** for updating

◆ Set the task **Type** for all tasks to **Fixed Units**

Choosing the Options for Updating Tasks

Choose **Tools, Options**.
Below you will find the options we recommend for updating tasks:

Tab	Option
Calculation	☑ **Updating task status updates resource status** Updating the tasks will update the actual work of the assignments. We recommend you keep this option checked for task updates.
	☐ **Edits to total task % complete will be spread to the status date** If a task is falling behind the progress entered will be evenly spread to the status date. This option is only relevant if you enter % Complete.
	☑ **Actual costs are always calculated by Microsoft Project** Updating the tasks will update the actual cost. It is up to you whether you want MS Project to do that.
	`Set as Default` Sets the options above as the default settings for any new schedules you create. The existing schedules are not affected because these options are stored in the project files (as you can see in the label of the section divider **Calculation Options for 'Project 1'**).
General	☐ **Automatically add new resources and tasks** Prevents a typo in a resource name from accidentally adding a new resource.
Edit	☐ **Allow cell drag and drop** Prevents accidentally dragging data on top of other data in your baselined schedule.
Schedule	☑ **Split in-progress tasks** Allows moving the uncompleted portion of a task to after the update date by splitting the task bar. The update date is the **Current Date** or the **Status Date** whichever is later (see **Project, Project Information**).
	`Set as Default` Sets the option above as the default setting for any new schedules you create. The existing schedules are not affected because this option is stored in the project files (as you can see in the label of the section divider **Scheduling Options for 'Project 1'**.)

Collecting the Data

In order to update your schedule with actual data you need to gather the actuals. You need the following information for a tasks update:

◆ Which task is started and on what date? (**Actual Start**)
◆ How many days are spent on the task? (**Actual Duration**)
◆ How many days to finish it from now? (**Remaining Duration**)
◆ If a task is finished, on which date was it finished? (**Actual Finish**)

As a project manager you will receive update information from the team leaders or the resources. If you do an update on the task level you can collect the information easily using paper Gantt Charts. Ask the team leaders to annotate their Gantt Charts with the new progress made on tasks. They can mark actual dates, and actual and remaining durations in extra columns you inserted in the spreadsheet. Or you can ask them to mark the progress in the timescale of the Gantt Chart. Collect these marked up Gantt Charts and enter the information into MS Project. Turn a new Gantt Chart around to them to inform them about the new forecasts, and then ask them to mark it up for the next reporting period.

Change the View to Tracking Gantt

1. Choose **View, Tracking Gantt**.
    The current schedule is shown in the top half of the task bars (colored blue or red). The baseline is shown as the gray, bottom half.

2. Choose **View, Table <name of current table>, Variance** to see the current schedule and baseline dates. The screen should now look similar to:

Using the Tracking Table

The tracking table has all the fields in which to enter data for a tasks update.

Choose **View, Table <name of current table>, Tracking**. The table looks like the following snapshot:

	Task Name	Act. Start	Act. Finish	% Comp.	Act. Dur.	Rem. Dur.	Act. Cost	Act. Work
1	⊟ REQUIREMENTS	NA	NA	0%	0 days	7.4 days	$0.00	0 days
2	research staff requirements	NA	NA	0%	0 days	4 days	$0.00	0 days
3	summarize requirements	NA	NA	0%	0 days	4 days	$0.00	0 days
4	⊟ LOCATION	NA	NA	0%	0 days	16.5 days	$0.00	0 days
5	select the realtor	NA	NA	0%	0 days	4 days	$0.00	0 days
6	visit the sites	NA	NA	0%	0 days	1 day	$0.00	0 days
7	evaluate the sites	NA	NA	0%	0 days	1 day	$0.00	0 days
8	meet to select the location	NA	NA	0%	0 days	1 day	$0.00	0 days
9	legal review	NA	NA	0%	0 days			

Tracking table to enter actual progress.

The tracking table is easy for entering actual information.

Using the Tracking Toolbar for Updating

1. Point to a toolbar and click the right mouse button.

2. Choose **Tracking**; it has all the handy tools for updating. The tracking toolbar is displayed:

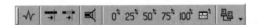

For an explanation of these tools, please refer to page 526: Tracking Toolbar.

Setting the Status Date for Updating

Change the status date to the date as per which you want to compare the schedule against the baseline. You may want to present an up-to-date status in a progress meeting, and you will have to prepare the status report before the meeting. We will set both the current date and the status date, because some of the update tools use the one or other.

1. Choose **Project, Project Information**.

2. Change the date in the **Status Date** field to the date as per which you want to update. The status date does not yet appear as a vertical line in the timescale.

3. Set the **Current Date** to the day after the **Status Date**. The reason for this is that the status date falls at the end of the day and the current date at the start of the next day. This will make the two dates coincide. We recommend this extra step because some update features in Project 2000 use the status date, and others use the current date.

4. Choose **Format, Gridlines** and select **Status Date** as the line to change, choose a dashed line in a bright color. Click [OK]; the status line is visible in the time scale:

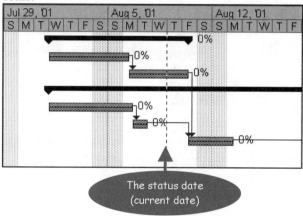

The status date
(current date)

MS Project uses the system date of your computer to continuously update the current date. Tomorrow, you will see two vertical date lines, the static status date and the current date line on tomorrow's date.

Set the Task Type for all Tasks

The task type has to be set in such a way that it triggers the right recalculations. When we update tasks, we change the durations. Fixed duration is therefore not the right type of task. When you update tasks, you typically want to keep the units of resources that work on the task the same, and see the total work (effort) change. **Fixed units** seems to be the most appropriate type of task.

1. Click on any column heading in the Tracking Gantt sheet to select all the tasks.

2. Click the **Task Information** 📇 tool; the **Multiple Task Information** dialog appears:

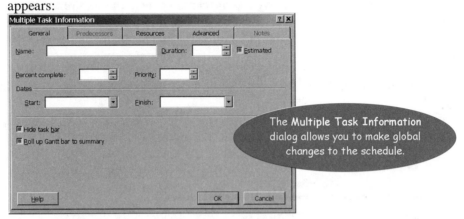

3. Click the **Advanced** tab and select from the list **Task type** [   ] ▼ the item **Fixed Units**. Changing the task type does not trigger a recalculation, only a change in a variable in the formula: *Duration x Units = Work* will do that.

4. Uncheck ☐ **Effort driven** and click [OK].

The Formulas Behind the Screen

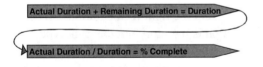

When we update the tasks in our project we should keep these formulas in the back of our minds. They explain the values that Project 2000 calculates and displays when we enter actuals.

In a tasks update, you typically enter the **Actual Duration** and allow Project 2000 to calculate the **Remaining Duration** and the **% Complete** using the formulas shown in the illustration. In many situations that is all you have to do.

In some situations, you realize the remaining duration calculated by Project 2000 may be too little time left. In this case, you should revise the remaining duration. Project 2000 will then recalculate the scheduled **Duration** and lower the **% Complete**.

Task Updating Situations in Practice

The following six situations are all you will come across:
◆ Tasks that Ran as Scheduled
◆ Tasks that Run as Scheduled
◆ Tasks that Run Behind (or Ahead)
◆ Tasks that Will Run Longer (or Shorter)
◆ Tasks that Started Late (or Early)
◆ Tasks that Finished Late (or Early)

You will encounter all of these situations. They each have their own best way to enter the update information. We will discuss each situation.

Tasks that Ran as Scheduled

You want to mark these as 100% complete.

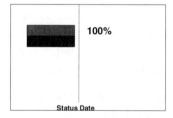

1. In the Tracking Gantt view, select the tasks that were completed as scheduled by dragging or holding down [Ctrl] and clicking.

2. Click the **100% Complete** tool:
   OR
   Enter 100% in the **% Complete** field of the tracking table.
   OR
   Click 🖼 and enter 100% under **% Complete**.

Tasks that Run as Scheduled

In this situation you want to show actual progress that goes up to the status date.

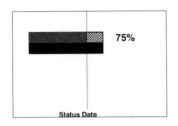

1. Select the tasks that are on schedule by dragging or by holding down ⌨Ctrl⌨ and clicking on it.

2. Click **Update as Scheduled** ⊞; this updates all the selected tasks as if they are exactly on schedule. The tool is not very precise but precise enough.

Tasks that Run Behind

This situation will require more updating effort. You will need to capture the actual progress, but because the task is behind, you will also have to bring the incomplete

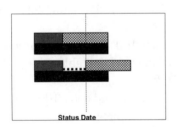

portion of the task bar forward to after the status date. Lastly, you have to review the forecast of the remaining duration. If the task was underestimated, you may have to increase the remaining duration.

In the illustration, you can see that the progress is falling behind because the solid color of the actual progress does not run up to the status date in the task bar at the top. The bottom task bar is a split showing that the incomplete portion of work has been rescheduled after the status date.

The steps to do this are:

1. Set the **Type** of task to *Fixed Units* or *Fixed Work*. If it is a *Fixed Duration* task, first change the type to either Fixed Units or Fixed Work. If you choose Fixed Units, the work will change upon revising the remaining duration. If you choose Fixed Work, the units assigned will change.

2. Enter the **Actual Duration** of the task (the number of days you have worked on the task) and revise the **Remaining Duration** (the number of days still to go). Project 2000 will calculate the **% Complete**.

3. Reschedule the complete portion of the task, the **Remaining Duration**, to after the status date. You can do this by dragging the light blue part of the task bar.
OR
Select the task and click the **Reschedule Work** button on the tracking toolbar. This will split the task bar if the option ☑ **Split in-progress tasks** is in effect in **Tools, Options, Schedule**. Notice that this tool uses the **Project, Project Information…, Current Date** instead of the **Status Date**. That is why we suggest entering the Current Date and the Status Date.

This way of depicting lack of progress by splitting is best if there was an interruption in the work, such as a power outage, or if resources were temporarily taken off the task to do some troubleshooting elsewhere.

Nevertheless, you still have to ask yourself if you are depicting the forecasted finish date accurately. If you look at the rate of progress in the illustration, you will notice that the rate is more or less half of what it should be (half of the work that should have been finished by the status date, is accomplished). If all stays the same (i.e., there will be more interruptions) this means that the eventual duration will be double the baseline duration. You can see that currently the forecasted duration is less than double the baseline duration; and the remaining duration should be increased even more (if you expect more interruptions).

Many people forget the last considerations in this situation. You have to move the remaining duration out to the future, because unfortunately you can't schedule work to be done for last week. (If only we could…) Only if you move it out and revise it, will the dependent successors be rescheduled. If you forget this, you end up with a status report instead of a forecast report. A status report is a report on yesterday's weather instead of a forecast on the weather for tomorrow, as shown in the cartoon at the start of the previous chapter.

Tasks that will Run Longer or Shorter

In this situation, good progress was made, but the realization sinks in that the remaining duration will not suffice. We need to increase the remaining estimate. Or, we may realize that the remaining duration is too long. (Hey, it has been known to happen!)

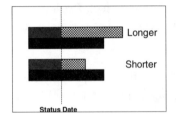

Make sure you have the **Type** of the task set such that the recalculation you will trigger reflects reality. You should not leave it set to **Fixed Duration**, because this will give hard-to-predict results since we are stretching the duration. If you choose **Fixed Units**, the work will increase, which is appropriate if the original estimates were too low and it turns out to take more effort. If you choose **Fixed Work**, the units on the task will be increased. This is appropriate if you will correct the slippage by adding people.

1. Set the **Type** of task to *Fixed Units* tasks or *Fixed Work*. Change *Fixed Duration* tasks first to either Fixed Units or Fixed Work. If you choose Fixed Units, the work will change. If you choose Fixed Work, the units assigned will change.

2. Enter the **Actual Duration** of the task and revise the **Remaining Duration**.
   OR
   Enter the **Actual Duration** and change the remaining duration with the mouse by pointing to the right side of its blue task bar, and when you see a single-headed arrow mouse pointer ⊩ , drag to change the remaining duration.

3. You may have to use the methods discussed in Chapter 9 Optimizing the Schedule to compensate for the slippage.

The steps reflect the simplest way to update tasks that fall behind. If you want to enter **% Complete** rather than the **Actual Duration**, it will be a longer, two-step process that follows the formulas in the next illustration.

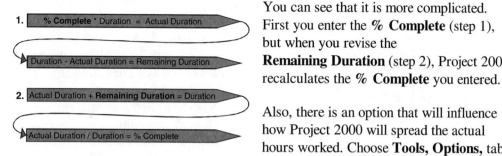

1. % Complete * Duration = Actual Duration

   Duration - Actual Duration = Remaining Duration

2. Actual Duration + **Remaining Duration** = Duration

   Actual Duration / Duration = % Complete

You can see that it is more complicated. First you enter the **% Complete** (step 1), but when you revise the **Remaining Duration** (step 2), Project 2000 recalculates the **% Complete** you entered.

Also, there is an option that will influence how Project 2000 will spread the actual hours worked. Choose **Tools, Options,** tab **Calculation**; the option is **Edits to total task % complete will be spread to the status date**. If you enter a % Complete Project 2000 can calculate the actual hours and spread them out to the status date with the option on. When it is off, the actual hours will be entered where they were scheduled, and splits will often appear.

When you tend to enter % Complete instead of having it calculated by Project 2000, use fairly rough %-increments only, such as: 0,25,50,75,100% as shown on the **Tracking** toolbar. After all, what does *90% progress* on a task mean? Does it mean:

◆ *I am almost finished!,* or
◆ *I have just figured out how to do this, and now I will do it*, or
◆ *I want you to think that I am at 90% complete!,* or
◆ *I have just started to work on the task!,* or
◆ *Leave me alone, so I can do my work!*

I often ask groups of project managers what they think it means, and inevitably they think that *90% complete* means any of the above! So ask for facts rather than fiction when collecting update information. Using **% Complete** is less objective than entering the actual number of business days that people worked on a task (**Actual Duration**). These days can easily be counted and are factual.

You can get to the facts more easily if you created tasks that are small enough, but not too small. See our discussion on the right level of detail on page 116: The Right Level of Detail. If you create tasks that are small enough, you can simply ask *Are you finished with it, or not?* This question does not leave much room for wishful thinking (or outright manipulation).

Tasks that Started Late or Early

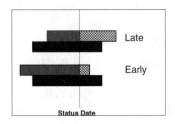

Late

Early

Status Date

In this situation the task did not start on the day that was planned. If you updated your schedule regularly and if you had a dynamic schedule (with all dependencies) the start date may have moved already to the right date. If that is not the case, you have to enter it. In the illustration, you can see that in the *Late* situation, the actual start date (left side of top half) is later than the baseline start date (the left side of the black bottom half).

1. Point to the middle of the blue task bar, and if you see a four-headed arrow mouse pointer ✥ drag the task bar to its new start date.
    OR
    Enter the date in **Act. Start** of the tracking table.
    OR
    Select the task with a delayed start, click 📇, and fill in the **Actual Start** date and click [OK].

2. You may have to use the methods discussed in Chapter 9 Optimizing the Schedule to compensate for the slipped finish date.

Tasks that Finished Late or Early

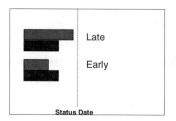

In this situation, you need to enter the finish dates. If you updated your schedule regularly, however, you often don't need to enter the finish dates. When you revise the remaining duration, Project 2000 already changes the finish date to the right date. If it still isn't the right date, you have to enter it into the project file.

1. Point to the right side of its blue task bar, and when you see a single-headed arrow mouse pointer ↦ , drag the finish to its new date. Set the task to 100% complete.
    OR
    Enter the date in **Act. Finish** of the tracking table.
    OR
    Select the task with a slipped finish date, and click ▦ and fill in the
    Actual Finish date and click OK .

2. You may have to use the methods discussed in Chapter 9 Optimizing the Schedule to compensate for the slipped finish date.

"My Reality is More Complex... "

Combinations of Situations

Often your situation is more complicated. No matter what, it is always a combination of the six situations we discussed before. For example, the start date is different from the baseline start and the progress is behind. Let's say the situation on a two-day task on May 2nd 2000 at 5PM is:

◆ the Actual Start date is May 2nd with a Baseline Start May 1st

◆ the Remaining Duration is revised from 1 day to 2 days

In a situation like this, you enter what you know first. We recommend you start with updating the **Actual Start**, then the **Actual Duration** and the **Remaining Duration** last. Graphically speaking, you enter the data going from left to right over the task bar.

The resource worked only May 2nd on the task; the Actual Duration is one day. The *% Complete* will be calculated at *50%*. Before entering the Remaining Duration, the schedule will look like:

Task Name	% Complete	Duration	Remaining Duration	Start	Apr 30, 00
					Apr 30 | May 1 | May 2 | May 3 | May 4 | May 5
write report	50%	2 days	1 day	May 2	50%

When you enter the Remaining Duration, you trigger a recalculation of the *% Complete* and it will be *33%*; you have completed one day of what will now be a three-day task instead of a two-day task. See the schedule below:

Task Name	% Complete	Duration	Remaining Duration	Start	Apr 30, 00
					Apr 30 | May 1 | May 2 | May 3 | May 4 | May 5
write report	33%	3 days	2 days	May 2	33%

Updating Out of Sequence

Occasionally, you may need to show progress on a task that is scheduled for the future. Its predecessors that are not yet finished, may hold it there. If work has started on a task you need to show progress on it, regardless of the logic of the dependencies. This is known as *out-of-sequence updating*. Normally, a task can only start when its predecessors are finished.

Updating out of sequence is simple. Entering actuals overrides the logic of the dependencies, so you can go ahead and update normally as though the tasks were done in sequence. In this situation, however, the option **Split in-progress tasks** (in **Tools, Options, Schedule**) will affect the result:

◆ If selected, the remaining duration is scheduled to start on the current date

◆ If not selected, the remaining duration may be scheduled before the current date

Notice how this option also uses the Current Date rather than the Status Date.

Checks on a Tasks Update

Here are some checks to apply after updating the schedule:

◆ Don't leave unfinished work earlier than (i.e. to the left of) the status date.
If you leave unfinished work before the status date, you are scheduling work to be done in the past. Even though this will show a pending slippage, the work should be moved to the future if you want to show new forecast dates. If you don't do this you have created a status report, not a forecast report.

◆ If the task progresses slower than planned, revise the **Remaining Duration**.
If you take corrective action and think you can catch up, keep the remaining duration the same. If you do nothing, the remaining duration should be increased.

Assignments Update

Preparing for an Assignments Update

Here are the things you need to do for updating the assignments:

◆ Choose the **Tools, Options**.

◆ Prepare the view:
  ◇ Change the view to **Resource Usage** and customize it.
  ◇ Apply the table **Work** and customize it.

◆ Set the task **Type** for all tasks.

◆ Collect the actual hours worked and the remaining hours forecast (using paper or electronic timesheets) using the workgroup features. If you use the workgroup features the process will be:
  ◇ Displaying the **Workgroup** toolbar
  ◇ Send messages from Project 2000
  ◇ Review the responses
  ◇ Transfer the data from the responses to Project 2000

◆ Report the status of the project and latest forecasts.

Choosing the Options for an Assignments Update

Page ta b	Set to:	Why?
Calculation	☑ **Updating task Status updates Resource Status**	We recommend you keep this option on so that Project 2000 calculates the **% Complete**. However, if you enter a % Complete yourself Project 2000 will calculate and override timesheet information data you entered. If you choose to do an assignments update, you should never enter % Complete for tasks.
	☑ **Actual Costs are always calculated by Microsoft Project**	If selected, the percentage complete will update the actual costs accordingly.
General	☐ **Automatically add new resources and tasks**	This prevents accidentally adding resources during updating and re-optimising.
Schedule	☑ **Split in-progress tasks**	Allows you to split the task bar and move the remaining duration to after the status date.
	☐ **Autolink inserted or moved tasks**	Disabling **Autolink** will prevent accidental changes to the network logic.

Creating the View

We will first explain which view you will need to enter the data by hand. Even if you will use the workgroup features, this is still useful knowledge in case you need to make corrections to the timesheet information that is automatically transferred into your project file.

In case you receive updates from each resource individually, you should probably use the **Resource Usage** view. Unfortunately, the view cannot display the status date line. Instead, click on the timescale on that date; it stays selected and can act as a status date. The tools **Update as Scheduled** and **Reschedule Work** are not available in the Resource Usage view.

1. Choose **View, Resource Usage**.

2. Create a new table by choosing **View, Table: <name of current table>, More Tables**; the **More Tables** dialog appears:

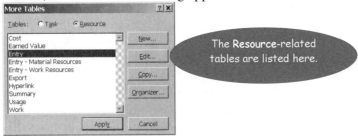

The **Resource**-related tables are listed here.

3. Select the table **Work** and click [**Copy...**]; the **Table Definition** dialog appears:

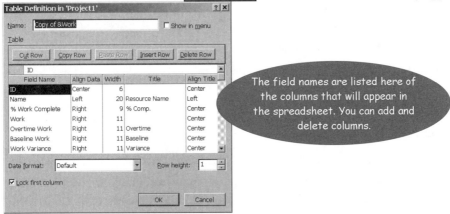

The field names are listed here of the columns that will appear in the spreadsheet. You can add and delete columns.

4. Give the table a name, for example, *Update Assignments*. After the field **Name**, insert the fields **Baseline Work, Work, Actual Work, Remaining Work** and **% Work Complete**. Abbreviate their column titles in the cell **Title** to, for example, *Bas.Work, Work, Act.Work, Rem.Work* and *%Work Comp.* respectively to save space.

5. Change the time to a one-character time unit in **Tools, Options,** tab **Edit,** under **View options for time units** to save space.

6. In the timescale, only the field **Work** is shown. Right-click anywhere in the yellow area below the timescale and select **Detail Styles...**; the **Detail Styles** dialog appears:

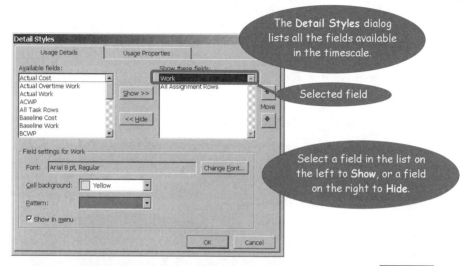

The **Detail Styles** dialog lists all the fields available in the timescale.

Selected field

Select a field in the list on the left to **Show**, or a field on the right to **Hide**.

7. In the list **Available Fields** click on **Baseline Work** and click on Show >> . Do the same for the field **Actual Work**. Click OK .

8. The view should now look like:

View ready for updating assignments.

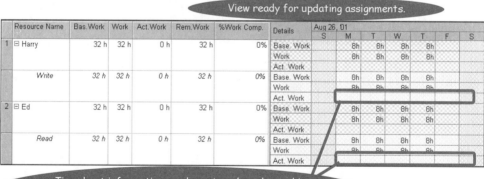

Timesheet information can be entered or changed in the **Actual Work** fields of the (italic) assignments.

Set the Task Type for all Tasks

The task type has to be set in such a way that it triggers the right recalculations. In all cases we will be entering **Work** values. Fixed work is therefore not the right type of task. When updating assignments, you typically want to see the effect on the **Duration** of the task (forecast), while keeping the **Units** of resources the same. **Fixed Units**, therefore, seems again the most appropriate type of task for an assignment update as it was for a task update.

1. Click on a column heading in the Gantt spreadsheet to select all the tasks.

2. Click the **Task Information** 📋 tool; the **Multiple Task Information** dialog appears:

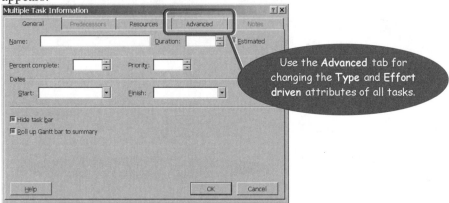

3. Click the **Advanced** tab and select from the list **Task type** [_____] ▼ the item **Fixed Units**.

4. Uncheck ☐ **Effort driven** and click [OK].

The Formulas Behind the Screens

The illustration shows the formulas that Project 2000 will use, when updating the assignments in your project. You should keep these formulas in the back of your mind because they explain the values that Project 2000 calculates and displays.

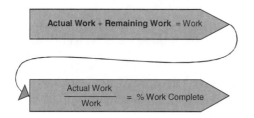

The formulas define the relationships between the four variables. If you enter only two out of the four, Project 2000 will calculate the rest. You should consistently fill in two fields and let Project 2000 calculate the rest. Notice that the field **Work** is the total work on the assignment.

In the following screen we show the difference between a resource and an assignment, and the cells for entering the timesheet data:

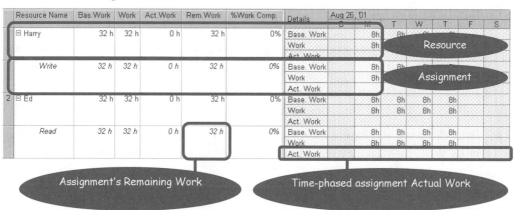

We recommend you enter timesheet data into the time-phased assignment **Actual Work** and also the assignment's **Remaining Work** *(Rem.Work)*. The time-phased **Act.Work** numbers add up to the total **Act.Work** on the assignment.

Notice that all fields mentioned here are the assignment-related fields, not the resource-related fields! You can recognize assignment rows by their italic font in the spreadsheet and a lighter yellow color in the timescale.

Less recommended combinations of fields to update are:

◆ The assignment's **Actual Work** *(Act.Work)* and the assignment's **Remaining Work** *(Rem.Work)*. It is harder to keep a running total of actual work on a task up-to-date, because you can't see what you added when.

◆ **Work** *(Work)* and **% Work Complete** *(%Work Compl.)*
It is harder to continuously estimate the total work than the remaining work.

◆ **% Work Complete** and **Actual Work**
As soon as you enter the actual work it increases the total work. This will recalculate and change the % Work Complete you entered.

◆ **% Work Complete** and **Remaining Work**: as soon as you type the remaining work, it increases the total work and this will recalculate and change the % Work Complete you entered.

Apart from the technicalities, it is better to ask for facts (Actual Work) than for fiction (% Work Complete), just as we recommend for updating tasks.

Collecting the Data

Collecting the data for an assignments update can be done in either of the following ways:

◆ Distribute paper fill-in forms to all team members.
For example, you can make weekly timesheets using the Resource Usage view. You will have to enter all the hours from the timesheet into Project 2000 by hand.

◆ Send electronic timesheets using the workgroup features. You can send them by email or by Web. By Web they will be posted on a website using the Project Central companion product.

All the collection of data and the data entry of actual information can be made easier if your team members have an email system or access to the Web. If that is the case, you can use the workgroup features of MS Project to transfer the actual hours automatically from the electronic timesheets.

One of the limitations of MS Project is that an MS Project file is not accessible by multiple users at the same time. The workgroup features alleviate this. Multi-user access is needed mostly for online updating by resources. The workgroup features allow this in an elegant fashion.

Paper Timesheets

Assignments Update Situations

The following situations can occur when you update assignments. You will notice that these situations are similar to the tasks update situations:

◆ Assignments that Ran as Scheduled
◆ Assignments that Run as Scheduled
◆ Assignments that Run Behind (or Ahead)
◆ Assignments that will Run Longer (or Shorter)
◆ Assignments that Started Late (or Early)
◆ Assignments that Finished Late (or Early)

We will discuss all these situations, but in less detail than we did for the tasks update. You will mostly need to know how to make corrections to the timesheet numbers, because entering them can be done automatically using the workgroup features.

Assignments that Ran as Scheduled

1. In the usage views, assignments have an italic font whereas the resources or tasks do not. Select the assignments that are completed as scheduled by dragging or by holding down ⌈Ctrl⌉ + clicking.

2. Enter *100%* in the **% Work Complete** field for that assignment.

 Notice that you can't click the ⌐100°⌐ tool on the tracking toolbar. This tool is for task updates; it would set the task and all its assignments to 100% complete.

Assignments that Run as Scheduled

1. Select the assignment that is on schedule.

2. Enter a percentage in the field **% Work Complete**. Make sure the hours are filled in up to the status date line.
   OR
   In the timescale of the view, select all the days in the row **Work** up to the status date. Use the drag-handle to drag when you see the cross-hair mouse pointer + and copy them down into the field **Act. Work**.

the drag-handle

Assignments that Run Behind

1. Find the assignments to be updated and enter a percentage in their field **% Work Complete**. Make sure the hours are not filled in up to the status date.

2. The remainder of the hours may have to be re-scheduled to start on the status date. You can do this by selecting the days on which no work took place in the timescale

   Work row and press ⬚Insert. The hours will move over to after the status date.
   OR
   Select by dragging in the timescale in the row **Work** the hours that need to be rescheduled. Then point to the border of the selection and when you see the mouse pointer ⬚ drag them to future days:

These assigned hours can now be rescheduled by dragging.

Assignments that Will Run Longer

You can fill in the **Remaining Work,** and Project 2000 will schedule this work in the timescale on extra days.
OR
In the row **Work** of the timescale enter hours on the extra days you plan to do the work.
OR
Fill in the first number and you can use the drag handle again to fill an even series of hours quickly. Point to it and when you see the cross-hair mouse pointer (+), you can

start dragging to copy the numbers.

OR

You can enter the first value, select the cells to fill into and choose the **Edit, Fill, Right** to copy the value to the extra days.

If the extension affects the fixed duration of the task you will get a prompt.

Assignments that Started Late

1. Select the assignment with a delayed start.

2. Select the days on which work should have been done (but wasn't) in the timescale

   Work row and press .

Assignments that Finished Late

Set the **% Work Complete** to 100% and enter actual hours in the timescale in the row **Actual Work** up to the date the resource finished the assignment.

Now that we have shown you how to work with paper timesheets, let's explore how we can make our lives easier with the workgroup features. Sending out paper timesheets and entering the data is a lot of effort that has to be repeated many times throughout a project. The workgroup features in Project 2000 can enter the data from the timesheets automatically. You may still need the steps we discussed above to make corrections, when needed.

Electronic Timesheets: the Workgroup Features

Workgroup Features

A *workgroup* is the group of people involved in a project. Typically the people involved are:
◆ Upper management
◆ Project manager
◆ Team leaders
◆ Team members
◆ The client (if different from upper management)
◆ Users (if different from client)

Project 2000 has workgroup features that facilitate the communication between the members of a workgroup. The project manager can easily send out different messages to team members to:
◆ Communicate assignments and get commitments: **TeamAssign** message
◆ Communicate changes to assignments: **TeamUpdate** message
◆ Collect actual progress data: **TeamStatus** message

The Workgroup Toolbar

When you want to send messages you may want to display the **Workgroup** toolbar that allows you to create them with one click:

1. Right-click on any toolbar.

2. Choose **Workgroup** from the pop-up menu; the workgroup toolbar is displayed:

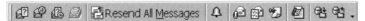

For an explanation of each tool on this toolbar, see page 527: Workgroup Toolbar.

 Messages can only be created from a task view.

Configurations

The workgroup features can be used in one of two configurations:

◆ **Workgroup by Email**
This uses the email system to carry custom project messages. This configuration requires less hardware and software.

◆ **Workgroup by Web: Project Central**
This establishes communication between Project 2000 and a website on the Intranet or the Internet. Project Central uses a database that holds the data and a Web server to display the data on the Web. This configuration offers more sophisticated features for project communications than email does, including specific viewing rights for different groups of users.

Workgroup by Email

In this configuration the messages are transferred using email. The illustration shows the process. The project manager sends email messages to the resources. The email messages arrive in the inbox of the resource. She replies and fills it in, then sends it back to the project manager. The project manager opens it from his inbox and can then accept the input from the resource and update his project file. Or, the project manager can enter into a discussion with the resource by replying to the message.

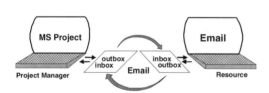

As the project manager, you will need an email system that can carry the MS Project-specific email messages, a 32-bit MAPI-compliant email system. MAPI stands for Message Application Programming Interface and MAPI-carriers are MS Mail, MS Exchange, or MS Outlook.

If the **Resource Name** is identical to the name in your email address list, you won't need to enter email addresses. Otherwise, enter the email addresses in the resource sheet into the field **Email Address**. Use the ⬚ Address... ⬚ button on the **Assign Resources** 🗘 dialog box for each resource, or better still, import all resources and email addresses at once using the **Address Book** tool 📖 on the **Resource Management** toolbar.

If your team members don't have MS Project, they need to run **WGSETUP.EXE** from the Project 2000 CD-ROM to enable their email systems to display and reply to the workgroup email messages. WGSETUP stands for **W**ork**G**roup **SETUP**.

Workgroup by Web: Project Central

In this configuration there is one focal point for all stakeholders, the Project Central website. The messages are kept in the database that lies underneath the Project Central interface. The database can be Oracle, SQL Server or its little brother, MSDE. The project manager generates the email messages from within Project 2000 and directs them

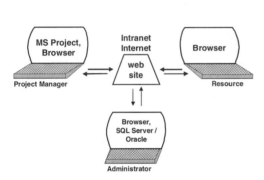

to the resources. The resources can read their messages by browsing to the Project Central website and logging in. The interface lists the messages. When resources respond to the messages, they are stored in the database. The project manager needs to log into the Project Central website to retrieve the responses. He can then decide to reply or to transfer the answers and data from the resource into the Project 2000 MPP-file.

However, Project Central is more than a postal service for messages. Below is a complete list of the benefits you can enjoy by using Project Central:

◆ Informing the entire team:
The Project Central homepage can act as the central message board for the project team.

◆ Collaborating:
As a project manager you can collect input from team members, like new tasks, changes to the work day and vacation time. The Project Central interface is a two-way street:

   ◇ project data from the project manager, and
   ◇ personal data from the team member.

◆ Integrating project planning with personal planning:

   ◇ One single integrated to-do list of project and non-project tasks. The to-do-list can be maintained in MS Outlook.

◇ You can synchronize the Outlook calendar with the resource calendar in Project 2000.

◇ You can make Project Central one of the views in MS Outlook such that team members only need to go to one place.

◆ Delegating tasks:
Project Central can accommodate large projects and more than two hierarchical levels of the project manager and his team members. There can be an intermediary level of team leaders. A team leader can delegate a task to one of his team members through the delegation feature.

◆ Reporting progress electronically in both hours worked and/or a narrative:

◇ Timesheets:
The big benefit of electronic timesheets is one-time data entry. Project Central allows the timesheets to be filled in online or offline and the timesheets in Project Central can include project and non-project tasks. Project managers can send out reminders.

◇ Textual status reports:
The project manager can send out freeform status reports or create template status reports that have the fields he expects to be filled in.

◆ Automatic updating of the project file:

◇ A project manager can create message rules that allow messages from trusted sources to be processed automatically.

◇ The project manager can even choose to manage by exception using this feature; if certain thresholds are exceeded, the message is not processed automatically but called to his attention.

◆ Providing visibility of the project to other groups of stakeholders:

◇ The project manager can create categories of target groups: team member, project manager, resource manager, and executive manager. Each category comes with a set of access rights.

◇ The project manager can give access to certain projects through portfolios of projects.

◇ The project manager can give viewing rights to certain data in the project database through custom views.

Types of Workgroup Messages

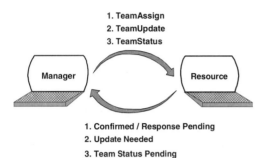

1. TeamAssign
2. TeamUpdate
3. TeamStatus

1. Confirmed / Response Pending
2. Update Needed
3. Team Status Pending

You will find three different types of messages in the **Tools, Workgroup** menu: **TeamAssign, TeamUpdate** and **TeamStatus**. The illustration shows all three and their corresponding task fields in which Project 2000 does track the messages. The tracking is entirely automatic even though you can make changes to certain fields.

◆ *TeamAssign*:
To ask a team member to commit to a task. When the team member replies and agrees, the commitment to the assignment will be shown in the assignment-related field *Confirmed*. When all assignments on a task are confirmed the task-related field **Confirmed** will be toggled to **Yes** by Project 2000.

◆ *TeamUpdate*:
When changes happen to the assignment, such as a cancellation, a change in start date, or the amount of work, Project 2000 will immediately notice this and automatically toggle the field *Update Needed* to **Yes**. You can easily keep track of communications with the resources by observing this field.

◆ *TeamStatus:*
To send a timesheet to collect hours worked. MS Project tracks whether a timesheet is outstanding in the field *Team Status Pending*. If you still need to receive a timesheet, the field will show **Yes**. When you incorporate the timesheet information, Project 2000 will automatically toggle the assignment related field **Team Status Pending** to **No** for that assignment.

The project manager sends messages to the project team members. The team member sends the response back to the project manager. After the project manager reads the response, he can decide:
◆ to continue the conversation by replying
◆ to incorporate the response into his project file by updating the project
◆ to decide later and close the message

Communicating Assignments and Getting Commitments

Creating a TeamAssign Message

1. Make sure you have all assignments that you want to communicate completed in your schedule. Notice that when you assign the first resource to a task, the field **Confirmed** toggles from **Yes** to **No**. A **No** means that a resource has yet to accept the assignment. For tasks without assignments (milestones), the field shows **Yes**.

2. Select the tasks for which you want to create assign messages and click on **TeamAssign** 🖼️.
    OR
    Click on **TeamAssign** 🖼️ and Project 2000 will prompt you in the **Workgroup Mail** dialog appears:

    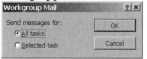

    Select ⦿ **All Tasks** or only the ⦿ **Selected Task** and click | OK |.

3. The **TeamAssign** dialog appears:

    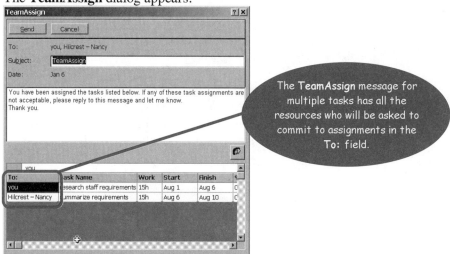

    The **TeamAssign** message for multiple tasks has all the resources who will be asked to commit to assignments in the To: field.

4. Review the message and click | Send |; the message(s) will be sent to the recipient(s). The field **Response Pending** is toggled from **No** to **Yes**, the field **Confirmed** stays on **No**.

The steps are identical for messages sent via email and via Project Central.

The Resource Replies to the TeamAssign Email

Each team member should regularly check his or her email inbox and reply to the messages.

The **TeamAssign** email as the resource receives it, looks like this:

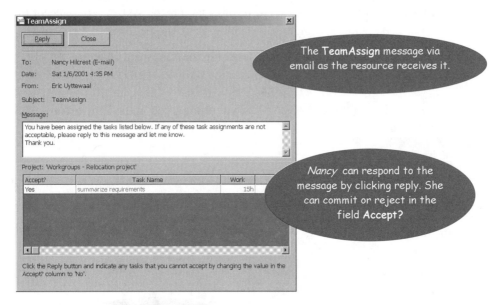

The resource can click [Reply] and indicate in the column **Accept?** whether she accepts or rejects the assignment with a simple **Yes** or **No**. In the column **Comment**, she can add any conditions or explanations. These comments will end up in the project file as permanent documentation on the assignment, another great benefit of the workgroup features.

The Resource Replies to the TeamAssign in Project Central

Each team member should regularly check his or her messages on the Project Central website and reply to the messages.

1. To browse to the Project Central website, click the **Teaminbox** tool on the workgroup toolbar.
   OR
   Choose **Tools, Workgroup, Teaminbox**.
   The Project Central logon website is displayed (unless you use the Windows authentication, which will take you into Project Central immediately using your LAN-login identity):

Microsoft Project Central

What is Microsoft
Project Central?

Setting up a
Microsoft Project
Central Account

Log on using your
Microsoft Windows
user account

Welcome to Microsoft Project Central

Please log on.

User name: [Administrator ▾]

Password: [_____] [Enter]

Select your name from the list above. If you do not see your name in the
list, click Setting up a Microsoft Project Central Account in the list on the
left.

Copyright© 1990-2000 Microsoft Corporation. All
rights reserved. License Agreement.

*The Project Central website is
a secure website with user
accounts and passwords.*

---

2. Log on to Project Central by selecting your **User name** from the list

   Administrator ▼ and typing your password. If the team member cannot find her name in the list, she has not been sent any messages. Project Central creates new users when messages are addressed to them.

   Click Enter and the page appears:

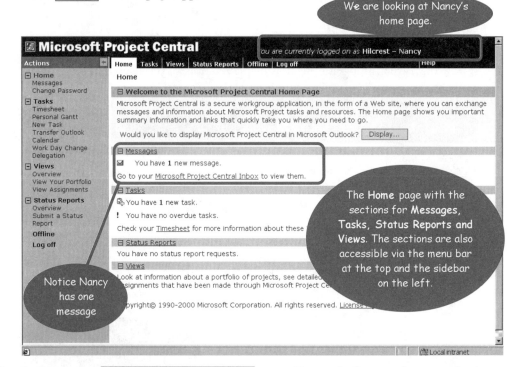

> We are looking at Nancy's home page.

> Notice Nancy has one message

> The Home page with the sections for **Messages, Tasks, Status Reports** and **Views**. The sections are also accessible via the menu bar at the top and the sidebar on the left.

3. In the section ⊟ Messages you will see whether you have received new messages from the resources. The number of messages received is indicated.

4. Click on the word ⊟ Messages and you will see your message inbox:

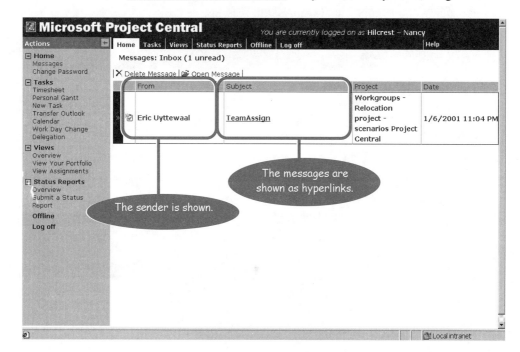

The sender is shown.

The messages are shown as hyperlinks.

5. In the **Subject** column, click on the underlined description `TeamAssign` and the message will open up. The **TeamAssign** message as the resource sees it, looks like this:

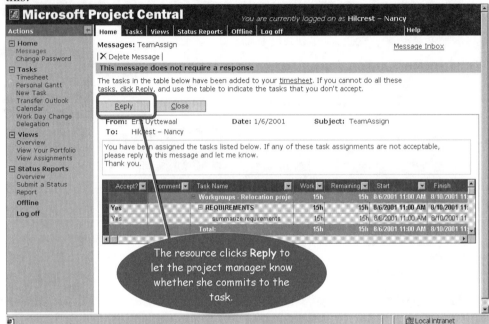

6. The resource could decide later and click | Close |.
    OR
    She can write a response, by clicking | Reply | and indicating in the column **Accept?** if she accepts or rejects the assignment with a simple **Yes** or **No**. In the column **Comment**, she can add any conditions or explanations. These comments will end up in the project file as permanent documentation on the assignments.

The following screen appears:

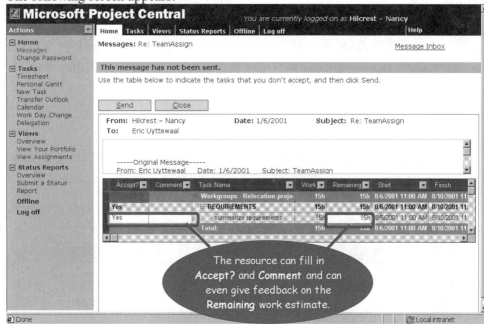

The resource can fill in **Accept?** and **Comment** and can even give feedback on the **Remaining** work estimate.

7. Click ⟨ **Send** ⟩, the message will arrive in the inbox of the project manager.

How the Resources can Keep Track of Tasks Confirmed

If the resource accepts the tasks and uses MS Outlook, the tasks are automatically copied into her task list in MS Outlook. The resource can view her list by choosing **View, Go To, Tasks**. It helps the resource keep track of tasks. Each task has a check box to keep track of tasks completed and, when checked, the task is struck out. Tasks in red are overdue.

The **Tasks** list in MS Outlook

☐ ☑	Subject	Start Date ▵	Due Date	Actual Work
	Click here to add a new Task			
☑ ☑	~~write~~	~~Fri 12/1/2000~~	~~Mon 7/16/2001~~	~~4 weeks~~
☑ ☐	edit	Thu 1/4/2001	Fri 1/5/2001	0 hours
☑ ■	print	Sat 1/6/2001	Sat 1/6/2001	0 hours
☑ ☐	research staff requirements	Wed 8/1/2001	Mon 8/6/2001	0 hours
☑ ☐	select the realtor	Wed 8/1/2001	Mon 8/6/2001	0 hours
☑ ☐	visit the sites	Fri 8/10/2001	Mon 8/13/2001	0 hours

To print the list from MS Outlook, she can choose **Actions, New TeamStatus Report**.

Checking the Replies from the Resources in Your Email System

1. Open your email application and check your inbox. Responses to **TeamAssign** messages will have **RE: TeamAssign** in the subject line.

2. Double-click on it to review the responses and:

   click [Reply] if you have questions or remarks for the resource, or

   click [Update Project] if you want to transfer the responses into the MPP-file. The comments will be copied into the **Notes** field in Project 2000.

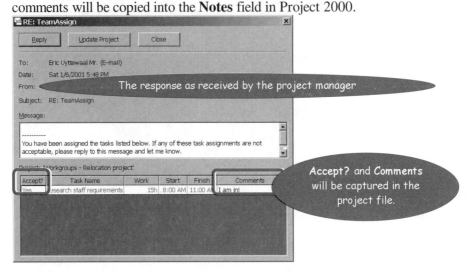

Checking the Replies From the Resources in Project Central

1. Click the **Teaminbox** tool on the workgroup toolbar.
    OR
    Choose **Tools, Workgroup, Teaminbox**.
    The Project Central logon website is displayed (unless you use the Windows
    authentication, which will take you into Project Central immediately using your LAN-
    login identity):

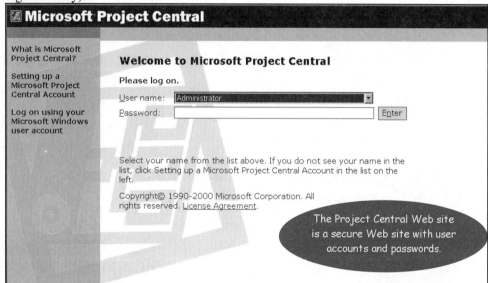

2. Log on to Project Central by selecting your **User name** from the list `Administrator ▼` and type your password. If you cannot find your name in the list, you have to create an account for yourself by switching back to Project 2000 and choosing **Tools, Options, Workgroup** and clicking `Create Account`. Project Central creates the team members as new users when you send them messages. Click `Enter` and the page appears:

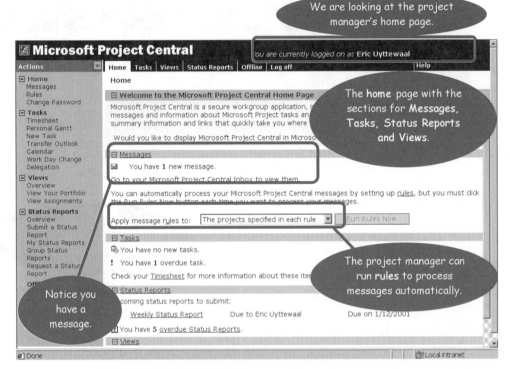

We are looking at the project manager's home page.

The home page with the sections for **Messages**, **Tasks**, **Status Reports** and **Views**.

The project manager can run **rules** to process messages automatically.

Notice you have a message.

3. In the section `⊟ Messages` you will see whether you have received new messages from the resources. The number of new messages is indicated.

4. Click on the word ⊟ Messages and you will see your message inbox:

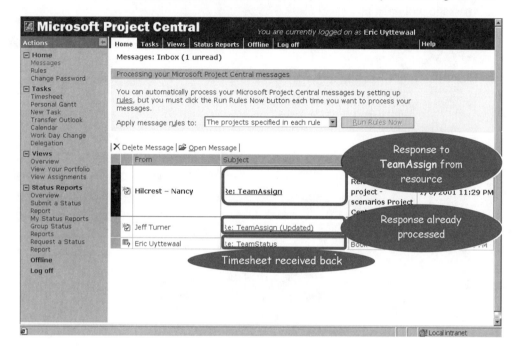

5. In the **Subject** column, click on the underlined description `Re: TeamAssign` and the message will open up:

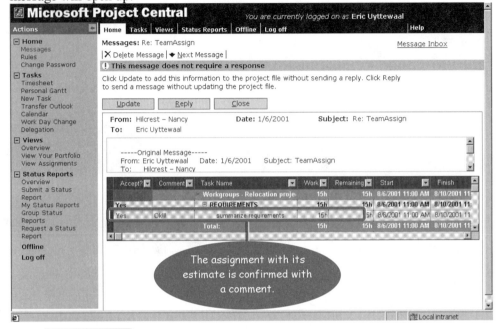

6. Click [Update] to transfer the commitment and comment to your project file.
   OR
   Click [Reply] and write a response.
   OR
   Click [Close] to decide later.

7. Notice that after you have updated your project file, the field **Confirmed** in Project 2000 shows a **Yes** for all the assignments that were committed to.

Viewing all Commitments in MS Project

Commitments are made on the assignment level. Project 2000 will summarize the commitments on the task level when a task has more than one assignment. Only when all resources assigned to the task have committed themselves, will Project 2000 toggle the task-related cell **Confirmed** to **Yes**.

For example, when two resources Harry and Ed are both assigned to the same task, the possibilities are:

Harry	Ed	Task field **Confirmed** will show:
Accepted	Accepted	Yes
Accepted	Rejected	No
Rejected	Accepted	No
Rejected	Rejected	No

The task-related cells summarize their assignment cells. As you can see, Project 2000 summarizes the assignments in a pessimistic fashion. Only if all resources are committed, will **Confirmed** show **Yes** on the task level. Similarly, the field **Response Pending** shows a **Yes,** even if just one of the TeamAssign messages is not back yet.

In the Task Usage view, you can see on the assignment level who responded in the **Response Pending** field, who rejected and who accepted in the **Confirmed** cells. This works in a similar fashion for the other two fields, **Updated Needed** and **TeamStatus Pending**.

If you want to see the exact commitments by assignment, view the commitments in the Task Usage view with the assignments expanded and the fields **Confirmed** and **Response Pending**. The following screen shows this:

	❶	Task Name	Duration	Confirmed	Response Pending	Update Needed	TeamStatus Pend
1		⊟ **REQUIREMENTS**	7.4d	**Yes**	**No**	**No**	**No**
2	📝	⊟ research staff requirements	4d	Yes	No	*Response received, assignment accepted*	
		you		Yes	No		
3	✉?	⊟ summarize requirements	4d	No	Yes	*Response pending*	
	✉?	Hilcrest – Nancy		No	Yes		
4		⊟ **LOCATION**	16.5d	**Yes**	**No**	**No**	**No**
5		⊟ select the realtor	4.6d	No	No	*TeamAssign message still has to be sent.*	
		you		No	No		

You can see the comments that were written by the team member in the **Indicators** field as a note attached to the task. Point to the icon 📝 or 📨 for one full second and read the notes in the pop-up:

📝 Notes: 'Jeff Turner (Dec 5 '00): I will be very busy around that time...'	📨 There has not yet been a response to all the TeamAssign messages for this task.

Notice that it captured the name of the respondent and the date. If you can't see all the text, select the task, click **Task Information** 📋 on the **Standard** toolbar and click on the tab **Notes**.

Toggling the Confirmed Field Manually

The **Confirmed** field can also be edited manually, but you can only edit the field in the assignment-related cells, not in the task-related cells. You can do this to make corrections, or to resend messages when they did not arrive.

Communicating Changes in Assignments

Checking if Updates are Needed

Project 2000 will immediately toggle the field **Update Needed** from **No** to **Yes** for accepted assignments as soon as the start date, duration, amount of work or finish date changes. The task field **Update Needed** will tell you if update messages are due.

You can see the icon 📨 in the **Indicators** column when you need to send out update messages to your team members. Point to the icon 📨 for one second and read the reminder or press 📋 and click on the tab **Notes**.

Creating a TeamUpdate Message

1. Check the **Indicators** column for the icon 📨.
    OR
    Scan the field **Update Needed** for **Yes**.
    OR
    Apply the filter **Update needed**.

2. Click **TeamUpdate** on the workgroup toolbar to create the message. The **TeamUpdate** dialog appears:

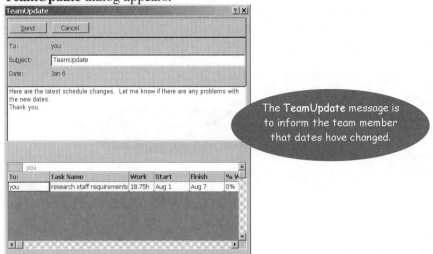

The **TeamUpdate** message is to inform the team member that dates have changed.

3. Review the message and notice that it will be sent out to all resources that need to be informed of changes in their assignments. Click ⟨ Send ⟩; the message(s) will be sent to the recipient(s).

These steps are identical for messages sent via email or Project Central.

The Resource does not need to reply to the **TeamUpdate** message; it is a one-way affair. Project 2000 just captures whether an update message was sent out or not and it knows this with 100% certainty. As a consequence, Project 2000 does not allow you to manually change the **Update Needed** field. The tool just assumes that if an update message is sent, it will arrive. However, some of my email messages have been in orbit for years and still haven't arrived. Not to mention that it also assumes that update messages will be read…

If you Remove a Resource From a Task

Project 2000 will notice automatically when an assignment was removed and will prompt you if you would like to send a **TeamUpdate** message. The message the resource receives in the email will look like:

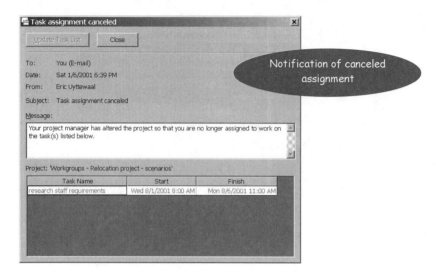

Collecting Actual Progress Data

Customizing the Timesheets

You can customize the timesheet dialog by choosing **Tools, Customize, Workgroup....**
The **Customize Workgroup** dialog appears:

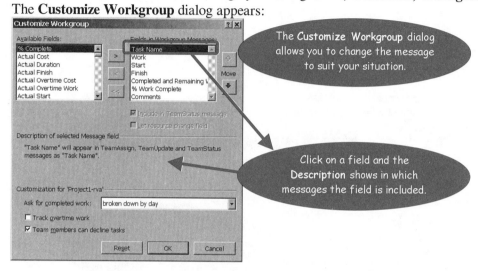

The **Customize Workgroup** dialog allows you to change the message to suit your situation.

Click on a field and the **Description** shows in which messages the field is included.

The default **TeamStatus** timesheet message has all the fields shown in the list on the right. These fields cannot be removed; they are the standard timesheet fields. You can add fields from the list on the left to the timesheet. Realize, though, that the space is limited on the messages and the recipient will have to scroll more.

Creating a TeamStatus Message

1. Select the tasks for which you want to create timesheets and click on **TeamStatus** 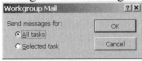 on the workgroup toolbar.
    OR
    Click on **TeamStatus** and Project 2000 will prompt you in the **Workgroup Mail** dialog to send messages for **All Tasks** or only the **Selected Task**:

2. The **TeamStatus** dialog appears:

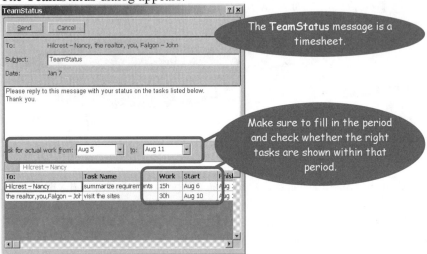

3. Enter the period for which to collect actuals in the fields:
    Ask for actual work from: Mar 13 '00 ▼ **to:** Mar 19 '00 ▼. Review the message and click Send ; the message(s) will be sent to the recipient(s).

4. Notice that the field **TeamStatus Pending** is toggled to **Yes** for the tasks. Also the **Indicators** column has the icon ▦ for them. If you point to the icon for one full second, you will see the pop-up:

> ▦ There has not yet been a
> response to all the TeamStatus
> messages for this task.

These steps are identical for email and Project Central.

The Resource Fills in the TeamStatus Email

The resource receives the timesheet by email as follows:

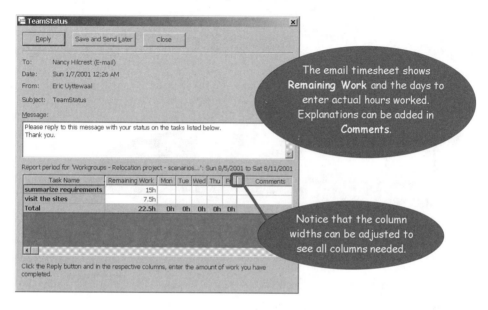

The email timesheet shows **Remaining Work** and the days to enter actual hours worked. Explanations can be added in Comments.

Notice that the column widths can be adjusted to see all columns needed.

After the resource fills in the actual hours, she should revise the **Remaining Work**. In the email system, the resource will have to decrease the remaining work herself. The resource should provide you with a new estimate, if appropriate. If needed, she can add an explanation in the **Comments** field.

A filled-in email timesheet looks like this:

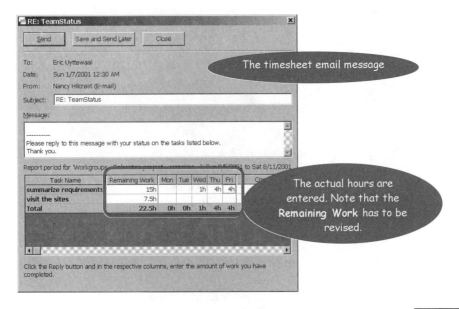

After the resource has completed the **TeamStatus** message, she clicks Send and the timesheet will be delivered to the project manager.

The Resource Fills in the Project Central TeamStatus

A resource can log into the Project Central website as, discussed on page 481, on the TeamAssign messages except that now the resource needs to look for **Re: TeamStatus** messages in your inbox. She receives the timesheet in Project Central as follows:

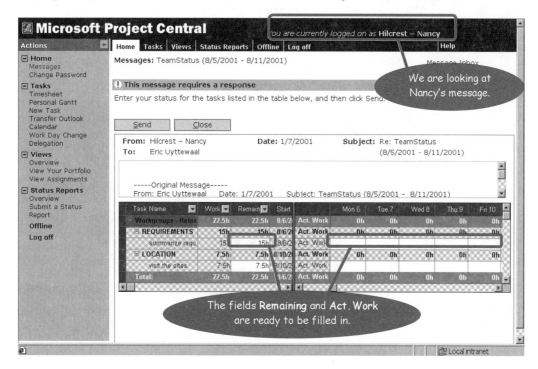

 Resources can fill in the **Act. Work** per day (the hours the resource worked on each day of the week, if it is weekly timesheet) OR the **% Work Complete** (hidden in the screen above) but not both. As soon as the resource fills in the one, the other is grayed and disabled. As we discussed before, on page 469, filling in both does not make sense and Project 2000 would only get confused. The **Remaining Work** hours are automatically decreased in Project Central every time actual hours are entered.

A filled in timesheet in Project Central looks like this:

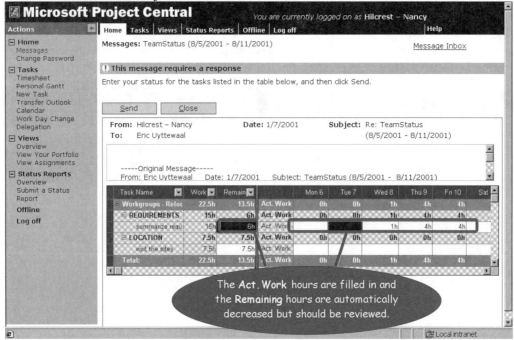

After the resource has completed the TeamStatus message, she clicks [Send] and the timesheet will be delivered to the project manager.

Checking the TeamStatus Emails

In your inbox you will find the timesheets from the resources by looking at the subject line that says **RE: TeamStatus**. The TeamStatus email messages look like this:

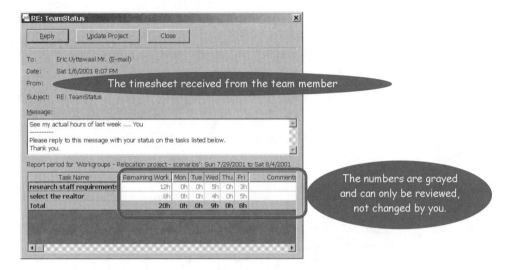

When you review the timesheets as the project manager, you have three options:

◆ Click [Reply] to ask questions or ask for clarifications

◆ Click [Update Project] to transfer actual hours and comments into the project file

◆ Click [Close] to decide later

Checking the TeamStatus Messages in Project Central

See page 486 for detailed steps on how to access messages received in Project Central. You now have to look for TeamStatus replies **Re: TeamStatus** instead of TeamAssign replies. The timesheet as the project manager receives it looks like this:

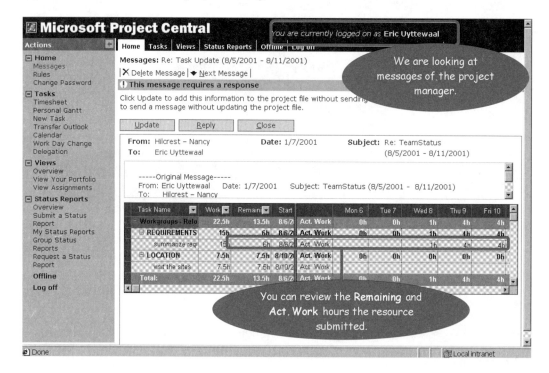

When you review the timesheets as the project manager, you have three options:

◆ Click [Reply] to ask questions or ask for clarifications

◆ Click [Update] to transfer the actual hours and comments into the project file

◆ Click [Close] to decide later

Viewing the Timesheet Data in Project 2000

After transferring the timesheet hours, you can view the actual hours entered in the Resource Usage view with the assignments expanded. Choose **Format, Details, Actual Work** to see the exact numbers typed in by the resources as illustrated in the next screen:

O	Resource Name	Bas.Work	Work	Act.Work	Rem.Work	%Work Comp.	Details	01 M	T	W	T	F
3	⊟ Hilcrest – Nancy	37.5h	37.5h	9h	28.5h	24%	Base. Work	2.25h	3.75h	3.75h	3.75h	6h
							Work			1h	4h	8.5h
							Act. Work			1h	4h	4h
	summarize requirements	15h	15h	9h	6h	60%	Base. Work	2.25h	3.75h	3.75h	3.75h	1.5h
							Work			1h	4h	4h
							Act. Work			1h	4h	4h
	visit the sites	7.5h	7.5h	0h	7.5h	0%	Base. Work					4.5h
							Work					4.5h
							Act. Work					
	evaluate the sites	7.5					Base. W					
							Work					
							Act. W					

*Project 2000 calculated the total **Actual Work** and the **% Work Complete**.*

These were the hours Nancy filled in. Notice they are fewer than baselined.

Toggling the TeamStatus Pending Field Manually

After updating the project file, Project 2000 toggles the field **TeamStatus Pending** back to **No** for the timesheets received. Check this field to find out if there are still timesheets outstanding before you create a status report on the entire project. You will have to chase after the resources that did not return their timesheets before you can report the status of your project.

The **TeamStatus Pending** fields can be edited manually. This is useful for:
◆ Verbal updates
◆ Lost messages when the power goes out or the email system breaks down
◆ Making corrections

The task-related cells summarize the assignment cells. If one of the resources assigned to the task did not submit his timesheet, the **TeamStatus Pending** will show **Yes**. Again, Project 2000 is pessimistic in summarizing on the task level.

Reporting Status and Latest Forecast

Regardless of whether you chose to update tasks or assignments, the Tracking Gantt Chart is good for reporting progress and new forecasts. The Tracking Gantt depicts progress using the calculated date field **Complete Through**. In the Tracking Gantt Chart you can see this by choosing **Format, Barstyles** and looking under **To**. The Complete Through field:

◆ follows closely the **Actual Duration** that is entered by you, when you update tasks
◆ is the number of days for which actual hours are entered, when you update assignments.

In the screen below, you will find the status and forecast report from an assignments update as explained above:

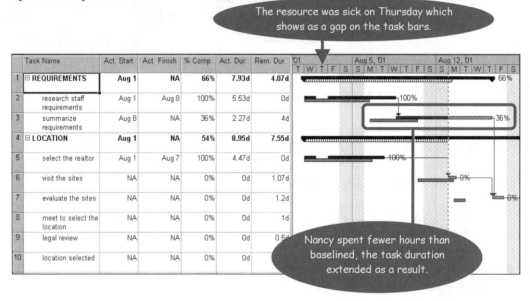

Notice that the Tracking Gantt does not show progress, if you turned the option ☑ **Updating Task Status updates Resource Status** off in **Tools, Options,** tab **Calculation**. With the option off, the **% Complete** and the **Complete Through** are not calculated. If you update the assignments with the option on, you have to make sure to never enter % Complete for tasks, because this will override the timesheet information.

Updating the Costs

Cost Updating Strategies

This is similar to updating the schedule:

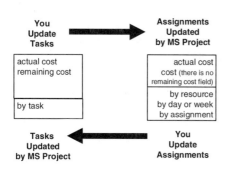

◆ You can update the tasks and have the assignment details updated by Project 2000.

◆ You can update the assignments. If you enter the data into the time-phased fields, you can model the actual cash flow very precisely. In order to do so, you have to change a default option.

Setting the Options for Assignments Cost Updates

You can enter actual costs in the time-phased **Actual Cost** fields for the assignments in Project 2000. This can be a useful way of keeping your project up-to-date on a daily or weekly basis, because you can enter information for a particular day or week in your schedule.

In its default options, Project 2000 automatically updates actual costs. It calculates them based on the accrual method you set and the % Complete. If you want to enter actual costs yourself, you must first turn off the automatic updating of actual costs. Then you can enter your own actual costs.

1. Choose **Tools, Options**, and then click the **Calculation** tab.

2. Uncheck ☐ **Actual costs are always calculated by Microsoft Project**.

3. Click   OK .

Preparing the View for Updating Costs

1. Choose **View, Task Usage**.

2. Choose **View, Table: <name of current table>, Tracking**; the fields for updating tasks are displayed.

3. Choose **Format, Detail Styles…**, in the list **Available fields** select **Actual Cost** and click the ⬚ Show >> . Click ⬚ OK ⬚ . The **Act. Cost** field is now also displayed in the timescale.

4. Update tasks: add the new cost to the running total displayed in the spreadsheet column **Act. Cost** and enter the new total actual cost.
   OR
   Update assignments: in the timescale enter expenditures in the **Act. Cost** row on the day you incurred the actual costs.

Exercises

Review

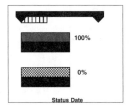

100%

0%

Status Date

A team leader submits the following report to you as shown in the illustration. Would you accept this report:

◆ as a status report? Why?

◆ as a forecast report? Why?

If you would not accept it, indicate what needs to be changed.

Relocation Project – Updating Tasks

Open the file *11 Updating the Schedule 1.MPP* in the sub-directory *Relocation Project* on the CD-ROM.

1. Change to the **Tracking Gantt** view.

2. Set the baseline for the entire project.

3. Set the **Status Date** to *September 14th* and create a gridline for the status date in the Gantt timescale.

4. Display the **Tracking** toolbar.

5. Set the following options in **Tools, Options, Calculation**:
   ☑ **Updating Task status updates resource status**
   ☑ **Actual Costs are always calculated by Microsoft Project**

6. As of *September 15th* the situation is:
   All the tasks until *Remodeled Location* are done. The contractor started late because he finished his previous contract late. The contractor supplied the following update:

Task	Started	Actual Duration	Revised Estimate of total Work
relocate walls	*10 Sept.*	*3d*	*150 d*

The rest of the tasks are not started yet.

7. Enter the status of the project by updating the tasks.

8. Describe the status of the project in your own words.

9. Compare your file with the solution file *11 Updating the Schedule 2.MPP* in the sub-directory *Relocation Project* on the CD-ROM.

Relocation Project – Optimizing for Time Again

Open the file *11 Updating the Schedule 2.MPP* in the sub-directory *Relocation Project* on the CD-ROM.

You find this schedule too risky; you need to meet the deadline of November 1st and, on top of that, you need a time buffer to meet the project deadline. You decide to explore whether working overtime offers solutions. The overtime rates are:

Name	Std. Rate	Overtime Rate
employees	*$ 25/h*	*$ 50/h*
contractor	*$ 30/h*	*$ 50/h*
LAN consultants	*$ 75/h*	*$ 100/h*
Realtor	*$ 35/h*	*$ 45/h*

1. Which people would you ask to work overtime to meet the November 1st deadline? Why?

2. You want to explore whether overtime during the weekends can solve the schedule conflict. Which weekends do you propose to work overtime?

3. Does it solve the schedule conflict? If not, which resource would you ask to work overtime during the weekends next?

4. Does it solve the schedule conflict? What do you propose to do?

5. Compare your file with the solution file *11 Updating the Schedule 3.MPP* in the sub-directory *Relocation Project* on the CD-ROM.

Chapter 12 Evaluating the Project

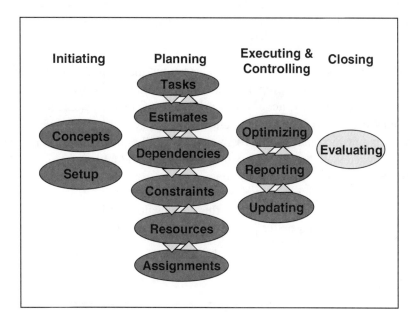

After this chapter you will:

◆ Know why project evaluation is important.

◆ Have a list of evaluation points that will help you to learn from a finished project.

Project Evaluation

Evaluating a project when it is completed is often seen as a waste of time. The reason for this seems to be that the atmosphere during an evaluation can be loaded with animosity. When things did not run the way they should have, pointing fingers quickly appear. These evaluations are indeed a waste of time.

Evaluation is useful when the focus is on, and stays on, the future. Only by learning from the past can you become better prepared for the future. Lessons learned can lead to improvements to the WBS, the accuracy of estimates, the use of dependencies, the use of resources and the appropriateness of assignments in the schedule. The meeting must be directed in such a fashion that people focus on gain for the future instead of on pain from the past. If managed well, the meeting can be a source of valuable information. Evaluating prevents running into the same troubles again.

Of course many projects run well. Even in this case evaluating is important because it is the only way to become yet a better project manager. There is always room to deliver projects better.

Evaluation Points

After the project is over you can ask questions. These are a few:

1. Was the schedule clear to all stakeholders? How can it be made clearer in future projects?

2. Was the WBS complete? Was it easy to understand? Did it function as a tool for delegation? How can it be improved for similar projects in the future?

3. Were the estimates optimistic or pessimistic? What factors caused schedule and cost variances? Can these factors be better predicted in future projects?

4. Was there enough time buffer in the schedule to compensate for unforeseen events? What types of tasks consumed most of the buffer?

5. Was the schedule easy to maintain during project execution? Could accurate status and forecast reports be generated at each reporting period? Was the network of dependencies complete? How can the reports be produced in an easier fashion in future projects?

6. Were the right resources available at the right times? How can availability be ensured in future projects?

To prevent learning painful lessons, you should use a checklist to ensure the quality of your schedule. We will provide a list of questions in the next chapter for use in evaluating the schedule. This list can be used to check the quality of the schedule as soon as it is created.

Chapter 13 Summary

Checklist for Dynamic Project Models

As a summary of this book we will provide a list of criteria for good schedules. Throughout the chapters, we have made many recommendations. These recommendations are compiled in this checklist. The list can be used to evaluate the quality of a project schedule. At the International Institute for Learning, we use this list to evaluate the quality of the schedules that are submitted for certification on the Orange Belt level of *Managing a Single Project with Microsoft Project*.

If your schedule meets these guidelines, you have created a dynamic model of your project. Schedules that meet the requirements not only need the least maintenance during the execution of the project, they are also ready for consolidation into master schedules on a program or department level. The next level of the IIL certification curriculum, *Managing Multiple Projects* or Blue Belt level, is targeted at people who manage more than one project. Managing multiple projects is a sheer impossible task if the single schedules, as the building blocks for the program schedule, do not meet the following requirements.

The checklist has the following categories that correspond to chapters in this book. The checklist can be seen as a succinct summary of this book:
◆ Work Breakdown Structure (WBS)
◆ Estimates
◆ Dependencies
◆ Scheduling Constraints
◆ Resources
◆ Assignments
◆ Optimizing
◆ Reporting
◆ Updating

Work Breakdown Structure (WBS)

❑ Is the WBS deliverable-oriented? If no, could the WBS be changed to a deliverable orientation?

❑ Is the list of deliverables complete?

❑ Does the WBS have a logical and hierarchical structure? Is the WBS an indented task list instead of one long list of tasks?

❑ Is the formulation of the task names following these guidelines:
  ❑ Phases are formulated using the imperfect tense (-ing).
  ❑ Deliverables are formulated using nouns.
  ❑ Detail tasks are formulated using present tense verbs.
  ❑ Milestones are formulated using nouns plus a verb in past or perfect tense or the words 'ready' or 'complete'.

❑ Are the task names consistent in the WBS?

❑ Are there enough milestones i.e., at least one for every deliverable or phase (summary task)?

❑ Does the WBS have the right level of detail?
  There may be too little detail in the WBS if:
  ❑ You can't estimate the durations or work on the detail tasks.
  ❑ You have difficulties finding the dependencies between the detail tasks.
  ❑ There are tasks that are longer than 10% of the project duration (1%-10% Rule).
  ❑ There are tasks that are longer than a reporting period.

  There may be too much detail in the WBS if:
  ❑ You think there are too many tasks; if you think the task list is too long.
  ❑ You can't guarantee you will be able to maintain all the detail in the schedule during the execution of the project.
  ❑ There are tasks that are shorter than 1% of the project duration (1%-10% Rule).

❑ Is the WBS clear to all stakeholders: client, upper management, team members, and support staff?

❑ Do the status meetings, as recurring tasks, continue over the entire duration of the project?

Estimates

❏ Are the estimates reasonable given the work that needs to be performed?

❏ Are the estimates within the boundaries of the 1%-10% rule?

Dependencies

❏ Is the network of dependencies complete? The following four questions will help determine this.

  ❏ Do all tasks have at least one successor?
  Exceptions for this are the project end milestone, summary tasks, recurring tasks and overhead/hammock tasks.

  ❏ Do all tasks have at least one predecessor?
  Exceptions for this are: tasks that can start when the project starts, and external deliveries (should have a milestone with a **Start-No-Earlier-Than** date).

  ❏ Are there tasks with an unreasonably large amount of **Total Slack**?

  ❏ When a change occurs in the project and the change is entered into the schedule, does it update the rest of the schedule automatically through the dependencies? If you have to go through the entire schedule every time when you enter a change, you don't have a dynamic schedule.

❏ Are there redundant dependencies that make the network too difficult to understand and maintain?

  ❏ No dependencies that leap-frog one another, and

  ❏ No dependencies that run in parallel on detail tasks and summary tasks. Keep the detail dependencies.

❏ Does the logic of the network make sense?

Deadlines and Scheduling Constraints

❏ There are as few as possible schedule constraints. Constraints make the schedule rigid. However, constraints are allowed on:

  ❏ External dependencies, such as delivery of supplies or materials.

  ❏ Activities that have to take place on a certain agreed-upon date, like presentations and training. In general these are activities in which a group of people is involved.

13

❏ Recurring detail tasks, like status meetings.

❏ Do-or-drop-dead deadlines, like the Dec.31, 1999 deadline for Y2K projects (but not on target dates; use the Deadline feature in Project 2000 for those).

❏ Activities affected by (winter) weather conditions i.e., task "asphalt streets" starts-no-earlier-than April 1st. (You can also use the feature of Task Calendars for these situations In Project 2000).

Resources

❏ Are all resources that could have a potential impact on the duration or the cost of the project identified?

❏ Is the right level of detail found for the resources: part-time, full-time, and/or consolidated resources?

❏ Is the availability of the resources adequately captured in the **Max. Units** field and on the resource calendar?
   ❏ Are the vacations of the individual resources captured?
   ❏ **Max. Units** for individuals should not exceed 120%

Assignments

❏ Is the appropriate Type of task chosen for each task?
   (**Fixed Duration**, **Fixed Units** or **Fixed Work**)

❏ Are the assignments complete: in the **Resource Usage** view there should be no detail tasks listed under the first category '**Unassigned**'.

Optimizing

Workloads

❏ Are the workloads for the resources reasonable?
   ❏ For individuals, the workload should not exceed 150% of their regular availability within any week. The workload should not exceed 120% for periods longer than a week.
   ❏ The workload should not exceed the availability of consolidated resources.
   ❏ The workloads are fairly smooth.

Costs

❏ Is the total cost within the budget of the project?

❏ The cost is modeled adequately using the right fields:
- ❏ In the Resource Sheet: **Standard cost**, **Overtime cost**, **Cost per use** and **Accrual**.
- ❏ In the Gantt Chart: **Fixed cost** and **Fixed cost accrual**.

Time

❏ Are the deadlines met in the schedule?

❏ Does the schedule have a Critical Path or a Resource-Critical Path? Is it highlighted in the **Gantt Chart** or **Tracking Gantt**?

Reporting

❏ Are the status/progress/forecast reports ready to go as **View** objects in the file?

❏ Do the reports give an appropriate impression of the health of the project? Are the appropriate health indicators chosen for the type of project?

Updating

If the project is supposed to be started already:

❏ Is the baseline of the schedule
- ❏ present
- ❏ original
- ❏ complete
- ❏ relevant

❏ Are the appropriate options selected for the updating strategy chosen (task updating or assignment updating)?

❏ Is the schedule up-to-date as per the **Status date** (or as per the **Current date**)?

❏ Is there no remaining duration or work (that has to be done still) scheduled before the status date? Otherwise, the schedule does not reflect up-to-date forecasts.

In Closing

If you have any further questions, don't hesitate to contact us. If you have any feedback on this book, please call 613-692-7778 or email me at: EricU@iil.com.

Thanks for the time you spent reading this book and thank you for choosing this product from the International Institute for Learning.

Eric Uyttewaal, PMP
Director, Microsoft Project Certification
International Institute for Learning
www.iil.com

Appendix 1: Shortcuts of Project 2000

To Move Around in a Project

The following convention is used in the table:

⌨Alt + ⌨→ means hold down ⌨Alt and press ⌨→.

Move to	By keyboard	By mouse
Next row	⌨Enter	Click
Next column	⌨Tab	Click
Next time unit in time scale	⌨Alt + ⌨→ or ⌨Alt + ⌨←	Click on an arrow button of the scroll bar ▶
Next screen in time scale	⌨Alt + ⌨Page Up or ⌨Alt + ⌨Page Down	Click at the left or right of the scroll box ■ on the scroll bar
The start date of the project	⌨Alt + ⌨Home	Left-align the scroll box ■ on horizontal scroll bar
The end date of the project	⌨Alt + ⌨End	
The beginning of the project	⌨Ctrl + ⌨Home	Drag the vertical scroll box ■ to the top
The end of the project	⌨Ctrl + ⌨End	Drag vertical scroll box ■ to the bottom
A specific task, resource or date	⌨F5 OR ⌨Ctrl + ⌨F	**Edit, Go To** OR **Edit, Find**
The other split window	⌨F6	Click in the other split window to make it active
The task bar of a selected task		Click 🖐 **Go To Selected Task**

Standard Toolbar

Button	Tool Tip	Similar to choosing menu items
	New	**File, New**
	Open	**File, Open**
	Save	**File, Save:** saves the project without prompting for file name
	Print	**File, Print:** Prints the active view using the current settings in the **File, Print** dialog without showing it
	Print Preview	**File, Print Preview**: previews the pages in the active view as they will be printed
	Spelling	**Tools, Spelling**
	Cut	**Edit, Cut**: removes the selected information and stores it on the Clipboard
	Copy	**Edit, Copy**: copies the selected information and stores it on the Clipboard
	Paste	**Edit, Paste**: inserts the information from the Clipboard
	Format Painter	Copies the format of the selected cell onto a target cell
	Undo	**Edit, Undo**: undoes the last action only and is not always available
	Insert Hyperlink	**Insert, Hyperlink**
	Link Tasks	**Edit, Link Tasks**: links the selected tasks with finish-to-start dependency
	Unlink Tasks	**Edit, Unlink Tasks**: breaks the dependency between selected task
	Split Tasks	**Edit, Split Task**: splits the task bar of the selected task

Button	Tool Tip	Similar to choosing menu items
	Task Information	Select a task, resource or assignment, hold down ⌜Shift⌟ and press ⌜F2⌟ OR choose the **Project** menu **Task Information Form**, **Resource Information Form** or **Assignment Information Form** Use these dialogs to change details
	Task Notes	**Project, Task Notes** or **Resource Notes** or **Assignment Notes**
	Assign Resources	**Tools, Resources, Assign Resources**: displays the **Assign Resources** dialog to add, change, or remove resource assignments for the selected tasks
No Group ▾	**Group By**	**Project, Group By**: allows you to group the tasks (resources) by their characteristics
	Zoom In	**View, Zoom…**: shows a smaller time unit on the timescale
	Zoom Out	**View, Zoom**: shows a larger time unit on the timescale
	Go to selected task	Displays the task bar of the task you have selected
	Copy Picture	**Edit, Copy Picture…**: copies the active view as an object
	Microsoft Project Help	**Help, Microsoft Project Help**
▾	**More Buttons**	

Formatting Toolbar

Button	Tool Tip	Similar to choosing menu items
Outdent	Outdent	Project, Outline, Outdent
Indent	Indent	Project, Outline, Indent
Show Subtasks	Show Subtasks	Project, Outline, Show Subtasks
Hide Subtasks	Hide Subtasks	Project, Outline, Hide Subtasks
Show ▾		Project, Outline, Show: shows the outline level of your choice
Arial	Font	Format, Font
8	Font Size	Format, Font
B	Bold	Format, Font
I	Italic	Format, Font
U	Underline	Format, Font
Align Left	Align Left	double-click on the column heading
Center	Center	double-click on the column heading
Align Right	Align Right	double-click on the column heading
All Tasks	Filter	Project, Filtered for:
▽=	AutoFilter	Project, Filtered for: AutoFilter
Gantt Chart Wizard	Gantt Chart Wizard	Format, Gantt Chart Wizard: helps formatting the Gantt Chart
▾	More Buttons	

Network Diagram Toolbar

Button	Tool Tip	Similar to choosing menu items
Align ▾	Align	Format, Layout, Box layout
	Hide/Show Summary Tasks	Format, Layout, ☑ Show Summary Tasks
	Hide/Show Progress Marks	Format, Layout, ☑ Mark in-progress and completed
	Hide/Show Page Breaks	Format, Layout, ☑ Show page breaks
	Show/Hide Link Labels	Format, Layout, ☑ Show link labels
	Straight Links / Rectilinear links	Format, Layout, ◉ Rectilinear ◉ Straight
	Hide Fields	Format, Layout, ☑ Hide all fields except ID
	Layout Now	Format, Layout Now
	Layout Selection Now	
▾	More Buttons	

Resource Management Toolbar

Button	Tool Tip	Similar to choosing menu items
	Resource Allocation View	View, More Views, Resource Allocation
	Task Entry View	View, More Views, Task Entry
	Go To Next Overallocation	
	Assign Resources	Tools, Resources, Assign Resources
	Share Resources	Tools, Resources, Share Resources
	Update Resource Pool	Tools, Resources, Update Resource Pool
	Refresh Resource Pool	Tools, Resources, Refresh Resource Pool
	Address Book	
	Resource Details	
	Windows User Account from Address Book	
	Using Resources	Project, Filtered for, More Filters, Using Resources
	Leveling Help	Help, Contents and Index
	More Buttons	

Tracking Toolbar

Button	Tool Tip	Similar to choosing menu items
-∿-	**Project Statistics**	**Project, Project Information,** Statistics...
→	**Update as Scheduled**	**Tools, Tracking, Update Project**
→	**Reschedule Work**	**Tools, Tracking, Update Project**
◀	**Add Progress Line**	
0% / 25% / 50% / 75% / 100%	0, / 25, / 50, / 75 or / 100% complete	**Tools, Tracking, Update Tasks**
▦	**Update Tasks**	**Tools, Tracking, Update Tasks**
▦	**Workgroup Toolbar**	**View, Toolbars, Workgroup**
▾	**More Buttons**	

Workgroup Toolbar

Button	Tool Tip	Similar to choosing menu items
	TeamAssign	**Tools, Workgroup, TeamAssign**
	TeamUpdate	**Tools, Workgroup, TeamUpdate**
	TeamStatus	**Tools, Workgroup, TeamStatus**
	TeamInbox	**Tools, Workgroup, TeamInbox**
Resend All Messages	**Resend All Messages**	**Tools, Workgroup, Resend All Messages**
	Set Reminder	**Tools, Workgroup, Set Reminder**
	Send to Mail Recipient (as Attachment)	**File, Send To, Mail Recipient**
	Send to Routing Recipient	**File, Send To, Routing Recipient**
	Send to Exchange Folder	**File, Send To, Exchange Folder**
	Insert Project	**Insert, Project**
	Open from Database	**File, Open**
	Save to Database As	**File, Save As**
	More Buttons	

File Page Setup Tools

Button	Tool Tip	For
A	**Format Text Font**	the font, size and style In order to format the text in the header select the text first and then click **A** .
	Insert Page Number	page number
	Insert Total Page Count	total number of pages
	Insert Current Date	date: the system date
	Insert Current Time	time: the system time
	Insert File Name	the path and filename
	Insert Picture	This button takes you into a dialog for inserting a graphic image into header, footer or legend. It is often used to insert the project logo.

Appendix 2: Certification Curriculum Sample Exam Questions

The Testing Process for Certification

In this appendix you will find exam questions that are representative of the Blue Belt exam in the certification curriculum of the International Institute for Learning. The Blue Belt exam covers the course materials of the Orange Belt workshop and the Blue Belt workshop. The Orange Belt course materials are completely covered by this book. The Blue Belt workshop has a separate course manual that is handed out to course participants when they attend the Blue Belt session in the certification curriculum. The following sample exam questions relate <u>only</u> to the text in this book, i.e. only to the Orange Belt course materials.

Answering these sample questions will not only help you pass the certification exam at the International Institute for Learning, but will also help in passing the Project 2000 Microsoft Office User Specialist exam (MOUS), see <u>www.mous.net</u>.

The exam:

◆ Tests your <u>readiness</u> to use the basic features of MS Project in practice.
   In other words, it tests your knowledge of the complete how-to steps of the basic features. Basic features are those features most people need in order to model their projects, regardless of their industry.

◆ Tests your <u>practical</u> knowledge and skills.
   It tests on how to model real-life situations rather than theoretic examples.

◆ Tests your <u>understanding</u> of MS Project.
   It tests the understanding of the behind-the-screens working of the tool, instead of details you normally look up in references.

The certification curriculum is designed such that it would comply with the standards of the American Council on Education (ACE). See <u>www.acenet.edu</u>.

Each exam is carefully crafted in terms of the chapters and difficulty of the exam questions. The testing is not just an evaluation activity, but also a learning activity. It is a learning activity in that participants mark their own exam immediately after taking it and then are given the opportunity to discuss any exam questions they would like to discuss. The participant knows the score before leaving the premises, and the final score is confirmed within five business days. The passing mark is 60%.

The questions are stored in a secure database, and the database is subject to continuous improvement. The issues that arise in the discussions with participants are captured and on a regular basis, used to review the exam questions. When a question is modified, it receives a new ID-number so it can be tracked as if it were a new question.

All answers given by participants are captured in the database and periodically the performance of the questions is analyzed. If a question has too many wrong or right answers the question is either dropped from the database, or modified to become a new question. New questions are introduced gradually, there will only be four or fewer new questions on an exam. New questions are only used for groups of ten or more participants.

The complete certification exam consists of 40 questions on the Orange and Blue Belt materials to be answered in one hour. Sixty percent, or 24 questions, come from the Orange Belt materials, which is this book. Below, you will find 24 sample exam questions. The correct answers can be found on our website www.iil.com. If you want to see whether you are ready to go for certification, you should be able to answer these questions in 36 minutes (60% of 60 minutes) and attain a score of 60% or higher. Pace your work at 1.5 minutes per question.

The answers to the questions have a good-better-best characterization. You should read all answers before picking the best one. If you don't know the answer, you have a 25% scoring chance if you just fill in any answer.

Orange Belt Sample Exam Questions

1 How can you change the contents of a project template?
   A. You open the template file and make the changes then you choose File, Save.
   B. You cannot edit the contents of a project template; you can only replace the template file.
   C. You can change a project template using the Organizer.
   D. You open the template file in a special way that opens the original template file.

2 The summary tasks summarize their detail tasks. Which of the following fields of detail tasks do NOT necessarily add up to a total shown on the summary task?
   A. Duration
   B. Cost
   C. Work
   D. none of the fields mentioned

3 If you want to transfer a view from one project file to another, how many objects may you have to copy at most in the Organizer?
   A. 1 view object
   B. 2 objects: 1 view object and 1 table object
   C. 3 objects: 1 view object, 1 table object and 1 filter object
   D. 4 objects: 1 view object, 1 table object, 1 filter object and 1 report object

4 What is a true statement about slack?
   A. The amount of Total Slack is always greater than or equal to the amount of Free Slack.
   B. Delaying a task and using its Total Slack will never affect its successors.
   C. Free Slack is synonymous to Float.
   D. The task bars of critical tasks are always shown in red.

5   The type of resources that is normally excluded from leveling is:
    A. Group Resources
    B. Individual Resources
    C. Facilities
    D. Materials

6   You want to create a schedule that needs the least maintenance while the
    project is executed, because you will be busy enough managing the project.
    You decide to follow these guidelines:
    A. Enter as many dependencies and schedule constraints as possible.
    B. Enter as few dependencies and schedule constraints as possible.
    C. Enter as many dependencies as needed and as few schedule constraints as
        possible.
    D. Enter as few dependencies as possible and as many schedule constraints as
        possible.

7   Which statement is true?
    A. Optimizing of the schedule should preferably be done only once.
    B. Creating a Gantt Chart should be done only once to win the bidding
        process.
    C. Setting the Baseline should be done only once in a project.
    D. Entering milestone constraint dates should preferably be done only once in
        a project.

8   .MPP-files can contain:
    A. Tasks, estimates, dependencies, constraints, resources and assignments.
    B. Schedule data (such as tasks, estimates) and objects (such as views, filters,
        tables, maps).
    C. Schedule data, but no objects. Objects are contained in .MPT-template
        files only.
    D. Schedule data (such as tasks, estimates) and generic options.

9   You want to shorten your project by creating an overlap between two tasks
that are Finish-to-Start (FS) dependent on each other. How can you best
accomplish this?
   A. You set a lead time on the dependency or you change the type of
      dependency.
   B. You set a negative lag time on the dependency or you change the type of
      the dependency to SS or FF.
   C. You cut the FS dependency; this will schedule both tasks in parallel
   D. You change the dependency to a SS with a 100% lag.

10 You are using forward scheduling and you have to install new computers,
install software on the computers and train people in the use of the software.
You want the users to be trained just before they receive the software.
Everything has to be finished before May at the latest. How would you
schedule this situation?
   A. The task "train people" needs an ALAP constraint and a milestone is
      needed with a Must-Finish-On constraint on May 1st.
   B. All tasks need ALAP constraints and a milestone is needed with a Must-
      Finish-On constraint on May 1st.
   C. The task "train people" needs an ALAP constraint and a milestone is
      needed with a Finish-No-Later-Than constraint on May 1st.
   D. The task "train people" needs an ALAP constraint and a milestone is
      needed with a Finish-No-Later-Than constraint on April 30th.

11 You have a task with a Fixed Duration of 5 days. Two resources are working full-time on the task. The Work field shows 10 days. You want to change the duration while keeping the work on the task the same. How can you accomplish this?

   A. You change the task type to Fixed Work, then you enter the new duration. MS Project will adjust the number of resource units working on the task.

   B. You change the task type to Fixed Units, then you enter the new duration. MS Project will adjust the number of resource units working on the task.

   C. You keep the task type Fixed Duration and you enter the new duration. MS Project will adjust the number of resource units working on the task and keep the Work the same.

   D. The task type does not matter. You enter the new duration. MS Project will adjust the number of resource units working on the task and keep the Work the same.

12 When you have to level workloads you can do this manually or you can have MS Project do it automatically. Which of the following statements is true?

   A. Automatic leveling results in tighter schedules than leveling manually.

   B. With automatic leveling you can create three different scenarios: no leveling, leveled by a target date and full leveling. You can go back and forth between the scenarios. Having the scenarios makes automatic leveling better than manual leveling.

   C. Leveling manually involves more work than automatic leveling, but can lead to shorter schedules.

   D. Manual leveling methods are re-assigning resources, moving vacations, assigning in overtime and delaying tasks. Automatic leveling is assigning in overtime and delaying tasks.

13 The differences between Views and Reports are:
   A. The data in Views is editable, not in Reports. Views are customizable, Reports are not customizable.
   B. Reports always show numeric information, Views do not. The Reports are highly customizable, Views are less customizable.
   C. The Views are highly customizable, Reports are less so. The data in Views is editable, not in Reports.
   D. Reports are quicker and easier to print Gantt Charts and Time-Phased Budgets than Views .

14 A person complains that it always takes too much effort to create print-outs of the schedule regularly, such as Gantt Charts and to-do lists for each resource. What would you recommend?
   A. Use Reports instead of Views.
   B. Create separate views for each print-out you need. Separate the views in which you do the scheduling from views you use for reports. Use the Calendar view and the "Using Resource..." filter for the to-do lists.
   C. Use the workgroup features to communicate to-do lists for resources. Use the Reports feature to create the Gantt Charts.
   D. Use the fit-to-one page feature to make the data quickly fit on one page.

15 A scheduler left some uncompleted work scheduled before the status date. The updated schedule shows that all the deadlines are met. What statement is appropriate about this status report?
   A. The report is wrong, the work should be brought forward to after the status date using the "Update as Scheduled" button on the Tracking toolbar.
   B. Who cares as long as the deadlines are met?
   C. The portion of work should be moved to after the status date using the "Reschedule Work" button, because this may affect meeting future deadlines.
   D. As long as the scheduler has entered all the Actual hours worked for each resource, the report is OK.

16 Suppose you want to enter the actual hours worked for each resource weekly during the execution of the project. You want MS Project to calculate the actual costs automatically. You have to set the following options:
A. in Tools, Options, Calculation:
de-select "Updating task status updates Resource Status"
select "Actual Costs are always calculated by Microsoft Project"
B. in Tools, Resource Leveling...:
de-select "Updating task status updates Resource Status"
select "Actual Costs are always calculated by Microsoft Project"
C. in Tools, Options, Calculation:
de-select "Edits to total task % complete will be spread to the status date"
select "Actual Costs are always calculated by Microsoft Project"
D. Actual Costs are always calculated by MS Project; you don't need to set this option.
in Tools, Options, Calculation:
de-select "Updating task status updates Resource Status"
de-select "Edits to total task % complete will be spread to the status date"

17 In order to create a Gantt Chart that is easy to maintain, you would enter AT LEAST:
A. Tasks, Dependencies, Estimates, and Constraints if necessary
B. Tasks, Schedule Logic, Estimates, Constraints, Resources, and Reports
C. Tasks, Dependencies, Schedule Constraints, Resources, and Assignments
D. Tasks, Start and End Dates, and Estimates

18 You are monitoring two milestones:
"Report sent" shows a Total Slack of 2 days.
"Test done" shows a Total Slack of -5 days.
These figures indicate:
A. both milestones will slip
B. the milestone "Report sent" can be met easily, but "Test done" cannot be met without taking corrective action
C. the milestone "Test done" can be met easily, but "Report sent" cannot be met without taking corrective action
D. both milestones can easily be met

19 Does the start date of the successor change if the dependency is changed from a Finish-to-Start with a 40% lead to a Start-to-Start dependency with 60% lag?
   A. No, never.
   B. No, but only if there are no other predecessors.
   C. Yes, the Finish-to-Start dependency schedules the successor earlier.
   D. Yes, the Finish-to-Start dependency schedules the successor later.

20 In which ways can you set schedule constraints?
   A. By driving a nail through a task bar on the Gantt Chart that hangs on the wall in your office.
   B. By dragging task bars to set Start-No-Later-Than constraints, or by entering start or finish dates, or by using the Advanced tab on the Task Information dialog box.
   C. By dragging task bars to set Start-No-Earlier-Than constraints, or by entering actual start or finish dates, or by using the Task Information dialog box.
   D. By dragging task bars, using the Advanced tab on the Task Information dialog box or using the task fields "Constraint Type" and "Constraint Date".

21 Two resources are working full-time on the task with 10 days of Work. You want to add an extra resource to the task, but keep the Work the same. How can you accomplish this?
   A. First you change the task type to Fixed Work, then you add the extra resource and the duration will decrease as a result.
   B. First you set the task to Fixed Duration, then you add the extra resource.
   C. First you change the task type to Fixed Units, then you set the task to non Effort-Driven and add the extra resource.
   D. First you set the task to Fixed Duration and non Effort-Driven, then you add the extra resource.

22 What do the "maximum units" of a resource represent?
    A. The number of resources in a group resource.
    B. The percentage availability of a part-time resource.
    C. The maximum availability of the resource.
    D. The overall workload of the resource.

23 When setting up a new project in which you will NOT need resources, it is important to:
    A. Specify a start date for the project, name the project, and choose the generic options.
    B. Fill in the Project Information dialog box and the File Properties dialog box.
    C. Enter the tasks and dependencies, then enter the resources and the assignments.
    D. Specify a start date for the project, choose the project-specific options and the generic options.

24 What factors should you consider, in general, when deciding whether or not to add a resource to the resource list?
    A. whether the resource will add to the total cost of the project
    B. the impact the resource will have on the duration of the project
    C. the impact the resource will have on the workload histograms
    D. whether the resource is available and whether the resource will have an impact on the duration or the cost of the project

Glossary

Activity see *task*. In this book the terms *task* and *activity* are used interchangeably.

Actuals The actuals is the set of data that represents how the project was realized. It shows the real durations (Actual Duration), the hours that were spent (Actual Work), the real start (Actual Start) and finish dates (Actual Finish), and the final cost (Actual Cost).

Assignment An assignment is a combination of a task and a resource. It can be a resource scheduled to work on a particular task or a task assigned to a specific resource. Assignments have their own specific fields, such as start and finish, work, units, work contour and cost rate table.

Baseline The baseline is the original, approved schedule, plus the approved changes. The baseline schedule is meant to be compared against. The Baseline contains the original set of start and finish dates, as well as total work and cost numbers. As soon as you have a version of the schedule that you want to use to compare progress against, you copy it into the baseline fields. The baseline is static unless you re-baseline. See also, *Interim Plan*.

Business Day A business day is a working day, normally a weekday.

Critical Path The Critical Path is the series of tasks that determines the duration of the project. The tasks on the Critical Path are often scheduled tightly; upon finishing one, the next one immediately starts. In other words, there is no slack between critical tasks. The Critical Path is based on the assumption that there is access to unlimited resources. See also, *Resource-Critical Path*.

Critical Resource A critical resource is a resource that drives the duration of the project because of its limited availability. It can be a driving assignment on a critical task, or it can be a task that becomes resource-critical when delayed during resource leveling.

Critical Task A critical task is a task on the Critical Path. See also *Critical Path* and *Resource-Critical Task*.

Delaying Delaying is rescheduling to a later date one of two tasks that compete for the same resource in order to resolve a resource over-allocation. The over-allocation is caused by the concurrence of both tasks and the use of the same resource.

Dependency A dependency is a logical cause-and-effect relationship between two tasks. A task often cannot start until another task is finished; the task is 'dependent' on completion of another. For example, the start of printing a report is dependent on finishing writing it. Entering logic is called setting dependencies. See also *Resource Dependency*.

Detail Task A detail task is a task on the lowest outline level or any task without sub-tasks. Detail tasks are done by a person, and it should be possible to estimate the duration and cost for each detail task. See also *summary tasks*.

Duration The duration is the number of business hours or business days estimated to perform a task or deliverable. See also *Work*.

Earned Value The earned value is (the value of) the completed physical work. Earned value analyses are often made during the execution of the project to evaluate the progress and to forecast the trend of the progress and cost.

Effort see *Work*.

Elapsed Duration Elapsed duration is the duration it takes to perform a task expressed in calendar time (which includes evenings, weekends and holidays). Elapsed time is used for tasks like *dry paint* or *back up computers*. See *Duration*.

Filter A filter is a condition that determines whether a task or resource is displayed in the view. A filter is an object that can be transferred between project files using the organizer.

Fixed Duration Task A fixed duration task has a duration that will stay the same regardless of how many additional resources are assigned to the task. For example: *drying of paint, teaching a course*.

Fixed Units Task A fixed units task keeps the number of resources assigned constant when a change is made to the *duration* or the *work* of a task. If the work changes the duration will change and vice versa. A task for which you only have one resource available, for example, can be a fixed units task.

Fixed Work Task A fixed work task is a task that is effort-driven; the amount of *effort* (*work*) will be the same regardless of the number of resources doing the task. For example, *coding a computer program, writing reports* and *painting walls* have an amount of effort that can be estimated up-front.

Float See *Free Slack* and *Total Slack*.

Free Float see *Free Slack*.

Free Slack Free Slack is the time that a task can be delayed without influencing the start of dependent tasks. On the *Critical Path* there is no free slack. Free slack is synonymous to *free float*.

Gantt Chart A Gantt Chart is a graphical presentation of tasks over time. Bars in a timescale represent the durations of the tasks. The chart is named after Henry L. Gantt who invented it early in the 20th century.

Global.MPT The Global.MPT file is the default template file that is always open when MS Project is running. It contains the default objects that are visible in new and existing project files, unless there is an object with the same name in the existing project file.

Group A group is a categorization of task or resource records in the MS Project database. A group is an object that can be transferred between project files using the organizer. There is also a resource-related field *group* in which, typically, the department or workgroup of a resource is captured.

Interim Plan An interim plan is a set of start and finish dates that is worthwhile preserving for comparison. An interim plan only contains start and finish dates and is therefore only a partial schedule. See also, *Baseline*.

Lag Time Lag time is the duration of a dependency. It is the time you have to wait after the independent task is finished, and before the dependent task can start in a Finish-to-Start dependency. Lag shows as a gap between the task bars in the Gantt Chart timescale. Lag time pushes the dependent task later in time.

Lead Time Lead time is the amount of time the independent task starts earlier than the finish of the independent task in a Finish-to-Start dependency. Lead time is like a negative duration of the dependency. The two task bars will overlap and create a partial dependency. Lead time puts the dependent task earlier in time. See, *Partial Dependency*.

Leveling Leveling the workload of resources is bringing the workload of resources down within their availability. A resource can have too much work when (s)he happens to be assigned to two tasks at the same time. Re-assigning to another resource is one of the solutions. A last resort solution is to reschedule one of the two tasks to later in time. This is called delaying a task. See *Delaying*.

Milestone A milestone is an event with a zero duration. A milestone is an important point in time, often an evaluation point. It can be a date on which a deliverable has to be ready or a meeting in which Go/No Go decisions are made. Events like the opening of a new facility can be milestones. Milestones appear as diamonds in the Gantt Chart and are visual reminders of these important dates.

Network Diagram The network diagram shows all the logical dependencies between the tasks. Dependencies are shown in the network diagram as arrows between the task boxes. Each arrow depicts a dependency and runs from the driving task to the follower task. See *Dependency*.

Object Objects are things that change the appearance of the schedule data (tables, filters, groups, views, fields, reports, maps, calendars) or that enhance the Project 2000 interface (modules, toolbars, menu bars). All objects can be seen in the Tools, Organizer.

Open DataBase Connectivity (ODBC) ODBC is a standard set to foster the exchange of data between database applications. Databases that adhere to the ODBC standard, allow other database software to read and write the data.

Organizer The organizer is a feature in Project 2000 through which objects can be transferred between project files and even the *global.mpt* file. Examples of objects are: tables, filters, groups, views, calendars and toolbars. You can access the organizer by choosing Tools, Organizer.

Outline Structure The outline structure refers to the profile of the indented task list. Detail tasks are indented under their summary task, to form an indented list of tasks or outline structure. See *Work Breakdown Structure*.

Partial Dependency When a task is dependent upon the partial completion of its predecessor, it is called a partial dependency. As a result, the tasks will overlap each other in the Gantt Chart. A Finish-to-Start dependency with lead time is an example of a partial dependency. See *Lead*.

Person Day A person day is one person working for one full business day. See *Business Day*.

PERT Chart PERT stands for Program Evaluation and Review Technique. The PERT chart was a view in previous versions of MS Project, which was renamed to Network Diagram in Project 2000. The PERT chart showed the network of dependencies between the tasks, similar to the current network diagram.

Predecessor The predecessor is the independent task or driver in a dependency relationship. In the example of *writing* and *printing*, the task *writing* is the predecessor of *printing* and *printing* is the successor of *writing*. See also, *Successor*.

Project Calendar It is the same as the standard project calendar. The project calendar is the calendar on which you can specify which days are working days and non-working days for everybody involved in the project. It constrains the scheduling by Project 2000. The calendar can be passed around as an object to ensure that everybody works with the same business days and working times. It is a time-saving device for creating resource calendars, because you can base these *resource calendar*s on the standard project calendar, which will copy all the holidays into the resource calendar.

Project Database All the data that are entered in the project are stored in the project database. Data can be extracted from this database as needed for a view or a report.

Project Summary Task The project summary task is the project title at the top of the task list with totals for the entire project. It has task ID number zero and all other tasks IDs indented below it, such that it summarizes the duration, work and cost for the entire project.

Project Template A project template is a standard schedule that is typical of projects run by an organization. It contains a standard WBS with dependencies, and often generic resources and assignments. A contractor who builds houses uses the same schedule over and over again when building houses. He could use a project template that is a boilerplate schedule. Template files can decrease the necessary data entry for creating similar schedules over and over again, and are protected from accidentally being changed.

Recalculation A recalculation is a refreshing of the entire schedule based upon changes made. Whenever a task is inserted or changed, the cost and work changes, as well as the dates of other tasks. These figures have to be calculated again by Project 2000.

Report A report is a ready-to-go numeric presentation of (part of) the project. Many reports are shipped with MS Project. Reports are customizable to a certain degree.

Resource-Critical Path The resource-critical path is the series of tasks that determines the duration of the project given a limited availability of resources. The resource-critical path takes logical dependencies and resource dependencies into account. Unlike the Critical Path the Resource-Critical Path is not based on having access to unlimited resources. See also, *Critical Path*.

Resource Critical Task A resource critical task is a task on the resource-critical path. See also, *Resource-Critical Path* and *Critical Task*.

Resource Dependency A resource dependency is a relationship between two tasks through a resource that is assigned to both tasks. If the resource needs more time to finish the first task, it will cause the resource-dependent task to start later.

Resource A resource is a person, team, facility, machine or material, used in a project to accomplish tasks. Anything that can influence the timing or the cost of tasks should be defined as a resource to the project.

Resource Leveling see *Leveling*.

Responsible A responsible person is the person who is accountable for deliverables of the project. A responsible person only becomes a resource to the project, if (s)he works on any tasks in the task list of the project.

Schedule A schedule is a set of start and finish dates of deliverables, tasks and milestones that will accomplish the project objective. A Project 2000 schedule typically contains the WBS, the dependencies between tasks, and the resources and assignments, based upon which it calculates the start and finish dates.

Sequential Dependency When two tasks are sequentially dependent upon each other, it means that the first has to be finished entirely before the second can start.

Slack see *Total Slack* and *Free Slack*.

Sort A sort is a new order in which the tasks or resources are displayed based on one or more fields.

Standard (Project Calendar) It is calendar named *standard* that acts as the project calendar. See *Project Calendar*.

Successor The successor is the dependent task, or follower, in a dependency. In the example of *writing* and *printing,* the task *writing* is the predecessor of *printing* and *printing* is the successor of *writing*. See also, *Predecessor*.

Summary Task A summary task is a task with sub-tasks that shows the duration, the total cost and the total amount of work of its sub-tasks. To make a schedule easier to understand by outsiders, you can group tasks and give each group a descriptive summary task name. Summary tasks are often deliverables. These summary tasks give the plan a logical structure. If tasks are scheduled in parallel, the summary duration is not necessarily the sum of the sub-task durations. See also, *Detail Tasks*.

Table A table is a selection of task- or resource-related fields that will appear as columns in the spreadsheet of MS Project. A table is an object that can be transferred between project files using the organizer.

Task Bar Each task has a task bar in the timescale of the Gantt Chart that represents the duration of the task.

Task A task is a concrete piece of work that has to be done and that can be assigned to a resource. It should be possible to estimate the duration of a task.

Total Float see *Total Slack*

Total Slack Total slack is the total time a task can be delayed without influencing the end date of the project (or any constraint date before the project finish date). On the Critical Path there is no total slack. Total slack is synonymous to *total float*.

Tracking Progress Tracking progress is comparing the current schedule to the original baseline. Comparisons can be made on the duration of the project, the work of the resources and on expenditures.

Updating Updating a project is entering what really happened in the project; what progress was made in terms of the actual start date, the work/time spent on a task and the finish date or the percentage of its completion.

View A view is an arrangement of project data in Project 2000 that applies a table, a filter and a group object, and that also contains the sort order, format settings and page layout choices. A view is an object that can be transferred between project files using the organizer.

WBS or Work Breakdown Structure The WBS is a deliverable-oriented grouping of project elements that organizes and defines the total work scope of the project [35]. See also *Outline Structure*.

What If analysis This is a way of finding out by trial and error what a better schedule may be.

Work Work is the estimated number of person hours or person days a resource spends on a task or deliverable. Work is synonymous to *effort*. See also, *Duration*.

---

[35] See the PMBOK® Guide, 2000 Edition, published by the PMI.

Index

%

% complete, 282

1

1%-10% rule, 117

A

activity, 539

actuals, 539

assignment, 539

    full-time assignment, 269

    part-time assignment, 269

availability, 248

B

backward scheduling, 311, 316

baseline, 539

    baseline schedule, 444

business days, 95, 139, 145, 539

C

calendar view, 70, 71

calendars

    base calendar, 242

    project calendar, 95

    resource calendar, 95, 99, 543

    task calendars, 95, 131

confirmed, 478

consolidated resources, 247

constraint, 209

cost, 49

cost rate table, 253

crashing, 322, 323

Critical Path, 189, 192, 539

early finish, 307

early start, 307

fast-tracking, 323, 371

late finish, 308

late start, 308

resource-critical tasks, 360

Critical Path Method, 305

critical resource, 539

critical task, 539

D

deadline, 209, 210, 215

decision points, 114, 215

delaying, 540

deliverable, 46

dependencies, 171, 540

decision point dependencies, 177

driver, 171

external dependencies, 177

FF, 174

finish-to-finish, 174

finish-to-start, 174

follower, 171

FS, 174

hard and soft dependencies, 177

logic, 189

network, 189

partial dependency, 175, 542

predecessor, 171

resource dependencies, 177

SF, 174

SS, 174

start-to-finish, 174

start-to-start, 174

successor, 171

detail task, 112, 119, 540

driver, 171

duration, 145, 282, 540

E

early finish, 307

early start, 307

earned value, 540

effort, 145, 154, 540

effort driven, 282, 289

elapsed duration, 540

estimates

    business days, 145, 154

    calendar days, 154

    gross work time, 156

    person days, 145, 154

    pure work time, 156

F

fast-tracking, 322

fields

    confirmed, 478

    team status pending, 478

    update needed, 478

filter, 240, 410, 540

finish, 282

fixed duration, 148, 272, 273

fixed units, 148, 272, 273

fixed work, 148, 272, 273

float, 541

follower, 171

forward scheduling, 311, 316

free float, 541

free slack, 309, 541

G

Gantt Chart, 70, 74, 222, 541

global.mpt, 58, 541

group, 422, 541

H

hammock tasks, 190

holidays, 95

I

interim plan, 541

L

lag, 175, 324, 541

late finish, 308

late start, 308

lead, 175, 324, 541

leveling, 541

    can level, 357

    priority, 160

logic, 189

M

merge-bias, 335

milestones, 112, 113, 120, 542

    ceremonies, 114, 216

    decision points, 114, 215

    deliveries, 114, 215

    do-or-die dates, 114, 215

    project end date, 114, 216

    target dates, 114, 215

Monte Carlo Simulation, 333

N

negative slack, 309

network diagram, 542

Network Diagram, 70, 76

O

object, 542

ODBC, 542

options

    global options, 91

    project options, 91

organizer, 542

outline structure, 542

out-of-sequence updating, 462

over-allocation, 94

overhead tasks, 190

overtime, 249

P

path-convergence, 335

person days, 139, 145, 542

PERT, 305

PERT chart, 543

PMO, 25

predecessor, 171, 543

priority, 160

program evaluation and review
technique, 305

project calendar, 543

project database, 543

project management office, 25

project summary task, 543

project template, 62, 543

Q

quality, 49

R

rate profile, 253

recalculation, 543

recurring tasks, 122, 190

report, 543

resource critical task, 544

resource dependency, 544

Resource Graph, 70, 80, 346, 423

resource histogram, 346

resource leveling, 544

Resource Sheet, 70, 81

Resource Usage, 70, 82

resource-critical path, 303, 359, 544

resource-limited schedule, 235

resources, 49, 544

   consolidated resources, 247

   full-time, 247

   overtime, 247

   part-time, 247

   temporary, 247

   variable availability, 247

responsible, 544

rolling wave, 157

S

schedule, 544

schedule constraints, 215

scheduling

   scheduling backward, 90, 210

   scheduling forward, 90, 210

scope, 49

scope creep, 108

sequential dependency, 544

slack, 544

free slack, 309

negative slack, 309

total slack, 309, 313

sort, 544

standard (project calendar), 545

start, 282

successor, 171, 545

summary task, 111, 112, 119, 126, 545

T

table, 545

task, 545

task bar, 545

task type, 282

    fixed duration, 148

    fixed units, 148

    fixed work, 148

Task Usage, 70, 78

tasks

    detail tasks, 112, 113, 125

    fixed duration, 276, 456, 458, 540

fixed units, 456, 458, 540

fixed work, 456, 458, 540

hammock tasks, 190

milestones, 112, 113

overhead tasks, 190

recurring tasks, 113, 122, 190, 285

split task bars, 113, 124

summary tasks, 111, 112, 113, 125

task type, 282

team status pending, 478

TeamAssign, 478

TeamStatus, 478

TeamUpdate, 478

time, 49

total slack, 309, 313, 545

Tracking Gantt, 70, 79

tracking progress, 545

U

update needed, 478

updating, 37, 545

% complete, 282

V

views, 545

    Calendar, 71

    combination view, 83, 407

    Gantt Chart, 74

    Network Diagram, 76

    Resource Graph, 80

    Resource Sheet, 81

    Resource Usage, 82

    single view, 83, 407

    task usage, 78

    Tracking Gantt, 79

W

WBS, 546

    1%-10% rule, 117

    chart, 108

what if analysis, 546

work, 145, 154, 238, 546

work breakdown structure, 546

work contour, 270, 278

workgroup, 474

working hours, 95

Contents of the CD-ROM

On the CD-ROM attached to the back cover page you will find the following subdirectories:

◆ **\Certified Schedules**
This subdirectory contains a selection of excellent schedules that have proven valuable to the individuals that created them and their organizations. The criteria used to select the schedules are:

◇ The schedules meet the requirements for Orange Belt certification in the Certification Curriculum of the International Institute for Learning. The summary chapter contains an overview of all the scheduling criteria discussed throughout the book. All of them have been passed for certification and are excellent schedules.

◇ The schedules display a wide variety of projects and industries in which MS Project and our scheduling guidelines are implemented.

◇ The schedules may have value for you personally for your own projects.

I wish to extend a special thank you to all individuals and organizations that were so kind as to allow me to share their schedules with you. Making them available to you provides insight into how the corporate world uses Project 2000 to deliver their projects successfully.

◆ **\Relocation Project**
This subdirectory contains the start- and finished-exercise files for the Relocation Project that is featured throughout the exercises in all the chapters in the book. The Relocation Project is taken through a complete project life cycle from inception to updating.

◆ **\Troubleshooting**
This contains files that are used for the troubleshooting exercises. Each file has a problem. The problems are representative of the kind for which technical support might be called.

The Certified Schedules

The certified schedules are categorized by industry. Each industry has a subdirectory under the **\Certified Schedules** directory.

Automotive Projects

Creator	Organization	Filename
Patty Amsden	EPW, Inc., USA	Dew Model – Patty Amsden.mpp
Carl Koerschner	Simpson Industries, Inc., USA	Steering Knuckle Design – Carl Koerschner.mpp
Steve Magee	Dura Automotive, USA	Recliner – Steve Magee.mpp
Rob Miller	–	Standard Draft Concept Demonstrator – Rob Miller.mpp

Construction Projects

Creator	Organization	Filename
Dale Dawson	Central Lincoln PUD, USA	Transformer House – Dale Dawson.mpp
Alberto Alcala	General Services Administration, Auburn, WA, USA	Phased Construction – Alberto Alcala.mpp
Eric Marois	Algonquin College, Canada	Voice and IP Installation – Eric Marois.mpp

Hardware Projects

Creator	Organization	Filename
Wayne Broich	–	Install PCs – Wayne Broich.mpp
Bill Reinhart	SBC/Ameritech, USA	Router Installation – Bill Reinhart.mpp
Tim Schell	–	Install Web Hardware – Tim Schell.mpp
Eddie Perez	–	Office Move – Eddie Perez.mpp
Charlie Milstead	–	IT Infrastructure – Charlie Milstead.mpp
Robertson Young	–	PC Deployment – Rob Young.mpp

Home Projects

Creator	Organization	Filename
Joy Barnitz	–	House sale –Joy Barnitz.mpp
John Rouster	–	Vacation – John Rouster.mpp
Tom Cappel	–	First Floor Remodel – Tom Cappel.mpp
John Koepke	–	Build Fence – John Koepke.mpp
Kevin Gore	–	Build Deck – Kevin Gore.mpp

New Product Development Projects

Creator	Organization	Filename
Chris Benson	–	Autonomous Lawn Mower – Chris Benson.mpp
Lisa James	Pharmacia	Design and build air compressor – Lisa James.mpp

Plant Development & Maintenance Projects

Creator	Organization	Filename
Steven Stricklin	–	Heat Rolls Rebuild – Steven Stricklin.mpp
Daniel Zook	–	Process Plant – Daniel Zook.mpp
Donald Martin	Walker & Associates, Inc., USA	Plant Development – Donald Martin.mpp

Project Management

Creator	Organization	Filename
Greg Callahan	–	Planning Process Development – Greg Callahan.mpp
–	–	Project Portfolio Mgmt.mpp
Stephanie Iverson	Marriott Vacation Club International, USA	Project Mngt System Implementation – Stephanie Iverson.mpp
Daniel Vitek	–	HW&SW Purchase Process – Daniel Vitek.mpp
Linda Lawlor	Linda Lawlor Consulting, Canada	Automated Project Office – Linda Lawlor.mpp
Ann Russell	–	Project Charters – Ann Russell.mpp

Software Projects

Creator	Organization	Filename
Carla Carter	Levi,Ray & Shoup, USA	Monthly checkwriting – Carla Carter.mpp
Kathy Convery	Levi,Ray & Shoup, USA	Database – Kathy Convery.mpp
–	–	SW Selection and Procurement.mpp
–	–	Requirements and Specifications.mpp
–	–	SW Development.mpp
David Kempster	Centrefile, Ltd. UK	Customer Database – David Kempster.mpp
Charlotte Mensah	Centrefile, Ltd. UK	Develop Cube – Charlotte Mensah.mpp
Ron Ainsworth	Centrefile, Ltd. UK	Software Development – Ron Ainsworth.mpp
Michael Jordan	Great American Insurance, USA	Claims Software – Michael Jordan.mpp
Beth Pollard	–	Emulation Evaluation – Beth Pollard.mpp

Training Projects

Creator	Organization	Filename
Michael Starkey	–	Training Process Development – Michael Starkey.mpp